Multicultural Couple Therapy

To three extraordinary couples:
Vir Bala and Balram Rastogi
Arnawaz and Jimmy Havewala
Karen and Richard Wampler

—Mudita Rastogi

To my wife Edie Pierce-Thomas, who taught me how to survive
and thrive in a cross-cultural relationship, and to all the couples
with whom I have had the privilege to work over the years who granted me
the space to learn about and appreciate cultural and racial differences.

—Volker Thomas

Multicultural Couple Therapy

Edited by

Mudita Rastogi
Argosy University, Schaumburg Campus

Volker Thomas
Purdue University

Los Angeles • London • New Delhi • Singapore • Washington DC

For information:

SAGE Publications, Inc.
2455 Teller Road
Thousand Oaks, California 91320
E-mail: order@sagepub.com

SAGE Publications Ltd.
1 Oliver's Yard
55 City Road
London EC1Y 1SP
United Kingdom

SAGE Publications India Pvt. Ltd.
B 1/I 1 Mohan Cooperative
    Industrial Area
Mathura Road, New Delhi 110 044
India

SAGE Publications
    Asia-Pacific Pte. Ltd.
33 Pekin Street #02-01
Far East Square
Singapore 048763

Printed in the United States of America

Library of Congress Cataloging-in-Publication Data

Multicultural couple therapy/edited by Mudita Rastogi, Volker Thomas.
      p. cm.
Includes bibliographical references and index.
ISBN 978-1-4129-5958-2 (cloth : alk. paper)
ISBN 978-1-4129-5959-9 (pbk. : alk. paper)
    1. Marital psychotherapy—United States. 2. Cultural psychiatry—United States. 3. Minorities—Mental health services—United States. I. Rastogi, Mudita. II. Thomas, Volker, 1948-
[DNLM: 1. Couples Therapy—methods—United States. 2. Marital Therapy—methods—United States. 3. Cultural Characteristics—United States. 4. Ethnic Groups—psychology—United States. 5. Minority Groups—psychology—United States. 6. Professional-Patient Relations—United States. WM 430.5.M3 M961 2009]

RC488.5.M846 2009
616.89'156—dc22   2008026115

This book is printed on acid-free paper.

14   15   16   10   9   8   7   6   5   4   3   2

Acquisitions Editor:	Kassie Graves
Editorial Assistant:	Veronica K. Novak
Production Editor:	Carla Freeman
Copy Editor:	Susan Jarvis
Typesetter:	C&M Digitals (P) Ltd.
Proofreader:	Theresa Kay
Indexer:	Jean Casalegno
Cover Designer:	Tony Lemos
Marketing Manager:	Carmel Schrire

Contents

List of Tables and Figures

Tables

Figures

Foreword

Good Counsel in Turbulent Times

Douglas H. Sprenkle

In producing the first volume specifically devoted to multicultural couple therapy, Mudita Rastogi and Volker Thomas have made an important contribution to the MFT literature. Since the typical "family" therapist does much more work with couples than with families that include children (Sori & Sprenkle, 2000), a volume that hones in on couple dynamics in multicultural therapy fills a significant gap. It is also very timely.

In the past three decades, there has been an exponential increase in the non-White population in the United States, and it is estimated that by 2050, Whites will be in the minority (Reuters, February 12, 2008). There are actually more Muslims in this country today than there are Presbyterians and Episcopalians combined (Eck, 2001). By 2010, there will likely be more Muslims in the United States than there are Jews (Al-Krenawi & Graham, 2005). Interracial and interfaith marriages have grown exponentially (see Greenman, Young, & Johnson, this volume). While still stigmatized in many places, public acceptance of same-sex couple relations has grown markedly, as have the numbers of same-sex couples seeking therapy (Nichols & Shernoff, 2007; Pew Research Center, 2006). The therapist who is not prepared to work in a multicultural world is, to put it bluntly, not prepared.

When I became a credentialed couple therapist in 1973, I was certainly ill-prepared. My graduate program, even though located in a major city, taught me nothing about multiculturalism, and in the early years I—a Euro-American male therapist—worked mostly with Euro-American couples. Yet even before I knew or had read anything about multicultural therapy, and even when I was working with ethnically homogeneous couples, I had some sense that their conflicts were rooted in "culture clashes" based on family of origin differences. One of my first cases was with a Euro-American couple in which the wife grew up in a family whose members frequently yelled and screamed at each other and then 15 minutes later were embracing. The husband's background was an emotionally reserved family where conflict was expressed indirectly and emotions were generally stuffed. What Christine thought of as voicing mild concerns, Arthur interpreted as over-the-top antagonism. Not surprisingly, this led to a withdrawer–pursuer dynamic that I then did not have the tools to address. Furthermore, given my family background that favored directness, I was more comfortable with Christine and, in retrospect, was much less empathic with Arthur—who felt somewhat "ganged up on" by his wife and me.

The couple and I were ethnically similar, and we even happened to belong to the same Protestant denomination: Presbyterian. Yet cultural dimensions loomed large in our work. Now, after years of working with a more diverse clientele, I think wistfully about the relative simplicity of this case from a multicultural standpoint. Like many therapists today, I am frequently seeing couples with differing ethnicities, sexual orientations, religions, and major life experiences such as immigration. The complexity of these cases, and the challenges to developing a strong therapeutic alliance with both partners and devising effective therapeutic strategies, are sometimes staggering. So, even though I am a very experienced therapist, I found this volume to be very helpful. It faced these complexities head on and helped me to sort them out and make them more manageable.

I believe this volume has a number of strengths. First, the authors assume a broad understanding of culture so that clients are understood in the "entirety of their context." At the macrolevel, culture includes racial, ethnic, national, sexual preference, and religious differences; however, it also includes, at the microlevel, a range of cognitive (e.g., values, beliefs, and attitudes), affective (e.g., emotional styles, affect regulation and attachment), and behavioral (e.g., communication patterns, gender role behavior) dimensions (Greenman, Young, & Johnson, this volume; Sevier & Yi, this volume). There is also diversity within diversity. One cannot assume that because we know people are Black or Jewish, for example, they will conform to a stereotype. Multicultural counseling is what the editors call a "multilayered reality." The rich and diverse topics covered in the volume are a witness to the breadth of this understanding of culture.

Just trying to understand an individual client on all of these dimensions is challenging enough. But to learn to work with the permutations and combinations of partners who differ on these variables can feel overwhelming. Fortunately, without oversimplifying the challenge, this volume demonstrates that this work can be both effective and satisfying. Closely related to this broad view of culture, the editors and the authors make it abundantly clear that multiculturalism is a "main course" in therapy and not some optional "dessert" that can be added to therapy training as an afterthought, or confined to a course on training in cultural competence.

Second, the volume makes it abundantly clear that multicultural couples therapy is not just learning about diverse clients (developing cultural knowledge). It also includes therapist (or educator or researcher) variables and belief systems. Throughout this volume, the reader is challenged to be aware of his or her own culture and how this impacts how one views clients, reacts emotionally to them, develops alliances with them, makes clinical decisions, and implements clinical strategies. The editors were also courageous enough to describe some of their therapeutic "failures" when they did not recognize the ways in which their own cultures blinded them. This gave me permission to reflect on my own failures and to normalize them.

Multicultural therapy, then, challenges the therapist to put as much energy into "knowing thyself" as learning about "other" cultures. It also entails being humble in the face of the clients' expertise about their cultures, asking respectful "not-knowing" questions, and making appropriate self-disclosure about one's limitations and preconceived ideas. In the spirit of being "personal," all the authors in this volume clearly identify themselves, their cultural heritage, and their context. This unusually rich self-description by the authors underscores the importance of the therapist's own culture in multicultural couple therapy.

Third, the volume is more cohesive than many edited volumes in that all authors follow the same outline. Each addresses the same nine topics (delineated in Chapter 1) related to theory, research, practice, and training. This common outline facilitates comparisons across topics and prevents the disjointed nature of some edited volumes.

Fourth, unlike many clinical books, the editors asked all authors to report on recent research on their themes. Hence, where possible, opinions are grounded in data. Even more impressive from my perspective is that authors report on the application of four evidence-based models (Emotionally Focused Therapy, Brief Strategic Family Therapy for Couples, Traditional Behavior Couple Therapy, and Integrative Behavioral Couple Therapy). These are the four couple therapy approaches with the strongest empirical records. In each case, the authors offer strong evidence that these approaches can be adapted to, and work effectively in, multicultural contexts.

Fifth, the case examples in the chapters are very compelling and make the treatment principles come alive. That each of the authors has a depth of experience in working with a given population is quite evident, as is their passion for the communities they serve. I thought the cases were challenging enough to keep a senior clinician interested and thirsty for new knowledge, but also clear enough to keep a novice excited. No easy feat!

Sixth, the volume is a treasure trove of information that the reader can keep as a handy reference. Each chapter includes exercises for clinicians, as well as reflection suggestions and additional resources, such as films, Web sites, and music, along with a comprehensive reference list.

In summary, Mudita Rastogi and Volker Thomas's book can be seen as a wise guide to an extraordinarily complex and challenging task—multicultural couple therapy. Depending on one's cultural preference, you can think of it as a trusted friend, a Native Elder, a sage aunt or uncle, the embodiment of a growing tradition, or whatever metaphor represents good counsel in turbulent times.

—Douglas H. Sprenkle
Professor of Couple and Family Therapy
Purdue University

References

Al-Krenawi, A., & Graham, J. R. (2005). Marital therapy for Arab Muslim Palestinian couples in the context of reacculturation. *The Family Journal: Counseling and Therapy for Couples and Families, 13*, 300–310.

Eck, D. (2001). *A new religious America*. San Francisco: Harper.

Nichols, M., & Shernoff, M. (2007). Therapy with sexual minorities. In S. R. Lieblum (Ed.), *Principles and practice of sex therapy* (4th ed., pp. 379–415). New York: Guilford Press.

Pew Research Center. (March 22, 2006). *Less opposition to gay marriage, adoption, and military service*. Retrieved July 7, 2008, from people-press.org/report/273/less-opposition-to-gay-marriage-adoption-and-military-service.

Reuters (February 12, 2008). *Whites to become minority in U.S. by 2050*. Retrieved July 8, 2008, from www.reuters.com/article/domesticNews/idUSN1110177520080212.

Sori, C. F., & Sprenkle, D. H. (2004). Training family therapists to work with children and families: A modified Delphi study. *Journal of Marital and Family Therapy, 30*, 497–496.

Acknowledgments

Numerous individuals have helped us as we worked on this book. We are very thankful to Kassie Graves, our editor at SAGE, for supporting this project from the very beginning and for making it possible. Veronica Novak, Carla Freeman, and Susan Jarvis have our deep gratitude for their patience and attention to detail. All of them have been a pleasure to work with.

The authors who contributed to this book have written remarkable chapters. We are thankful for their research acumen, their clinical insights, and their wisdom regarding multicultural couple therapy. We would especially like to express our deep gratitude to Dr. Douglas Sprenkle for being generous and gracious in writing the Foreword to this book.

We would like to thank our reviewers for giving us valuable feedback at the inception of this project. Their thoughtful comments helped us to expand the scope of this book and make the content more focused:

Gonzalo Bacigalupe
University of Massachusetts

Steven A. Meyers
Roosevelt University

Megan J. Murphy
Iowa State University

Neal Sheeley
Iowa State University

Robert Werner-Wilson
University of Kentucky

Jon Winek
Appalachian State University

I (Mudita Rastogi) would like to thank the following people:

Dr. Volker Thomas has been an amazing friend and coeditor. His knowledge, caring, and passion are evident throughout this book. I feel very fortunate to have collaborated with him and have learned a great deal from him in the process.

My mentors, colleagues, and students have contributed to this book by engaging me in discussions on multiculturalism and teaching me to think critically about diversity. I especially want to thank Drs. Rachana Johari, Satish Saberwal, Gwen Sorell, Karen Wampler, Richard Wampler, and Liz Wieling for years of support and friendship. I am humbled by the lessons my clients have taught me by sharing their lives and struggles with me. To all of them, I owe deep gratitude.

My parents, Vir Bala and Balram Rastogi; family members Arnawaz and Jimmy Havewala, Manish, Meenal, Neha, and Megha; and friends across many countries continue to inspire and encourage me. I am deeply indebted to them for their love and warmth. My life partner Aspi Havewala has always cheered me on. He inspires me with his creativity and vision. I can't thank Aspi enough for the love and sense of humor that sustain me, and for being so generous with his technology skills. My sons Zubin and Romil fill my life with love, Legos, Star Wars, and soccer. They challenge me to be more present in the moment and they make the journey more joyful.

—Mudita Rastogi

I (Volker Thomas) would like to thank the following people:

Dr. Mudita Rastogi had the confidence in me to be her partner and coeditor for this project. Her patient leadership and gracious friendship have made even the tedious parts of completing such a wonderful book a great joy.

I am indebted to my colleagues, students, and clients from different cultures who have inspired and challenged me in my humanity to look beyond cultural stereotypes. They allowed me to struggle with them through the process of me learning and appreciating cultural and racial differences. As a German immigrant, I am particularly grateful to all my Jewish friends and colleagues who permitted me to work through my guilt and shame associated with the Holocaust. I am thankful to the many African American colleagues, students, and clients for their patience with my ignorance of the enormous power slavery and its aftermath have had and continue to have on the relationships between African Americans and Whites in this country. Finally, I want to thank all members of the various minority groups represented in this book for having to put up with the power and privilege that I as a White straight male still hold by default in this culture.

Finally, I want to thank my parents, Rosemarie and Emil Thomas, for the opportunities they provided me to become who I am, and for enduring the pain my emigration caused them. My life partner of the past 25 years, Edie Pierce-Thomas, has always supported me in living across continents and cultures, and helped me to stay connected with my German roots. I am grateful to my "German" daughter Tina, who has stuck with me despite moving away from her across the big ocean when she was only 10 years old, and to my "American" children, Erika and Philip, who continue to teach their father "proper American English."

—Volker Thomas

PART I

Overview

One

Introduction to Multicultural Couple Therapy

Mudita Rastogi and Volker Thomas

A few years ago, a client[1] walked into my (MR's) clinic. He seemed to be a White man in his 40s, tall and well dressed. After filling out the paperwork, Joe talked for a few minutes about his symptoms of depression and his conflict with his wife. Then, rather abruptly, he sat up and said: "Dr. Rastogi, this may not be obvious to you but my father is Black. My mother is White. Most people can't tell from looking at me. I just want to mention it." Then he sat back, looking somewhat tentatively at me.

He was very light-skinned, and I would most definitely not have guessed his biracial identity had he not told me. I was also embarrassed because I had failed to read this fact on his intake form; he had clearly checked the "biracial" category under ethnicity. I thanked him for informing me, apologized for not noting the information earlier, and proceeded to ask detailed questions about his background, his current relationship, and his symptoms of depression. Before the session ended, I specifically probed his feelings about his biracial identity, the fact that he can "pass as White," and also his feelings about being in therapy with someone ethnically different from him.

The following week, he and his wife Ginny came in for couple therapy. She was White, of European origin, and was raised in a very economically privileged family. The couple had been married for one year, and prior to that had been engaged for seven months while in a long-distance, transcontinental relationship. They discussed their conflict patterns and their feelings of "stuckness" with me. They had been in couple therapy with a previous therapist but had dropped out after two sessions.

Using an Emotionally Focused Therapy (Johnson, 2004) framework, it became clear that he was the "pursuer" in the relationship and she was the "distancer." He picked fights with her, she withdrew, and he panicked and tried to back-pedal. As I observed them getting stuck in their cyclical pattern, I tried to think of ways to inject new information into their interactions. I asked how their different backgrounds impacted their relationship. There was silence in the room for about 30 seconds. Joe started to say something intellectual about "growing up biracial in the '60s." He stopped, blinked back tears, and described how he frequently dealt with racism as a child. Patrons stared when his family would walk into a restaurant. Friends were not allowed to come over to play after their parents had met his father. Kids called him names at school. His current experiences were not much better. At bars, with acquaintances and coworkers, he had learned to be on guard. "Invariably, they make racist jokes and throw the N-word around," he said. Joe articulated how much he automatically expected rejection and dreaded having to "out" himself under hostile circumstances. He also hinted that the previous two therapists had empathized with his childhood but minimized his more recent experiences.

In this context, Joe then shared with Ginny that every time they argued, he was convinced she would leave him. This was information he had not shared with her before because he felt she would not understand his views. Further, growing up as a biracial man, he had learned to be both tough and to suppress his feelings. As I listened to Joe's pain, sadness, and anger, it became clear that Ginny could not immediately relate to some of his experiences and feelings. As a new immigrant, she missed her mother and sisters, and she was also preoccupied with decoding this new environment. Growing up with considerable privilege, and as a White woman in the United States, her experiences were very different.

For several sessions, the clients and I struggled with getting them both to hear each other's vulnerabilities and needs. In addition, I had to be mindful of my own reactions to the clients' diverse experiences, and their reading of my reactions.

Race relations, ethnic identity, oppression, gender, social class, immigration, and cultural differences played a pivotal role in this couple's relationship. Intersecting with these variables were my own identity as a female therapist of color, my views on multiculturalism, and the clients' perceptions of me. Clearly, the case required a "meta" consideration of cultural variables in defining the couple's problems, sensitivity to multiculturalism in conceptualizing the case, and integrating the above factors in treatment. Further, doing therapy with this couple required skills both to form alliances with the clients and to work effectively with them, while integrating my own awareness of my identity, feelings, and privileges. A novice therapist could have taken a skills-based "textbook approach" by mistakenly focusing on Ginny and Joe's pursue–withdraw interactions alone and excluding the discussion of larger systems, the therapist–client relationship, and the therapist's own identity and belief system.

More than 20 years ago, after I (VT) had immigrated from Germany to the United States, I had an intake session with a couple in my private practice who presented with the common issue of "lack of communication" and "excessive arguments" that never got resolved. I felt comfortable with the couple and was confident that I could successfully work with them in addressing their issues. They were highly educated, insightful, and very motivated to make the changes necessary to improve their relationship. During the session, they brought up an argument that had repeatedly occurred on their way to the *temple*. Perplexed, I looked up and noticed the black hair and brown eyes, which reminded me of people from the Mediterranean (e.g., Spain, Italy, and Greece) that I had encountered many times during my frequent travels from Germany. However, most people in the Mediterranean are Catholic and go to church, not to the temple. For a moment, panic struck me. Fortunately, I was able to contain and hide my affect, while realizing that the couple with whom I was talking was Jewish.

Growing up in Germany right after World War II, I had never met a Jewish person. Yet, being acutely aware of the terrible Nazi atrocities and the Holocaust, I was overcome by guilt and shame. I felt helpless about how to deal with the couple who, in my perception, had changed from a couple with "ordinary" marital problems to one with an "extraordinary" context. They were used to being Jewish and living in a country with several million fellow Jews. But I was not, and I had no idea how to deal with the emotions that the context of our encounter had triggered in me. I mustered all my courage and, combined with desperation, revealed to them my German background and how I felt about meeting Jews for the first time in my life. Both husband and wife smiled at me and, to my surprise, shared with me that my first name (Volker) had given away my German background to them when I had talked to the wife on the phone to set up the appointment. Having had family killed in the Holocaust, they had talked about whether or not they could and wanted to work with a German therapist. Graciously, they had decided to give it a try and came in for the first session. Both expressed to me their appreciation that I had identified myself as German to them and had shared my affective reactions. They took that as me owning my part of the responsibility of the cultural context in which we had met to work together in resolving their "ordinary" couple problems.

Doing this "ordinary" work was a healing experience for all of us—one that went far beyond the communication problems and arguments that had brought the couple to therapy. The cultural, ethnic, political, and historical context of our work shed such a different light on their experience as a middle-aged couple. From this experience (and many other similar ones that followed), I learned that taking the cultural context of therapists and clients into account is not only a necessary condition for successful couple therapy but a sufficient condition and a moral imperative for all mental health services.

As educators and therapists committed to multiculturalism, we believe that *all* clients deserve to be understood in the entirety of their context. This context includes therapist (or educator/researcher) variables and belief systems. We passionately believe that mental health professionals lose the valuable opportunity to anchor relational data within a systemic framework if we do anything other than multicultural therapy. All of us, whether we are therapists, researchers, educators, students, supervisors, trainees, or clients, are deeply impacted by multiple, intersecting contextual variables, even as we create categories such as race, gender, sexual orientation, social class, ability, and religious beliefs, and interpret them.

This book addresses a very large gap in the couple therapy literature. Couple therapy books (including textbooks) focus primarily on theories that represent a Eurocentric perspective, and research and clinical work based mainly on White couples. Such scholarship often marginalizes issues of diversity; typically, a book will have a chapter each on gender, sexual orientation, and ethnicity added toward the end. Whether we approach multicultural couple therapy from a purely practical perspective of effectiveness, or as a moral imperative, it is clear that diversity ought to be integrated in therapy, training, and supervision so that it is the "main course" and not an afterthought. Every chapter in this book makes the argument that multiple areas of diversity intersect with each other and should be considered at every step of learning or conducting couple therapy. Multicultural therapy includes reflecting on and gaining skills on how to form that all-important alliance with clients in the context of both the therapist's and the clients' multilayered reality. This book also addresses the specific knowledge base and culturally sensitive approaches that would be essential to mental health professionals in dealing with different cultures. Finally, some of the culturally focused research published in this book challenges us to expand existing couple research to use representative samples of participants, so as to increase the external validity of our core research. All of us educators, clinicians, students, researchers, and other stakeholders in the field ought to push for these win–win changes to become a priority.

This book is designed for researchers and clinicians, beginning trainees and experienced counselors/therapists, and readers interested in multicultural therapy and in couple therapy. In order to address all these different perspectives, the book is divided into three parts. Part I includes thoughts on developing a multicultural competence; addresses issues of power, privilege, and oppression to be considered by White therapists working with minority couples; and discusses the emotional experience of immigration, which is a central issue for many minority couples presenting for therapy. Part II of the book, Intersections of Diversity, is focused on therapy with interracial couples, interventions with religious minority couples, and evidence-based models of couple therapy with minority populations. The final section, Part III, highlights approaches to working with couples from different racial/ethnic backgrounds, including various perspectives on therapy with African American and Black couples, Asian American couples, Latino/a and Hispanic couples, and Native American and First Nations couples.

In order to cover the pertinent research, examine state-of-the-art treatment approaches, make it meaningful for clinicians, and provide practical resources in the topic areas, all authors have followed the same outline and included nine distinct sections in their chapters: (1) introduction of the topic, the population under discussion, and the contextual context of the author(s); (2) a summary of the most recent research; (3) presentation of novel approaches to working with couples under consideration, using a multicultural and systemic perspective; (4) presentation of clinical material to illustrate the approach (i.e., case example); (5) specific tips for clinicians; (6) implications for training, supervision, future research, and personal growth; (7) exercises for clinicians and suggestions for reflections; (8) additional resources (e.g., films, Web sites, music, books); and (9) a comprehensive reference list.

We hope that this book will be attractive to the wide range of readers for whom it is intended, and that it will contribute to increasing couple and family therapists' multicultural knowledge and sensitivity with regard to couple therapy. We welcome your feedback and comments. We can be reached at MuditaRastogi@hotmail.com and thomasv@purdue.edu.

Note

1. Client details have been changed to protect confidentiality.

Reference

Johnson, S. (2004). *The practice of emotionally focused marital therapy: Creating connection.* Philadelphia: Brunner/Mazel.

Two

Power, Privilege, and Oppression

White Therapists Working With Minority Couples

Sheila Addison and Volker Thomas

Understanding how race works in the United States doesn't seem like rocket science to me. There are clues everywhere if white people want to see them.

—Kendall, 2006, p. 1

For the most part, other chapters in this volume are written to address the therapist–client relationship based on client characteristics or presenting problems. This chapter, on the other hand, addresses a "problem" that clinicians may not even be aware of, or one that they may not agree exists: the issue of racial privilege, particularly White privilege, and how it impacts the work of White[1] clinicians from the therapist's side of the relationship. In short, this is a chapter that is essentially saying "White clinician, treat thyself."

9

We assume this is likely to be the most-often-skipped chapter of this book. What hardworking, dedicated, sensitive professional wants to be told that he or she is part of the problem? However, it is our belief as clinicians, educators, and researchers that addressing privilege is as essential to helping clients, to being an effective therapist, as is having all the rest of the knowledge and skills contained between the covers of this book. Perhaps it is even more important. In our work, we have become convinced that issues of power and privilege, and their influence on the therapeutic process, matter. We have had the experience—both enlightening and humbling—of realizing that these issues matter most deeply when the therapist is identified with one or more dimensions of the majority culture. And we have come to suspect that, while some clinicians have more obvious privileged identities than others, all of us to some degree or other represent institutional and societal power when we sit down with our clients. But in cross-cultural therapy, these dynamics are particularly salient. Given the demographics of the mental health professions, which are overwhelmingly White (Northey, 2005), it is likely that the majority of this book's readers will also be White. Thus, it is impossible for us to imagine the existence of this book without a chapter on White privilege.

We anticipate that readers who have made it this far will be at a wide variety of places along the journey to becoming not just aware of White privilege, but also sensitive to the ways in which it affects our clients. The subjects of race and White privilege can be difficult to address, because White clinicians generally want to see themselves as good people—which in some circles has been defined as "people who don't 'see color'" (Bonilla-Silva, 2006). Hardy and Laszloffy (1998) suggest the following:

> One of the reasons it is difficult to acknowledge seeing color is that it will automatically be equated with *discriminating* against another on the basis of color. Many people, Whites especially, live with the fear that they will be accused of being a racist. Because many of these same people believe themselves to be . . . committed to racial justice, they find it difficult to acknowledge anything that might lead to the accusation that they are racist. (pp. 119–120)

As the authors also note, often words or actions that reinforce racial inequality are unintentional, or even invisible to the person behind them, who may well identify as someone who abhors racism. Similarly, we believe that White privilege is usually exercised outside the conscious awareness of White people; so, too, is male privilege invisible to men, straight privilege unseen by heterosexuals, and class privilege exercised unthinkingly by those in the middle and upper classes. Indeed, invisibility is an inherent quality of privilege. Kimmel (2003) compares having a privileged identity to walking with a strong wind at your back, rather than having to face it and fight it with every step. "You do not feel the wind; it feels you . . . Only when you turn around and face that wind do you realize its strength" (p. 1). McGoldrick (1998) refers to the "unspoken secrets" about the cultural, racial, and class- and gender-based hierarchies "that are the underpinnings of our society" (p. 5). In fact, for every identity category—sexuality, religion, size—there are at least two possible identities, often an apparently opposing pair (straight/gay, Christian/non-Christian, thin/fat), and it is usually crystal clear to those who share a culture which of the pair is favored, preferred, and privileged (Wilchins, 2003). This knowledge is obvious on an unconscious level. It is also so deeply ingrained as to appear totally natural.

To further complicate discussions of privilege, none of us occupies only one identity. We all have a gender, and a race, and an ethnicity. (Some of us may have more than one!) Often, discussions of privilege and oppression center on only one dimension of identity, opening the door for us to protest "but I don't *feel* privileged," to focus on our oppressed identities and exclude our privileged ones from our view. Identity categories "are not hermetically sealed from each other"—note Heldke and O'Connor (2004, p. 420) in their volume on the many varieties of privilege—but the resistance to looking at both the powerless and the powerful within us goes deep, beyond us as individuals to systemic movements such as feminism, which long resisted an analysis of its racism (Collins, 2004); gay rights, with its entrenched sexism (Beneke, 2004); and the historic racist and homophobic tensions that have pitted gays and lesbians against people of color, usually to the advantage of White heterosexuals (Bérubé, 2003).

The challenge we are offering in this chapter is, first, to resist the urge to dismiss the idea of privilege that readers may be uncomfortable searching out in themselves; second, to remain open to critically engaging with the idea of White privilege and its effects in therapy, particularly multicultural couple therapy; and third, to consider how other dimensions of difference, and therefore privilege, may be present with clinicians in the therapy room, even if they experience themselves as keenly, painfully oppressed along other dimensions.

Having opened with the royal "we," the authors do intend to introduce ourselves and speak of our personal journeys with privilege. I (SA) am a queer White woman in my early 30s. More specifically, I am a bisexual woman of no particular religious affiliation, from a predominantly White Midwestern state, born into a family whose ethnicity I would describe as "middle-class Yankee," a group of de-ethnicized Whites with a strange mix of affection for individualism, capitalism, social service, and conscience, but little understanding of the systemic effects of oppression. While I was raised to have progressive ideals by a feminist single mother, I was—like most White people in the United States—unaware of the implications or even the existence of my Whiteness. While I was eager to explore issues of gender and sexual identity in my scholastic and clinical work, I had to be reluctantly awakened to the need to incorporate race and ethnicity. At times I was resentful toward those who suggested I needed to attend to race, to "see color" and to recognize the privileges associated with my racial background. I believed they were trying to complicate things unnecessarily, to force their agenda on me, to take time and energy away from "my issues." In retrospect, I understand my resistance as an attempt to stay safe from having to acknowledge my privilege, from confronting racist implications of my own words and actions, and from examining the hidden racism in the feminist and gay-liberation movements that were so important to my understanding of my own identities. Seeing myself as marginalized empowered and energized me; seeing myself at the center, as the wielder of power, was terrifying.

I (VT) am a White, straight man in my late 50s, in my second marriage with three children and one grandchild. As an immigrant to the United States from Germany in the mid-1980s, I was hypersensitive about my German ethnicity and naively colorblind to racial differences, and to my own power and privilege associated with my skin color and ethnic background. I grew up in post–World War II Germany with parents who used the economic growth of the postwar era to advance from the status of poorly educated farm families to middle-class urban business people. When I came to the United States, I thought I knew all about racial power and privilege growing up in a country that had committed genocide to fulfill its "dream" of racial dominance. Although I was highly aware of my German ethnicity, it took me some time to open my eyes to the racial privileges I was awarded by my Whiteness (which I did not even want). Over the years, I learned in sometimes painful encounters that we are afforded certain privileges (for me, that included being White, male, straight, married, well educated, middle class, and able-bodied) for which we have to take responsibility and hold ourselves accountable if we are serious about working against injustice and helping others.

White Privilege

Even culturally sensitive clinicians may wonder what relevance such a discussion has to a book about couple therapy. To answer that question, we must ask two more: first, what is White privilege? And second, how might it affect work with our clients?

What Is White Privilege?

In her discussion of the ethics of privilege, Hobgood (2000) talks about the "unearned benefits" that come with membership in "elite class, race, and gender groups" (pp. 2–3). She argues that these benefits are not connected to individual circumstances—a fortunate introduction here or a merit pay raise there—but instead come "as a result of our dominant positions in interlocking class, race, and sex/gender systems . . . Unearned benefits come when our group has the power to increase the social burden on other groups" (p. 3). So, for Hobgood, privilege is linked to dominance.

Dyer (2003) looks more specifically at White privilege, pointing out that while people of color are often identified by their race or ethnicity, both in real life and in the media ("a Black student," "my Japanese friend"), Whites are almost never referred to as "White," but by some other characteristic ("a second-year student," "my friend who works downtown"). "There is no more powerful position than that of being 'just' human . . . The claim to power is the claim to speak for the commonality of humanity. Raced people can't do that—they can only speak for their race" (Dyer, 2003, p. 22). In other words, if you want to hear "what the Black community thinks," ask a Black person. But if you want to know what "people" think, you ask someone who is White.

Brown et al. (2003) discuss racial privilege in terms of the power to exclude, pointing out how laws have historically allowed Whites to exclude people of color from certain neighborhoods, and how the over-representation of Whites in executive and managerial positions has allowed them to set policies that have subtly controlled minority access to loans and other forms of credit, stores, and health care. Jensen (2005) calls racial privilege a social phenomenon, one that plays out within a complex network of other identities such as gender and class, but that includes differing treatment shown to Whites versus people of color in situations such as purchasing a car, renting an apartment, and hailing a cab.

Johnson (2006) gives an example on a more personal level. "If people take me more seriously when I give a speech than they would someone of color saying the same things in the same way, then I'm benefiting from White privilege" (p. 21). He points out that privilege operating in this situation would likely be invisible to him—after all, he does not know whether someone congratulating him on his presentation would be "more critical and less positive if I were Latino or female or gay. I don't *feel* privileged in the moment. I just feel that I did a good job, and I enjoy the rewards that are supposed to go with it" (Johnson, p. 21). But he gets both the rewards of speaking well and the benefits of positive attitudes toward Whites from those in the audience.

Probably the most widely cited essay on White privilege is "White Privilege: Unpacking the Invisible Knapsack," by Peggy McIntosh (1998), because its list of invisible, unearned benefits of Whiteness is so memorable. McIntosh observes: "I can turn on the television or open to the front page of the paper and see people of my race widely represented" (p. 149). She goes on:

> Whether I use checks, credit cards, or cash, I can count on my skin color not to work against the appearance of financial reliability . . . I can do well in a challenging situation without being called a credit to my race . . . I can be pretty sure that if I ask to talk to "the person in charge," I will be facing a person of my race . . . I can choose blemish cover or bandages in "flesh" color and have them more or less match my skin. (pp. 149–150)

Yet McIntosh's (1998) list also seems a popular target for those who would deny the importance or existence of White privilege. Perhaps some of its assumptions have not aged well; in 2007, African American and Latino people can certainly "go into a music shop and count on finding the music of my race represented" (McIntosh, 1998, p. 149), for example. But educators often find themselves arguing the validity of specific assertions, as if microlevel change eradicates racial privilege on a macrolevel, while students avoid addressing the systemic privileges McIntosh documents. "Instead," Lipsitz (2006) writes, "they complain that 'reverse discrimination' against Whites makes their race a liability, and that . . . society . . . delivers unfair gains and unjust rewards to communities of color" (p. 105). Jensen (2005) describes showing a 1991 *Nightline* program on discrimination to his White students, who turned out to be more interested in complaining about how they might be treated if they were to enter a Black neighborhood—something most of them rarely, if ever, did.

Indeed, I (SA) was left speechless by a White male graduate student's assertion that "I'm just so sick of having to read that stupid 'knapsack' article," as if his boredom (which he blamed on the article, not his lack of engagement with it) were more important than the conversation the article was intended to provoke.

By the very nature of their invisibility, the barriers that protect White privilege and reserve it for White people resist critical examination. The barriers seem so natural to Whites, and so unrelated to race, that they defy discussion. White people may see instances of difference, but fail to understand their connection to Whiteness and its inherent privileges. But, as Kimmel (2003) points out, "Barriers have different meanings to those on opposite sides of them, even though they are barriers to both" (p. 20). Just as the walls of a prison represent captivity to the inmate and safety to those outside it, "a set of social and economic barriers . . . separating two groups may be felt, even painfully, by members of both . . . and yet may mean confinement to one and liberty and enlargement of opportunity to the other" (p. 21). This is how White privilege acts on us, and on our cross-cultural clients, confounding our search for mutual understanding while preventing us from realizing or acknowledging that it is doing so.

How Does White Privilege Affect Work With Our Clients in Multicultural Couple Therapy?

Readers of this volume presumably have come to some kind of relationship, uneasy or not, with the idea that culture matters in therapy, and in fact this conclusion seems to be informing the field more each year (McDowell & Jeris, 2004). Other authors have explored the ways in which clients' cultures matter in great depth elsewhere in this book. And yet, although the idea of "self-of-the-therapist"—or, expressed in older, more psychoanalytic terms, "countertransference"—is hardly new to our profession, there still seems to be some hesitancy in concluding that indeed we too have our role to play in the therapy process, and our identities come with us into the therapy room.

Blow, Sprenkle, and Davis (2007) present a comprehensive look at what is known about how individual therapist qualities affect outcomes, and conclude that evidence suggests these factors may be even more important than the use of any particular therapeutic model. Even in manualized treatments, individual therapist qualities seem to be critical. In addition to reminding readers that "it is in the therapeutic relationship that therapists either make or break therapy" (p. 306), the authors state that "therapists who are knowledgeable about and highly sensitive to the unique cultural worlds of their clients . . . do a far better job of engaging and retaining clients in therapy and as a result achieve better outcomes" (p. 305). Evidence suggests that this is true not only for ethnic or racial minorities, but for sexual minorities as well (Phillips, 2000).

Our investigation of White privilege leads us inexorably toward the conclusion that it is part of the "unique cultural worlds" of our minority clients, as visible to them as it should be invisible to those of us who are White. Ignoring the effects of privilege in the world at large allows us to ignore our clients' experiences of how privilege works against them, leading us to minimize or quibble with their concerns. Kivel (2003) offers the example of a Latino student who expresses to a White teacher that he believes he was passed over for a job offer because of his ethnicity. The teacher, though well meaning, downplays the possibility of racism and questions the student's assessment of the situation, perhaps in an attempt to soothe the student's feelings. But the interaction may also represent the teacher's lack of awareness about how his White privilege has informed his experience with job interviews, as well as his discomfort with the student's anger. "He begins to defend himself, the job recruiter, and White people. He ends up feeling attacked for being White. Rather than talking about what happened, he focuses on [the student's] anger and his generalizations about White people" (pp. 403–404). It is not hard to picture a similar action taking place, not in the hallway of a school but in the privacy of the therapy room.

Mahmoud (1998) uses the classic MRI term *double bind* to apply to the conflicting strictures people of color experience when they experience oppression at the hands of those who are allegedly acting benevolently toward them. One way in which oppression enters the therapy room is when the therapist fails to see the relevance of race to clients and their problems. Mahmoud points out that when "oppression is not directly addressed . . . a key dynamic in . . . a client's life and its concomitant pathology will be ignored" (p. 263). She also identifies the therapist's behavior as potentially oppressive; by displaying an "anxiety-provoking neutrality" around issues of race and culture, clients may feel discounted, or like the clinician is defending those who are creating the double binds in the client's life.

Hardy and Laszloffy (1998) take the analysis even further, noting that "many people of color learn early in life to censor [comments on racism] while in the presence of White people. Therefore . . . it is more likely for clients in similar situations to remain silent" (p. 123). Silence in the face of a

White therapist's ignorance or privilege merely reinforces the double binds of racism, the "crazy-making" experience of wondering, "Is there something wrong with them, or with me?" Under such conditions, an effective therapist–client relationship cannot possibly flourish, and indeed McGoldrick (2005) notes that "the more power and privilege we have, the harder it is to think about the meaning of the rage of the powerless" (p. 34).

Research on the topic of race and the therapeutic relationship offers both frustration and hope. A recent focus group study revealed that many African Americans still picture typical psychotherapists as "older White males who [are] unsympathetic, uncaring, and unavailable" (Thompson, Bazile, & Akbar, 2004, p. 23). Participants shared worries that White therapists do not understand the realities of African American life, that clinicians would be biased, and that they would be negatively labeled as "crazy" because of their emotional expressiveness. They expressed the belief that most therapists were of a higher socioeconomic status, and some even avoided talking about financial and work problems because of fears that the therapist "would not understand" (Thompson et al., 2004, p. 24). The cues participants looked for to indicate that a mixed-race therapy relationship was safe were often subtle—reading material in the waiting area, art on the walls, and therapists' reactions when clients "tested the water" with concerns about issues such as employment or discrimination.

Another recent qualitative study suggested that White therapists often did not bring up the subject of racial difference with their minority clients, instead leaving that job to the clients themselves (Knox et al., 2003). A larger, even more recent, study still reported mixed results, with most clinicians acknowledging that they discussed race and ethnicity some of the time, but the typical respondent had done so with fewer than half of their cross-ethnic or cross-racial clients. Still, noticeable subgroups connected bringing up the topic with improving treatment outcomes, or with recognizing the connections between minority identities and clients' experiences (Maxie, Arnold, & Stephenson, 2006).

According to McDowell and Jeris (2004), "Many Whites believe only others are racist, and that racism is only demonstrated by overt, mean-spirited acts that occur in isolated instances" (p. 90). The authors point out the hidden assumption that eliminating racist acts and stereotypes will eliminate racism, and assert the need for clinicians to "challenge their own racial perspectives and dismantle racism in themselves" (p. 91), while also questioning the norm of Whiteness within the Marriage and Family Therapy (MFT) field that reinforces White privilege in therapy.

CASE EXAMPLE

The following case example addresses not only the therapeutic level—that is, the therapist–client relationship—but also the supervision level—that is, the therapist–supervisor relationship—and the metavision level—the supervisor candidate–mentoring supervisor relationship. In fact, the issue of White privilege plays out at all three levels. As a White male supervisor of European descent, I (VT) provided mentoring supervision to two supervisor candidates, Carl and Jim. They in turn provided supervision of entry-level Marriage and Family Therapy students. One of the supervisor candidates, Carl, was Black while the other, Jim, was White.

During one of our mentoring supervision sessions, Carl consulted with us on his supervisory work with a first-year master's-level MFT student doing couple therapy. During our session, Carl repeatedly praised the student for doing an excellent job with the couple. As their supervision progressed, the therapist became more skillful in conceptualizing her therapeutic work and applying it to her therapy sessions. I was very impressed with Carl's ability to support the therapist in her work and, at the same time, to challenge her in ways that moved the supervision process forward. Toward the end of our session Carl mentioned—which I perceived as an afterthought—that the couple with whom the White therapist had been working was African American.

Surprise was my initial reaction, and I found myself saying to him: "Here am I, a White mentoring supervisor, finding myself wondering why you, a Black supervisor, neglected the crucial racial context of your supervision and the therapeutic arrangement. Your supervision session would have been a great opportunity for you as an African American supervisor to have praised a White therapist for doing a good job with Black clients. What kept you from making the racial context isomorphicly overt in the supervision session so that the therapist could use it in her therapy sessions?" Overwhelmed by a mixture of excitement, embarrassment, and a slight irritation, I barely heard Carl's response, which he delivered in a calm voice, sharing with me that he did not place importance on the couple's race in the context of therapy because the therapist was so well connected with, and supportive of, the couple that he did not want race to become an issue that might threaten their excellent working alliance. Carl continued to talk about his experience of racism that had taught him when to confront it and when to leave it alone. He maintained that the successful therapy of his supervisee was an example of a time when raising the issue of race could have done more harm than good to the therapeutic and supervisory relationship.

I could not believe what I had heard. "Is Carl colorblind when it is opportune? Why does he not consider the isomorphic processes on the therapeutic and supervision level and seize the opportunity?" I wondered. I gave a mini-lecture on isomorphism and race relationships. Carl held his ground, insisting that he knew what he was doing and that he could not see any plausible reason to raise the topic of race. I quickly realized that we were stuck, and that I had to do something else to "convince" Carl. I turned to Jim, knowing that he and Carl were good friends. "Jim, please help me out. Carl does not understand what I am talking about. You are White; maybe you as his buddy can explain to him what I mean." Jim looked at me hesitantly, but complied with my request.

As the tension in the room continued to rise, the situation became increasingly awkward. I knew something had gone wrong during the session. I felt helpless and very uncomfortable. I clearly sensed that Carl and Jim did too. Because we were at the end of our time, I made some summarizing remarks about the complexities of isomorphism and supervision in the context of racial issues. I suggested we talk about the case more during our next supervision session.

The following day, I received an e-mail from Carl in which he openly expressed his frustration with my statements and particularly with the process of our session. I felt relieved that Carl had felt safe and courageous enough to express his reactions. His comments were consistent with my processing of events during the session. I had been so focused on the racial context of the therapy context (Black client–White therapist) and the supervision context (White therapist–Black supervisor) and their isomorphic relationship that I lost sight of our mentoring supervision/metavision context (Black supervisor candidate–White mentoring supervisor and White supervisor candidate). I was blind to how I had used my position of power as White mentoring supervisor to disregard my Black supervisor candidate's considerations of the racial context in therapy. Additionally, I pulled in the other White supervisor candidate to "convince" his Black "buddy" that I was "right."

I lectured Carl on racial sensitivity in relation to his supervisee without seeing my own racial insensitivity in relation to him and his White colleague. I had also tried to recruit Carl into congratulating a White therapist on being successful with Black clients—an act that would overemphasize the White therapist's "goodness" for demonstrating simple baseline multicultural competence, and would put Carl in the position of making a White person feel virtuous for not acting in a racist way. Black people are often called upon, overtly or covertly, to make White people feel good about their racial politics and to assure them that they are "not racist," and my expectation that Carl would do the same for his supervisee came more from my White privilege (and my desire to appear racially sensitive) than from a sense of what would be clinically helpful.

The complexity of considering multiple interactional levels (i.e., therapy, supervision, mentoring supervision) simultaneously was not a sufficient explanation for my lapse in recognizing the effects of my privilege and power as a White mentoring supervisor on our process, and taking responsibility for changing it. I felt embarrassed, and realized once again how subtle racist processes can easily interfere and become less and less subtle as the interaction cycle escalates. I also realized that processes that were "subtle" and invisible to me were, in all likelihood, highly visible to Carl, who as a Black person was trained from birth to recognize racially charged situations and dominating White behaviors.

Realizing that my White racial developmental process (Helms, 2000) was not as advanced and that I was not as culturally sensitive (Hardy & Laszloffy, 1998) as I had hoped, I accepted responsibility for my behavior and responded to Carl with an e-mail of apology. I also asked Carl whether he agreed that we share our e-mail exchange with Jim, since he had been part of our session. With Carl's approval, I forwarded both e-mails to Jim, suggesting to both that we talk about our processes more during our next session.

When we met the following week for mentoring supervision, I still felt embarrassed, but was relieved when it seemed that the awkward stuckness of our last session had been replaced with dialogue. The e-mail exchange between Carl and me had reopened conversational space between us. Carl accepted my apology as me taking responsibility for the use of my White and institutional power and privilege. Each of us shared our struggles with the situation and racism in the past and present, while Jim talked about his role and affect as a White "bystander" to our exchange.

Discussion

At the beginning of this chapter, we acknowledged that there are many types of privilege and oppression—and indeed it is possible, even probable, that readers will have both dominant and subordinate identities in relationship to many clients. The concerns and principles outlined above with regard to White privilege are also applicable to heterosexual therapists working with GLBT clients, able-bodied therapists with disabled and chronically ill clients, thin therapists working with fat clients, and client–therapist religious differences (Greene, 1995). The overriding principle is that it is incumbent upon us as clinicians to manage our anxiety so that we can accept the possibility of invisible privilege at work.

For example, I (SA) have begun seeing more clients seeking "size positive" therapy, mostly women who are looking for services from a clinician who will not stigmatize them for being "overweight" or "obese" and try to pressure them to lose weight as a panacea for their problems. Although I identify as "fat," I am smaller than many of my clients seeking such acceptance, and I make it a point to acknowledge that, even with our similarities, my "fat experience" at a size 16 is not the same as another person's experience at a size 32. The responsibility is on me to accept that, despite my experiences of being excluded or singled out because of my body, some of my clients may look at me and think "she has it easier than I do."

Our job as therapists is to overcome our fear of discussions of race and other dimensions of privilege/oppression, and to become comfortable not only hearing out our privileged identities, but to be able to initiate discussions of them as well rather than leaving the risks for our clients to take (a privilege in and of itself) as illustrated in the case example above. Resources provided at the end of this article may be helpful to clinicians who are seeking guidance for how to take accountability for one's unearned privilege, and how to translate this accountability into a responsible use of one's situationally granted power as a therapist or supervisor.

Now, while we would like to have the luxury of taking only a strengths-based approach to the thorny problem of White privilege, we must point out the many seductive, yet unhelpful, responses that present themselves when we are asked to confront our alliance with dominant identities. A few examples follow, inspired in part by McGoldrick, Giordano, and Garcia-Preto's (2005) exploration of "how Whites often attempt to discuss racism" and Johnson's (2006) chapter "Getting Off the Hook: Denial and Resistance."

"My grandparents came over during the Great Irish Famine/I got free school lunches growing up/I'm married to a person from South America." As we acknowledged previously, it is possible to be simultaneously privileged on some dimensions of identity and oppressed on others. This simply makes the conversation more complex—oppression and privilege are not like positive and negative numbers that cancel each other out. There is plenty

of opportunity to honor our experiences with struggle, while also using that experience to create compassion for others. When we have felt victimized by others, it is difficult to see ourselves as potential victimizers ourselves, but the best way to avoid doing so is to acknowledge the possibility that we may not always walk as softly in this world as we would like.

"I think racism is terrible/I voted for same-sex marriage." Even good people are entangled in systems of power and privilege. We, the authors, could attempt to renounce every scrap of White privilege afforded to us by the system, but we would still be perceived in racially advantaged terms when out in public, and we would nonetheless owe a portion of our current educational and professional status to advantages granted to our ancestors. While we badly want to be judged as individuals and found to be good people, we cannot afford to exclude ourselves from an examination of power and privilege, and remain congruent with our values.

"I do feminist/client-centered/postmodern therapy. I try not to have any hierarchy with clients." Chantler (2005) eloquently points out the flaws of a strictly Rogerian approach to therapy, noting that "the power differences between therapist and client are an inherent part of the relationship— despite attempts to equalize it" (p. 247). She writes,

> Focusing on one dimension of power within person-centered counseling relationships, can lead to an insistence that therapeutic relationships are equal when all manner of unspoken equalities are also part of the relationship. . . . This encourages a culture of silencing power relations, which has a direct impact on the therapeutic endeavor. (p. 247)

"If couples want therapy without White privilege, they should just see a therapist from their own ethnic/racial group." As mentioned in the Introduction, the demographics of our field make this an impossibility: There are simply not enough clinicians of color to meet the needs of all minority clients. This frustrated response also denies the possibility for deeply satisfying, clinically helpful cross-identity relationships. Murphy, Faulkner, and Behrens (2004) found that clients did not need a therapist with the same racial identity in order to feel satisfied with treatment. Bernstein (2000) argues that the same is true when it comes to sexual minority clients. And for opposite-sex, mixed-religion, or cross-race couples, it is impossible for a single therapist to have the same identity as both clients.

"I'd like to talk about this, but it feels unsafe." It is crucial to remember that the ability to participate in or withdraw from a discussion is a privilege in

and of itself. People who wear their disadvantaged identities out into the world do not have the option to only consider race, sex, size, class, and sexual identity when they feel it is safe to do so. Even less visible identities, such as sexual identity, religion, or socioeconomic status, still impact how subjugated people experience the world. The anti-gay joke or the question "How are you celebrating Christmas?" inflicts pain, whether apparent to the privileged speaker or not. Taking the risk of choosing to address your privilege, even when it is uncomfortable to do so, is one way to actively decline the benefits of a privileged identity.

Conclusion

In closing, we as the authors hope that White readers will take this chapter as encouragement toward further challenges and growth, rather than as a blanket condemnation of White therapists. We hope that all readers will consider how they may be privileged along some dimension(s) of identity, and how this privilege enters the clinical picture regardless of our good intentions and kind hearts. We hope that our passion for integrating social justice with clinical work, beginning with an unflinching critical examination of our own identities, will inspire others to do the same. As Kendall (2006) wrote in our opening quote, this is not rocket science. We believe in the capacity of every clinician to undertake this work and, in doing so, to promote healing on many systemic levels through our own fearless desire to do better and do what is right.

Note

1. The term *White* refers to persons with light skin color who have European background; we use it interchangeably with the term *Caucasian*. We capitalize the term to differentiate it as a racial, socially constructed category from the color.

Additional Resources

Films

Chasnoff, D., & Cohen, H. (Directors). (1996). *It's Elementary.* Available from www.womedia.org. Aimed at schools and teachers, this film illustrates how heterosexism and homophobia penetrate the consciousness of even young children, and how confronting stereotypes makes school safer for Gay, Lesbian, Bisexual, and Transsexual (GLBT) kids.

Lee Mun Wah (Director). (1994). *The Color of Fear*, Parts 1–3, and *Last Chance for Eden*. Available from www.stirfryseminars.com. These documentaries feature diverse groups of people exploring racism and sexism through the personal relationships they develop while having "difficult dialogues."

Nanako, D. (Director). (1995). *White Man's Burden*. Staring John Travolta and Harry Belafonte. Set in an alternative America where Blacks are the majority and Whites are marginalized, this film powerfully illustrates the hidden ways in which privilege operates.

Peters, W. (Director). (1985). *A Class Divided*. Available on the PBS Web site, www.pbs.org/wgbh/pages/frontline/shows/divided for online viewing or purchase. The film features Jane Elliott's "blue eyed/brown eyed" exercise, dividing her third-grade class by eye color to help teach them about the effects of discrimination, as well as a repeat of the exercise with employees of the Iowa prison system.

Readings

Heldke, L., & O'Connor, P. (2004). *Oppression, privilege, & resistance: Theoretical perspectives in racism, sexism, and heterosexism*. Boston: McGraw-Hill. An extensive anthology of writings on many types of privilege and how they operate in a framework of dominance. Excellent discussions of how oppressed and privileged identities can intersect in individuals.

Hobgood, M. E. (2000). *Dismantling privilege: An ethics of accountability*. Cleveland, OH: Pilgrim Press. An ethical perspective based in, but not limited to, Christianity on the importance of increasing social justice by disrupting systems of oppressive power.

Johnson, A. F. (2006). *Privilege, power, and difference* (2nd ed.). Boston: McGraw-Hill. An accessible book linking theories of power and difference to real-life examples that gently but deeply challenges readers' assumptions about privilege.

Kendall, F. E. (2006). *Understanding White privilege: Creating pathways to authentic relationships across race*. New York: Routledge. An examination of privilege based both in scholarship and in the author's experiences as a White woman, this book is an excellent primer for "those who have tried to build authentic professional relationships across race but have felt unable to do so."

Kivel, P. (2002). *Uprooting racism: How White people can work for social justice* (Rev. ed.). Gabriola Island, BC: New Society. This is a book "designed to help White people act on the conviction that racism is wrong." An excellent guide for how to give up the privilege to sit on the sidelines of the struggle for racial justice.

Stone Fish, L., Harvey, R., & Addison, S. (2000). Don't ask, don't tell: Supervision and sexual identity. In *Readings in family therapy supervision: Selected articles from the AAMFT Supervision Bulletin.* Washington, DC: American Association for Marriage and Family Therapy. A discussion of stages of supervisor identity development around preparation for addressing sexual identity in the supervision process.

Tatum, B. D. (1997). *Why are all the Black kids sitting together in the cafeteria?* New York: Basic Books. A jargon-free book examining racial divisions in America, and how they are created and maintained.

Web Sites

Ally Work: http://allywork.solidaritydesign.net. A group blog "dedicated to helping White people fight White Supremacy."

AP Racism: http://community.livejournal.com/ap_racism/profile. A live journal community for discussion of privilege and unexamined aspects of racism. Moderated membership.

Beyond White Guilt: http://community.livejournal.com/debunkingwhite. A live journal community for examining aspects of White identity as they relate to institutional oppression.

Tim Wise: www.timwise.org. Home page for the well-known White anti-racism speaker and educator Tim Wise.

White Privilege: www.whiteprivilege.com. A free resource for antiracism education and activism. A group blog offering personal essays and deconstruction of news events.

Why am I not surprised? http://whyaminotsurprised.blogspot.com. Blog written by a sociologist about social constructions of race.

References

Beneke, T. (2004). Gay sexism. In L. Heldke & P. O'Connor (Eds.), *Oppression, privilege, & resistance: Theoretical perspectives in racism, sexism, and heterosexism* (pp. 544–552). Boston: McGraw-Hill.

Bernstein, A. (2000). Straight therapists working with lesbians and gays in family therapy. *Journal of Marital and Family Therapy, 26,* 443–454.

Bérubé, A. (2003). How gay stays White and what kind of White it stays. In M. S. Kimmel & A. L. Ferber (Eds.), *Privilege: A reader* (pp. 253–283). Boulder, CO: Westview Press.

Blow, A. J., Sprenkle, D. H., & Davis, S. D. (2007). Is who delivers the treatment more important than the treatments itself? The role of the therapist in common factors. *Journal of Marital and Family Therapy, 33,* 298–317.

Bonilla-Silva, E. (2006). *Racism without racists: Color-blind racism and the persistence of racial inequality in the United States.* Lanham, MD: Rowman & Littlefield.

Brown, M. K., Carnoy, M., Currie, E., Duster, T., Oppenheimer, D. B., Shultz, M. M., & Wellman, D. (2003). *White-washing race: The myth of a color-blind society.* Berkeley, CA: University of California Press.

Chantler, K. (2005). From disconnection to connection: "Race," gender, and the politics of therapy. *British Journal of Guidance and Counselling, 33,* 239–256.

Collins, P. H. (2004). Toward a new vision: Race, class, and gender as categories of analysis and connection. In L. Heldke & P. O'Connor (Eds.), *Oppression, privilege, & resistance: Theoretical perspectives in racism, sexism, and heterosexism* (pp. 529–543). Boston: McGraw-Hill.

Crohn, J. (1998). Intercultural couples. In M. McGoldrick (Ed.), *Re-visioning family therapy: Race, culture, and gender in clinical practice* (pp. 295–308). New York: Guilford Press.

Dyer, R. (2003). The matter of Whiteness. In M. S. Kimmel & A. L. Ferber (Eds.), *Privilege: A reader* (pp. 21–32). Boulder, CO: Westview Press.

Greene, B. (1995). Addressing racism, sexism, and heterosexism in psychoanalytic psychotherapy. In J. M. Glassgold & S. Iasenza (Eds.), *Lesbians and psychoanalysis: Revolutions in theory and practice* (pp. 145–159). New York: Free Press.

Hardy, K. V., & Laszloffy, T. A. (1998). The dynamics of a pro-racist ideology: Implications for family therapists. In M. McGoldrick (Ed.), *Re-visioning family therapy: Race, culture, and gender in clinical practice* (pp. 118–128). New York: Guilford Press.

Heldke, L., & O'Connor, P. (2004). *Oppression, privilege, & resistance: Theoretical perspectives in racism, sexism, and heterosexism.* Boston: McGraw-Hill.

Helms, J. E. (2000). *Black and White racial identity: Theory, research, and practice.* New York: Greenwood Press.

Hobgood, M. E. (2000). *Dismantling privilege: An ethics of accountability.* Cleveland, OH: Pilgrim Press.

Jensen, R. (2005). *The heart of Whiteness: Confronting race, racism, and White privilege.* San Francisco, CA: City Lights.

Johnson, A. F. (2006). *Privilege, power, and difference* (2nd ed.). Boston: McGraw-Hill.

Kendall, F. E. (2006). *Understanding White privilege: Creating pathways to authentic relationships across race.* New York: Routledge.

Kimmel, M. S. (2003). Toward a pedagogy of the oppressor. In M. S. Kimmel & A. L. Ferber (Eds.), *Privilege: A reader* (pp. 1–10). Boulder, CO: Westview Press.

Kivel, P. (2002). *Uprooting racism: How White people can work for social justice* (rev. ed.). Gabriola Island, BC: New Society.

Kivel, P. (2003). Being a strong White ally. In M.S. Kimmel & A. L. Ferber (Eds.), *Privilege: A reader* (pp. 401–411). Boulder, CO: Westview Press.

Knox, S., et al. (2003). African American and European American therapists' experience addressing race in cross-race therapy dyads. *Journal of Counseling Psychology, 50*, 466–481.

Lipsitz, G. (2006). *The possessive investment in Whiteness: How White people profit from identity politics* (rev. ed.). Philadelphia, PA: Temple University Press.

Mahmoud, V. M. (1998). The double binds of racism. In M. McGoldrick (Ed.), *Re-visioning family therapy: Race, culture, and gender in clinical practice* (pp. 255–267). New York: Guilford Press.

Maxie, A. C., Arnold, D. H., & Stephenson, M. (2006). Do therapists address ethnic and racial differences in cross-cultural psychotherapy? *Psychotherapy: Theory, Research, Practice, Training, 43*, 85–98.

McDowell, T., & Jeris, L. (2004). Talking about race using critical race theory: Recent trends in the *Journal of Marital and Family Therapy. Journal of Marital and Family Therapy, 30*, 81–94.

McGoldrick, M. (1998). Introduction: Re-visioning family therapy through a cultural lens. In M. McGoldrick (Ed.), *Re-visioning family therapy: Race, culture, and gender in clinical practice* (pp. 3–19). New York: Guilford Press.

McGoldrick, M., Giordano, J., & Garcia-Preto, N. (2005). *Ethnicity and family therapy* (3rd ed.). New York: Guilford Press.

McIntosh, P. (1998). White privilege: Unpacking the invisible knapsack. In M. McGoldrick (Ed.), *Re-visioning family therapy: Race, culture, and gender in clinical practice* (pp. 147–152). New York: Guilford Press.

Murphy, M. J., Faulkner, R. A., & Behrens, C. (2004). The effect of therapist–client racial similarity on client satisfaction and therapist evaluation of treatment. *Contemporary Family Therapy, 26*, 279–292.

Northey, W. F. (1985). Studying marriage and family therapists in the 21st century: Methodological and technological issues. *Journal of Marital and Family Therapy, 31*(1), 99–105.

Phillips, J. C. (2000). Training issues and considerations. In R. M. Perez, K. A. DeBord, & K. J. Bieschke (Eds.), *Handbook of counseling and psychotherapy with lesbian, gay, and bisexual clients* (pp. 337–358). Washington, DC: American Psychological Association.

Tatum, B. D. (1997). *Why are all the Black kids sitting together in the cafeteria?* New York: Basic Books.

Thompson, V. L. S., Bazile, A., & Akbar, M. (2004). African Americans' perceptions of psychotherapy and psychotherapists. *Professional Psychology: Research and Practice, 35*, 19–26.

Wilchins, R. (2004). *Queer theory, gender theory: An instant primer.* Los Angeles, CA: Alyson Books.

Three

The Emotional Experience of Immigration for Couples

Sol D'Urso, Sandra Reynaga,
and Jo Ellen Patterson

According to the 2000 U.S. Census, 11.1% of the U.S. population, or 31.1 million people, are foreign-born individuals. Approximately half of the U.S. foreign-born population is from Latin American countries. The number of individuals born outside of the United States has more than doubled between 1990 and 2000. As a result of current immigration trends, American hospitals and organizations are being asked to deliver health care services, including mental health, to immigrants and their families. Given the increase in the number of immigrants in the U.S. population, therapists need knowledge of the complexity of this experience and how it influences the family system. This chapter concentrates specifically on describing how immigration influences couples' relationships.

All couples face issues of parenting, division of labor, gender roles, the role of extended family, and other normative tasks. However, the immigrant couple faces an extra layer of complexity when addressing these issues. For example, division of household labor may vary greatly between their native country and new country because culture informs a couple's beliefs about gender roles. When an immigrant couple faces contradictory perspectives, the partners are left to solve these discrepancies by themselves, which can result in conflict.

Another unique issue faced by immigrant couples is differences in adaptation of family members to the new culture. Immigrant parents may know that their children are often exposed to unwanted influences and can feel powerless to stop the process. In addition, the couple may disagree about the seriousness of the children's challenges to family values. Finally, immigrant couples who might previously have depended on extended family support may find themselves isolated and lonely in their new culture. While transitions—including immigration—often present new opportunities, fresh challenges to the couple's historical norms often arise.

As marital and family therapists, our clinical work involves treating immigrant couples who live in San Diego, California. Most of the couples are first- or second-generation immigrants from Latin America who, as foreigners in the United States, face struggles similar to those discussed above. Other themes that are unique to the immigration experience are missing one's homeland, family members being left behind, language barriers, discrimination, and violence. Many of these issues have psychological and emotional effects on the couple's relationship.

Therapists who consider immigration as a variable in the assessment and treatment of couples recognize that the stress between the partners could be the result of any one of these factors or a combination of these factors with the couple's dynamics. In addition, financial strain including poverty can add additional stress to the immigration process, and to the couple's relationship dynamics. While it is beyond the scope of this chapter to address the effects of poverty on immigrants, in general this chapter focuses on immigrant couples struggling with financial challenges in addition to the acculturation process.

The couples receive services at a clinic that provides primary care and mental health services to individuals, couples, and families with no health insurance in an underserved community of San Diego. The therapists are two Spanish-speaking Latina women. Sol D'Urso was born and raised in Argentina and immigrated to the United States in 2000. Sandra Reynaga is a first-generation Mexican American from San Diego. Both therapists have personal experiences with the immigration process, which have influenced their curiosity about and interest in working with immigrant couples. The case study that will be illustrated in this chapter is a couple they saw as cotherapists while working toward their master's degree in marital and family therapy at the University of San Diego. The supervisor did not speak Spanish and had a different ethnic background; this created an enriching experience for both trainees and supervisor that was reflected in the couple's care.

In this chapter, we provide an outline of a narrative therapy approach used to work with immigrant couples. Narrative therapy suggests that we are born into cultural stories that shape our perception of what is possible (Freedman & Combs, 2002). Therapy then becomes a process of helping couples to create new stories that take into account their immigration experience.

Existing Research

The cross-cultural literature addresses different aspects of immigration: how immigration affects mental health; how this process intertwines with family issues; and how families make sense of this transition. Immigration initiates many challenges that can bring on mental health problems. For example, some of the challenges immigrants face include failure to succeed in the country of origin, dangerous border crossings, limited resources, restricted mobility, marginalization/isolation, blame/ stigmatization and guilt/shame, vulnerability/exploitability, and fear/ fear-based behaviors (Sullivan & Rehm, 2005). Leaving one's country of origin is associated with substance abuse, depression, crime, delinquency, family conflict and violence, school dropout, and other forms of individual and family breakdown (Falicov, 1998). Many articles identify the mental health effects of immigration and differences among ethnic groups; however, very few provide approaches to working specifically with the immigrant population.

Falicov (1998) developed an approach to working with immigrant families within the context of Family Therapy. Falicov's answer to providing attuned services to immigrants is to supplement information from Family Systems Theory and Family Therapy with concepts from migration theory. In her book *Latino Families in Therapy*, Falicov (1998) writes about the dilemmas immigrants face. She presents new ideas about the process of acculturation and assimilation into American culture, and she argues that instead of having to choose between their two cultures, couples can draw from both. She refers to the idea of living in two worlds as "both/and" solutions, and to the idea of having to choose between cultures as "either/or," or living between two worlds. Therapy then concentrates on helping families to navigate between the two worlds and utilizes positive aspects of each so the family can reach a point of stability and continuity. During therapy, clinicians can encourage immigrant couples to share their story, normalize their experience, and help the couple negotiate between demands from both cultures.

The idea of uprooting entire systems of meaning—physical, social, and cultural—can also be explored in therapy. Uprooting means an individual is taken out of his or her reality and placed in a different one. This idea can best be understood using Falicov's (1998) "root" metaphor of migration. When a plant is uprooted, the soil that remains on the root of the plant is vital for its survival when it is replanted. The key concept behind the uprooting metaphor is that immigrant families can use what they carry with them from their country of origin to adapt to their new life.

Gottman (1999) also talks about the creation of shared meaning in his work on marriages and marital therapy. Gottman points out that shared meaning is the couple's own culture—symbols, rituals, and goals that lead each partner to understand the meaning of being part of their marriage. Creating shared meaning often helps couples to overcome adversity but can also create conflict when the couple's "hidden agendas" go unrecognized or unarticulated. The immigrant couple may have many hidden agendas that become intertwined with their immigration experience, or that were created during this complex process. Helping the couple identify their hidden needs and purposes, and helping them articulate how they have overcome previous challenges, is one method for bringing the couple closer together.

Model

Our approach integrates concepts from the literature on immigration and marriage (Falicov, 1998, 2003). The therapist expands these concepts by using deconstructive questions from narrative therapy to help couples make sense of their experience. To use our approach, therapists first have to empathize and connect with the couple's experiences from a place of deep understanding and compassion.

To establish rapport, the therapist must understand the common prejudices and discrimination that immigrants endure daily. The therapist must also understand changes in immigration patterns and current possibilities for immigrants within the U.S. system. For example, a common belief is that immigrants are taking Americans' jobs. Other pundits point out that the U.S. economic system depends on immigrant labor to survive. Some Americans believe that all immigrants are eligible to receive government funding and health insurance. However, to qualify for these services, one must usually be a resident or citizen. The current Immigration Reform Laws (www.whitehouse.gov/infocus/immigration) will affect immigrant families and couples, and the therapist should know how these laws and regulations influence their clients.

Immigrants are often resourceful people who are beset by cultural norms and financial situations that undermine the values they bring from other countries. Immigrants decide to take risks in the hope of making a better life. They have left behind their systems of meaning, their familiar surroundings, and their extended families to come to a new country. When surrounded by uncertainty, immigrants can lose sight of their resources or points of reference; thus, feelings of confusion emerge. In many cases, this loss occurs because immigrants idealize the new system. In other cases, they idealize what was left behind (Estrada, Wiggins Frame, & Braun Williams, 2004). Many times, immigrants find themselves looking at what others have back home and what people in their new country have that they cannot attain. Therapy can help couples recognize and utilize their strengths in the new system, as well as help them find their own perspectives and values in their new context.

Narrative Therapy Approach

Narrative therapy (Freedman & Combs, 2002; White & Epston, 1990) values the clients' perspectives and helps them feel empowered. It also creates responsibility on the part of both the client and the therapist. Through therapy, the clients have more responsibility for their new choices and self-definitions. In contrast, the therapist is responsible for understanding how societal stereotypes harm individuals and help clients understand their situation in a different way.

Narrative therapy strives to create more equality between the clients and the therapist. A narrative approach allows therapy to be less hierarchical and creates a curious stance, concentrating on the client and thus creating a different way of listening, respecting, and stimulating change with clients. A narrative therapist respects immigrants' values and allows the couple to be the principal agent of change. In addition, the therapist is ready to provide, when necessary, different points of view that promote equality and respect.

In the process of creating a new narrative, the therapist both joins the couple in a respectful and collaborative way, and listens to the couple's story and what it means for them. The therapist does not assume to have the "truth" or "solution" to the problem. The therapist understands himself or herself as a "co-researcher," working in collaboration with the couple to create new knowledge. The therapist's role is to listen and search for strengths rather than deficits. Therapists also take a less hierarchical stance; at some point, they may situate their ideas in their own experience and subsequently make their intentions transparent. The therapist also encourages the couple to ask questions about his or her professional comments and work. The therapist may ask, "Is the work we have been doing helpful for you?" "Could I do something different that could be more helpful?" or "Do you have any questions for me?" (Freedman & Combs, 2002).

Based on postmodern ideas, narrative therapy supposes that all knowledge is constructed rather than discovered, and individuals are always participants in their interpretations of reality. This means that there is no truth or objective reality to observe; we are part of the interpretations we create (Freedman & Combs, 2002). The narrative therapist listens with the framework that there are many interpretations and meanings to the same story. In the case of immigration, each member of the couple may have a different view about the immigration experience. At times, partners are not able to see each other's interpretations and get stuck in a pessimistic view of their relationship. From this perspective, a narrative therapist collaborates with the couple to modify their narratives from problem-saturated to positive stories, or stories that make sense to the couple, helping them feel empowered and in control of their lives.

The therapist takes a "curious" stance and does not make any prior assumptions about the couple's earlier experiences (Anderson, 2000). For example, if a client comes to therapy and tells the therapist that she is a "person of color," the therapist may ask her to define what that means for her and how it affects her life, instead of assuming the therapist's own meaning of what a person of color is. In working with immigrant couples, the therapist is "curious" about their immigration experience and how the couple makes sense of that experience. Thus, the therapist has to ask the couple about their personal stories of immigration as part of the "description of the problem" during the assessment phase.

A therapist can invite a couple to discuss their immigration experience by using deconstructive questions. The therapist asks questions that may point out contradictions in the couple's story, or that may bring forth examples when the couple resisted the problem. Therefore, questions in narrative therapy make the couple aware of different viewpoints. The therapist also has to ask himself or herself deconstructive questions to understand personal biases and what the therapist brings to therapy.

Deconstructive Questions Specific to Immigration

The following are some examples of deconstructive questions that can be used to open up the exploration of each partner's immigration narrative to allow each individual to share his or her version of the story so they can hear each other's perception of their immigration experiences. Keep in mind that some couples may have come at different times, and will share different stories. Make sure that positive as well as negative aspects of immigration are explored. Again, the purpose of asking these questions is to make the couple aware of their experiences, their differences in experience, and how their differences in interpretation affect their relationship.

These are some examples of questions that will elicit the immigration narrative:

- When did you immigrate to this country? How long have you been here?
- Whose idea was it to come to the United States? Did you both want to come?
- How did you decide to come?
- How have you been adapting to the new culture?
- Who came first? Or did you come together?
- If immigration was a person that came to visit your family and knocked on your door, what would she or he look like and why?

The following questions can be used to highlight the differences in terms of perception of the immigration experience. These differences may give the therapist a sense of where the couple differs in a variety of areas and how they choose to work around those areas. Themes in which couples may differ include degrees of adaptation, future plans as a couple, financial issues, and parenting.

- Did you have a plan on how long you were going to stay here?
- Have both of you respected this plan?
- How do you view your spouse/partner adapting to this new culture?
- Which one of you feels more adapted to the culture you are in now? Why?
- Do you ever talk about how immigrating to this country has influenced your relationship as a couple? How would you relate this to the conflict you are having as a couple right now?
- Do you ever imagine how your relationship would be different if you had not come to the United States? Do you ever talk about this together as a couple? Do you allow your imagination to wander to that possibility?
- If you had never come to the United States, what do you envision your relationship would be like right now? What do you think you would be struggling with as a couple? What would be your differences?

As stated before, immigrants live in a reality where they are constantly balancing two cultures. The following questions are useful to elicit a person's ideas about this.

- How do you see that these cultural values clash with your own cultural values?
- How has your social identity changed since you came to the United States?
- Do you ever think of yourselves as navigating between two worlds?
- Do you feel that you have to choose one or the other?
- Do you feel that it will always have to be about choosing one versus the other? Do you think it is possible to have both?
- Can you have "both/and" solutions as a couple in regard to your adaptation process and the way you understand your experience? (Falicov, 1998)

The therapist should strive to use language that makes sense to the couple, or adopt the language that they use to describe their experience. Some common expressions used to address the adaptation process are "navigating two cultures," "being between two worlds," "feeling torn," and "not belonging." If necessary, encourage the couple to discuss the fact that some people believe immigrants should adapt to the new culture and other people believe they should try to keep their own cultural values. Where do they stand on these issues? Propose the possibility that both can happen, and present to them the "both/and" solutions.

Immigration also creates changes as to how people relate to their immediate and extended family. Below are some questions that can help facilitate a discussion about changes they see in relation to different family members.

- How has immigration affected your relationship with your children? Are they here with you?
- If children were left behind, how did that process go? Who takes care of them now?
- How do you see your children adapting to this culture? If the children were born in this country, how do you think they make sense of the fact that their parents are immigrants?
- How has immigration changed your relationship with different members of your family of origin? How do you keep in touch with family members in your country of origin? Do you send them money? If yes, how often?
- What does your family of origin expect of you now that you are in the United States?
- Do you have family members in this country?
- Do you have a community that you relate or belong to? How do they help you make sense of your experience?

Ideally, these questions make couples aware of the choices they have made and the ways they can change their story. Through talking about their immigration experience, the couple may realize how they are adapting to the new system and country. These questions also help the couple think about the larger social context and how culture is affecting their relationship. The therapist may help the couple find ways to question the social context and find alternatives for themselves as a couple.

In exploring the couple's immigration narrative, it is also useful for the therapist to normalize all the ambiguous feelings that come with immigration. Normalizing all losses, continuous change, stress, and so on is important so that the couple does not feel that they are experiencing something pathological. A case study illustrates ways to implement these suggestions.

CASE EXAMPLE

Lucia and Marcos attended couple therapy with two Latina marital and family therapy trainees. Lucia is a 53-year-old Mexican woman who was referred to therapy by the nurse at the clinic. Her motivation to come to therapy was based on her individual symptoms, which included poor sleep, decreased energy and motivation, and depressed mood. Lucia reported that she had been taking Zoloft for three years, prescribed by her primary care physician, but did not start therapy at the time based on lack of services in Spanish. Initially, her husband Marcos, a 52-year-old Mexican man, came to therapy to accompany his wife and became interested in participating once he learned how therapy could help them as a couple. Marcos reported worrying over his wife's health and how her symptoms were affecting their relationship as a couple. Marcos reported that Lucia did not show affection toward him as she used to before they came to the United States. He also reported that they had not been physically intimate for a long time as a result of their relationship problems and also living arrangements.

At the beginning, the couple concentrated on describing Lucia's symptoms and what they had done to decrease them. She had started taking medication and was trying to go for walks to exercise. During the assessment, the therapists listened to the couple's story and started asking deconstructive questions to elicit their immigration stories. They started with simple questions to obtain details and open up the exploration process. They asked the couple when they migrated to the United States, whose idea it was to come, whether they both wanted to come, whether they came together, and how they made the decision to come. The therapists allowed each partner to share a personal version of the story so each member of the couple could hear the other's perception of the experience. From these initial questions, Lucia reported that they lived in Guadalajara, Mexico, until they came to the United States four years ago. She reported that they both wanted to leave Mexico to be with their children, who had migrated six years earlier. Lucia wanted to meet her grandchildren. She also reported that she was not clear about how long they were going to stay. In Marcos's opinion, they both wanted to come but it had been harder for him to adapt once they arrived in San Diego because his lifestyle and role in the family changed completely. He reported that the reason he had made the effort to stay in the United States was to be with his wife and children. During this conversation, the therapists asked more questions and took note of how each partner perceived his or her experience. The couple had significant differences in adaptation and perception of their plan to stay in the United States.

Because Marcos brought up his difficulty adapting to the United States, and his role change in his family, the couple's therapists explored this subject in depth. The therapists used the couple's language and explored with them what it meant for them when they talked about roles and adaptation. The therapists asked questions including: How are you adapting to the new culture? What was your role when you were in Mexico? Marcos reported that in Guadalajara he was the provider for his wife and family. He had his own business selling homeopathic medications, and had prestige and a good reputation in his community. Once he came to this country, he did not work for several months because of the language barrier, lack of knowledge of the system, and document status. He reported that he had lost his status in his community and in his family. Now he was working in a fast-food restaurant, and he was in charge of transporting his family. He had lost self-respect. This discussion prompted a conversation with Marcos about how his view of himself was being influenced by cultural expectations for men in his culture. Discussions also focused on how he could use the strengths he had developed in Mexico in the United States, to regain his self-respect.

The therapists became curious about how gender roles and expectations had affected Lucia as well. Lucia described her culture's expectations of women, and how she viewed herself in respect to these expectations. Lucia described how in Guadalajara she had been a house-wife all her life and was dedicated to raising her children. Then, once they had grown up, she became very involved in her church and community. Since she had come to the United States, being a grandmother was a very important role in her life but she had also started working to help her family financially. The fact that Lucia was working created conflict for Marcos, because he felt that he had always provided for her, and now they needed her to earn income. The couple explored how Lucia had changed since arriving in the United States, and they realized how these changes related to navigating a new system and culture.

The therapists and the couple then analyzed how the immigration experience had affected their views of themselves and unbalanced the couple's structure. They explored the type of conflict they had before coming to the United States, and how they imagined their relationship would be if they had never come to this country. They worked on finding "both/and" solutions to the changes and adaptation process, and on using their best skills as individuals and as a couple.

In the process of therapy, the couple realized that before coming to the United States they were responding to more traditional cultural expectations. They were also preparing to launch their last child and face each other as a couple without children. Coming to the United States, they had returned to living with their children and taking responsibilities and roles they had never had in their own country. The therapists helped the couple to normalize their experiences and understand how this process had been part of adapting and navigating between two cultures. The therapists also helped the couple understand how this process had helped them adapt to the demands of their new circumstances, but had also created tension between them.

The couple started sharing their unspoken expectations they had carried with them since they immigrated. In therapy, the couple realized their choices and started discussing whether they wanted to go back to Mexico and how to negotiate this decision. Once they understood how changes in cultural context brought by the immigration process had affected their relationship, the couple was able to concentrate on working on the meaning of this process in their relationship. Each partner stopped defending his or her own view, and stopped blaming the other. The couple was then willing to work on their communication and the transitions they faced.

Discussion

For therapists to feel comfortable asking questions like the ones provided above, they need to be aware of their own biases regarding immigration. There are many stereotypes about immigrants that may influence therapists' views. Therapists-in-training can also address issues of immigration in supervision. Thus, it is important that supervisors are also informed about the impact immigration can have on couples.

Supervision

Awareness and skills about immigration affect both the therapist–client (an immigrant couple in this case) relationship and the therapist–supervisor relationship. In supervision, minority marital and family therapy trainees report experiencing "the tension" created by unspoken differences between the supervisor and the supervisee. They also experience these differences between themselves and the couples. The "unspoken tension" represents racial, cultural, ethnic, and ideological differences that are present in the supervisor–supervisee–client triad (Estrada, Wiggins Frame, & Braun Williams, 2004). Along with the literature on cross-cultural supervision and the experiences mentioned above, it is imperative to address cultural diversity as part of supervision. It is even more important to do this when immigration is considered as a sociocultural variable in the conceptualization of the therapy cases. The following section focuses on ways to address cultural diversity—specifically immigration—in supervision with immigrant couples.

The supervisor should be aware of his or her own perspective and biases regarding immigration. Does the supervisor agree or disagree with immigrants coming into this country? Does the supervisor have any knowledge about the process of migrating? The supervisor also has to have an understanding of his or her personal perspectives about immigrants adapting to the dominant culture. Does the supervisor know the difference between the models of assimilation, hybridization, and acculturation? What is the supervisor's own personal theory about how immigrants should adapt to the host culture? The supervisor's competence in diversity issues will help the trainee in case conceptualization, and serve as a launching point to help the trainee explore similar questions.

The supervisor who knows about these topics and is aware of any personal biases can encourage conversations about culture within the supervisory experience. Having conversations about culture, ethnicity, and immigration includes, among other topics, the supervisor cautioning the therapist about stereotyping; supervisor and supervisee reflecting on their own beliefs about people of different ethnic background and immigration status; and trying to imagine the loss immigration brings. The supervisor must share honest views about his or her own beliefs about immigration, and be honest about his or her level of knowledge about immigration. The supervisor can ask the therapist what kinds of questions or thoughts come up for the therapist in working with immigrant and ethnically diverse clients. If the therapist is of a similar background to the couple, the supervisor can initiate conversations about the therapist's experience in working with couples of the same ethnic background. The supervisor can ask for feedback from the therapist about what may be happening to the client from a cultural perspective. The supervisor should also acknowledge when the therapist has more knowledge than the supervisor, and explore how the therapist can use his or her expertise to help the couple.

In addition, the supervisor and therapist can talk about their own ethnic backgrounds and belief systems because their personal experiences will have an impact on the effectiveness of therapy. If the supervisor does not attend to these issues in the supervisory experience, it is likely that the trainee will not attend to them in the client–therapist relationship (Estrada, Wiggins Frame, & Braun Williams, 2004).

When it is time for the trainee to address ethnicity and immigration issues in therapy, the supervisor may help the therapist transform his or her lack of knowledge into respectful curiosity. However, this does not mean that it is the couple's responsibility to educate the therapist about their culture. Instead, the therapist must acknowledge that he or she does not know much about the client's culture and ask the couple to share points of view and cultural expressions.

Cultural Immersion Experiences

To learn about diversity, a therapist and supervisor can immerse themselves in experiences and situations where they feel unfamiliar with the situation. For example, students can participate in an event in which they know nothing or very little about a culture. Students report that these experiences create the possibility to learn about themselves, their biases, and their perspectives. By immersing themselves in a new culture, therapists gain some insight into what it must be like to be an outsider. Upon arriving at the location of the cultural event (or, in some cases, in preparation for the event), therapists may find themselves looking different from everyone else, not knowing the rules that everyone else knows, or what to expect next. In this way, the immersion experience is a powerful tool because it challenges the therapist to be more flexible.

The supervisor can also aid in the development of metaphors that help the therapist relate to the couple's experience. If the therapist has never been in another country or experienced another culture, the therapist can draw from other situations in which he or she has felt vulnerable and has had to question perceived reality. For example, the supervisor can help the therapist discuss a situation in which he or she was part of a minority in terms of gender, class, race, sexual orientation, or religion.

Other exposure experiences to learn about immigration and a client's culture include watching movies, eating food from that culture, and having conversations with people from the client's culture. The therapist can also read books, magazines, and newspapers, conduct Internet research, and attend talks about the couple's culture. There are many other ways to learn about a couple's culture. The next section offers resources for therapists who want to learn more about immigration. It is up to the trainee and supervisor to become creative and learn from these enriching experiences. In learning about a couple's culture, one often recognizes stereotypes and assumptions.

The immigration experience is fraught with challenges and stress. Even couples with strong marriages can be exhausted by the process of assimilation because it challenges their core purposes and meanings. Culturally sensitive therapists have the opportunity to facilitate a couple's transition during this period of upheaval. But first the therapist must be aware of his or her own beliefs and biases about both immigration and cultural differences.

Additional Resources

Films

Black, T., Navarro, B., & Thomas, A. (Producers), & Nava, G. (Director). (1983). *El Norte.* Cinecom International Films/Island Alive.

Coppola, F. F. (Producer), & Nava, G. (Director). (1995). *Mi Familia* [My Family]. New Line Cinema.

DeVivo, D. (Producer), & Mathew, J. (Director). (2006). *Crossing Arizona.* Available from www.crossingaz.com.

James, S., & Quinn, G. (Producers). (2003). *The New Americans.* Available from www.pbs.org/independentlens/newamericans.

Lappin, A., & Sheridan, J. (Producers), & Sheridan, J. (Director). (2002). *In America.* Available from www.foxsearchlight.com/inamerica.

Mylan, M. (Producer & Director). (2004). *Lost Boys of Sudan.* Available from www.lostboysfilm.com.

Nair, M. (Producer & Director). (2007). *The Namesake.* Available from www.foxsearchlight.com/thenamesake.

Stone, O. (Producer), & Wang, W. (Director). (1993). *The Joy Luck Club.* Buena Vista Pictures Distribution.

Readings

Barkan, E. R. (1996). *And still they come: Immigrants and American society, 1920 to the 1990s.* Wheeling, IL: Harlan Davidson.

Chavez, L. R. (1997). *Shadowed lives: Undocumented immigrants in American society: Case studies in cultural anthropology.* Fort Worth, TX: Wadsworth.

Espiritu, Y. L. (2003). *Home bound: Filipino American lives across cultures, communities, and countries.* Berkeley, CA: University of California Press.

Falicov, C. (1998). *Latino families in therapy: A guide to multicultural practice.* New York: Guilford Press.

Martinez, R., & Rodriguez, J. (2004). *The new Americans: Seven families journey to another country.* New York: New Press.

Nazario, S. (2006). *Enrique's journey: The story of a boy's dangerous odyssey to reunite with his mother.* New York: Random House.

Portes, A., & Rumbaut, R. G. (1996). *Immigrant America: A portrait.* Berkeley and Los Angeles: University of California Press.

Portes, A., & Rumbaut, R. G. (2001). *Ethnicities: Children of immigrants in America*. Berkeley and Los Angeles: University of California Press.

Web Sites

Murthy Law Firm, Immigration and the Movies: www.murthy.com/films.html
Sentimental Refugee: www.sentimentalrefugee.com/index.html
The New Americans: www.pbs.org/independentlens/newamericans

References

Anderson, H. (2000). Becoming a postmodern collaborative therapist: A clinical and theoretical journey. *Journal of the Texas Association for Marriage and Family Therapy, 5,* 5–12.

Arminio, J. (2001). Exploring the nature of race-related guilt. *Journal of Multicultural Counseling and Development, 29,* 239–252.

Arredondo-Dowd, P. (1981). Personal loss and grief as a result of immigration. *The Personnel and Guidance Journal, 13,* 376–378.

Besley, A. C. (2002). Foucault and the turn to narrative therapy. *British Journal of Guidance & Counseling, 30,* 125–143.

Chiu, T. (1996). Problems caused for mental health professionals worldwide by increasing multicultural populations and proposed solutions. *Multicultural Counseling and Development, 24,* 313–328.

Delgado-Romero, E. A. (2001). Counseling a Hispanic/Latino client—Mr. X. *Journal of Mental Health Counseling, 23,* 207–221.

Estrada, D., Wiggins Frame, M., & Braun Williams, C. (2004). Cross cultural supervision: Guiding the conversation toward race and ethnicity. *Journal of Multicultural Counseling and Development, 32,* 307–319.

Falicov, C. (1998). *Latino families in therapy: A guide to multicultural practice*. New York: Guilford Press.

Falicov, C. (2003). Immigrant family processes. In F. Walsh (Ed.), *Normal family processes: Growing diversity and complexity* (pp. 280–300). New York: Guilford Press.

Falicov, C. (2005). Emotional transnationalism and family identities. *Family Process, 44,* 399–406.

Freedman, J. H., & Combs, G. (2002). Narrative couple therapy. In A. S. Gurman & N. S. Jacobson (Eds.), *Clinical handbook of couple therapy* (pp. 308–334). New York: Guilford Press.

Garcia-Preto, N. (1998). Latinas in the United States: Bridging two worlds. In M. McGoldrick (Ed.), *Re-visioning family therapy: Race, culture, and gender in clinical practice* (pp. 330–343). New York: Guilford Press.

Gottman, J. (1999). *The seven principles for making marriage work*. New York: Three Rivers Press.

McGoldrick, M. (Ed.). (1998). *Re-visioning family therapy: Race, culture, and gender in clinical practice.* New York: Guilford Press.

McGoldrick, M., & Giordano, J. (1996). Overview: Ethnicity and family therapy. In M. McGoldrick, M. J. Giordano, & J. K. Pearce (Eds.), *Ethnicity and family therapy* (pp. 1–25). New York: Guilford Press.

Napier, A. (1988). *The fragile bond: In search of an equal, intimate and enduring marriage.* New York: Harper Perennial.

Nichols, M. P., & Schwartz, R. C. (2004). Narrative therapy: Restoring lives. In M. P. Nichols & R. C. Schwartz (Eds.), *Family therapy: Concepts and methods* (pp. 329–346). Boston: Pearson Education.

Roberts, J. (2005). Migrating across literature, stories, and family therapy. *Family Process, 44,* 407–411.

Schmalzbauer, L. (2004). Searching for wages and mothering from afar: The case of Honduran transnational families. *Journal of Marriage and Family, 66,* 1317–1331.

Sciarra, D. T. (1999). Intrafamilial separations in the immigrant family: Implications for cross-cultural counseling. *Journal of Multicultural Counseling and Development, 27,* 31–41.

Stone, E., Gomez, E., Hotzoglou, D., & Lipnitsky, J. (2005). Transnationalism as a motif in family stories. *Family Process, 44,* 381–398.

Suarez-Orozco, C., Todorova, I. L. G., & Louie, J. (2002). Making up for lost time: The experience of separation and reunification among immigrant families. *Family Process, 41,* 625–643.

Sullivan, M. M., & Rehm, R. (2005). Mental health of undocumented immigrants: A review of the literature. *Advances in Nursing Science, 28,* 240–251.

U.S. White House. (n.d.) *Comprehensive immigration reform.* Retrieved September 6, 2007, from www.whitehouse.gov/infocus/immigration.

Waldinger, R., & Fitzgerald, D. (2004). Transnationalism in question. *American Journal of Sociology, 109,* 1177–1795.

White, M., & Epston, D. (1990). *Narrative means to therapeutic ends.* New York: Norton.

PART II

Intersections of Diversity

Section A

Interracial Couples

Four

Integrating Socially Segregated Identities

Queer Couples and the Question of Race

Sheila Addison and Deborah Coolhart

As a Black lesbian feminist comfortable with the many different ingredients of my identity, and a woman committed to racial and sexual freedom from oppression, I find I am constantly being encouraged to pluck out some one aspect of myself and present this as the meaningful whole, eclipsing or denying the other parts of self. But this is a destructive and frightening way to live. My fullest concentration of energy is available to me only when I integrate all the parts of who I am, openly.

—Lorde, 2004, pp. 557–558

When those who have power to name and to socially construct reality choose not to see you or hear you, whether you are dark-skinned, old, disabled, female, or speak with a different accent or dialect than theirs, when someone with the authority of a teacher, say, describes the world and you are not in it, there is a moment of psychic disequilibrium, as if you looked into a mirror and saw nothing.

—Rich, 1986, p. 199

McGoldrick (1998) discusses the evolution in thinking about marginalized people within the field of family therapy. She quotes McIntosh's five stages of cultural diversity development, moving from a total absence of women and minorities from academic discussion, to an expansion via "token" inclusion, to minorities being regarded as "special problems," and then leading to a transformation that includes the historian as part of the history and produces critical consciousness. While the fifth stage, a total reconceptualization in which "history will itself be reconceived to include us all" (p. 12), is beyond our grasp today, the fourth seems a reasonable goal—an "interactive process" (p. 12) where perspectives on history and its participants are more fluid. In essence, McIntosh and McGoldrick are proposing to move away from the "ghetto mentality" that breaks our training, research, and writing about "diversity" into separate, discrete groups. This series of tiny "multicultural villages" has disturbing echoes of colonialism, as each "village" is visited and then left behind when facts about the local minority group have been "adequately" documented by visitors from the dominant group. And yet here we are, writing for an anthology on diversity and couple therapy, where "diversity" is really code for "non-Whites." The importance of a book like this, standing as a proud counterpoint to the many books that proclaim to be about couples, when in fact they are largely about White couples, is immense. But the fact that, in 2008, it is still the norm to divide our field into White people and Everyone Else weighs heavily on us as authors.

In taking up this chapter, we are agreeing to occupy a ghetto within a ghetto, to confine the topic of gay, lesbian, bisexual, and transgender relationships among people of color (POC) to a special area of the book, to admit that, for the most part, the term *couples* means "opposite-sex and cisgendered[1] couples." We are complicit in marking these queer relationships as "other" by virtue of putting them in their own village, rather than questioning why all chapters in this book do not consider the many different types of couples. We are guilty of making it easier to exclude queer relationships from the rest of the book, just as non-White relationships are excluded from most chapters of other books on couple therapy. Yet without this chapter, we believe that there would be little room for queer couple relationships between these covers.

We are also aware that the choice of two White women to write a chapter on queer people of color (QPOC) and their relationships is far from ideal. White people habitually attempt to speak for those from other racial and cultural groups, denying members of those groups their own voices and effectively colonizing their experiences. White people are also often called on by those in power to speak about people of color (sometimes in the hope that we will be "less angry" or have a less challenging "tone"), and our words are taken more seriously and given more gravity than the words of the people we are displacing (Johnson, 2006). Neither of us can claim to be indigenous experts on the many and varied lives of POC; however, we both identify as White allies, dedicated to achieving anti-racist and social justice goals, being accountable for our own racism and unearned privilege, and taking responsibility for decentralizing Whiteness in our teaching, supervision, writing, and clinical work.

In this chapter, we will use the term *queer* to describe diverse sexual and gender identities including, but not limited to, gay, lesbian, bisexual, and transgender identities. *Queer* is controversial, political, and often generational; many whom the term attempts to describe still hear it as an epithet, despite efforts to reclaim it as a broad identity that creates possibilities and alliances (Rust, 2003). However, other language that tries to describe subjugated sexual identities is insufficient and problematic (Torres Bernal & Coolhart, 2005). The term *homosexual* was invented in the nineteenth century to describe same-sex sexual behavior (Jagose, 1996), and to medically define it as abnormal, whereas *heterosexual* was only later coined to describe what was already defined as normal (Fausto-Sterling, 2000). In addition to pathological historical roots, the terms *homosexual* and *heterosexual* suggest a dichotomy and mutual exclusivity. In reality, there are countless diverse sexual and gender identities, desires, and behaviors that do not fit neatly into two categories. The medicalized roots of *homosexual* also resonate with the "scientific" use of racial differences to justify White domination (Somerville, 2000).

More recent terminologies have also proved lacking. During the movement for "gay civil rights" that took shape during the 1960s and 1970s in the United States, the term *gay* described White men who engaged in same-sex sexual behavior; however, the term typically neglected the experiences of women, transgender people, bisexuals, and POC. More recently, *gay, lesbian, bisexual, and transgender*—or the acronym GLBT—has been used as an umbrella term to try to unite groups with supposedly similar interests and concerns. While somewhat more inclusive, the GLBT acronym still limits people to its four (exclusive, nonoverlapping, definable) categories, all of which are still simultaneous in the dominant discourse with Whiteness. Nonbinary or less "decorous" identities (like pansexual, dyke, butch/femme, intersexed, and genderqueer) are left out, as are identities particular to POC, such as two-spirited, Same Gender Loving (SGL), stud, and *hijra*[2] (Garcia, 1996; Valdes, 2004). Rather than create another fallible acronym, we believe the term *queer* strikes a balance of functionality and inclusiveness, while still acknowledging its problems. *Queer* also suggests the difficult relationship of same-sex and transgender couples of color to the dominant discourse. If *queer* implies difference from a norm, then the socially prescribed heterosexuality and Whiteness upon which most couple counseling texts rest is, in effect, held up for inspection every time we use the word.

We, as authors, also implicate ourselves with the word *queer*. I (SA) am a bisexual woman who was married to a man for nearly 10 years, yet I am active in organizations supporting and advancing the rights of queer people. Though single at the time of this writing, I date people of many genders and gender presentations. I (DC) am a queer woman whose sexuality is characterized by attraction to and love for people with diverse gender expressions, including but not limited to male, female, and transgender. I recently separated from my lesbian-identified genderqueer partner of seven years.

Neither of us has identities or lives that would fit most assumptions about queer women. Both of us, with nonbinary sexual identities and as advocates for transpeople, have experienced hostility and discrimination from gays and lesbians, as well as heterosexuals. And yet, for both of us, sexual and gender identities are a prevailing theme in our professional lives; we have published articles, presented at conferences, and infused our work as supervisors and teachers with information about queer people. We find the umbrella term *queer* sheltering as well as descriptive.

Separation in the Literature of Multicultural and Queer Identities

In the past two decades, there has been a tremendous increase in the body of literature about queer people and their loved ones. However, it is important to note that the majority of this new "knowledge" has been "whitewashed," based almost exclusively on the experiences of White people. Most clinical and empirical research has been conducted with not only White but also middle-class and college-educated samples. Additionally, many studies fail to mention race as a variable at all, obscuring understanding of racial and cultural influences on the lives of queer people (Greene, 2003). Textbooks on working with queer people typically segregate POC into their own chapter or two (e.g., Laird & Green, 1996; Perez, DeBord, & Bieschke, 2000; Ritter & Terndrup, 2002). The literature specific to couple therapy also habitually separates queer and multicultural issues. For example, textbooks on couple therapy commonly approach the two topics in separate chapters, with no intersection between queer and non-White identities (e.g., Bobes & Rothman, 2002; Gurman & Jacobson, 2002; Young & Long, 1997). Additionally, literature about same-sex couples often leaves out culture, as if all queer couples are White (e.g., Berzon, 2004; Greenan & Tunnell, 2003).

Literature on counseling with racial and ethnic minorities also either ignores sexual identity (e.g., Atkinson, 2004; Boyd-Franklin, 2003; Mishne, 2002) or confines it to its own chapter (e.g., Wing Sue & Sue, 2002). Studies on intimate relationships among POC have similarly ignored or marginalized same-sex relationships, even in studies of alternative family forms (e.g., Peplau, Cochran, & Mays, 1997). Morrow (2003) suggests that for QPOC, race is more visible and salient, and to address race and sexuality together may "doubly jeopardize the individual's professional standing" (p. 70).

This assumption of separateness both comes from and reflects back onto queer and minority communities. It requires little effort to find examples of inattention to POC in popular magazines devoted to gays and lesbians. QPOC are similarly often absent from mass media directed at racial and ethnic minorities. Neglecting to discuss the intersection of minority sexual and racial identities is problematic because QPOC face unique tasks in integrating and balancing multiple subjugated identities. The challenges of such intersectionality have been described as a "double whammy" for queer Latinos/as (Valdes, 2004), and "triple jeopardy" for Black lesbians, who are also marginalized by their gender (Greene, 1994). Morales (1990) calls QPOC "a minority within a minority" (p. 219), confronting racism from Whites, while their sexuality is viewed by their culture of origin as "White people's problem." It is crucial for clinicians to understand how this specific set of intersections impacts the lives of QPOC.

While race and sexual identity are so often separated, transgender identities are most often ignored altogether. Transgender relationships are typically nonexistent in discussions on therapy with POC (e.g., Atkinson, 2004; Boyd-Franklin, 2003), therapy with sexual minorities (e.g., Greenan & Tunnell, 2003; Ritter & Terndrup, 2002), and therapy with couples (e.g., Bobes & Rothman, 2002; Gurman & Jacobson, 2002; Young & Long, 1997). Discussions of transgender relationships, in turn, typically focus on White experiences, and leave out clients' racial identities (Israel, 2004; Malpas, 2006).

The Cultural Context of Queer People of Color

Understanding the cultural context of QPOC and their intimate relationships is vital to providing sensitive, effective clinical services (Garcia, 1996; Greene, 1997). Greene (1997) warns that "generalized descriptions of cultural practices may never be applied with uniformity to all members of any ethnic group" (p. 216), but provides some frameworks for broadening clinical perspectives on QPOC. Most queer youth develop in a bicultural context, as the vast majority are still raised by heterosexual, cisgendered parents (Ritter & Terndrup, 2002). As Greene (1997) points out, for ethnic minority youth, identification with their parents' culture is likely to be a source of strength and a sense of belonging, but these same family mirrors have often also provided negative images of queer people, "gleaned from loved and trusted figures, [which] complicate the process of gay or lesbian identity development and self-acceptance" (p. 233). The sense of being "caught between two cultures" can be overwhelming and persistent. Morales (1990) proposes a model of QPOC identity development that takes into account individuals' cultural identity development. He points out how distressing it may be for a young POC who already confronts the daily reality of life as an ethnic/racial minority to become aware of their multiminority status.

Those identifying as QPOC frequently face racist attitudes in the White gay community. While QPOC are subtly excluded from mainstream gay imagery, more overt forms of racism persist as well. For example, Manago (1998) challenges the White gay community's habit of rallying around anti-gay violence against White victims such as Matthew Sheppard, while ignoring racially motivated hate crimes. At the same time, minority communities have long struggled to accept queer members. Clarke (2004) documents examples of queer exclusion and targeting of queer relationships by Black organizations, including one group's description of queer couples as "an accelerating threat to our survival as a people and a nation" (p. 249). Greene (1997) identifies similar dynamics within families, and the community and familial tensions this creates for QPOC are immense. Espin (1997) notes that immigrant lesbians have often encountered discrimination from their own families and culture prior to migration, which is then compounded by racism and anti-immigrant sentiment once they cross a border.

While it is often perceived that communities of color are more homophobic than Whites, these assumptions must be critically analyzed. For example, hooks (2000) notes that Black communities may "verbally express in an outspoken way antigay sentiments" (p. 69), but also often support QPOC in their own families. Greene (1997) and Ritter and Terndrup (2002) describe how minority families accommodate queer members, though the outcome may not always resemble the idealized White model of openness. Perhaps verbalized ambivalence about sexuality, rather than a higher level of homophobia, is what is truly more common in Black communities (hooks, 2000).

Specific Issues in Queer Coupling

Green and Mitchell (2002) suggest that all gay and lesbian couples face four basic challenges: (1) coping with homophobia and heterosexism; (2) maintaining a sense of couple identity, despite the lack of role models and supports; (3) creating social networks that provide emotional support and connections; and (4) maintaining flexible gender roles to avoid fusion in female couples or disengagement and competition in male couples. The authors propose that, although work with queer couple, may often be similar to work with heterosexuals, clinicians must keep these in mind at all times as they may covertly influence the presenting problems.

The impacts of cultural oppression—a fact of daily life for POC—are no less salient for queer people, particularly when they are in relationships. Stigma against queer people is pervasive, ranging from negative cultural messages to workplace discrimination, and including violence from strangers and even family members (Ritter & Terndrup, 2000). The lack of role models showing well-adjusted, long-term queer relationships, while subtle, can feed into a deeper sense of invisibility and defectiveness, undermining a couple's faith in the future of their relationship (Connolly, 2004).

Queer people "come out," or identify themselves as queer to other people, at a wide variety of ages. "Consequently, a couple with similar chronological ages may have very different experiences as 'out'" (Brown, 1995, p. 282). These differences in "out time" can lead to tension in queer relationships. For example, a partner may feel anger or resentment about not being invited to work functions or included in family activities, and may doubt the other partner's commitment to the relationship. Smith (1997) states that a clinician sensitive to these differences may "support one member of the couple in a 'holding pattern' while facilitating the other in her or his [readiness] for a next step" (p. 297). Smith also cautions that, in interracial same-sex couples, different expectations and beliefs about coming out may be operating in a context already unbalanced by pressures and privileges around race. Clinicians must recognize that there can be serious, even life-threatening consequences for coming out about a queer identity, and that in the case of QPOC, loss of family connections may also involve loss of cultural connections as well.

Systemic, institutionalized heterosexism means that queer relationships are often not supported through legal and social structures such as marriage. Currently in the United States, only one state allows same-sex couples access to the benefits of marriage administered at the state level. Six states offer "separate-but-equal" civil unions or domestic partnerships with most of the benefits of marriage, while five more offer arrangements that come with only some benefits. However, none of these arrangements is guaranteed recognition out of the state's jurisdiction. Nor do they come with the same federal rights and responsibilities as heterosexual marriage in the cases of relationship breakdown, medical decision-making, and child custody (Ossana, 2000).

In the absence of unambiguous, widely accepted methods for defining relationship commitment, many queer couples experience what Green and Mitchell (2002) call "relational ambiguity": difficulty defining the boundary around the couple relationship, poorly articulated expectations, and struggle over what each partner perceives to be his or her obligations to the relationship. The couple may have trouble bonding and functioning as a unit, with covert power struggles taking place over whose expectations are the "correct" ones. It can be difficult to tell whether, for example, a couple refrains from public affection because of fear, personal preferences about how to show affection, or because they have not mutually defined the relationship as one that includes "dating/coupled" behaviors. But the arguments that happen as a result may present in the therapy office (Green & Mitchell, 2002; Ossana, 2000).

Queer couples, according to Johnson and Keren (1996), face two major problems with their family-of-origin relationships, both centered around boundaries: "(1) lack of visibility and invalidation of the couple relationship in the family of origin, and (2) intrusions and disrespect in terms of how the family of origin relates to the couple" (p. 240). Families who refuse to include same-sex or transgender partners in rituals, gatherings, and photos, or who insist that couples sleep in separate bedrooms because they are not married (when they cannot legally marry) send a clear message to the couple that their relationships are considered second best, if they are acknowledged at all. When families assume that a queer member is single because he or she is not married, they may feel justified in demanding that they date and marry someone they consider "appropriate" (Green & Mitchell, 2002), or put aside plans with their partners to spend time with the family, or serve as caregivers. Queer couples may instead seek out a "family of choice" made up of sympathetic extended family, friends of the couple, and even ex-partners who remain on good terms (Siegel & Walker, 1996). Clinicians must not underestimate the importance of these relationships—in fact, queer couples who have few supports may benefit if therapy helps them expand their connections and build a family of choice (Connolly, 2004). Smith (1997) notes that the idea of families of choice fits with the Afrocentric notion of "fictive kin," in which nonblood relatives may be considered, and even labeled, siblings, cousins, aunts, uncles, or grandparents. Encouraging the development of a support network also fits with the emphasis in Latino and many Asian cultures on the importance of family closeness and interdependence (Greene, 1997).

Finally, relationships that do not include two "opposite-gendered" participants require clinicians to consider the impact of gender roles. In heterosexual, cisgendered couples, both partners have been socialized very differently. However, in lesbian and gay couple relationships, partners have typically had more similar gender role models around emotional intimacy, sexuality, and power (Connolly, 2004). Most notably, same-sex female couples may face "a problem with boundaries, often manifested as intolerance for distance and difference within the couple" (Brown, 1995, p. 283). This fusion occurs as a result of the importance placed on intimacy and connectedness in female socialization; women are taught to nurture, care, and to take on responsibility for the success or failure of their intimate relationships (Brown, 1995). Conversely, male partnerships are often described as "disengaged" (Green, Bettinger, & Zacks, 1996), which is attributed to men being socially rewarded for individualism and for emphasizing sexual connection before emotional intimacy (Connolly, 2004). While these guidelines may be useful, they are simply that: guidelines. Research suggests that same-sex relationships are less polarized than previously imagined. Green et al. (1996) found that "compared to heterosexual married couples, both lesbian and gay male couples are more cohesive and much more flexible" (p. 202), with female couples scoring even higher than male couples. These very qualities appear to correlate with greater relationship satisfaction, making them a strength rather than a liability. Peplau and Spalding (2003) cite Kurdek's 1998 study of gay and lesbian relationships, which revealed levels of closeness in queer relationships similar to those found by Green et al. but also indicated they may have more autonomy than heterosexuals, suggesting that these couples may have an advantage when it comes to achieving a balance of togetherness and separateness.

Ritter and Terndrup (2002) note that gender norms from one's family and culture of origin are rarely internalized fully, and point out that "other issues, such as ethnicity, culture, religion, class, age cohort, and education, also contribute to the socialization process" (p. 320). This last point is particularly salient when working with QPOC, who come from racial and ethnic backgrounds with gender norms that may differ from those of Whites. However, recognizing that underlying gender schemas may shape the course of a relationship differently for queer couples is still clinically useful. Research has shown that a more "feminine" psychological profile appears to correlate with the tendency to try to fix a failing relationship, while a more "masculine" profile seems to speed up the tendency to leave or allow things to deteriorate (Ritter & Terndrup, 2002). This can influence how therapy proceeds with a troubled couple because, whether or not the outward gender of the partners involved matches their gender schema, they may still be influenced by internal gender messages in terms of their interest in resolving problems or "cutting their losses" and working toward a humane breakup.

Other challenges for queer couples may be less common but no less important for the clinician to understand. Transgender individuals may transition from one gender to another while they are in a relationship. This can have implications for the other partner and how they understand their own sexual identity (Coolhart, Provancher, Hager, & Wang, in press). For example, for a woman previously self-identified as lesbian who now has a partner transitioning to male, her sexual identity as lesbian may need to expand to encompass her partner's new gender if she wants to remain in the relationship. Further, transition in one partner may impact how the couple is perceived by society (Coolhart et al., in press). A heterosexual couple may later be perceived as queer and experience homophobia, while a previously same-sex couple may lose its queer identity post-transition (Lev, 2004).

Bisexuals face discrimination from both heterosexuals and gays/lesbians. In mixed-orientation couple relationships, where one partner is bisexual and the other identifies as gay, lesbian, or straight, biphobia can take the form of the other partner's jealousy. Bisexuals, often stereotyped as promiscuous and unfaithful (Peplau & Spalding, 2003), may be accused of cheating due to their partners' fears of being left for a person of the other gender. Relationships that include bisexuals may also experience alienation from members of the gay and lesbian community who regard bisexuals with suspicion, yet opposite-sex relationships that include bisexual partners may not fit well into the "straight world," which erases their identity and re-labels them as heterosexual. Yet the label "bisexual" may be more acceptable to ethnic and racial minority queer people, particularly in the early stages of identity acceptance (Morales, 1990), meaning that clinicians working with QPOC must be prepared to engage with the potential implications of this label for the relationship as well as the individual.

Sexual monogamy or lack thereof is a topic of special importance when working with queer relationships. The sexual exclusivity and emotional fidelity assumed to be part of heterosexual couple relationships may or may not be present in queer couples, particularly for gay men. Some studies suggest that more gay men are in "open" or non-monogamous relationships than in "closed" or monogamous ones (Bettinger, 2006). However, such studies often predate the HIV epidemic, and patterns appear to be changing with between 48% and 63% reporting monogamous relationships as of the early 1990s (Ossana, 2000).

While a full discussion of the distinctions among such relationship styles as polyamory and open relationships is beyond the scope of this chapter, it is crucial for clinicians to understand that queer couples may be non-monogamous. Working with these clients requires that the therapist put aside biases about what type of sexual relationships she or he might prefer, and accept clients' definitions of their relationship so long as it is meeting both partners' needs. Clinicians cannot assume that having multiple sexual partners is evidence of dissatisfaction, cheating, or problems with intimacy.

Other issues of special note include the ongoing HIV epidemic and its role in the lives of gay, bisexual, and same-gender-loving men (Ossana, 2000). Domestic violence affects queer relationships, with its legacy of terror, silence, and abuses of power, but can take on added complexity when violence is between two people of the same or indeterminate gender (Peplau & Spalding, 2003; Ritter & Terndrup, 2003). Queer couples can also have the usual variety of sexual issues, compounded by poor or inaccurate information about queer sexual practices, differing expectations about how sex is defined and who initiates sexual intimacy, and bias or lack of knowledge by providers of sex therapy (Ossana, 2000; Ritter & Terndrup, 2002).

Finally, it is important to recognize the specific relational challenges that may be faced by intercultural queer couples, particularly when one member of the relationship is White. Crohn (1998) points out that anxieties around discussions of race may prevent cross-racial couples from acknowledging their differences, even though culture can affect attitudes toward "time, family, eating, money, sex, and monogamy . . . how anger and affection are expressed . . . and what roles men and women play" (p. 295). Connolly (2004) reports that queer couples are more likely to involve partner differences in terms of race, ethnicity, socioeconomic status, age, and education than heterosexual couples. While intercultural queer couples show levels of relationship satisfaction comparable to same-race queer couples (Ritter & Terndrup, 2003), the prevalence of cross-racial coupling means that clinicians must be prepared to address this specific dynamic in therapy. Because queer identities can have very different meanings in different cultures (Greene, 1997), and because a White partner has access to cultural privilege and power that is denied to a partner of color (McIntosh, 1998), the many intersections of identities in these couples must be addressed so the anxiety, tension, and conflict they can potentially create can be depathologized and worked with in the couple (Crohn, 1998). It is particularly important that the clinician keep in mind the complexity of the clients' lives. Failing to do so assumes that all queer couples are basically the same.

An Intersectional Model for Therapy

To effectively work with QPOC in couples, clinicians must be able to talk about cultural influences. Laird (1998) writes that "we need to know enough to ask good questions, to 'notice' culture in its many guises" (p. 22). She urges therapists to "learn how to learn about culture" (p. 23), rather than focusing on gaining sufficient in-depth knowledge about every possible minority group to be an expert. She suggests that clinicians need to know about cultures beyond their own in order to guide their questions and suggest possibilities outside their experiences, but that they must also recognize the possibility that this knowledge may limit them. The intersectionality of identities in QPOC makes this approach particularly important, since the experiences of "most" members of their racial or sexual identity group may or may not fit. Bernstein's (2000) cultural literacy model focuses on self-of-the-therapist work for heterosexual therapists working with queer clients. She prescribes an "attitude inventory" (p. 446), strategies for managing anxiety with clients, examining heterosexist assumptions in therapy, and being honest about their sexual identity if asked. She emphasizes the need to build trust with clients who may be accustomed to being on guard for covert signs of homophobia, a point similar to that made by Hardy and Laszloffy (1998), who argue that race is always salient for POC when interacting with Whites, whether Whites are aware of this or not. Finally, Bernstein echoes Laird's focus on respectful, collaborative inquiry, cautioning against assuming queer relationships should mimic heterosexual ones, or minimizing in-group differences among queer people.

This combination of increasing knowledge and respectful inquiry has also been suggested for working with clients of color (Bean, Perry, & Bedell, 2001). Critical examination of self-of-the-therapist issues around race, and education regarding the impact of social forces on minority clients' lives, are also identified as useful strategies for White clinicians (Bean et al., 2001). Hence, we suggest these approaches as a kind of "umbrella" for working with QPOC in couples. Underneath this umbrella, clinicians can choose specific theories and techniques for couple work based on their training, experience, and comfort with various models. Our experience generally relies on combining well-tested couple treatment models, such as Gottman's (1999) focus on functional and dysfunctional couple processes and Johnson's (2004) Emotionally Focused Therapy (EFT), with more multiculturally sensitive approaches. For example, Gottman's initial assessments and interviews (1999) can be combined with questions from Hardy and Laszloffy's (2002) multicultural assessment model or a cultural and sexual genogram (Addison & Brown, 2003) to get a picture of the couple that foregrounds, rather than ignores, race, ethnicity, and sexual identity. We have found EFT (Johnson, 2004) techniques that build empathy between partners and work toward soft, vulnerable engagement to be helpful as couples discuss their experiences with racism, gender, homophobia, and other oppressions, allowing them to see the impact these forces have on the relational problem(s) presented for therapy.

CASE EXAMPLE

In this example, I (SA) will discuss my work with a queer mixed-race couple in my private practice. Diane and Margot were both in their early 30s; Diane, an African American woman, worked in a low-level management position at a local health care company while slowly finishing her dissertation in sociology, and identified as "lesbian, or maybe queer." Margot, White and bisexual, had been laid off in the past year and was barely managing to get half-time work at a friend's small business. Both were unhappy in their jobs, but Margot's financial distress, combined with a toxic interpersonal environment at work, contributed to a deep depression. The couple had discussed her returning to school for a graduate degree in speech therapy with Diane's support.

The presenting problem at the time of our first meeting was Margot's depression. However, it soon became clear that both women were unhappy about the couple relationship, which seemed quite disengaged and had not involved sex in months. Though they rarely fought, when they did arguments were volatile, escalating rapidly to critical, contemptuous, and defensive interactions that were followed by intense withdrawal, all characteristic of Gottman's "Four Horsemen of the Apocalypse" (1999).

I used questions from Gottman's Oral History Interview (1999) to elicit the story of how their relationship developed, and what they perceived as its strengths and weaknesses. I could not put my finger on what was causing tension between the couple as they talked about their many positive memories, but finally Margot named it: At the depth of her depression, Diane had conducted an "emotional affair" with another woman, Tracy. Though they had not had sex, Margot felt that Diane and Tracy had become "too close for comfort" and that Diane had begun to put the majority of her emotional energy into Tracy while distancing herself from Margot. Tears welled up in Margot's eyes, while Diane sat quietly, though she seemed to be staying present rather than "checking out."

Early in our sessions, Diane was habitually quiet, giving short answers with little affect and often allowing Margot to answer for her (a pattern in which I quickly intervened). Diane seemed most comfortable remaining at an intellectual distance from therapy. She agreed with Margot's concerns about Tracy and did not object to the word "affair." She reported she had cut off all ties with Tracy and was interested in rebuilding trust with

Margot. Margot was also invested in this goal, which became central to our therapy.

As a clinician concerned with privilege, power, and difference, I identified several themes that were of interest, whether or not they were to Diane and Margot. First, the racial difference between Diane and Margot set up the likelihood of a power imbalance between the two. Margot's White identity gave her privileges not available to Diane, including the privilege to identify as bisexual, experience depression, and go through unemployment without having these seen as reflections on her whole race (McIntosh, 1998). Second, in the gay community, Diane's identity as "lesbian, or maybe queer" was likely preferred over Margot's bisexual identity, since many gay men and lesbians are suspicious of bisexuals and see them as "fence-sitters." However, the city in which we all lived had a predominantly White queer community, which in turn privileged Margot.

Third, Diane had the "upper hand" in terms of educational level, since she was close to finishing her PhD, while Margot only had an undergraduate degree. As the primary wage earner, Diane also wielded more economic power in the relationship. And yet, while Margot felt "guilty and angry at myself" over her dependence on Diane, she also had free time that Diane envied—time she sometimes spent taking care of their home but also sometimes spent in the throes of her depression. If Margot were to return to school, she would rely even more on Diane's income, but Diane would also be putting off completing her PhD and searching for a more enjoyable, better-paying job.

Fourth, Margot was completely out to her family of origin, and experienced significant support and affirmation from them about her relationship with Diane. Diane told me that she felt welcomed by Margot's family and had a good relationship with them, particularly Margot's mother. But Diane herself was mostly still "in the closet" with her family. She thought her mother and father might have "connected the dots," but did not believe they would accept her if she were to come out to them. She maintained a distant but connected relationship with them, which she valued, and "did not see what would be gained" by disrupting that. As a result, Margot had no relationship with them at all, and was labeled "Diane's roommate" by Diane's family.

These dimensions of difference were part of Diane and Margot's relationship on a daily basis, even if they were largely hidden. I began to use a variety of tools, including Hardy and Laszloffy's (2002) multicultural couple assessment model, to encourage more direct discussion. As we did so,

Diane began to talk more frequently and to show more affect. She stopped letting Margot interrupt or talk for her, while Margot got more chances to take the listening role, something she said she liked because "it's exhausting being the one who has to air all the concerns for us both."

When the couple came to me, they had never discussed their differences. They preferred to focus on their similarities that made them feel more connected. Diane said she was uncomfortable with her identity as an African American woman, because her family's middle-class status and her success in school always made her feel different from other Blacks. As a result, she was unsure how important the cross-racial aspect of her relationship with Margot was. Margot envied Diane's educational achievements and relative economic security, which she saw as far more salient than her own Whiteness. Both of them agreed that, although they had a good network of gay and lesbian friends nearby, it was both largely White and biphobic. They had each heard versions of "cheat on her before she cheats on you" said about bisexual women, and Diane admitted that she had sometimes worried that she would not be "enough" for Margot in the long run.

Throughout my work with this couple, I used the gentle, questioning stance suggested by Johnson's (2004) EFT to encourage both partners to speak for themselves and to talk not only about their thoughts on difference, but also the feelings it evoked. Taking a slow and inquisitive pace also allowed me to use the "informed not-knowing" stance advocated by Laird (1998), in which I used my knowledge about racial minority and queer identities to guide my questions, but also was guided by the clients' responses as they told me about their specific experiences.

In short enactments, I encouraged Margot and Diane to identify and share the emotions brought up by these conversations, and helped each partner to self-soothe her anxieties so she could listen to and validate the other. Diane identified feelings of worthlessness that had roots in her childhood experiences of racism, sexism, and heterosexism, as well as her disconnect from the Black community and her own family of origin. She shared with Margot her fears that Margot secretly wanted a White male partner, or at least a female partner who would come out to her family and "fight the battles" rather than "going along to get along." She also revealed how unfair it felt to her that Margot was "sheltered" from the racial tensions Diane experienced in her life, and that Margot got to be "the dysfunctional one" while Diane had to "keep it together all the time." Margot connected with powerful feelings of shame and guilt evoked by her White privilege, and shared how they could "get messy and ugly" when combined with her shame over her depression and unemployment. She also identified rage at Diane for the affair, and her own feelings of worthlessness that the affair tapped into, which were exacerbated by Diane's refusal to introduce Margot to her family as her partner.

Diane and Margot were sensitive and open to hearing each other's primary emotions, and particularly connected around their shared experience of feeling worthless. As they took turns engaging with each other emotionally, and experiencing one another as a "safe haven" for expressing their most vulnerable parts, the level of trust in their relationship increased dramatically. The more connected they got as a couple, the less depressed Margot felt, and slowly their sex life revived as well. By the time they terminated therapy, although they had not decided whether Margot would return to school, they both described their relationship as "more like the kind of relationship I've always wanted to have." At one year post-treatment, they were still happily together.

Discussion

This case study demonstrates that effective clinical work with QPOC couples requires the therapist to pay close attention to hidden dynamics of privilege and oppression, as well as the overt presenting problems and couple conflicts. Simply treating this couple for Margot's depression, or Diane's affair, would have been of limited effectiveness—perhaps a short-term improvement, but not addressing their deeper needs. The couple had begun to enter the Distance and Isolation Cascade identified by Gottman (1999) as a predictor of relationship failure and did not seem to experience the kind of intimacy and trust that Johnson (2004) associates with a secure relational bond. They had taken concrete steps to deal with Diane's emotional affair, yet did not seem to feel that things were better. My assessment was that their unspoken differences were both diagnostic of, and contributing to, their lack of safety and connectedness. My goal was to help the couple reestablish a secure bond by assisting them in sharing and witnessing the vulnerable primary emotions that lay underneath their anger and withdrawal (Johnson, 2004). The topic of their identities both addressed an area previously ignored in their relationship, and allowed them quick access to intense emotions that they had never shared, ideal for encouraging the reengagement and softening moments of EFT (Johnson, 2004). Thus, the therapy was successful because we addressed difficult topics that had previously been silenced, but also did so via a process that went beyond intellectual insight and engaged Diane and Margot's emotional needs.

The "informed not-knowing" stance was also crucial to success, because there were many ways in which both Diane's and Margot's experiences differed from the dominant narratives about their identities. While Diane's Black family was, she believed, intolerant of homosexuality, they were also middle class, educated, and not particularly close. Margot had never experienced negative messages about her sexual identity from her family of origin, and the couple had a close relationship with her parents rather than being marginalized by them. And in defiance of the stereotype, it was not Margot the bisexual partner who had the affair, but Diane. It was important for me to be culturally literate enough to ask good questions, but to listen for unexpected answers as well.

Tips for Clinicians, Educators, and Supervisors

Bernstein (2000) points out that work with queer clients is not a specialty practice—over 80% of therapists in a study of marriage and family therapists reported working with gays and lesbians in therapy. So long as the field is dominated by White, heterosexual clinicians, QPOC will turn up on these majority therapists' caseloads. Clinicians must be prepared to provide quality services to them. Clinicians cannot assume that queer couples of color are either exactly the same as, or totally different from, White heterosexual/cisgendered relationships, White queer relationships, and heterosexual/cisgendered couples of color. Therapists must be prepared to not just tolerate, but embrace and celebrate complexity.

Educators and supervisors must lead the way on this journey. Long, Bonomo, Andrews, and Brown (2006) point out that, despite studies showing that clinicians do not feel trained to work with queer clients, training programs have been slow to improve in this area, perhaps because "supervisors and professors are reluctant to deal with this topic or are themselves ill-prepared" (p. 29). Phillips (2000) connects the poverty of clinical training regarding queer people with the perpetuation of heterosexist biases in therapy, and points out that specialized training for work with ethnically and culturally diverse populations is also considered crucial in order to provide competent clinical services. Long et al. (2006) suggest that if faculty and supervisors also suffer from a lack of knowledge, the problem is then self-perpetuating until leaders in the field address it in themselves. Plainly, such an update in skills and information would have to include information on QPOC, or the institutional separation of race/ethnicity from sexual and gender identities will continue.

Phillips (2000) suggests helping trainees develop a broad base of knowledge about queer people's lives, and gives ideas on how to incorporate such information into classes on ethics, research, assessment, and general clinical skills as well as specific, separate courses. Long and Lindsey (2004) offer the Sexual Orientation Matrix for Supervision (SOMS) as a tool for evaluating levels of heterosexual bias (beliefs) and acceptance of nonheterosexual orientations (clinical behavior). They suggest that supervisors use the SOMS for self-evaluation as well as for assessing supervisees' readiness for work with queer clients, using additional training and other supervisory tasks to remedy bias and heterosexism. A refinement of the SOMS (Long & Bonomo, 2006) expands it to include attitudes toward transgender and questioning clients.

Stone Fish, Harvey, and Addison (2000) challenge supervisors to go through their own identity development in the process of becoming aware of and sensitized to the ways in which sexual identity can impact clients, trainees, and supervisors themselves. Drawing from Sophie's (1985) four-stage identity development model, they suggest that supervisors take the journey from first awareness, through test and exploration, identity acceptance, and finally identity integration as they learn to honor the topic of sexual identity as a given, a necessary part of the supervisory process.

Conclusion

We hope we have managed to convey some of the complexities and challenges, but also some of the joys and opportunities, that arise when working with queer couples. In the end, helping clients to integrate socially segregated aspects of themselves, while working to meet their relational needs with one another, can create powerful change that facilitates deep intimacy.

Rather than asking clients to "pluck out some one aspect" of self, or to look into Rich's empty mirror that fails to reflect their realities, we as clinicians can offer queer couples validation, acceptance, curiosity, and hope.

Notes

1. The term *cisgendered* is a neologism that indicates a match between an individual's biological sex and socially assigned gender role. The root *cis* comes from Latin and means "on the same side," in contrast to *trans*, "across," as in "transgendered." This word is chosen in order to avoid contrasting transgendered people with "normally" or "correctly" gendered people, as is often the case in the medical and psychological literature.

2. *Two-spirit* is a term used by some of Native American/First Nations descent to describe an individual who has both a male and female spirit, which influences their gender and sexual identities. *SGL* is a term adopted by some Black men who feel marginalized by the Whiteness of "gay/bisexual." *Stud* is a description popular among some Black lesbians who have a masculine or "butch" gender presentation. *Hijra* is a third gender acknowledged in some parts of India, Bangladesh, and Pakistan.

Additional Resources

Films

Lee, A. (Director). (1993). *The Wedding Banquet* (1993), directed by Ang Lee. Samuel Goldwyn Films.

Lee, S. (Director). (1996). *Get on the Bus* (1996), directed by Spike Lee. Sony Pictures.

Riggs, M. (Director). (1989). *Tongues Untied*. Frameline Distribution.

Simmons, J. (Director). (2005). *TransGeneration*. New Video Group.

Wu, A. (Director). (2005). *Saving Face*. (2005). Sony Pictures Classics.

Readings

Boykin, K. (1996). *One more river to cross: Black and gay in America*. New York: Doubleday.

Greene, B. (Ed.) (1997). *Ethnic and cultural diversity among lesbians and gay men*. Thousand Oaks, CA: Sage.

Heldke, L., & O'Connor, P. (Eds.). (2004). *Oppression, privilege, & resistance: Theoretical perspectives on racism, sexism, and heterosexism*. Boston: McGraw-Hill.

Whitman, J. S., & Boyd, J. C. (Eds.). (2003). *The therapist's notebook for lesbian, gay, and bisexual clients: Homework, handouts and activities for use in psychotherapy.* New York: Haworth Press.

References

Addison, S. M., & Brown, M. (2003). Creating a cultural and sexual genogram. In J. S. Whitman & C. J. Boyd (Eds.), *The therapist's notebook for lesbian, gay, and bisexual clients: Homework, handouts and activities for use in psychotherapy* (pp. 101–105). New York: Haworth Press.

Atkinson, D. R. (2004). *Counseling American minorities: A cross-cultural perspective.* New York: McGraw-Hill.

Bean, R. A., Perry, B. J., & Bedell, T. M. (2001). Developing culturally competent marriage and family therapists: Treatment guidelines for non-African-American therapists working with African-American families. *Journal of Marital and Family Therapy, 28,* 153–164.

Bernstein, A. C. (2000). Straight therapists working with lesbians and gays in couple therapy. *Journal of Marital and Family Therapy, 26,* 443–454.

Berzon, B. (2004). *Permanent partners: Building gay and lesbian relationships that last.* New York: Plume.

Bettinger, M. (2006). Polyamory and gay men: A family systems approach. In J. J. Bigner (Ed.), *An introduction to GLBT family studies* (pp. 161–181). Binghamton, NY: Haworth Press.

Bobes, T., & Rothman, B. (2002). *Doing couple therapy: Integrating theory with practice.* New York: W. W. Norton.

Boyd-Franklin, N. (2003). *Black families in therapy.* New York: Guilford Press.

Brown, L. (1995). Therapy with same-sex couples: An introduction. In N. S. Jacobson & A. S. Gurman (Eds.), *Clinical handbook of couple therapy* (pp. 274–291). New York: Guilford Press.

Clarke, C. (2004). The failure to transform: Homophobia in the Black community. In L. Heldke & P. O'Connor (Eds.), *Oppression, privilege, & resistance: Theoretical perspectives on racism, sexism, and heterosexism* (pp. 197–208). Boston: McGraw-Hill.

Connolly, C. M. (2004). Clinical issues with same-sex couples: A review of the literature. In J. J. Bigner & J. L. Wetchler (Eds.), *Relationship therapy with same-sex couples* (pp. 3–12). New York: Haworth Press.

Coolhart, D., Provancher, N., Hager, A., & Wang, M. (in press). Recommending transsexual clients for gender transition: A therapeutic tool for assessing readiness. *Journal of GLBT Family Studies.*

Crohn, J. (1998). Intercultural couples. In M. McGoldrick (Ed.), *Re-visioning family therapy: Race, culture, and gender in clinical practice* (pp. 295–308). New York: Guilford Press.

Espin, O. (1997). Crossing borders and boundaries: The life narratives of immigrant lesbians. In B. Greene (Ed.), *Ethnic and cultural diversity among lesbians and gay men* (pp. 191–215). Thousand Oaks, CA: Sage.

Fausto-Sterling, A. (2000). *Sexing the body: Gender politics and the construction of sexuality.* New York: Basic Books.

Garcia, A. (1996). Foreword. In J. F. Longres (Ed.), *Men of color: A context for service to homosexually active men* (pp. xiii–xvi). New York: Harrington Park Press.

Gottman, J. M. (1999). *The marriage clinic: A scientifically based marital therapy.* New York: W. W. Norton.

Green, R. J. (2004). Foreword. In J. J. Bigner & J. L. Wetchler (Eds.), *Relationship therapy with same-sex couples* (pp. 185–227). New York: Haworth Press.

Green, R. J., Bettinger, M., & Zacks, E. (1996). Are lesbian couples fused and gay male couples disengaged? Questioning gender straightjackets. In J. Laird & R. J. Green (Eds.), *Lesbians and gays in couples and families.* San Francisco: Jossey-Bass.

Green, R. J., & Mitchell, V. (2002). Gay and lesbian couples in therapy: Homophobia, relational ambiguity, and social support. In A. S. Gurman & N. S. Jacobson (Eds.), *Clinical handbook of couple therapy* (3rd ed., pp. 546–568). New York: Guilford Press.

Greenan, D. E., & Tunnell, G. (2003). *Couple therapy with gay men.* New York: Guilford Press.

Greene, B. (1994). Lesbian women of color: Triple jeopardy. In L. Comas-Diaz & B. Greene (Eds.), *Women of color: Integrating ethnic and gender identities in psychotherapy* (pp. 389–427). New York: Guilford Press.

Greene, B. (1997). Ethnic minority lesbians and gay men: Mental health and treatment issues. In B. Greene (Ed.), *Ethnic and cultural diversity among lesbians and gay men* (pp. 216–239). Thousand Oaks, CA: Sage.

Greene, B. (2003). Beyond heterosexism and across the cultural divide—developing an inclusive lesbian, gay, and bisexual psychology: A look to the future. In L. D. Garnets & D. C. Kimmel (Eds.), *Psychological perspectives on lesbian, gay, and bisexual experiences* (2nd ed., pp. 357–400). New York: Colombia University Press.

Gurman, A. S., & Jacobson, N. S. (2002). *Clinical handbook of couple therapy* (3rd ed.). New York: Guilford Press.

Hardy, K. V., & Laszloffy, T. A. (1998). The dynamics of a pro-racist ideology. In M. McGoldrick (Ed.), *Re-visioning family therapy: Race, culture, and gender in clinical practice* (pp. 118–128). New York: Guilford Press.

Hardy, K. V., & Laszloffy, T. A. (2002). Couple therapy using a multicultural perspective. In A. S. Gurman & N. S. Jacobson (Eds.), *Clinical handbook of couple therapy* (3rd ed.) (pp. 569–596). New York: Guilford Press.

hooks, b. (2000). Homophobia in Black communities. In D. Constantine-Simms (Ed.), *The greatest taboo: Homosexuality on Black communities* (pp. 67–75). New York: Alyson Books.

Israel, G. E. (2004). Supporting transgender and sex reassignment issues: Couple and family dynamics. In J. J. Bigner & J. L. Wetchler (Eds.), *Relationship therapy with same-sex couples* (pp. 53–64). New York: Harrington Park Press.

Jagose, A. (1996). *Queer theory: An introduction.* Washington Square, NY: New York University Press.

Johnson, A. F. (2006). *Privilege, power, and difference* (2nd ed.). Boston: McGraw-Hill.

Johnson, S. M. (2004). *The practice of Emotionally Focused Couple Therapy: Creating connection.* New York: Routledge.

Johnson, T. W., & Keren, M. S. (1996). Creating and maintaining boundaries in male couples. In J. Laird & R. J. Green (Eds.), *Lesbians and gays in couples and families* (pp. 231–250). San Francisco: Jossey-Bass.

Laird, J. (1998). Theorizing culture: Narrative ideas and practice principles. In M. McGoldrick (Ed.), *Re-visioning family therapy: Race, culture, and gender in clinical practice* (pp. 20–36). New York: Guilford Press.

Laird, J., & Green, R. J. (Eds.). (1996). *Lesbians and gays in couples and families.* San Francisco: Jossey-Bass.

Lev, A. I. (2004). *Transgender emergence: Therapeutic guidelines for working with gender-variant people and their families.* Binghamton, NY: Haworth Clinical Practice Press.

Long, J. K., & Bonomo, J. (2006). Revisiting the Sexual Orientation Matrix for supervision: Working with GLBTQ families. In J. Bigner & A. R. Gottlieb (Eds.), *Interventions with families of gay, lesbian, bisexual, and transgender people* (pp. 151–166). New York: Harrington Park Press.

Long, J. K., Bonomo, J., Andrews, B. V., & Brown, J. M. (2006). Systemic therapeutic approaches with sexual minorities and their families. In J. Bigner & A. R. Gottlieb (Eds.), *Interventions with families of gay, lesbian, bisexual, and transgender people* (pp. 7–37). New York: Harrington Park Press.

Long, J. K., & Lindsey, E. (2004). The Sexual Orientation Matrix for Supervision: A tool for training therapists to work with same-sex couples. In J. J. Bigner & J. L. Wetchler (Eds.), *Relationship therapy with same-sex couples* (pp. 123–135). New York: Haworth Press.

Lorde, A. (2004). Age, race, class and sex: Women redefining difference. In L. Heldke & P. O'Connor (Eds.), *Oppression, privilege, & resistance: Theoretical perspectives on racism, sexism, and heterosexism* (pp. 553–560). Boston: McGraw-Hill.

Malpas, J. (2006). From otherness to alliance: Transgender couples in therapy. In J. J. Bigner & A. R. Gottlieb (Eds.), *Interventions with families of gay, lesbian, bisexual, & transgender people: From the inside out* (pp. 183–206). New York: Harrington Park Press.

McGoldrick, M. (1998). Introduction: Re-visioning family therapy through a cultural lens. In M. McGoldrick (Ed.), *Re-visioning family therapy: Race, culture, and gender in clinical practice* (pp. 3–19). New York: Guilford Press.

Mishne, J. (2002). *Multiculturalism and the therapeutic process*. New York: Guilford Press.

Morales, E. S. (1990). Ethnic minority families and minority gays and lesbians. In F. W. Bozett & M. B. Sussman (Eds.), *Homosexuality and family relations* (pp. 217–239). New York: Haworth Press.

Morrow, S. L. (2003). Can the master's tools ever dismantle the master's house? Answering silences with alternative paradigms and methods. *The Counseling Psychologist, 31*, 70–77.

Ossana, S. M. (2000). Relationship and couples counseling. In R. M. Perez, K. A. DeBord, & K. J. Bieschke (Eds.), *Handbook of counseling and psychotherapy with lesbian, gay, and bisexual clients* (pp. 275–302). Washington, DC: American Psychological Association.

Peplau, L. A., Cochran, S. D., & Mays, V. M. (1997). A national survey of the intimate relationships of African-American lesbian and gay men: A look at commitment, satisfaction, sexual behavior, and HIV disease. In B. Greene (Ed.), *Ethnic and cultural diversity among lesbians and gay men* (pp. 11–38). Thousand Oaks, CA: Sage.

Peplau, L. A., & Spalding, L. R. (2003). The close relationships of lesbians, gay men, and bisexuals. In L. D. Garnets & D. C. Kimmel (Eds.), *Psychological perspectives on lesbian, gay, and bisexual experiences* (pp. 449–474). New York: Columbia University Press.

Perez, R. M., DeBord, K. A., & Bieschke, K. J. (Eds.). (2000). *Handbook of counseling and psychotherapy with lesbian, gay, and bisexual clients*. Washington, DC: American Psychological Association.

Phillips, J. C. (2000). Training issues and considerations. In R. M. Perez, K. A. DeBord, & K. J. Bieschke (Eds.), *Handbook of counseling and psychotherapy with lesbian, gay, and bisexual clients* (pp. 337–358). Washington, DC: American Psychological Association.

Rich, A. C. (1986). *Blood, bread, and poetry: Selected prose 1979–1985*. New York: W. W. Norton.

Ritter, K. Y., & Terndrup, A. I. (Eds.). (2002). *Handbook of affirmative psychotherapy with lesbians and gay men*. New York: Guilford Press.

Rust, P. C. (2003). Finding a sexual identity and community: Therapeutic implications and cultural assumptions in scientific models of coming out. In L. D. Garnets & D. C. Kimmel (Eds.), *Psychological perspectives on lesbian, gay, and bisexual experiences* (pp. 227–269). New York: Columbia University Press.

Siegel, S., & Walker, G. (1996). Conversations between a gay therapist and a straight therapist. In J. Laird & R. J. Green (Eds.), *Lesbians and gays in couples and families* (pp. 28–68). San Francisco: Jossey-Bass.

Smith, A. (1997). Cultural diversity and the coming-out process: Implications for clinical practice. In B. Greene (Ed.), *Ethnic and cultural diversity among lesbians and gay men* (pp. 279–300). Thousand Oaks, CA: Sage.

Somerville, S. B. (2000). *Queering the color line: Race and the invention of homosexuality in American culture.* Durham, NC: Duke University Press.

Sophie, J. (1985). A critical examination of stage theories of lesbian identity development. *Journal of Homosexuality, 12*(2), 39–51.

Stone Fish, L., Harvey, R., & Addison, S. (2000). Don't ask, don't tell: Supervision and sexual identity. In *Readings in family therapy supervision: Selected articles from the AAMFT Supervision Bulletin.* Washington, DC: American Association for Marriage and Family Therapy.

Torres Bernal, A., & Coolhart, D. (2005). Learning from sexual minorities: Adolescents and the coming out process. *Guidance and Counselling, 20(3/4),* 128–138.

Valdes, F. (2004). Notes on the conflation of sex, gender, and sexual orientation: A queercrit and latcrit perspective. In L. Heldke & P. O'Connor (Eds.), *Oppression, privilege, & resistance: Theoretical perspectives on racism, sexism, and heterosexism* (pp. 466–475). Boston: McGraw-Hill.

Wing Sue, D., & Sue, D. (2002). *Counseling the culturally diverse: Theory and practice.* New York: Wiley.

Young, M. E., & Long, L. L. (1997). *Counseling and therapy for couples.* Pacific Grove, CA: Wadsworth.

Five

The Unspoken Power of Racial Context

What's Race Gotta Do With It?

Larry Jin Lee

Then too, you're constantly being bumped against by those of poor vision. Or again, you often doubt if you really exist. You wonder whether you aren't simply a phantom in other people's mind. Say, a figure in a nightmare which the sleeper tries with all his might to destroy. It's when you feel like that, out of resentment, you begin to bump people back. You ache with the need to convince yourself that you do exist in the real world, that you're a part of all the sound and anguish, and you strike out with your fists, you curse and you swear to make them recognize you. And alas, it's seldom successful.

—Ellison, 1972, pp. 3–4

A good friend and colleague of mine once told me many years ago, "True insanity is a person of color . . . fully aware." It was a chilling reality to me then, and still cuts me to the core now. I frequently find myself caught in this internal struggle of catching and noticing the frequent unconscious and subtle racial slights directed at me, but also experience the wish to filter them out of my awareness at the same time. However, in spite of the pain of registering these experiences, I still hold the belief that it is far better to be aware and conscious rather than to be in a numbing state of denial. In particular, as a psychotherapist, to internalize pervasive racial injury and hurt can lead to potential unconscious harm and projection on to clients (Hardy & Laszloffy, 1992). To illustrate further, I would like to use a poignant example from my life. I had been invited to facilitate a workshop in a national diversity conference in Monterey, California, several years ago. "Great venue, great town," I thought to myself and happily accepted the invitation. It was about a half hour before the workshop was scheduled to begin in the morning, and I wanted to get a little something to eat. I walked across the street to a small cafe to buy a muffin. What ensued and unfolded left me stupefied and in disbelief. The irony was surreal.

Permit me to frame the scene once again: A Chinese American male diversity trainer, dressed professionally, enters a cafe that is directly across from a causeway of a big-name hotel to buy a muffin. No other customers are in the establishment. There is a White male proprietor at the other end of the counter who does not acknowledge my presence. I stand there for about two or three minutes, patiently waiting to have the server notice me. Then a White woman dressed in a casual velour gym suit runs in and approaches the counter and steps in front of me. The White male proprietor immediately approaches the other side of the counter and, with a smile on his face, serves her and finishes her transaction. The White customer actually turns to me as she is walking out and says, "Oh, I'm sorry. You gotta understand, I have three hungry kids waiting for me." She laughs and walks briskly away. I then walk right up to the counter immediately after her, ready to make my purchase. To my utter disbelief, he walks away without serving me. I have a flash of anger. I even have a brief out-of-body experience, because I was in such total shock. A screenwriter couldn't have written a more ironic script. As I am preparing to leave in disgust, another employee, a Latina server, comes up to the counter and offers to assist me in my purchase.

Later that morning in my workshop, still reeling from this incident, I shared how I consistently struggle with the double edge of expecting racial clashes to occur yet always being surprised and dismayed when it happens. As I write about this incident, I reexperience the same outrage and helplessness of that day. I find myself holding much of this pain as unspoken truths, and they become secret invisible wounds, internalized until it is safe to bring them into the light of day. These micro and macro experiences shape and inform my "context" personally, and consequently professionally. I frequently wonder whether others, especially White people, share the same struggle—and if not, why not? If I were to disclose this incident to a White therapist in session, would the therapist possibly tell me I was imagining this scenario, or even blame me for my own victimization (Tatum, 1997; Wise, 2005)?

I imagine that White European Americans do not live with these persistent painful reminders of being the "other," where one has persistent internal conversations after a racial incident: where I am left to second-guess whether what I experienced indeed did happen, or if I imagined it or misinterpreted what occurred. Over time, you begin to either lose trust in your own perception, voice, and intuition, or develop a cumulative insulation of anger and guardedness. As expressed so powerfully and precisely by Ralph Ellison over 50 years ago in his book, *Invisible Man:*

> You ache with the need to convince yourself that you do exist in the real world, that you're a part of all the sound and anguish, and you strike out with your fists, you curse and you swear to make them recognize you. (Ellison, 1952/1972, p. 4)

The potency and empowerment expressed in this quote by Ellison's protagonist brings to the fore a core theme in the case examples I will use later in this chapter: *Anger as Survival.*

It highlights the importance of "anger" as the key binding catalyst for the wounds of racial injury and the preservation of voice and dignity for people of color. This is especially poignant and significant for African American men. I can vividly recall an African American male client express to me in a therapy session how essential it was for him to be able bring his rage and anger into the room: "Anger is how I survive out in the real world. It is very important that I can express that rage and outrage here without feeling as though I am being judged as an 'out of control' angry Black man." I must add, however, that a pervasive state of anger is damaging to one's health and well-being (Tatum, 1997; Wise, 2005). Therefore, cultivating and fomenting anger is not the ultimate goal; rather, anger is a defense against the humiliation and degradation of racism. The goal is to support and validate the rage and anger to facilitate its release (Wise, 2005). The other option, suffering in silence, is a false choice: Without anger as the shield, you have despair, depression, and loss of self—perhaps even insanity.

However, I can recount innumerable occasions where colleagues have expressed strong negative opinions about seeing African American men in therapy, especially if they are construed as being aggressive and angry (Hardy, 1993). I have participated in many case discussions where clinicians would pathologize the client and deem them resistant or non-compliant to treatment.

The Preeminence of Context

Everything we do is embedded within multiple contexts of collective and individual historical events that culminate in present day encounters. Unfortunately, the historical impact of racism still reverberates in our daily lives today.

—Lee, 2005, p. 94

One of the most essential components of a culturally literate practice is a clinician's proficiency in and perceptivity to the racial context and templates that are active in any client narrative or interaction (Tatum, 1997). Therefore, one needs to be attuned to the parallel process of the specific contexts and ecology within a client's life story, and also to the context invoked in the therapy room itself between therapist and client. This can be especially challenging in treatment with interracial couples with a therapist of color or with a White therapist, where there are multiple personal, racial, gender, and historical contexts brought into the therapeutic encounter (Dolan-Del Vecchio, 1998). A word of caution, however: While it is good for a clinician to have access to a contextual lens, it is equally important not to automatically impose that perspective onto a client prematurely and jump to conclusions. Thus, another aspect of cultural competence is the mindful stance of the therapist simultaneously holding both the awareness of racial context(s) and yet not becoming too committed or attached to it where it can inadvertently silence the client.

This occurred when I saw an interracial couple, a Japanese American woman and an African American man, in my initial session with them. Both shared how they grew up in primarily White-dominated schools and towns. Each shared that they were "tracked" into specific academic programs in school. Now, you might speculate what racial/historical templates began to appear on my clinical radar. Of course, the African American man was probably tracked into the lower performing reading groups and the Japanese American woman was most likely tracked into the academically gifted ones, I thought. Attempting to validate the African American man's experience, I expressed how sadly common it was for me to hear my African American clients share how they were unfairly placed in lower performing categories in spite of how much promise and ability they exhibited in the classroom (Kozol, 1991; Meier, 1990). Much to my chagrin, he diplomatically corrected me in my presumption that in fact he was not tracked into the lower performing group, but that he went to a progressive school that was mindful of giving children of all racial and ethnic backgrounds opportunities to excel. His Asian American counterpart had been assigned to a higher performing reading group despite the fact that she had undiagnosed dyslexia as a child. Her story proved to be the more emotionally charged and painful as a result of the pressure placed on her from the assumption and stereotype that Asians American are all academically inclined. She apparently was automatically assigned to a higher math and reading group based purely on her being Japanese American. She shared her memories of her struggle to keep up with her work and how she compensated for her learning disability, constantly fearing failure.

As the session unfolded, my being professionally humbled notwithstanding, the African American man did disclose how it is an ongoing point of contention in his relationship that he chose to be a coach with youth in a neighborhood recreation center rather than pursue a more ambitious vocation. He expressed how his partner's family viewed him as lazy and a deadbeat living off of her significantly higher income. What can you identify as some of the predominant racial contexts pertinent in this case? What would be the contexts active in the therapy room between this couple and a Chinese American therapist, an African American therapist, or a White therapist? How great an impact do you believe this would have on the treatment outcome?

Identifying and Naming Contextual Themes

In brief, I will suggest some of the more salient racial templates imbedded in this case. First and foremost is the overarching impact of the Asian American model minority stereotype juxtaposed to the African American stereotypes. The irony demonstrated here is that, regardless of the fact that there was an unexpected twist where the stereotypes were the opposite of what was assumed, at the other end of it a central conflict for the couple led back to the usual racial attributions. The African American man had to confront the usual perceptions of being lazy and a deadbeat; the Japanese American woman was tormented by pressures to excel academically (Feagin & Sikes, 1994; Shipler, 1997). From this nexus emanated her family's expectations and their tacit, unconscious collusion with racist attributions that become problematic for this couple. In addition, we should not ignore the template of the difficulty experienced by academically gifted African Americans who run the risk of criticism, ridicule, and ostracism from other African Americans because getting good grades is perceived as "selling out" or "acting White" (Kelly & Boyd-Franklin, 2005).

Let us also examine what was happening in the therapeutic dance during the session between the clients and the therapist. There would be the unspoken power and impact of the sole African American man in a room with two Asian American women, or with an Asian American woman and me, an Asian American man. What potential is there for triangulation? One can imagine the variations that can come into play, not to mention issues related to having two males of color in the therapy room, the female Asian American client and her templates around Asian American men in her family of origin, traditional gender roles, class, even subtleties around language and accent. There may be a temptation to avoid and deny the clinical relevance of these dimensions in treatment because we were not provided with maps to navigate these waters during our training. One of my mentors challenged me to be willing to "lose sight of land" so I could find my way to my next developmental stage. I invite you to join me in that ongoing journey.

> It is a powerful realization that such a brief exchange can tap into the energy of multiple historical legacies and stories of our collective struggles with the issues of racial oppression, learned roles, and stereotypes . . . The unspoken question is, can these exchanges be opportunities for mutual growth and learning? (Lee, 2005, p. 95)

This case example is a good illustration of the slippery slope of racial/cultural contexts. Having stated this, I am concerned that this challenge would discourage many from diligently developing cultural lenses and perspectives. Although it is my intention to stress how "just a little knowledge" is not enough, and can even potentially be harmful, in working across differences the concept of possessing a "beginner's mind," from a mindfulness perspective, is particularly useful. In other words, the consistent cultivation of professional humility and inquisitiveness can create the conditions necessary for cultural literacy. Rather than being fearful, a practitioner can approach work with clients without absolutes or fixed formulas, holding on to a position of fluid awareness and openness to one's inner experience as a therapist while providing space for the client(s) to weave their narratives freely.

A Case From the Movies

I frequently use brief excerpts from popular media when I teach cultural literacy classes or workshops. One of my favorites is taken from the movie *The Joy Luck Club*. The cultural misunderstanding and clashes portrayed in this short vignette provide us with a rich metaphor to use in work with interracial couples. There is a humorous scene where a Chinese American daughter brings her European American fiancé to a family dinner to meet her mother. The back-story is that this daughter has an ongoing conflictual relationship with her mother and is resentful that, as an adult, she still yearns for her mother's approval. She desperately wants her mother to approve of her choice of a life partner. Everyone is sitting down for the meal, and of course her mother has gone to great lengths to perfectly prepare a multicourse meal.

What ensues is a series of cultural faux pas on the part of the fiancé. First, after a toast he guzzles his glass of wine, whereas everyone else takes a small sip. Then, as the dishes go around the table and he is the first to be served as a guest, he takes a large portion for himself before anyone else has been served. Last, the biggest blunder and insult of all is that he takes the liberty of sloshing soy sauce all over the dish his fiancée's mother took the most pride in preparing. In all fairness, we cannot fault him for any of his transgressions. After all, while placing her specialty dish on the table, her mother apologetically expressed disclaimers that the dish did not taste very good and that it lacked flavor. Little did he know that this was all a culturally expected and prescribed dance of false humility and standing on ceremony. He did not know that the appropriate response would have been for him to take a taste of the food and proclaim it the best he had ever had, to which she would have responded with more self-deprecating comments. At this point, one may say in frustration, "How on earth are you to know all of this?" and perhaps even think that ethnic and cultural matching of therapist to client is the only option. I believe that would be a tragic conclusion to draw. Rather, it is my hope that most would choose professional humility and accepting the challenge of learning the art of "not knowing" and "non-doing."

Different Realities: White Privilege

Although an in-depth analysis and treatise on cultural nuances are beyond the scope of this chapter, I wish to provide some highlights and distinctions that will be helpful to establish for subsequent cases I will present here. The value of the vignette from *The Joy Luck Club* is that it poignantly elucidates the frequent clashes and frustrating misperceptions between a culture with an "individualist" paradigm—for example, White European American—versus one with a "collectivist" Asian American paradigm. Another way of understanding this is by what I refer to as the "awareness of the other" (external locus) versus a "focus on the individual/self" (internal locus) continuum (Kelly & Boyd-Franklin, 2005). In the example of the fiancé at dinner, he is portrayed as a caricature of the self-focused oblivious White male who may be well intentioned but is totally unaware of the need to accommodate to a different reality and set of rules. The typical reaction I receive from White audiences when this excerpt is used is to blame the Chinese daughter for not adequately preparing and coaching her White fiancé. I usually counter with, "Would you have the same opinion if the scenario were reversed? Would you place the same onus on the White person to coach her or his partner for a visit to the White family?" I submit that it would be an unspoken assumption that it is the person of color's burden to accommodate and know the rules of conduct when in the company of White people (Tatum, 1997). Furthermore, I have also observed a tendency for White audiences to readily excuse the White person and blame the Chinese mother for her indirect, passive-aggressive stance, mirroring the systematized White supremacy that exists in mainstream American culture. Therein lies the face of White privilege. Additionally, I believe it is necessary to name sexism and male privilege as an underlying theme in this scenario. In our society, the burden to accommodate and defer falls primarily on women.

If the White male fiancé took the time to experience being the "other" in this family, he may have realized that just observing would have been a good default position to take. What if he does not have any points of reference around marginalization? Therein lies the problem. One of my clients gave me a wonderful metaphor that she learned while living in the Far East. She made the observation that people in Asian countries use their car horns to let others know that they are there; in this country, we honk to tell others to get out of our way. Such is the yin and yang of cultural styles. This is what I meant when I mentioned the art of non-doing. Our culture and profession seem to place a high premium on being very "direct." However, not all cultures express and communicate in this mode. I am sure that if you had the inclination to research the genesis of these cultural styles, you would discover clear explanations as to what has shaped the character of a culture (Tatum, 1997). We can all comprehend how events such as trauma, war, slavery, the Holocaust, the Great Depression, and natural disasters like Hurricane Katrina can have significant bearing over generations. This would enhance a deeper understanding of the origin of these cultural templates (Fadiman, 1997). The mother was conveying a very clear message understood by everyone but the White fiancé. If she were to have stated bluntly, "This is my best dish and I think it's pretty darn tasty," it would have been perceived as crass, shameful, and disrespectful. Conversely, I have heard White colleagues pejoratively label this aspect of Asian American clients as codependent.

I take the liberty of taking my use of this excerpt one step further and asking students to imagine this White male fiancé as a therapist working with this Asian American family. How would the family or couple perceive this therapist? How would they respond to him and his demeanor? Would they possibly be deferent and put on a mask of tacit compliance, agreeing to his treatment recommendations, nodding their heads and deciding never to return (Tatum, 1997)? I can cite many instances where White psychotherapists find themselves in unfamiliar cultural realities making no accommodation for difference, without acknowledging any clashes in context, acting shocked when they do occur, and turning around to blame the client(s) for treatment failure. At worst, therapists can even resort to shaming the client.

The current statistics reveal an ever-increasing prevalence of interracial relationships and marriages (Crohn, 1998), which underscores the ethical responsibility therapists have to learn the skill and art of culturally literate practice.

CASE EXAMPLE

In this case example, I will demonstrate the power of racial/oppression narratives in couple therapy. Let me begin by setting the stage with the most pertinent psychosocial history for both clients. This is a case of a Chinese American man, Peter, and a White European American woman, Megan, both in their mid-30s. Their presenting problem was that they had been in their relationship for six years and Megan was pressuring Peter to set a timetable for marriage. Peter's excuses were that his monetary goals had not yet been met and he had just started a new job. Megan's urgency was fueled by her ticking biological clock. With increasing tension and resentment, they were bickering over myriad seemingly minor issues. Peter was relentlessly nagging Megan about her weight and fitness, and the fact that she was not making enough money at her job. Peter felt that he was doing more than his share of improving their financial future by taking on this new job. He saw Megan as weak and as just making excuses for her weight and settling for a low compensation in her job. He also expressed little sympathy or compassion for Megan's one-year bout of depression, during which she was unable to work. His response to Megan's struggle was, "She should have done something, even if it was part-time. I can't imagine just not doing anything." Permit me to interject a brief comment here about the clear sexist and male privilege paradigm underlying Peter's attitudes. Statistics have proven for decades that women make 60–70% of what men earn for equivalent jobs. Furthermore, the "glass ceiling" is still very much a reality for women in the workplace. In spite of his own privilege, Peter alluded to his perception that Megan had it "too easy" growing up, fully supported by her family and "privileged." This issue looms large as an unspoken basis for much of Peter's critical, almost harsh, parental stance toward Megan. I will elaborate on this further after I provide a bit more background about each of their family histories.

Peter grew up as a first-generation—born in the United States—Chinese American. He is the second son in a family of three. He has an older brother and younger sister. His father owned a grocery store and immigrated to this country with his wife and parents in the 1940s. He disclosed that his father was very harsh and critical, almost to the point of being emotionally and verbally abusive. His older brother was the favorite eldest son who always did better in school, excelled in all things, and was held up as the model for him to emulate. However, it was quite obvious that Peter could never obtain his father's or brother's approval, regardless of how hard he tried. And he pushed himself very hard. Peter would get any job he could at a very young age, exercised zealously to be in shape, and pursued many sports with the hope of being a "star" in something; however, he never attained what he needed: recognition. The fact that Peter chose a White girlfriend was more grist for the mill.

Most infuriating to Peter, however, was that he described an early awareness that, in many arenas, he had to try significantly harder just because he wasn't White. He expressed in a session, "I know that I had to look better, try harder, and be impeccably articulate to be taken seriously. I have experienced it so much, it isn't funny." He described that all of the management at his new place of employment were White men. He recounted many meetings where he would express an opinion or share an idea and not be heard or acknowledged, just to have a White person say exactly the same thing and receive instant kudos. This, along with having to endure frequent racial innuendo about Asian drivers and hearing coworkers mimic sing-song Chinese accents, would infuriate Peter, but he would internalize his rage since he was a new employee on probation. Again, his pervasive attitude was, "You can't let them get to you. You gotta show that you're strong enough to take it and still succeed. That's where I get my satisfaction."

When Peter shared his experiences with racism and unfairness in his life, Megan would be understanding and openly acknowledge how she was fortunate not to have to endure this as a White person. She described how she grew up in an upper middle-class, primarily White, homogeneous community in the Southwest. Her father was a community college professor and her mother was a homemaker. Megan reluctantly disclosed that her mother was a closet alcoholic. She was the responsible, parentified oldest daughter of four children. She had an older brother and two younger sisters. She had to compensate for her mother's unavailability as a parent to her younger siblings. She shared that she was a late bloomer and was not in the popular group in high school, where she experienced exclusion by cliques. However, she did feel that she came into her own in college, and did very well academically and socially after leaving home. Her father was her role model and she felt she learned acceptance and tolerance from him. She met Peter at a party thrown by her college roommate.

The Racial Context/Compassionate Witness Model

Early in my work with Peter and Megan, I attempted to build a foundation around parallels and points of connection around each of their experiences of oppression. In my experience, I have discovered the use of oppression/racism narratives can provide a powerful bridge to understanding and reconciliation in couple therapy. I have also chosen to weave in the compassionate witness model I presented in a previous paper into

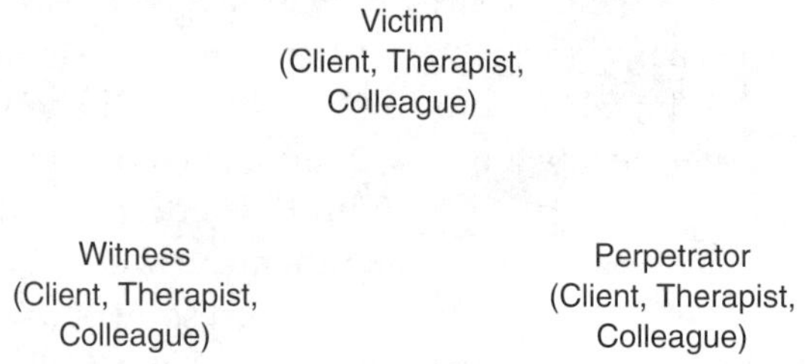

Victim
(Client, Therapist,
Colleague)

Witness   Perpetrator
(Client, Therapist,   (Client, Therapist,
Colleague)   Colleague)

Figure 5.1   Compassionate Witness Model

this case (Lee, 2005) to illustrate the healing power of retelling/revisiting traumatic oppressive incidents in the presence of authentic, fully present compassionate witnesses (see Figure 5.1).

In working with a client of color who has experienced racial trauma—as with all trauma—the therapist needs to be aware that there exist symbolic representations of three entities that were present in the original perpetration of the injury or crime: the victim, the perpetrator, and the witness. In the clinical encounter, a therapist can embody and act from any one of these three positions, either through verbal, nonverbal, or metacommunication. Clearly and obviously, a therapist seeks to aspire to be an authentic compassionate witness to facilitate a corrective emotional experience. The therapist and White partner can join to become corrective emotional allies to the person of color in the couple's therapy as he or she revisits the scene(s) of the crime.

One of the primary challenges in work with interracial couples is not only to identify and define the possible racial and oppression themes, but more importantly to perceive where and when the windows of opportunity are to invoke and name the issue, bringing it into the room. Thus, art transcends skill. As you might expect, very few clients bring up racism or White privilege overtly, since we have been taught and conditioned to not discuss these issues openly. It is the therapist's facility and comfort with racial contexts that dictate the space for these healing conversations to unfold. I will illustrate this use of process narratives taken from my sessions with Peter and Megan. However, I must interject here that my greatest challenge in writing this chapter is to discover clear and effective ways to describe the "art" of practice with interracial couples. Therefore, I will begin by addressing the inner workings of how I approach my work with a couple like Peter and Megan. The next part of the process involves what I hypothesize may be on the radar around active racial templates that can be made explicit at some appropriate timing in the treatment. The last phase is to illustrate the art of using the compassionate witness model to facilitate building a metaphor for empathy and reconciliation between the couple, as well as to establish each as an ally for social justice around racism. Due to the limitations of scope and space for this chapter, I must limit my focus to the main contexts for this case. But I emphasize that it is tremendously valuable to have knowledge of greater macro contexts such as war or immigration laws and patterns, which have multigenerational ramifications on client character and beliefs.

Phase 1: Therapist Inner Workings/Dialogue

We have all been taught and trained to be attuned to biases—also known as *countertransference*. Obviously that awareness is fundamental in order to "do no harm" in all clinical encounters. However, as a result of institutionalized systems of prejudice and White supremacy, one has to be vigilant to remain conscious of these automatic reactions. I have provided a survey of what gets triggered in my work with this couple:

- A sense of competition with the Chinese American male partner, possibly splitting by presenting myself as the "benevolent, good" Chinese male and Peter as the "bad" one
- Getting pulled into countering Asian American male stereotypes to prove my competence and masculinity: activating my own insecurity regarding White women's perception of Asian American men
- Perception that a person who dates outside of their race has internalized racism/self-hate
- Assumption that Megan is enlightened about race issues and an ally/anti-racist versus the "My best friend is . . ." type
- A natural, learned tendency to rescue the White person and comfort him or her
- Strong opinions about White privilege and how Megan has benefited
- Feelings of anger toward Peter for his lack of insight into how he has become an oppressor to Megan
- Reactions to Peter's sexism as well as my own unconscious issues around male privilege

This is far from being an exhaustive list. What other trigger issues can you identify? What distinct differences would arise if the therapist were White, if Peter were African American, and so on? It is in one's willingness to ask and process these questions, tempered with professional humility, that a therapist can become more authentic, present, and effective. The converse, a lack of awareness, can lead to shaming, reinjury, invalidation, and feelings of invisibility.

Phase 2: Active Racial Templates/Contexts

It is my intention to illustrate the depth and breadth of the racial templates relevant to this case. I would encourage you to mindfully read and review the client history once again before you proceed to the list I have provided. In the process of comparing and contrasting, you may be able to focus in on how you may want, in your context(s), to approach this case versus how I would approach it as a Chinese American therapist.

- *Privilege/equity and fairness:* Even playing field versus advantages.
- *Misdirected anger/not colluding with your privilege:* I am going to make it as hard on you as White people have made it for me.
- *Pulling oneself up by the bootstraps:* Making excuses is weakness.
- *Tough love builds character:* You can't ever play a race card.
- *You are not an individual:* The burden of representing your race.
- *Being Chinese American is not as good as being White:* You always need to prove yourself (internalized racism).
- *You need to be better than White people/model minority:* Always try harder, it is never good enough.
- *It's a White man's world:* Don't ever believe otherwise—White people take advantage of you, don't trust anyone.
- *I am not the racist oppressor:* I'm not responsible for what happened to you.
- *Betwixt and between (caught between two cultures):* Not Chinese enough, not White/American enough—never whole or included.
- *A woman's role is to submit and defer to men:* to please her man.
- *You are a reflection and extension of me as my trophy:* objectification of women.
- *I am validated and legitimized by having a White partner.*

It would not be possible or effective to elaborate on how to address each of these racial templates. Instead, I will choose one main theme to examine in depth; this will provide a sense of the timing, flow, and rhythm of how to bridge racial narratives into treatment. I will also highlight and identify in the process dialogue some of the racial templates that come into the session, as well as including a second interaction that, in my opinion, led to Peter's decision to terminate our therapeutic relationship.

Phase 3: The Compassionate Witness Model: Addressing White Privilege, Equity, and Fairness

A persistent theme in arguments between Peter and Megan revolves around his perception that Megan has had it much easier in life. He usually stops just short of mentioning her White privilege. Coupled with his experiences with inequities and repeated racially based injustices, Peter feels justified—albeit unconsciously—in oppressing Megan with the very same treatment he has endured. He has an all-or-nothing view about carrying one's own weight and believes that making excuses is a sign of weakness. The following process narrative occurred in our fifth session.

M: It isn't helpful when you [Peter] say that I need to lose weight and that I need to get in shape (*Objectification of women*). Why is this so important? I am working at it and I already know how you feel about it [looking exasperated].

P: I just feel it's extremely important to be healthy and to feel the best about yourself. I hold myself by the same standard. How long is it going to take? You say you're going to do it but you never do [angry and frustrated].

M: That's not fair [angry and tearful]. I do try. I am still dealing with my depression. (*Possible point of common connection with Peter's own experience as far as rendering a part of one's experience invisible and invalid*)

P: That's exactly my point. You would feel less depressed if you felt better about your weight. It might also help if you got a better job that paid you better. You don't even like your job [Megan is shaking her head and crying]. (*Pulling oneself up by the bootstraps: Excuses equal weakness*)

TH: What are you feeling right now, Megan?

M: He just doesn't understand. He doesn't want to. It makes me feel worse and it doesn't matter what I say.

TH: Would you like to respond to that, Peter?

P: I *do* understand. I'm not trying to make you feel bad. I want you to be stronger and that's how I believe you can do it. You can't just sit there passively. (*Pull yourself up by the bootstraps*)

TH: [I find that I am also reacting to Peter's immovable position] Peter, I'd like you to slow down and tell me what you heard Megan say about feeling misunderstood?

P: [Reluctant] I know that she feels that I am too hard on her. I went through all last year where she stayed home unemployed . . . (*Alluding to sexist position that a woman's role is to defer and please her man*)

TH: [Interrupts] Pardon me, Peter. You're venturing off into another direction. I want to stay with this because I feel this is a key area to look at. I just wanted you to address your view of why Megan felt misunderstood and invalidated. I'm puzzled why this is difficult for you to focus on. *(Testing the timing to identify Peter's template around invalidation/making excuses)*

P: [Contemplative pause] I guess I don't like excuses. I think Megan had it too easy growing up and didn't have to push herself. She knew that her parents would bail her out. She can't be weak and give up on her responsibilities, on herself. *(Not colluding with White privilege)*

M: [Shaking her head] I'm not. You forgot what I had to go through with my family, with my mom the way she was.

TH: Would you mind retelling that part of your story? *(Invoking an oppression narrative that I'm hoping will intersect with Peter's own story)*

M: I felt I was given too much responsibility for my younger sisters at home. I had to put my own needs aside and be what everyone else wanted me to be. I tried so hard to fit in at school but I was too ashamed to bring friends home to see what my mother was really like. Sure, we had a nice home and things, but not emotionally—I felt really alone. I never felt like a whole person. I had to play the role of the responsible, low-maintenance daughter [crying but articulate]. One of the reasons I was attracted to Peter and drawn to him was the fact that we shared an understanding about not being fully able to be accepted for who we were. I know Pete had to grow up tough. I also know that he continues to feel that he has to prove himself all the time, but that's not my fault. *(I am not the oppressor.)* [Megan creates an opening for Peter's racial narrative to come into the room]

TH: I can see how much pain you still have from growing up in an alcoholic family. I do hear how much you had to sacrifice in order to keep your family together and functioning. I frequently refer to individuals in your role as the "heart and soul" of the family, or as the hero child. I want to highlight something you said, Megan, about feeling as though you and Peter had a common bond that drew you together and it had to do with common experiences with not being able to be whole, authentic individuals at home. If I may, perhaps we can say that both of you had to accommodate others all of your lives. [Pausing to check in with both clients] Are you with me on this? [Both nod]

P: Yeah, I want to say something. I just realized how much I hated it when my father would relentlessly tell me how stupid I was or how weak I was. It really hurt me when I was small, but I learned to use it to improve myself, but it still hurt and drives me to never feel good enough. I'm never satisfied with anything and I know that's bad *(Naming the model minority template)*. I also believe my dad was so hard on me to make me strong enough to compete in a White world, to be better than them. I really don't like bringing this into the equation because I know that my dad never wanted me to make excuses, because he never did. I know that he was mistreated by Whites and looked down on because he didn't speak English well. I felt ashamed about that too *(Internalized racism/never playing the race card)*. Customers used to take advantage of him and threaten him and I used to fume in anger watching him just take it [very upset and angry]. *(Naming the "it's a White man's world" context and genesis of his anger)*

TH: I can tell how angry it still makes you [Deciding to use self-disclosure]. I can actually connect with my own experience of watching my own father. I imagine that you can, unfortunately, now add your own experiences of racism and discrimination along with those of your father's. *(Compassionate witness model)*

P: Yeah. [Appearing to be more open—Megan is very attentively listening] The last thing I want to do is to make Megan feel bad about herself, because I really do understand her pain. I'm not sure if she "can" understand mine. I do believe she has and had more choices in her life. *(Naming the Privilege/Fairness template)*

TH: [Interrupting and asking Peter to address Megan directly, but naming White privilege explicitly] I am going to explicitly name what I think you're referring to but did not say. I think you're talking about Megan having White privilege? Is that correct to say? [Both nod.] Can you speak directly to Megan about this, rather than to me? *(Invoking the White privilege narrative directly)*

P: Sure. Back to what you said that it's not your fault that I have to push myself so hard to prove that I'm just as good, if not better, than some White guys—I know it isn't. But I don't think you really understand how hard it really is. It's always there. You don't live it.

It feels lonely to me, because I don't talk about it [Looks sad and ashamed]. I don't make excuses or play that card. *(Never good enough/betwixt and between)*

TH: [Megan is moving more closely toward Peter] Peter, what are you feeling right now?

P: [Eyes welling up] I'm feeling alone. Embarrassed, because I've never really said this to anyone. I could hear my dad's voice telling me I'm being weak, like a girl.

TH: Megan, could you tell Peter what you hear Peter saying and how you feel about it?

M: I hear and see Pete's sadness and his feeling alone in his experiences. Pete, you make me feel that way when you criticize me *(Initiating a compassionate witness experience)*. It makes me feel exactly what you feel. *(Identifying that Peter has become the oppressor)*

TH: Do you think Pete is trying to help you?

M: Sure doesn't feel that way when we're in the middle of it.

TH: I'm going to take a risk to say that, I believe two truths exist here. One is that this is a way Pete feels he can help you that was modeled to him by his father. Two, it is also misguided resentment and anger toward you for what Pete believes is an unfair advantage you and White people have had over people like him all his life *(Explicitly naming White privilege in the context of their relationship)*. This is a challenge passed on to you because you are in a relationship as a Chinese person and a White person. It is the racial context defined by historical and personal legacies outside of this room. Megan, are you willing to hear more about Pete's struggles and pain from racism in his life?

M: I'd like to understand how this affects him and us.

TH: Pete, was it helpful for you to put some of these feelings outside of yourself—to give them voice?

P: I can get used to it. It's not easy but I'm kinda surprised that it feels like a relief.

TH: I honor your survival and the energy it continues to take to live in a White world. You have initiated telling your story with Megan and me as witnesses, and we honor the trust you have in us to proceed as you feel comfortable [Both smile and nod]. What you initiated today is that you don't have to hold the pain and helplessness of racial injury alone. You might have quite possibly touched on some understanding of why your father treated you the way he did.

In our subsequent sessions, there seemed to be a marked shift in Peter's tone toward Megan. Although he still maintained a critical bent, it had less of an oppressive and angry edge. I believe that his gradual release of his shame and internalized inadequacy via compassionate witnessing provided more opportunities for Peter to be fully present with himself, and consequently with Megan.

CASE EXAMPLE

Both sexes are struggling for maturity in America where the rights of women are changing dramatically. White males, whose dominance has been based on female subjugation, must relinquish and share power with women. For Black males, who already feel subjugated by Whites, relinquishing dominance over women, especially Black women, is more problematic.

—Poussaint, 1993, p. 89

As I mentioned earlier, it is best to maintain a fluid stance in work with interracial couples. However, it would be useful to practice the framework I provided in my work with Megan and Peter on the following case. This is a case of an African American man, Charles, and a White woman, Nicole. They have two children, Charles Jr., age 12, and Maya, age 9. Nicole initiated couple therapy after Charles was diagnosed with severe hypertension. She was also concerned about how Charles handled the stress of his job as a manager of a car dealership. She reported that their daughter, Maya, asked her one day, "Why is Daddy always so angry?" Charles denies his anger, but says that he has a very difficult, demanding job. He emphasizes that he is a very good provider for his family—that his children are in private schools, and they own their home in an upper middle-class neighborhood. He makes a point of saying that he has an MBA and that three members of his family have MDs and PhDs. He feels he deserves more respect at home, from his kids and especially from

Nicole who he feels criticizes him in front of the children. Nicole expresses that she is unable to engage Charles in dialogue about his emotions and difficulties. He just tells her that she wouldn't understand and that it would create more problems with her.

> When some African American men feel threatened . . . Black men may turn inward, leading to withdrawal and a profound sense of resignation or a "Why bother?" attitude. (Kelly & Boyd-Franklin, 2005, p. 277)

Last, he discloses that he is very tired of people treating him like he is uneducated and from the streets (Kelly & Boyd-Franklin, 2005). He frequently encounters awkard responses when he is introduced as the manager. However, he refuses to elaborate. How would you begin to engage this couple, especially Charles? The exercise is to begin with employing the same process delineated in the previous section:

Phase 1: Identify the therapist's inner workings/dialogue.

Phase 2: What are the active racial templates/contexts relevant to this case (macro/micro)?

Phase 3: Facilitate compassionate witness model and racial narrative.

It is important to give strong consideration to the specific contexts you embody as the therapist. They can be spoken or unspoken—but they are frequently felt by clients who may have attenuated sensitivities from racial trauma. I must reiterate once again that this journey of work across difference is an ongoing developmental process. The work requires a personal commitment to your own racial/cultural narrative or lack of one, and your understanding of the impact of not having one in your practice with oppressed individuals. It is constant process of learning and unlearning.

Challenge to Educators and Supervisors

In our current professional milieu with HMOs and managed care, there is a high premium placed on specialization of practice. The expected advantages are efficiency in practice and promoting quantifiable measures of positive therapeutic outcome. However, I submit that the potential side effect and impact of this trend is that it inadvertently fuels an attitude of reductionism and may actually reinforce stereotypes. Specialized therapists may be encouraged to use "cookie cutter" paradigms and interventions in their practice. I wish to make some suggestions to supervisors and educators in their training of clinicians that can assist in balancing some of these side effects:

1. *Mindfulness and awareness:* Make it a priority to integrate an attunement to cultural/racial contexts in all lectures and case presentation/discussions.

2. *Employ an integrative model:* Most cultural competency/literacy courses are taught in a segregated/single-course fashion, in essence marginalizing diversity issues into one lone course requirement. All courses should incorporate issues of culture, difference, and privilege in a dynamic/organic way.

3. *Assignments to develop a cultural/contextual lens:* Tailor assignments that challenge privileged/White supremacist paradigms and unconscious oppression, and name privilege contexts.

4. *Maintenance doses of powerlessness and being the other:* Challenge students with experiential and exposure opportunities to being marginalized.

5. *Model professional humility:* Practice a beginner's mind and tolerance of "not knowing."

6. *Create safe space for compassionate witness and alliance building.*

Conclusion

I am a perpetual beginner as a therapist—therein lies the core of why this profession is so deeply rewarding to me. I experience regular doses of gratitude to my clients for honoring me with their patience as they share their stories of resilience and survival. I frequently hear my clients express, "You are the first one I have spoken to about . . ." Just take a moment to sit with and be aware of the level of trust invested in you as the client sits on the precipice of fear and vulnerability at that moment of trust. This investment of trust is an awesome responsibility, but it can also be a powerful window of opportunity to connect deeply with your client in a profound healing relationship. For some clients, this attempt can either be curative or re-wounding.

I challenge each of you to explore and embrace what it would mean for you to seek maintenance doses of being the other, to experience the powerlessness of that experience. This is the only way that you can resonate and mirror your couples and clients, enabling you to be truly present and authentic. Be present with your own narrative as you are present with your clients. Be a part of your own compassionate witness community, because we can experience secondary trauma; it is one of the ways we can expand our own capacity for empathy and kindness. Our profession has a shadow side that can cultivate shame and guilt. We must be vigilantly committed to not allowing that to predominate in our work. Last, I want to share an acronym with you that I came up with that has helped me in my work with marginalized individuals, TACT:

Truthful sharing of story and narrative

Authentic full presence in relationship

Connection via creating an accepting space, safety, and community

Trust is the fruit of all the above plus cultivating relationships on a reparative paradigm of fairness, justice, and equity.

Additional Resources

Films

Elliot, J. (Producer). (1970). *Eye of the Storm*. Available from www.newsreel.org/nav/title.asp?tc=CN0160.
Lee Mun Wah (Producer). (1994). *The Color of Fear*. Stir Fry Productions.
Lee Mun Wah (Producer). (2003). *Last Chance for Eden*. Stir Fry Productions.
Strigel, C., & Verhaag, B. (Producers), & Verhaag, B. (Director). (1995). *Blue Eyed* (with Jane Elliott). Available from www.newsreel.org/nav/title.asp?tc=cn0015.

Readings

Fadiman, A. (1997). *The spirit catches you and you fall down*. New York: Noonday Press.
Loewen, J. W. (1995). *Lies my teacher told me*. New York: Simon & Schuster.
McGoldrick, M. (1998). *Re-visioning family therapy*. New York: Guilford Press.
Rastogi, M., & Wieling, E. (2005). *Voices of Color*. Thousand Oaks, CA: Sage.
Tatum, B. D. (1997). *Why are all the Black kids sitting together in the cafeteria?* New York: Basic Books.
Thompson, C., Schaefer, E., & Brod, H. (2003). *White men challenging racism*. London: Duke University Press.
Wise, T. (2005). *White like me*. New York: Soft Skull Press.

Web Sites

Alternet: www.alternet.org
Tim Wise (anti-racist writer and educator): www.timwise.org

References

Boyd-Franklin, N., & Franklin, A. (1998). African American couples in therapy. In M. McGoldrick (Ed.), *Re-visioning family therapy* (pp. 268–281). New York: Guilford Press.

Crohn, J. (1998). Intercultural couples. In M. McGoldrick (Ed.), *Re-visioning family therapy* (pp. 295–308). New York: Guilford Press.

Dolan-Del Vecchio, K. (1998). Dismantling White male privilege within family therapy. In M. McGoldrick (Ed.), *Re-visioning family therapy* (pp. 159–175). New York: Guilford Press.

Ellison, R. (1972). *Invisible man.* New York: Vintage. (Original work published 1952)

Fadiman, A. (1997). *The spirit catches you and you fall down.* New York: Noonday Press.

Feagin, J. R., & Sikes, M. P. (1994). *Living with racism: The Black middle-class experience.* Boston: Beacon Press.

Hardy, K. V. (1993). War of the worlds. *Networker,* July/August, 50–54.

Hardy, K. V., & Laszloffy, T. A. (1992). Training racially sensitive family therapists: Context, content, contact. *Families in Society, 73,* 364–370.

Kelly, S., & Boyd-Franklin, N. (2005). African American women in client, therapist, and supervisory relationships. In M. Rastogi & E. Wieling (Eds.), *Voices of color* (pp. 67–89). Thousand Oaks, CA: Sage.

Kozol, J. (1991). *Savage inequalities.* New York: HarperCollins.

Lee, L. J. (2005). Taking off the mask. In M. Rastogi & E. Wieling (Eds.), *Voices of color* (pp. 91–115). Thousand Oaks, CA: Sage.

Loewen, J. W. (1995). *Lies my teacher told me.* New York: Simon & Schuster.

Meier, K. J. (1990). *Race, class, & education: The politics of second-generation discrimination.* Wisconsin: University of Wisconsin Press.

Poussiant, A. (1993). African American couples. *Ebony Magazine,* 88–89.

Shipler, D. K. (1997). *A country of strangers: Blacks and Whites in America.* New York: Alfred A. Knopf.

Tatum, B. D. (1997). *Why are all the Black kids sitting together in the cafeteria?* New York: Basic Books.

Thomas, V., Karis, T., & Wetchler, J. (Eds.). (2003). *Clinical issues with interracial couples: Theory and research.* New York: Haworth Press.

Thompson, C., Schaefer, E., & Brod, H. (2003). *White men challenging racism.* London: Duke University Press.

Wise, T. (2005). *White like me.* New York: Soft Skull Press.

Section B

Religious Minority Couples

Six

Couple Therapy With Muslims

Challenges and Opportunities

Manijeh Daneshpour

According to the U.S. State Department, Islam is one of the country's fastest-growing religions, and by 2010 Muslims will surpass the Jewish population as the country's second-largest religious group (Al-Krenawi & Graham, 2005). The latest statistics claim that the Muslim population in the United States numbers about eight million, of which 12.4% are Arab, 42% are African American, 24.4% are Asian, and 21% are "other" (Dadabhoy, 2004; Holmes-Eber, 1997), with immigrants making up two-thirds to three-quarters (Al-Krenawi & Graham, 2005; Dadabhoy, 2004). Furthermore, immigration to the United States from the Middle East has been heavy in recent years. This increase is expected to continue at such high levels that it is likely to have significant political and social implications. The number of Middle Eastern immigrants in the United States has grown from fewer than 200,000 in 1970 to almost 1.5 million in 2000. The portion identifying as Muslim has jumped from 15% in 1970 to 73% in 2000 (Census Data, 2000).

There has been a very small but growing literature (Daneshpour, 1998; Hedayat-Diba, 2000) that considers therapy with Muslim families. Of this growing literature, many consider clinical work with Arab (Abudabbeh & Aseel, 1999; Al-Krenawi & Graham, 1997, 2000, 2005; Chaleby, 1992) and Arab Muslim families (Eleftheriadou, 1997), but there is no comprehensive literature regarding couple therapy with Muslim immigrant families. This chapter is an attempt to identify, discuss, and clarify some important issues for mental health professionals working with Muslim immigrant couples using hermeneutic approaches and postmodernist perspectives. The main goal is to provide guidance and insights that can assist clinicians in working with this immigrant group apart from their ethnic backgrounds. Several case examples will highlight strategies for approaching and helping Muslim couples. It is important to note that this chapter focuses on just one portion of Western Islam, namely those Muslims who live in the United States and who are either immigrants or their descendants (hereafter referred to as "Muslim immigrants"). It does not deal with the other major component, the converts, nor does it deal with other Western countries. Also, even though there are numerous Shi'i, Sunni, Sufi, and African American institutions and organizations operating in America, as a minority the Muslim "sameness" is greater than their "differences," providing them with a sense of community, which in turn is an essential source of solace and support (Hedayat-Diba, 2000). It is also important to note that I have an insider perspective on Islamic ideology and culture as a native of Iran and a member of the Shi'i sect of Islam. I am also a licensed marriage and family therapist, and have been working with immigrant Muslim couples from a range of different sects and countries for many years. A major component of my teaching, presentations, and research projects also revolves around this population.

Postmodern Perspectives

Postmodernism embraces the contradictions and complexities of postmodern life, envisions nondichotomous possibilities, challenges cultural constructions of sex and gender, and ultimately reclaims and redefines couples' relationships by assuming that grand utopias are impossible (De Reus, Few, & Blume, 2004). It accepts that reality is fragmented and that personal identity is an unstable quantity transmitted by a variety of cultural factors (Flax, 1990). Postmodernism rejects grand narratives and favors "mini-narratives"—stories that explain small interactions, rather than large-scale universal or global concepts. In this view, culture and cultural differences are not transhistorical entities (Sandoval, 2000), nor are they homogenous (Grewal & Kaplan, 2002). Each culture is crisscrossed by internal class, religious, ethnic, and regional divisions. Therefore, even though Muslim "sameness" is greater than its "differences," each Muslim country is impacted by sociopolitical changes in many different ways, and each Muslim couple's relationship is impacted by systemic issues such as gender, power, extended family support, education, class, and age in many different ways as well.

Thus, the guidelines proposed in this chapter are an attempt to create some sense of "sameness" for Muslim couples so therapists can gain understanding regarding the Muslim populations living in America. In any specific situation, however, the postmodernist perspective should be used to understand Muslim couples' own "mini-narratives" to help them repair their relationships.

Hermeneutics

Hermeneutics is concerned with the process of interpretation (Gadamer, 1997; Qureshi, 2005; Risser, 1997). Philosophical hermeneutics shows promise as a theoretically grounded approach to multiculturalism in psychology (Qureshi, 2005). The focus on relationship and interpretation makes hermeneutics particularly suitable for working with Muslim couples. The hermeneutically conscious therapist recognizes that her sociohistorical situatedness and relationality are central to being human, and that the therapist–client relationship is dialogical and reciprocally effecting. From the perspective of philosophical hermeneutics, race and culture, among other identity domains, are implicated in psychotherapy, and therefore all psychotherapy is multicultural (Sue, Ivey, & Pederson, 1996). As such, any therapeutic endeavor must engage with the client's sociohistorical situatedness, experience, perspectives, and so forth, simply because they are elemental in forming the "who" of the client and psychotherapist. For these reasons, a hermeneutically sensitive therapist will dialogically apply her cultural knowledge, while recognizing that this knowledge is itself subject to her own prejudices as well as those of the source of the knowledge. It is up to the hermeneutically sensitive psychotherapist to be open to her clients so she can learn the client's particular style, and on that basis formulate an appropriate response predicated on her usual therapeutic approach without interpreting the client's experience from her cultural vantage point. This next section will discuss some common clinical issues for Muslim couples, with several case examples highlighting the use of postmodern and hermeneutic approaches.

Common Clinical Issues

Depression and Somatization

Non-European populations including Middle Eastern people display many more somatic and quasi-somatic symptoms, which include disturbances of sleep, appetite, energy, body sensation, and motor functioning as opposed to depressive symptoms including feelings of guilt, self-deprecation, suicidal ideas, and despair (Marsella, Sartorious, Jablensky, & Fenton, 1985). Physical symptoms are accepted as a way of dealing with emotional pain. Therefore, extreme fatigue and other psychomotor symptoms will be interpreted physically, and will not be interpreted as depressive symptoms. Thus, when approached for treatment, Muslim clients consider relational issues and their impact on depressive symptoms to be unimportant. Muslim clients, like many other Easterners, usually will seek a cure—usually of a medical nature—and will be reluctant to discuss their personal or interpersonal concerns or difficulties.

CASE EXAMPLE

Mrs. J was referred to me by her internist, who was concerned about her emotional state and was contemplating prescribing an antidepressant for her. Her complaints included lack of appetite, sleeplessness, and crying spells; however, she viewed her symptoms as signs of physical fatigue due to working hard at home and at her job. She was much more comfortable discussing her physical symptoms than any of her personal or relationship issues. Using the hermeneutics approach, her interpretation was validated while she was reminded of the importance of the mind–body connection. She was asked to describe her relationship with her husband and her children, followed by the possible contributing factors to her sleeplessness, lack of appetite, and lack of concentration. Mrs. J was able to describe her hopelessness with regards to many bad memories of the past. She claimed that her husband had married her against his parents' wishes, and they had to live with them for several years after they were married. His parents were very critical of her, and she believed that her husband did not care about her suffering enough to challenge them and protect her. She had built-up resentments against him from the past, which were preventing her from having a meaningful and positive relationship with him now. However, Mrs. J was not able to see a connection between her interpersonal difficulties and her depressive symptoms. After several sessions, she was able to understand that her husband was an active character in her life story and perhaps could help her construe some of his own family dynamics—or at least help her at home with her daily chores to alleviate some of her daily stresses. During a couple therapy session, to her surprise, her husband discussed his frustrations about those years and was able to understand the power dynamics between his mother and his wife. He was even able to own his part of not standing up against his parents and pretending that things were fine.

Mrs. J, in turn, was able to have a better understanding of her husband's relationship with his parents as he talked about being the second born and not getting enough attention from his mother as a child and his need to please her. He promised to write a letter to his parents and resolve some of his own childhood issues as well as the problem with their treatment of his wife. She eventually decided to let go of some of the past resentment issues to concentrate on the present and the future. After several sessions with her husband and deeper conversations about their life together, she reported that her depressive symptoms were slightly better but she admitted that there was a long history of nontreated and unrecognized depression in her family of origin, and said her mother also suffered from many similar symptoms. Both Mrs. J and her mother were referred to a psychiatrist. Mrs. J was also able to better understand the connection between her emotional state and her physical symptoms. From the postmodern and hermeneutics perspectives, Mr. J and Mrs. J felt that their "mini-narratives" were heard and interpreted in a way that could help their relationship dynamics, while Mrs. J received appropriate help for her depressive symptoms.

Anxiety Symptoms

There are many immigrant Muslims dealing with anxiety symptoms due to war, family misplacements, witnessing traumatic events, not having a supportive system of care, and most importantly being misunderstood by their host culture. It is important for clinicians to view these symptoms as part of the coping mechanism for clients, and understand that acute anxiety was once needed for survival but chronic anxiety needs to be processed with lots of support and care. Like depression, anxiety symptoms will also be dealt with on a physical level rather than a psychological one, and they need to be treated with great care and understanding.

CASE EXAMPLE

Mr. and Mrs. H were referred to me by Mrs. H's gynecologist. She was six months pregnant and was suffering from anxiety attacks. She described her symptoms as being stomachaches not related to ulcers or stomach flu and painful heartaches. She claimed that her thoughts were racing all the time, then she would start breathing faster and would have difficulty breathing. She was not in favor of psychotherapy but had lots of respect for her medical doctor; since I was also a doctor and Muslim, she agreed to see me. A few months before the appointment, her husband was badly beaten while she helplessly witnessed the attack. The attack was racially and religiously motivated, and the perpetrator confessed in court that he was upset about her head cover, or *hijab*. Her husband ended up with severe head injury and the person responsible was sentenced to only 25 hours of community service.

Mrs. H was outraged and was feeling extremely guilty because she believed that her *hijab* was the biggest contributing factor to the incident, and also that the judge did not fairly punish the attacker because she and her husband were from the Middle East. During the initial interview, she indicated that they did not need therapy but they needed justice, and wanted me to find the attacker's address so she could find him and somehow take revenge. She was insisting that the only way she could have the symptoms relieved was by confronting him. It became very clear later on that her anxiety symptoms were related to the fear that the attacker would find and hurt them again. Her perceptions of the event were validated and supported.

Mr. H, on the other hand, felt embarrassed and humiliated by the event. He was blaming himself for her anxiety symptoms because he was not strong enough to protect his family on the night of the incident. Both were stuck in a vicious cycle of not even being able to validate the other's perspectives, and were completely disconnected from each other. Both were finally convinced that, even though their situation was very unfair and the court system did not treat them well, they needed to at least talk to each other about their feelings and try to continue on with life.

Mrs. H saw a psychiatrist and a psychotropic medication was prescribed to help relieve her acute and emotionally related symptoms. Eventually, with the support of the Muslim community and by using the Koran as a source of support that teaches forgiveness, both were able to reconnect and feel better. Using postmodernist and hermeneutics approaches also helped a great deal in changing their perceptions of the situation. She was able to become closer to her husband and relieve her guilt and emotional pain. Mr. H also reevaluated his perspective and was able to reinterpret the situation to see himself as a victim of a senseless crime instead of a helpless husband who could not prevent the incident and protect his wife. Both were able to notice the attacker's contribution to their own marital disengagement and decided to unite against him and redefine their relationship.

Family Problems

Family is the most important source of support and connection for Muslim couples. Thus, it is very confusing and challenging when family members are having difficulty getting along or the couple's boundaries, their roles and rules, have been disrespected either by adult family members or by the younger generation. Also, it is very important to recognize that many immigrant Muslim couples deal with the same issues that other couples have to deal with. From the power dynamics in the couple's relationship to parent–child conflict to financial difficulties, they may have similar patterns and dynamics. The key differences are how couples discuss and portray their difficulties and the way family therapists are reacting to it that make it a challenge from a cross-cultural perspective.

CASE EXAMPLE

Mr. and Mrs. A were referred to me from another Euro-American therapist who conducted three sessions with them and felt that their situation needed more cultural understanding than she could offer. Both spouses were reluctant to see me. Mrs. A was worried that other Muslim families who were working with me might come to my office before or after their appointment and know that they were seeking help. They were also reluctant because they felt that their previous therapist was doing a good job and they were happy with their progress. Their presenting problem was related to finances, which had a strong impact on their own relationship, and those with their family of origin and their children. Mr. A was a highly educated man with a prestigious and successful career. His wife had also been employed for many years and had serious issues with the way her husband was handling their finances. She did not feel that they needed to save so much, and wanted to spend her money as she pleased. He, on the other hand, was worried about their retirement years and insisted that she always give him her entire paycheck. They had been married for 30 years and had three grown children who appeared to be much closer and more loyal to their mother—a very typical Middle Eastern pattern observed when the husband is more powerful or is more involved with his own family of origin. She was presenting him with the threat of leaving him to stay with their oldest son.

Mr. A, in turn, was feeling betrayed by both her and his children and did not understand the "new paradigm shift" in his wife's thinking. He was claiming that she used to be far more docile and understanding, and felt that her close friends might have influenced her and may be responsible for her new way of thinking. The wife, however, believed that developmentally they were both at a different stage in their lives, and she was demanding the same level of respect in decision making from him as he was demanding from her. Apparently, Mr. A came to the United States as a young man and, after finishing his education, went back to his country of origin, met his wife through his own family, and after a very brief stay brought her to the United States. He knew the language well and was very familiar with the host culture. She, on the other hand, had to work hard for years to learn the language and adjust to living in the United States.

Couple therapy revolved around their somehow renewed sense of couplehood from a more equal base and his strong ambivalence related to holding on to his traditional beliefs about his wife's unconditional respect and obedience on one hand, and believing in equality in work outside home on the other. Also, we discussed her ambivalence regarding him being the protector and provider without expecting her financial contribution according to traditional and cultural family systems while wanting the freedom to make decisions regarding her own finances. Once we were able to use their "mini-narratives" from their individual perspectives to reinterpret and reevaluate life-cycle transitional issues related to her paradigm shift, resolve the ambivalence related to loyalty to the culture of origin, and also to the host culture, and discuss the need for letting go of the power difference in their relationship, they were able to move beyond their conflict and negotiate new rules and boundaries.

Intergenerational Issues

Due to generational differences and living in a culture that does not value hierarchical family relationships, the younger generation challenges the older generation even in terms of Islamic values. Many Muslim immigrant couples often use what is purely cultural as the inherent definition of Islamic values. They do this to control their children and to refrain from losing them to the host culture. Teenagers, however, do not hesitate to call them out on this misconception. Other conflictual issues might be related to choice of school, dating, Islamic dress codes, and cultural assimilation. Each of these topics is important and needs to be addressed cautiously using postmodernist and hermeneutics perspectives accompanied by understanding and nonjudgmental perceptions and attitudes.

CASE EXAMPLE

Mr. and Mrs. M came to see me after a presentation in the mosque discussing the topic of raising confident children in a culturally dissimilar society. They had a high level of conflict in their marital relationship that was related to raising their children in Western society. Mr. M felt that he was losing his connection with his two sons and only daughter. His sons, aged 17 and 14, along with his daughter of 15, were frustrated with him and his use of their country of origin's culture as a way of teaching them right from wrong. He wanted them to continue going to an Islamic school and had a tendency to allow his sons to "explore life" more than his daughter. There was also a double standard related to dress code for his daughter that was considerably more conservative than the one applied to his sons. Mrs. M was not in agreement with her husband, and after years of being silent she was openly challenging him in front of their children. She perceived him as a very strict and rigid person and believed that she was also suffering from his authoritarian conduct. It was apparent that the more his family challenged his way of thinking, the more rigid he became.

We discussed the children's developmental stage regardless of their gender, separating cultural issues from generic Islamic values and accepting the existence of a generational gap between him and his children. We also discussed Mrs. M's frustration with him that was being channeled through their children, and the inherent need to separate these issues. A postmodern perspective helped all of us to listen to him and understand his frame of reference. Mr. M believed that it was his Islamic duty to keep everyone on the right path, and that his treatment of his wife and his daughter as second-class citizens was in line with the Islamic teaching he had received in his home country. Family-of-origin examination proved that his father was also very strict and had the same authoritarian dictatorial attitude, and that as a young boy he did not appreciate his father's interactions with him, his siblings, or even his mother. After validating the fact that his interactions with his family members were based on what he had learned from his father, he was challenged to look into some research-based Islamic literature about the prophet Mohammed's treatment of women and also his teachings about the treatment of children. It was also important to help this family understand the importance of a meaningful balance between valuing superior aspects of their culture of origin and also valuing the good aspects of the host culture.

In addition, the inappropriate and unfair use of double standards and how they have contributed to a host of problems in families were discussed. The couple was able to discus ways to challenge these double standards in their own home, in order to enjoy a better family connection. Through his own research, Mr. M became convinced that Prophet Mohammed wanted his followers to love one another and become a source of comfort for each other, and that he indeed respected women. Mrs. M was also able to understand that her husband's behavior was based on what he had learned from his own father, who depicted strong men as detached and authoritarian. Once they all felt that their perspectives were validated, the family members were able to negotiate a new set of rules and expectations more suited to their own family dynamics.

Gender and Power Dynamic Issues

Over the past few years, the U.S. media have had a tendency to deeply influence the public's view about gender equality. The issue of gender equality all around the globe is systemic, complex, and contextual, and cannot be perceived as linear with cause and effect relationships. Middle

Easterners and Asian woman, like many other Easterners, may not be comfortable with or seek the kinds of gender equity with which most Euro-American therapists are familiar (Moghaddam, 2000). Gender equity within this community may be more equated with being respected in the role that they have chosen—a role that may or may not include homemaker, mother, or employee. Many Middle Eastern women believe that Euro-American women working both inside and outside the home are greatly oppressed, and Euro-American men are not responsible or accountable enough to their families.

So, while being alert and attentive to all of these issues, therapists need to understand each couple's "mini-narratives." This includes paying more attention to the specific presenting problem and doing some one-on-one therapy with each partner in the couple to increase one's understanding of the individuals. In addition, this provides an opportunity for women partners to address concerns that may be difficult to raise within the couple session. This approach might be helpful for many cases, regardless of client's cultural background. In particular, Muslim women—like many other new immigrant families—may be in a vulnerable position if there is any form of violence in their homes, as they may have few support resources. Muslim wives may be dependent on their husbands financially and/or on their husband's sponsors to maintain their position in the United States as immigrants or international visitors.

CASE EXAMPLE

Mrs. B was referred to me by her friend. She did not want her husband to be aware of her discussing their relationship difficulties with anyone, including a therapist. Mr. B was a famous physician with a high status, both in his workplace and also in the Muslim community. Mrs. B was an educated young woman from an upper-class family. She described her marriage as one that was very loving and committed in the beginning but that changed completely following the death of her father-in-law and the addition of her mother-in-law to their home. This transition demanded much of her husband's devotion and unconditional attention be shifted to his mother. Mrs. B was angry, and reluctant to be flexible with the new dynamics in her home; she had several serious fights with her husband and mother-in-law. In retaliation, Mr. B decided to leave their bedroom and, over time, stopped talking to her completely. The couple had two small children, and, due to both her immigration status (still nonresident) and their very comfortable lifestyle, Mrs. B did not want to leave the relationship while not wanting to live with the existing problems either. She was afraid to include her husband or mother-in-law in any of our conversations for fear of their retaliation, and just wanted to figure out what she could do to improve her marriage. It was apparent that there were very powerful gender and generational dynamics present in her marriage. As a woman, she had significantly less power than her husband, but viewed her mother-in-law as much more powerful than her husband. So, even though the gender hierarchy was an important issue, the generational hierarchy was more serious.

Therapy concentrated on teaching her new ways of communicating with both her husband and her mother-in-law. She was able to stop the pursuing–distancing cycle with her husband because the more she was pursuing him the more he was distancing himself. In addition, she was able to enlist her mother-in-law as an ally. After much coaching she was able to convince her mother-in-law that, as a younger woman, she required the support of her elder female generation who has had more experience with men. Over time, she was able to utilize her mother-in-law as a support system, and reconnect with her husband by using the family's gender and generational dynamics in place of fighting against the situation.

Intergenerational and Extended Family Issues

Both the Koran and the Islamic teachings advocate strongly for the recognition of elderly wisdom and also the importance of elderly care. Older people are highly valued, regardless of gender, and their permission is often needed before the younger generation can make any independent decisions. Extended family also has high significance for Eastern and Middle Eastern families. Their opinion is important, and family members in therapy might mention them frequently even though they are not even living in the United States.

CASE EXAMPLE

Mr. and Mrs. S had been married for 17 years. Mr. S was from one of the Middle Eastern countries and Mrs. S was American. Mr. S's family immigrated to the United States five years ago. Mr. S's mother had been dealing with health issues for many years and, even though she was living with her youngest son and her daughter-in-law, Mr. S needed to be involved with her care almost on a daily basis. This created a great amount of tension in his marriage. When this couple began therapy, Mr. S's mother needed more care than was available at home due to recent surgeries she had undergone. However, placing his mother in a senior citizens' home was a very difficult decision for Mr. S. The couple sought therapy due to a high level of conflict in their relationship related to Mr. S's strong feelings of shame and guilt for not doing his best to care for his mother. He was getting long letters and e-mails from his uncle and other extended family members from overseas, reprimanding him and his siblings for not providing the best care. He was feeling overwhelmed and pressured because he felt that their criticisms were valid even though he did not know what else to do. Mrs. S, on the other hand, was pressuring Mr. S to leave his mother at a nursing home and stop being what she perceived as "too overinvolved with her." This conflict illustrates the core of their individualistic versus collectivistic value differences with regard to family relationships and care giving. While he viewed caring for his mother at his home as his responsibility, she felt that this was a sign of "overinvolvement" on his part.

After several couple therapy sessions spent on validating his pain and guilt and her confusion and helplessness, we began looking for ways to change the dynamics of the situation to achieve better results. First, given the extended family's involvement, it seemed essential to invite Mr. S's siblings to one family therapy session. They each talked about their overwhelming responsibilities toward their mother. They also talked about being afraid that if they did not take good care of their mother at home, God would not reward them or help them in their old age. The session revolved around the importance of elderly care and providing it in the best possible way. At the same time, they were challenged on their interpretation of providing the "best care" when their homes were not equipped to provide the necessary care. Second, Mr. S was encouraged to write a letter to his uncle explaining the medical condition while thanking him for his support and care. He also explained different ways that they try to be more supportive to their mother, and asked him for some feedback. In this way, he was respecting his elders and also getting more support from them instead of criticism. Finally, in couple therapy sessions, he was also able to talk to his wife explaining the cultural aspect of his "overinvolvement." It was apparent that he was caught between the demands of two cultures. One was pressuring him to let go and the other wanted him to do considerably more than he was capable of.

Eventually, Mr. S. was able to place his mother in a culturally sensitive nursing home. He also received help from the Muslim community to visit her more often, and was finally able to let go of his extensive guilt after being convinced that he was providing the "best care." Mr. and Mrs. S were able to reconnect with each other, while Mr. S. succeeded in keeping his ties with his extended family who lived overseas.

Clinical Implications

Most mental health professionals have little familiarity with Muslim couples. Their "otherness" status prevents many therapists noticing their "sameness." Many of the relationship issues for Muslim couples are similar to those facing other religious groups in this country, which are more widely understood, known, and accepted. Muslim couples, like all other couples, struggle with familiar issues around division of labor, parenting, finances, juggling roles and responsibilities, communication related to dynamics of the relationship, and decision-making issues. Furthermore, Muslim couples esteem and respect their parents and extended family members, just like many other ethnic national and international groups. Cultural competency for therapists should stress knowledge and awareness about similarities rather than differences.

At the same time, therapists working with Muslim couples must first be informed about the specific culture from which the family has emerged and how the culture has had an impact on the practice and application of the Muslim couple's belief system. Therapists can use postmodernist and hermeneutics perspectives to embrace a nonjudgmental, curious stance, and to ask the Muslim couples to provide them with information about their beliefs and attitudes. Furthermore, they should keep in mind that Muslim couples—like any other group—might use culture/religion as a mask so they do not have to deal with many issues. Finally, it is essential to attend to cross-cultural and acculturation issues for Muslim couples who have newly and recently arrived in the United States. In addition to the challenges that most international or immigrant families face with cultural and ethnic adaptations, Muslim couples must cope with the dominance of Judeo-Christian values and beliefs in the United States. This is often a surprising and difficult adaptation for those from countries where the institutionalized religion is Islam and the day-to-day rhythms (prayer times, holidays, foods) are in accordance with Muslim beliefs and traditions.

Mental health professionals should be mindful of the importance of the family and the extended family in the lives of Muslim couples, and strive to respect and be attentive to family hierarchies that are in place. They should consider inviting members of the extended family into sessions after checking with and ascertaining from the presenting couple whether this might be helpful. They also should approach the joining process as central to the therapeutic process and adjust to the pace with which their clients are comfortable.

From the hermeneutics and postmodernist approach, an essential part of the therapist's self-education when working with the Islamic religion is to understand commonly held stereotypes and prejudices regarding the American culture and to be able to process that well. Equally important is the therapist's willingness to reflect about his or her own stereotypic views of Islam and decide how this will impact the process of joining and establishing rapport as well as helping couples with their challenging issues.

Conclusion

As our society moves away from the melting-pot ideal and toward that of cultural and religious pluralism and a belief in a postmodern way of thinking, so must psychotherapy and couple therapy move from a secular assimilationist perspective back to more conventional and conformist ideologies in order to meet the varied needs of multicultural communities. Therefore, couple therapy should use the hermeneutics perspectives to include the interpretations of religious, cultural, social, and personal experiences of these couples. As a result, couple therapy can become holistic, rather than fragmented into body, mind, and social environment.

Further, Muslim couples may share a universal religion but they come from a diverse range of ethnic and racial heritage. In addition to an understanding of Muslim religious beliefs, it may be necessary to become familiar with the cultural expectations of the broader family system (Berg & Jaya, 1993; Carolan, Bagherinia, Juhari, Himelright, & Mouton, 2000). At the same time, it is important not to lose sight of the individuality of the persons within the system (Berg & Miller, 1992; Carolan et al., 2000). Contemporary wisdom advises the family professional to balance ethnic understanding and sensitivity with awareness of the commonality of human characteristics. This may require extending the time for joining with a Muslim couple in order to become more familiar and sensitive to their uniqueness—as a preliminary step to moving toward universal experiences. The information presented in this chapter will hopefully assist researchers, supervisors, educators, and practitioners using postmodernist and hermeneutics philosophies for understanding contemporary Muslim couples' relationships, and challenge practitioners to rethink and reinterpret their own assumptions about Muslim couples' relationships. It will be extremely helpful for educators and supervisors to encourage students and supervisees to learn more about this population using postmodernist and hermeneutics philosophy.

Experiential Exercises, Questions, and Topics for Reflection

1. What are some stereotypes about Muslim immigrant families? What is their basis, and what is the reality?
2. What is similar about the experiences of Middle Eastern Muslim immigrants and other minorities?
3. How do different conditions such as occupation, language, religion, and life cycle affect Muslim immigrant couples' adjustment in the United States?
4. What is the effect of the U.S. politics in the Middle East on Muslim immigrants—the families, marriages, and the community?
5. Compare the role of religion in the Muslim immigrant family to that in Mormon and Lutheran families. How are they similar and different?

Additional Resources

Films

Miller, L. (Producer), & Wilson, D. (Director). (1992). *Islam in America.* Available from Christian Science Monitor, 1 Norway Street, Boston, MA, 02115.

Readings

Aswad, B. C., & Bilge, B. (1996). *Family and gender among American Muslims: Issues facing Middle Eastern immigrants and their descendants.* Philadelphia, PA: Temple University Press.
Haddad, Y. Y., & Lummis, A. (1987). *Islamic values in the United States.* New York: Oxford University Press.

References

Abudabbeh, N., & Aseel, H. A. (1999). Transcultural counseling and Arab Americans. In J. McFadden (Ed.), *Transcultural counseling* (2nd ed., pp. 283–296). Alexandria, VA: American Counseling Association.

Al-Krenawi, A., & Graham, J. R. (1997). Spirit possession and exorcism in the treatment of a Bedouin psychiatric patient. *Clinical Social Work Journal, 25,* 211–222.

Al-Krenawi, A., & Graham, J. R. (2000). Culturally sensitive social work practice with Arab clients in mental health settings. *Health and Social Work, 25,* 9–22.

Al-Krenawi, A., & Graham, J. R. (2005). Marital therapy for Arab Muslim Palestinian couples in the context of reacculturation. *The Family Journal: Counseling and Therapy for Couples and Families, 13,* 300–310.

Berg, I. K., & Jaya, A. (1993). Different and same: Family therapy with Asian-American families. *Journal of Marital and Family Therapy, 19,* 31–38.

Berg, I. K., & Miller, S.D. (1992). Working with Asian-American clients: One person at a time. *Families in Society: The Journal of Contemporary Human Services, 17,* 356–363.

Carolan, M. T., Bagherinia, G. T., Juhari, R., Himelright, J., & Mouton, M. (2000). Contemporary Muslim families: Research and practice. *Contemporary Family Therapy, 22,* 67–79.

Chaleby, K. (1992). Psychotherapy with Arab patients: Toward a culturally oriented technique. *Arab Journal of Psychiatry, 3*(1), 16–27.

Dadabhoy, M. (2004). Islam in America: Who are American Muslims? *Minnesota Muslim, 3*(1), 1–3.

Daneshpour, M. (1998). Muslim families and family therapy. *Journal of Marital and Family Therapy, 24,* 355–368.

De Reus, L., Few, A., & Blume, L. (2004). Theorizing identities and intersectionalities: Third-wave feminism, critical race theory, and families. In V.L. Bengtson, A. Acock, K. Allen, P. Dilworth-Anderson, & D. Klein (Eds.), *Sourcebook of family theory and research* (pp. 447–469). Thousand Oaks, CA: Sage.

Eleftheriadou, Z. (1997). The cross-cultural experience: Integration or isolation? In S. du Plock (Ed.), *Case studies in existential psychotherapy and counseling* (pp. 59–69). New York: John Wiley.

Flax, J. (1990). Postmodernism and gender relations in feminist theory. In L. Nicholson (Ed.), *Feminism/postmodernism* (pp. 39–62). London: Routledge.

Gadamer, H. G. (1997). *Truth and method.* J. Weinsheimer & D. G. Marshall, Trans. (2nd rev. ed). New York: Continuum.

Grewal, I., & Kaplan, C. (Eds.) (2002). *Scattered hegemonies: Postmodernity and transnational feminist practices.* Minneapolis, MN: University of Minnesota Press.

Hedayat-Diba, Z. (2000). Psychotherapy with Muslims. In P. S. Richards & A. E. Bergin (Eds.), *Handbook of psychotherapy and religious diversity* (pp. 289–314). Washington, DC: American Psychological Association.

Holmes-Eber, P. (1997). Migration, urbanization, and women's kin. *Journal of Comparative Family Studies, 28*(2), 54–73.

Marsella, A., Sartorious, N., Jablensky, A., & Fenton, F. (1985). Cross cultural studies of depressive disorders: An overview. In A. Kleinman & B. Good (Eds.), *Culture and depression: Studies in the anthropology and cross-cultural psychiatry of affect and disorder* (pp. 299–324). Berkeley, CA: University of California Press.

Moghaddam, V. (2000). Transnational feminist networks: Collective action in an era of globalization. *International Sociology, 15*, 57–84.

Qureshi, A. (2005). Dialogical relationship and cultural imagination: A hermeneutic approach to intercultural psychotherapy. *American Journal of Psychotherapy, 59*(2), 119–129.

Risser, J. (1997). *Hermeneutics and the voice of the other.* Albany, NY: State University of New York Press.

Sandoval, C. (2000). *Methodology of the oppressed.* Minneapolis, MN: University of Minnesota Press.

Sue, D. W., Ivey, A. E., & Pederson, P. B. (1996). *Theory of multicultural counseling and therapy.* Pacific Grove, CA: Brooks/Cole.

Seven

Two Jews, Three Opinions

Understanding and Working With Jewish Couples in Therapy

Israela Meyerstein

The saying "two Jews, three opinions" euphemistically describes Judaism as a complex, interwoven, pluralistic religion and culture. Not only are there differences in beliefs and practices among the various denominations of Judaism, but Jews are also culturally diverse, living in many countries and speaking multiple languages. Whether from Ashkenazic or Sephardic descent, the historical migration experience of being "wandering Jews" has deeply impacted the collective psyche of the Jewish people.

The above quote also describes a 5,000-year-old intellectual heritage that introduced a core set of beliefs, values, and ethical behavior codes to the world. Talmudic legal debate characteristically involved decisions rendered by a majority of rabbis along with dissenting minority views. Thus, the tradition of different voices is woven into Jewish scholarship. Having a transnationally portable set of life guidelines provided stability during migrations, as well as stimulating independent thinking and questioning of the status quo.

The United States has afforded Jews the opportunity to immigrate, acculturate, integrate, and assimilate. While Sephardic Jews (from Spain and North Africa) have been in the United States for several hundred years, the largest proportion of Jews comprises East European Jews who came in the late nineteenth and twentieth centuries, with more recent immigrants including Jews from the former Soviet Union (Herz & Rosen, 1996).

Since the peak of anti-Semitism in the United States during the decades from the 1920s to the 1940s, Jews have entered mainstream American society with nearly all career paths open to them. As a predominantly White/European racial group, they have not endured the same level of prejudice experienced by non-White minorities (Green, 1998). While Jews, at under six million, comprise less than 2% of the U.S. population (Kornbluth, 2003), their visibility and contributions to the fields of medicine, science, education, humanities, and the arts are vastly disproportionate to their numbers.

Despite the rising "credit rating" of Jewishness in America, Jews often see themselves on the verge of disaster (Kornbluth, 2003)—perhaps an existential cultural anxiety due to a long history of suffering (Herz & Rosen, 1996), persecution, and exile. The Holocaust, an unprecedented disaster of the twentieth century, reinoculated Jews with the fear of being victims of extermination. While most Holocaust survivors and their families went on to lead productive successful lives (Marcus & Rosenberg, 1989), few escaped emotional scars (Epstein, 1979; Mostysser, 1975) or a perceived sense of vulnerability.

Recognizing the wide range of Jewish personal expression is essential in learning to work with Jewish clients, underscoring the importance of individualizing treatment with each couple. You do not have to be Jewish to work effectively with Jewish couples. However, it is helpful to be a "polyglot" who knows something about the culture. There is a humorous story told about a poor elderly Jewish couple who won the lottery and hired a non-Jewish butler. They asked him to set the table for lunch for four because the Cohens were coming. When the Cohens called to tell him they were bringing the Knishes and the Blintzes, he went ahead and set the table for eight, much to the consternation of the elderly couple.

A Window Into Jewish Culture and Religion

Values

All denominations of Judaism acknowledge the Torah (Tanakh, 1985) (i.e., Five Books of Moses, including the Ten Commandments) as the source of directives for living a holy life. Our purpose as human beings created in God's image is to share in the task of co-creation through *tikkun olam* (repairing the world) (Dorff, 2005). The human being, viewed as an integrated whole (body and spirit), is endowed with free will and the responsibility to make choices. Hence, the Bible is full of stories of human mistakes and suffering, alongside the enduring capacity to repair, sending a profound message about human resilience (Wolin, Muller, Taylor, & Wolin, 1999) and hope. Judaism's emphasis on a "justice seeking spirituality" (de Perry & Rolland, 1999) is evident in liberation stories such as the Exodus, celebrated during Passover to encourage sensitivity toward the oppressed.

Opportunities during the High Holidays for repentance, healing, and changing behavior patterns resemble a therapeutic process. Judaism is a heavily behaviorally oriented religion, not just one of faith and belief, with values operationalized through ritual practices. Judaism's reverence for learning, loyalty to family and community, and multigenerational continuity are values as well as vehicles for preserving identity and encouraging responsibility for one another (Fishbane, 1999).

Religious Denominations

In the absence of one central religious authority, several major denominational movements have flourished, which differ in theology as well as ritual practice. Orthodox Jews take a more fundamentalist, literal approach to the holy texts, and are the strictest in their observance of *halacha* ("the way"), 613 commandments dealing with a person's relationship to God and human beings in daily life. Eleven percent of Jews in the United States affiliate with Orthodox synagogues (Silverstein, 2007). Even within Orthodoxy, there are nuances of practice and thought. Very Orthodox Jews are more likely to practice customs and rituals that set them apart from modern culture in dress, food, scheduled observances, and interpersonal relationships. Their community is very tight, exerting pressure to conform to prescribed ritual, academic, and social pathways. The rabbi is an esteemed leader, whose wisdom and arbitration are consulted in religious, legal, personal, emotional, and family matters.

Of Jews who affiliate with a synagogue, 80% join non-Orthodox synagogues; in general, only 20% of Jews tend to affiliate at all in a free society (Silverstein, 2007). Conservative Judaism views the Torah as a divinely inspired narrative, and focuses on "conserving" traditional customs while allowing modification as an accommodation to modernity. Reform Judaism has the most liberal interpretation of the tradition, giving human beings the personal autonomy to modify customs according to personal choice. As in Reconstructionist Judaism, ethical values and social action are emphasized, along with flexible ritual observance.

American Jews vary in their level of attachment to Judaism over their lifetimes (Kornbluth, 2003), as they face the dilemma of living alongside the American, Freudian, individualistic culture and its difference from Jewish religious values (Fishbane, 1999). In the fertile soil of American diversity and multiculturalism, challenges to traditional patriarchal models in the general society, such as feminism and gender diversity, have found their way into Judaism as well.

Marriage and the Family

For the Jewish family, marriage and raising children are the central focus of life (Herz & Rosen, 1996). There are pressures to marry, as well as obligations to extended family. Couples are expected to "be fruitful and multiply" (Genesis 1:28), although only the Orthodox community tends to have significantly larger families. The cornerstone value of family life is *shalom bayit*, the "development of a peaceful and harmonious relationship among all members of a household" (Donin, 1991, p. 61), a noble ideal consistent with family therapy (Lipsitz, 1987), but one that is not easily reachable.

Jewish families have been characterized by heavy expectations for intellectual achievement and financial success (Herz & Rosen, 1996). At the same time, Jewish families tend to be less hierarchical, and also somewhat permissive and overprotective, with parents devotedly privileging children's self-expression, happiness, and well-being (McGoldrick,1982). Enmeshment is a frequent characteristic, with Jewish children rarely leaving home without some degree of conflict between liberation and family loyalty (Herz & Rosen, 1996). The heightened sense of parental devotion and sacrifice is humorously illustrated in the story of an elderly Jewish couple, unhappily married for 69 years, who seek a marriage counselor because they want a divorce. When the puzzled therapist questions why the couple waited so long, enduring misery together, the wife and husband look at each other, sighing, and say, "We wanted to wait until all the children had died."

Jewish couples present with a variety of symptoms (*Encyclopedia Judaica*, 1971). Common problems lean toward neurotic symptoms of mental illness, compared with more severe symptoms in other populations. In general, Jews have a lower rate of alcoholism, especially among Orthodox Jews. Emotional states characterized by heavy amounts of guilt, as well as different manifestations of worry and anxiety, have been the brunt of comedians' characterizations. Marital problems are frequently defined as poor communication, with husbands often seen as distancing and unaffectionate and wives as critical and pursuing.

In previous generations, men were traditionally the providers, enjoying greater status outside the home and expecting to be cared for by their wives at home, where they were more peripheral. Women were economically dependent on their husbands and subordinate, but powerful in controlling the household. Each partner, on entering marriage, expected the same caring they had received in their family of origin, which often led to conflicts and disappointment (Herz & Rosen, 1996).

The Jewish mother often devoted herself to the caretaking of others, living for her kids' achievements, with more of an emphasis on mothering than being a spouse. As more women entered the workplace, they faced competing demands between family and career, serving others versus personal striving (Goldenberg, 1973). In today's postfeminist dual-career families, gender roles and the sharing of parenting tasks appear more flexible, yet are also a frequent source of conflict between spouses.

Jews generally have a lower divorce rate than the general population (Mancher & Rankin, 1991), although intermarriages end in divorce at twice the rate of same-faith Jewish marriages (Kornbluth, 2003), supporting the role of homogamy in marital stability (Bumpass & Sweet, 1972). Intermarriage is almost twice as frequent in second marriages (Cowan & Perel, 1992). Despite pressures to marry within the faith, intermarriage has grown from 17% in 1960 to a majority norm in the 1990s of 52% (Council of Jewish Federation National Population Survey, 1990), with one out of three American Jews living in an interfaith household, although these rates vary by geography.

Insistence on marrying coreligionists may be viewed as prejudicial from a multicultural lens, and young Jews are often puzzled by their parents' severe reactivity in response to intermarriage, especially if the parents were not religious. Cross-cultural marriages face tensions stemming from partners' differing expectations on a wide variety of issues that are culturally embedded, as well as due to interpersonal dynamics. Religious differences are felt to be among the most challenging. Intermarriage may have multiple psychological meanings and functions within a family system (Cowan & Perel, 1992), besides the competition between individual love and self-determination versus Jewish collective continuity (Perel, 1990).

Jews have been major consumers and providers of mental health services, suggesting possible cultural roots of this reflective, interpretive tradition that privileges verbal expression, reasoning, and discussion of feelings. Often referred by a trusted helper in the community, such as a rabbi, teacher, or physician, Jews search for the best services, and will often seek as well as challenge expert authority figures (McGoldrick, 1982). In treatment, they seem to prefer complex analysis and explanations over simple behavioral change. At times, their verbal sophistication and psychological mindedness belie emotional reactivity evident in verbal aggression and resistance to change, perhaps recommending a structural or strategic approach (McGoldrick, 1982). Others have advocated intergenerational approaches fostering differentiated connections (Fishbane, 1998). Treatment approaches with Jewish couples and families have been reported by Wieselberg (1992), Margolese (1998), and Mirkin (1998).

Author's Background and Methods

I am a traditional Conservative Jew, familiar with practices of Orthodox, Conservative, Reform, and Reconstructionist Judaism, and interested in Jewish Spiritual Renewal. I have lived within the framework of organized Jewish communal life in the United States and have visited Jewish communities around the world. As an integrative systemic couple therapist in private practice for 30 years, I have worked with Jewish couples along the entire spectrum of Jewish practice, with interfaith couples, as well as with couples and families of other ethnic minorities and religions. With each couple, I try to be a respectful, curious, nonjudgmental visitor and explorer. Since psychotherapy is not a value-free enterprise (Aponte, 1985;

Laird, 1998), knowing my own values hopefully helps me to self-monitor and to avoid the pitfall of imposing values on clients. Each couple offers me opportunities to not only develop a helping relationship but also to grow personally in understanding myself and the other.

A Spiritually Sensitive Couple Therapy

I embrace a systemic model, incorporating structural, developmental, and intergenerational aspects. In contrast to the historically secular culture of therapy, I also espouse a "biopsychosociospiritual" perspective (Meyerstein, 1995), which privileges an awareness of the documented importance of religion and spirituality as valued resources to clients in their lives (Aponte, 2002; Larson, 2001; Levin, 2001; Pargament, 1997; Walsh, 1999). My "biopsychosociospiritual" approach has several main elements:

1. Understanding the particular couple's culture, level of religious practice, and role of spirituality in their lives. This focus is important (Walsh, 1998) and consistent with Joint Commission on Accreditation of Hospitals guidelines mandating the inclusion of spirituality in clinical assessment and treatment (2003). Asking questions early on in a first-session rough genogram about ethnic/religious background and open-ended questions about spirituality is part of learning the client's world-view (Meyerstein, 2004). It is helpful to understand clients' beliefs about the meaning of their problems, acceptable pathways for healing, and the degree to which spiritual resources could be useful. Viewing clients from a spiritual assessment dimension (Davidowitz-Farkas, 2001; Hodge, 2005a; Weintraub, 2000) tends to humanize their situation. My familiarity with cultural norms and idiomatic language helps clients feel understood, fostering engagement. When unfamiliar with the culture, adopting a curious and respectful stance is appropriate.

2. Differentiating when an issue is more driven by culture and religion and when it is driven by psychological factors and structural conflicts. The Just Therapy team's use of a "cultural consultant" (Waldegrave, 1990) underscores the importance of not pathologizing aspects of culture. Green (1998) warns of the pitfall of overfocus on intrafamilial relations to the exclusion of larger cultural factors. However, religious issues often stem from intra- and interpersonal conflicts, and are more often the effect than the cause of the conflict (Wikler, 1982). For example, conflicts over life-cycle celebrations or raising children may reflect spouses' loyalty to

family of origin in a divided household. Furthermore, one must not ignore ritualistic religious behaviors that are excessively emotionally charged or taken to an extreme, and may represent obsessive compulsive behaviors (Greenberg & Witztum, 1991). Friedman (1982) urges therapists not to be mesmerized by "cultural camouflage," underscoring universal family dynamics as the driving force in situations of intermarriage. Crohn (1986) notes the underlying complementarity in partners drawn to the very cultural traits the other is trying to escape. Others see intermarriage as an act of emancipation that readjusts undesirable characteristics associated with one's own culture, opening the system to new definitions and diversity (McGoldrick & Giordano, 1982). The complex mix of process and cultural dynamics in intermarriage recommends a specialized approach.

3. Utilizing the religious or cultural idiom as part of treatment, based on the researched belief that spirituality and religion can be useful resources (Pargament, 1997), whether through strengthening the client's hopefulness, providing spiritual coping tools, including clergypersons as part of the treatment, or involving clients in their faith community. The majority of clients are open to discussing spirituality, when broadly framed. Supporting clients in accessing their own values can be strengthening (Aponte, 2002). Certainly not all couples are open to spiritual exploration, but for those who are, the therapist and clients might cocreate a spiritual treatment plan (Weintraub, 2000) that blends therapeutic and religious tools such as psalms, prayer, or ritual. For example, the therapist can select a text that might relate to a client's situation. Spiritual coping tools (Meyerstein, 2005) can help reduce anxiety by providing comfort, a focus, or something to do. Utilizing rituals, symbols, and ceremonies built into the culture to mark transitions can create important shared therapeutic moments—for example, saying a prayer together, lighting a memorial candle, or using the *mikveh* (ritual bath) for purification or for highlighting a change in status.

4. Broadening the discussion to include the clash between expectations of a secular American culture and religious values, analyzing when cultural factors have bearing on the meaning of problems—for example, discriminating the meaning of emotional dynamics (separation/connection and generation/gender), depending on whether it is a collective traditional culture or an individualistic mentality (Falicov, 1998). Some would even suggest not creating cultural conflicts for clients, even if it

means settling for lesser therapeutic solutions (Heilman & Witztum, 1997). The therapist's understanding of family background, migration patterns (Mirkin, 1998), and geographical origins can help locate a couple's experience—for example, the impact of a legacy of Holocaust survival or recent migration to the United States. The therapist's sensitivity would make it more likely that interventions would be constructively received. In addition, the therapist's knowledge of the community might lead to encouraging clients to contact their religious leaders and community as resources (Bilu & Witztum, 1992).

CASE EXAMPLES

Early Marriage Surprises

A young Orthodox couple, Sarah (22) and Chaim (24), sought couple therapy soon after marriage because of constant fighting. Neither Sarah nor Chaim dated before it was time for mate selection, having attended same-sex schooling and being introduced by a *shadchan* (matchmaker). Chaim, a student in Yeshiva and part-time teacher, was the more *frum* (religiously knowledgeable) partner, an imbalance that affected couple dynamics. Chaim had become an ultra-Orthodox *baal teshuva* (one who returns, repents) as an adult, perhaps as a pathway to differentiate him from his family. Sarah worked part-time as a teacher's aide. The couple had limited income and received some support from Chaim's mother. Chaim, an only son to first-generation American parents who were Holocaust survivors, felt heavy emotional responsibility toward his widowed mother. Sarah came from a very large, religious family where she felt little support. She excelled as a student in a girl's *yeshiva* away from home, due to the mentorship of a teacher.

For this young couple, the intimacy of marriage and extended family loyalties created vulnerability and crisis. Conflicts triggered disproportionate rage in Sarah, especially when Chaim responded with an ultra-logical approach, acting angrily paternalistic toward Sarah to cover his own anxiety. Both Sarah and Chaim accepted the definition of Sarah as the primary client, while Chaim remained blind to his participation in the imbalance. Because of the fighting, the couple had sought rabbinic permission to wait before starting a family.

I began couple therapy respecting their traditional gender organization while redefining the problem from an internal one in Sarah to a relationship issue. I joined with Chaim's experience before challenging him to reflect on his own anxiety with the distance evoked by conflict, an issue with which he was still struggling in relation to his overly close mother. Sarah, guarded about close familial ties, was verbally quite blunt with Chaim's mother, trying to fight Chaim's battles for him.

My familiarity with language and customs helped reduce the awkwardness of translation, reducing the distance between us. Understanding the practices of *taharat hamishpacha* (family purity; Lamm, 1966) and *tzniut* (modesty; Ganzfried, 1961) made it easier for Sarah and Chaim to discuss issues of sexual behavior. Once Sarah felt my support for her heavy responsibilities as an *eyshet chayil* (woman of valor, responsible for creating the household atmosphere), she was able to examine her part in escalating conflicts, both with Chaim and her mother-in-law.

Couple therapy helped this new couple define their boundaries as a unit. Chaim began to set limits, connecting in a more differentiated adult way with his mother, and Sarah learned to relate to Chaim's mother more effectively around family visits. The couple negotiated religious differences, fulfilling his more rigorous requirements while also incorporating Sarah's preferred traditions. Sarah and Chaim were highly motivated to develop a positive emotional and spiritual relationship with each other so they would feel secure about starting a family.

Shalom Bayit and Spiritual Growth

Susan (45) and Larry (47), an American Jewish couple, came to therapy to reduce conflicts and improve the quality of their stressful, hurried, disconnected lives. They had each previously been in individual treatment. Susan had grown up with a bitter and critical mother and absent father. Larry's family suffered from mood disorders. Growing up in secular homes and under tight financial conditions, each strove to become high-wage-earning professionals: Larry a doctor and Susan a lawyer. Despite hard work and success in their respective careers, they regretted that family life had suffered in the process. Although a devoted father, Larry was prone to angry depression, and Susan was often critical, expressing disappointments like her mother. While they spent a lot of money on material possessions and trips, they felt unable to relax, or to experience joy or peace in the household. They were searching for something to enrich their lives and were open to growing spiritually.

I responded to Susan and Larry's interpersonal, family, and spiritual agendas. Susan felt pushed away by Larry's controlling harshness, not recognizing the sadness underneath. I offered Susan a spiritual tool to help her feel more centered and less reactive to Larry's moodiness. Reciting a psalm to herself helped her pause instead of overreacting to Larry. Helping Larry express the sadness and anxiety underneath his edginess, with Susan as a witness, allowed him to feel heard. Once Larry realized the impact of his harsh style, he vowed to gain better control over his behavior, especially in the face of Susan's empathy and yearning to be closer. When I invited Larry to recite a reading titled "Eyseht Chayl, A Woman of Valor," in honor of Susan each Friday evening at their family Shabbat dinner table as a way of expressing his true feelings, Larry seized this opportunity to repair and has proudly continued the practice.

Susan had felt a growing spiritual urge in her 40s and began studying more about Judaism. She decided to become a bat mitzvah as an adult in her synagogue. In honor of the occasion, Susan and Larry gave *tzedakah* (charity) and planted trees in Israel in memory of lost relatives who could not be present at the ceremony. Following the bat mitzvah, they wanted to overcome their difficulty in experiencing joy by cutting back on work hours and creating more family togetherness time, as well as focusing on greater intimacy with each other.

A Divided Household

Marie and Howard, an intermarried couple in their early 50s, entered couple treatment via family therapy with their youngest daughter, Deborah, 16 years old, who had been functioning poorly at school, disrespectful and uncooperative at home, and dating a non-Jewish boyfriend. As mother and daughter engaged in daily escalating skirmishes, Deborah's father, who had a shorter fuse, would jump in to criticize Marie and threaten Deborah. Marie admitted she had a hard time enforcing consequences because she did not want to be a "cold" mother, as she herself experienced growing up.

The verbal expressiveness of this family quickly led to Deborah stating that she and her mother struggled like typical mothers and teenage daughters, but she was upset about her father's temper. Howard was surprised to hear her pain, and expressed his aversion to being the heavy in the family. Wishing to improve his relationship with Deborah and to lessen the turmoil, he agreed to stop barreling into mother–daughter skirmishes unless invited to do so by Marie.

In a session with the parents, Marie expressed deep resentment about the lack of help with child rearing over the years, despite her working full-time; she even considered leaving the marriage when Deborah left home. Howard responded with hurt and anger, yet remained clueless about the impact of his blunt and sarcastic style. Since Deborah was going away for part of the summer, I offered Marie and Howard a few couple sessions to begin talking about their relationship.

Marie and Howard came from very different backgrounds, with opposite temperaments that initially drew them together. Marie was a reserved, intellectually oriented, nonreligious Christian from a large disengaged family, and Howard was from an intensely close and verbally combative Jewish family. When I asked about religious differences, I learned that Marie had willingly agreed to raise their daughter in the Jewish tradition, and that the real disagreements were in the realm of interpersonal communication. Both described years of distance, with friction and arguments over Deborah snuffing out their earlier closeness.

Marie's resentment toward Howard seemed quite deep, and she had withdrawn, feeling her voice was unheard. Marie pointed to Howard's harsh judgmental attitude, stubborn insistence on following his career path, and failure to pay attention and make Marie feel valued. As Marie shared and Howard listened with concerned attention, it was as if an infected abscess began to drain. Howard acknowledged Marie's need for personal time, apologizing with regret for his lack of cooperation over the years, and Marie recognized how her tight bond with Deborah had shut him out. Howard admitted that he did not fully understand Marie and asked her to give him candid feedback instead of withdrawing. Marie and Howard continued to meet to air misunderstandings and hurts, as well as to identify what each might want to revive in the relationship without Deborah at the center.

Discussion

These three vignettes illustrate the diversity that may greet a therapist working with Jewish couples. When encountering a culturally supported patriarchal system with highly defined gender roles, the therapist may have to temper feminist leanings in order to facilitate engagement, and orchestrate change from within the couple's value framework, focusing more on what is and is not working from each one's perspective. Also, with

Orthodox couples, therapists would be wise to accept rules of modesty and not automatically shake the hand of a member of the opposite sex, respect laws of the Sabbath and not telephone between Friday and Saturday evenings. Working with sexual intimacy issues needs to be informed by awareness of family purity guidelines (Lamm, 1966). Being aware of confidentiality in a small community might recommend not scheduling back-to-back appointments with religious couples who might meet in the waiting room. The therapist must be willing to address any hesitations couples may have about the therapist's degree of knowledge of their lifestyle.

Introducing spirituality into therapy is a relatively new arena, and one that must be approached in an open-ended way, with sensitivity, and balanced with therapeutic wisdom. When a couple is open to discussion about spirituality/religion, the therapist can share spiritual tools and collaborate on developing meaningful rituals, employ therapeutic exercises (Hodge, 2005b), or encourage the couple to seek resources in their faith community.

In intermarriage and other situations, tracking communication to decipher the cultural/religious aspect from interpersonal dynamics can create more flexible possibilities for partners to understand conflict in its larger context, foster differentiation, and negotiate differences (Perel, 2000). Not all religious differences are problematic, and not all religious differences are about religion only. Perel's metaphor of partners as anthropologists, tourists, or immigrants in the unfamiliar territory of the other, and as archeologists of their own history, is apt for both clients and therapist.

Helpful Hints for Clinicians

Being a sensitive listener and skilled clinician is not enough; it is important to learn about a couple's ethnicity. A true systemic view includes an expansive analysis of contexts, of how class, gender, race, religion, and immigrant status affect a couple's relationship. Therapists need to develop conversational tools to discuss aspects of diversity not typically addressed, such as race and class (McGoldrick, 1998). Learning characteristics of different ethnic groups may be necessary, but it is not sufficient, and at times it can create limiting stereotypes that oversimplify the diversity existing within each culture. To learn more about a culture, a therapist can consult with leaders and members of the community.

Therapists need to develop the facility to introduce questions about spirituality into treatment. Creative tools exist for assessment as well as therapeutic intervention to assist the therapist in this direction (Hodge, 2005a, 2005b; Meyerstein, 2005). While there are differences in beliefs, ceremonies, and rituals from group to group, all cultures have mechanisms to deal with misfortune. Moreover, therapists need to look for the humanity and emotional sameness shared by different ethnic groups in their respective experiences of suffering, poverty, and loss (Montalvo, 1992).

Implications and Further Tips for Educators

As the field has evolved, awareness of culture and other aspects of diversity has grown in sophistication. There are training curricula to help therapists think culturally and multidimensionally (Falicov, 1995; Montalvo & Gutierrez, 1990), as well as tools to help therapists question themselves and clients (Crohn, 1995; Laird, 1998). Through formal training, literature, movies, cross-cultural community experiences, and exposure to clients of different ethnicities, therapists can gain familiarity with different cultures.

Supervision can expand sensitivity to ethnic diversity by including how different culturally embedded family styles deal with problems, helpers, and institutions in the community. Sometimes trainees' discomfort describing characteristics of certain ethnic groups may reflect lack of familiarity, reluctance to be politically incorrect, or fear of prejudice expressed about their own ethnicity (McGoldrick & Giordano, 1996). Supervisors and educators need to reflect by example awareness of the inevitable subjectivity of therapists as human beings and the importance of understanding one's own values and identity. By encouraging therapists to do a genogram of their own families, highlighting ethnicity, religion, and other aspects of diversity, supervisors can increase therapists' understanding of their own historical roots. By cultivating an ethic of transparency (White, 1993) and a humble, collaborative, nonhierarchical stance, supervisors can initiate a process of self-discovery and self-definition crucial to helping students and clients achieve the same.

As therapists, we are agents of social and cultural order. Expanding the secular value framework of therapeutic wellness to include cultural, spiritual, and religious aspects can be supportive of clients' strengths. Learning about our clients' ways takes time and patience, but so does the development of trust. To a secular therapist, some religious views/behaviors may seem trivial, but it is important to respect their underlying importance to clients. It can be tempting to stereotype religious clients because of similar outward appearances or practices, but it is important to remember that they are just as varied in personality patterns as the rest of the population. *Therape* in ancient Greece involved treatment of the whole person and was a sacred task. Our challenge is to be open, reflective, flexible, and self-aware about our values and our emotional selves to remain loyal to our sacred mission in serving clients.

Additional Resources

Films

Dar, G. (Director). (2005). *Ushpizin.* Picturehouse. Features an ultra-Orthodox couple.

De Jong, A. (Producer), & Krabbé, J. (Director). (1998). *Left Luggage.* Castle Hill Productions. Addresses the Holocaust.

Marshall, S. (Director). (2006). *Keeping Up With the Steins.* Miramax. Features a contemporary Jewish family.

Readings

Cardin, N. B. (2000). *The tapestry of Jewish time.* New York: Behrmann House.

Dosick, W. (1998). *Living Judaism: The complete guide to Jewish belief, tradition, and practice.* New York: HarperCollins.

Kushner, H. (1994). *To life! A celebration of Jewish being and thinking.* New York: Warner Books.

Lamm, N. (1966). *A hedge of roses: Jewish insights into marriage and married life* (2nd ed.). New York: Feldheim.

Olitzky, K. M. (2003). *Making a successful Jewish interfaith marriage work.* Woodstock, VT: Jewish Lights Publishing.

Web Sites

Interfaith Family (Jewish community Web site): www.interfaithfamily.com
Jewish Outreach Institute: www.joi.org

Museums

Museum of Tolerance, Los Angeles
The National Holocaust Museum, Washington, D.C.

Experiential Exercises and Tools for Reflection

Crohn, J. (1995). Many voices within: Clarifying cultural and religious identity (self-guided questionnaire). In J. Crohn (Ed.), *Mixed matches: How to create successful, interracial, interethnic, interfaith relationships* (pp. 108–142). New York: Ballantine.

Hodge, D. (2005). Spiritual life map: A client centered pictorial instrument for spiritual assessment, planning, and intervention. *Social Work, 50,* 77.

References

Aponte, H. (1985). The negotiation of values in therapy. *Family Process, 24,* 323–338.

Aponte, H. J. (2002). Spiritually sensitive therapy. In F. W. Kaslow (Ed.), *Comprehensive handbook of psychotherapy* (Vol. 3, pp. 279–302). New York: John Wiley.

Bilu, Y., & Witztum, E. (1992). Working with Jewish ultra-Orthodox patients: Guidelines for a culturally sensitive therapy. *Culture, Medicine, and Psychiatry, 17,* 1–37.

Bumpass, L. L., & Sweet, J. A. (1972). Differentials in marital instability: 1970. *American Sociological Review, 37,* 754–766.

Council of Jewish Federations. (2001). *National Jewish population survey data: Strength, challenge, and diversity in the American Jewish population.* New York: United Jewish Communities.

Cowan, R., & Perel, E. (1992). A more perfect union: Intermarriage and the Jewish world. *Tikkun, 7,* 59–94.

Crohn, J. (1986). *Ethnic identity and marital conflict: Jews, Italians, and Wasps.* New York: American Jewish Committee.

Davidowitz-Farkas, Z. (2001). Jewish spiritual assessment. In D. A. Friedman (Ed.), *Jewish pastoral care: A practical handbook from traditional and contemporary sources* (pp. 104–124). Woodstock, VT: Jewish Lights Publishing.

De V. Perry, A., & Rolland, J. S. (1999). Spirituality expressed in community action and social justice: A therapeutic means for liberation and hope. In F. Walsh (Ed.), *Spiritual resources in family therapy* (pp. 272–292). New York: Guilford.

Donin, H. H. (1991). *To be a Jew: A guide to Jewish observance in contemporary life.* New York: Basic Books.

Dorff, E. J. (2005). *The way into Tikkun Olam/repairing the world.* Woodstock, VT: Jewish Lights Publishing.

Encyclopedia Judaica (1971, with subsequent supplements). (pp. 1372–1377, 1336–1341). Jerusalem: Keter Publishing.

Epstein, H. (1979). *Children of the Holocaust.* New York: Putnam.

Falicov, C. J. (1995). Training to think culturally: A multidimensional comparative framework. *Family Process, 34,* 373–388.

Falicov, C. J. (1998). The cultural meaning of family triangles. In M. McGoldrick (Ed.), *Re-visioning family therapy: Race, culture and gender in clinical practice* (pp. 37–47). New York: Guilford Press.

Fishbane, M. D. (1998). I, thou, and we: A dialogic approach to couples therapy. *Journal of Marital and Family Therapy, 24,* 41–58.

Fishbane, M. D. (1999). "Honor thy father and thy mother": Intergenerational continuity and Jewish tradition. In F. Walsh (Ed.), *Spiritual resources in family therapy* (pp. 136–156). New York: Guilford Press.

Friedman, E. (1982). The myth of the *shiksa.* In F. Walsh (Ed.), *Normal family processes* (pp. 156–172). New York: Guilford Press.

Ganzfried, S. (1961). *Codes of Jewish law: Vol. 4.* New York: Hebrew Publishing.

Goldenberg, J. O. (1973). The Jewish feminist conflict in identities. *Response, 7,* 11–18.

Green, R. J. (1998). Race and the field of family therapy. In M. McGoldrick (Ed.), *Re-visioning family therapy: Race, culture, and gender in clinical practice* (pp. 93–110). New York: Guilford Press.

Greenberg, D., & Witztum, E. (1991). Problems in the treatment of religious patients. *American Journal of Psychotherapy, 45,* 554–565.

Heilman, S. C., & Witztum, E. (1997). Value-sensitive therapy: Learning from ultra-Orthodox patients. *American Journal of Psychotherapy, 51,* 522–542.

Herz, F. M., & Rosen, E. J. (1996). Jewish families. In M. McGoldrick, J. K. Pearce, & J. Giordano (Eds.), *Ethnicity and family therapy* (pp. 364–392). New York: Guilford Press.

Hodge, D. R. (2005a). Spiritual assessment in marital and family therapy: A methodological framework for selecting from among six qualitative assessment tools. *Journal of Marital and Family Therapy, 31,* 341–356.

Hodge, D. R. (2005b). Spiritual life maps: A client centered pictorial instrument for spiritual assessment, planning, and intervention. *Social Work, 50,* 77–87.

Joint Commission Resources. (2003). *Comprehensive accreditation manual for hospitals: The official handbook:* Oakbrook Terrace, IL: Joint Commission on Accreditation of Healthcare Organizations.

Kornbluth, D. (2003). *Why marry Jewish?* Detroit, MI: Targum Press.

Laird, J. (1998) Theorizing culture: Narrative ideas and practice principles. In M. McGoldrick (Ed.), *Re-visioning family therapy: Race, culture, and gender in clinical practice* (pp. 2–36). New York: Guilford Press.

Lamm, N. (1966). *A hedge of roses: Jewish insights into marriage and married life* (2nd ed.). New York: Feldheim.

Larson, D. L. (2001). Spirituality—the forgotten factor in health and mental health: What does the research say? *Institute for Professional Development,* Jewish Family Services, Baltimore, MD.

Levin, J. (2001). *God, faith, and health: Exploring the spirituality–healing connection.* New York: John Wiley.

Lipsitz, G. J. (1997). *Practical parenting: A Jewish perspective.* New York: Ktav Publishing House.

Mancher, J. S., & Rankin, R. P. (1991). Religious affiliation and marital duration among those who file for divorce in California, 1966–71. *Journal of Divorce and Remarriage, 15,* 205–217.

Marcus, P., & Rosenberg, A. (Eds.) (1989). *Healing their wounds: Psychotherapy with Holocaust survivors and their families.* New York: Praeger.

Margolese, H. C. (1998). Engaging in psychotherapy with the Orthodox Jew: A critical review. *American Journal of Psychotherapy, 52,* 37–54.

McGoldrick, M. (1982). Normal families: An ethnic perspective. In F. Walsh (Ed.), *Normal family processes* (pp. 399–424). New York: Guilford Press.

McGoldrick, M. (Ed.). (1998). *Re-visioning family therapy: Race, culture, and gender in clinical practice.* New York: Guilford Press.

McGoldrick, M., & Giordano, J. (1996). Overview: Ethnicity and family therapy. In M. McGoldrick, J. K. Pearce, & J. Giordano (Eds.), *Ethnicity and family therapy* (2nd ed). New York: Guilford Press.

Meyerstein, I. (1995). *A tapestry of therapy conversations about medical illness.* Workshop presentation at the American Association for Marriage and Family Therapy National Conference. Baltimore, MD.

Meyerstein, I. (2004). A Jewish spiritual perspective on psychopathology and psychotherapy: A clinician's view. *Journal of Religion and Health, 44,* 329–340.

Meyerstein, I. (2005). Sustaining our spirits: Spiritual study discussion groups for coping with medical illness. *Journal of Religion and Health, 44,* 207–225.

Mirkin, M. P. (1998). The impact of multiple contexts on recent immigrant families. In M. McGoldrick (Ed.), *Re-visioning family therapy: Race, culture, and gender in clinical practice* (pp. 370–384). New York: Guilford Press.

Montalvo, B. (1992). Editorial: A conversation about diversity. *The Supervisor Bulletin VII:1,* 2–3, 7.

Montalvo, B., & Gutierrez, M. (1990). Nine assumptions for work with ethnic minority families. In G. Saba, B. Karrer, & K. Hardy (Eds.), *Ethnic minorities and family therapy* (pp. 35–50). New York: Haworth Press.

Mostysser, T. (1975). The weights of the past reminiscences of a survivor's child. *Response, 8,* 3–32.

Pargament, K. I. (1997). *The psychology of religion and coping: Theory, research, practice.* New York: Guilford Press.

Perel, E. (1990). Ethnocultural factors in marital communication among intermarried couples. *Journal of Jewish Communal Service, 66,* 244–253.

Perel, E. (2000). A tourist's view of marriage: Cross-cultural couples—challenges, choices, and implications for therapy. In P. Papp (Ed.), *Couples on the fault line: New directions for therapists* (pp. 187–198). New York: Guilford Press.

Silverstein, A. (2007). *The future of conservative Judaism in America.* Lecture at Adat Chaim Synagogue. Reisterstown, MD, April 22.

Tanakh (1985). *The Holy Scriptures: The new JPS translation according to the traditional Hebrew text.* Philadelphia: The Jewish Publication Society.

Waldegrave, C. T. (1990). Just therapy. *Dulwich Center Newsletter, 3,* 5–46.

Walsh, F. (1998). Beliefs, spirituality, and transcendence: Keys to family resilience. In M. Goldrick (Ed.), *Re-visioning family therapy: Race, culture, and gender in clinical practice* (pp. 254–266). New York: Guilford Press.

Walsh, F. (Ed.). (1999). *Spiritual resources in family therapy.* New York: Guilford Press.

Weintraub, S. Y. (2000). Unpublished presentation to National Association of Jewish Chaplains Conference.

White, M. (1993). Deconstruction and therapy. In S. Gilligan & R. Price (Eds.), *Therapeutic conversations* (pp. 54–73). New York: Norton.

Wieselberg, H. (1992). Family therapy and ultra Orthodox Jewish families: A structural approach. *Journal of Family Therapy, 13,* 305–336.

Wikler, M. (1982). Another look at the diagnosis and treatment of Orthodox Jewish family problems. *Journal of Psychology and Judaism, 7,* 42–54.

Wolin, S. J., Muller, W., Taylor, F., & Wolin, S. (1999). Three spiritual perspectives on resilience: Buddhism, Christianity, and Judaism. In F. Walsh (Ed.), *Spiritual resources in family therapy* (pp. 121–128). New York: Guilford Press.

Section C

Evidence-Based Models of Couple Therapy With Minorities

Eight

Emotionally Focused Couple Therapy With Intercultural Couples

Paul S. Greenman, Marta Y. Young, and Susan M. Johnson

In the past three decades, there has been an unprecedented increase in the number of intercultural marriages worldwide (Frame, 2004; Molina, Estrada, & Burnett, 2004; Waldman & Rubalcava, 2005). Intercultural relationships typically refer to a union between partners from different racial, ethnic, national, or religious backgrounds (Ho, 1990). Although all couples negotiate their individual differences to a certain extent, intercultural couples are faced with a "synergy of differences" that often taxes the relationship (Sullivan & Cottone, 2006). Despite the prevalence of intercultural marriages and the unique stresses of such relationships, including higher rates of divorce and a greater tendency to be in second marriages compared with intracultural couples (Gaines & Agnew, 2003; Gaines & Ickes, 1997; Gaines & Liu, 2000; Waite, Bachrack, Hindin, Thomson, & Thornton, 2000), the impact of cultural factors in couple therapy has largely been ignored, with a few notable recent exceptions (e.g., Bhugra & De Silva, 2000; Biever, Bobele, & North, 2002; Thomas, Karis, & Wetchler, 2003; Sullivan & Cottone, 2006).

The principal aims of this chapter are therefore to outline the impact of cultural issues on couples' interactions, and to describe the advantages of Emotionally Focused Therapy (EFT) in working with intercultural couples. Therapists who practice EFT focus on problems of direct relevance to couples who, in addition to dealing with issues common to couplehood, may also be challenged by cultural differences and by the stresses of acculturation. A discussion of the process and the empirical support for EFT will set the stage for a detailed case study of a couple in which one partner was of Middle Eastern background and the other was English Canadian. The case study will illustrate the usefulness of EFT with intercultural couples, the challenges EFT therapists face in their work with members of various ethnocultural groups, and the adjustments that need to be made to EFT interventions to ensure their effectiveness in multicultural contexts.

The Authors

Paul Greenman is a Professor of Clinical Psychology at the Université du Québec en Outaouais in Gatineau, Québec, Canada, and a practicing psychologist at the Ottawa Couple and Family Institute in Ottawa, Ontario, Canada. He specializes in EFT for couples in his teaching and clinical practice and conducts research on the emotional and interpersonal lives of individuals from a range of cultural backgrounds. Marta Young is a Professor of Clinical Psychology at the University of Ottawa in Canada. She also has a private practice providing assessment and treatment services to immigrants and refugees. Specializing in cross-cultural psychology, she conducts research on the acculturation and well-being of immigrants and refugees. Susan M. Johnson is one of the originators and main proponents of Emotionally Focused Therapy (EFT) for couples, now one of the best-validated interventions for couples in North America. She is a Professor of Clinical Psychology at the University of Ottawa and Director of the Ottawa Couple and Family Institute and the Center for Emotionally Focused Therapy.

Unique Experiences of Intercultural Couples

Although intercultural couples face many of the same stresses and challenges as their endogamous counterparts, there are unique experiences that shape and challenge their relationships. Bhugra and De Silva (2000) identified two primary sources of distress that intercultural couples may experience, namely macrocultural or systemic influences and microcultural individual differences. In addition, for those partners who have experienced migration, there are a number of acculturative stresses related to emigration and resettlement that may impact the couple.

Systemic Influences

At a more macro or systemic level, intercultural couples are subjected to three main types of influences: social messages, family influences, and acceptance from the community (Molina, Estrada, & Burnett, 2004). Many intercultural couples are affected by the implicit and explicit oppressive messages regarding exogamous relationships (Killian, 2001; Molina et al., 2004). Examples of such social messages include statements like "You know he only wants to improve his social status by marrying a White woman," or "You would be better off staying with one of our girls who will know how to honor her man." With respect to family influences, family opposition to marrying outside of one's cultural group is often a significant challenge. Intercultural couples may be subjected to discrimination, hostile and violent behaviors, banishment, and even death in some extreme cases. These unsupportive family influences can profoundly affect the social and emotional well-being of the couple. Community acceptance or rejection has also been found to be an important influence on intercultural couples that can have a negative impact on their relational adjustment (Hsu, 2001).

Throughout history, individuals have experienced rejection and oppression because of their membership in particular groups (e.g., Native peoples, immigrants, visible minorities). When couples experience exclusion from the community, they are often faced with additional stressors such as housing discrimination, problems with colleagues and employers, social isolation, and witnessing their multicultural children being ostracized. Furthermore, members of privileged groups may suddenly find themselves the target of discrimination because of their choice of a culturally different partner (Biever et al., 2002).

Microcultural Differences

Intercultural couples are, by definition, faced with negotiating differences they may have in terms of habits, beliefs, values, and customs.

Common challenges and conflict areas include gender-based role expectations, fidelity, attitudes toward work and leisure, orientations toward time, importance of fate versus control, individualism/collectivism, financial matters, sexuality, religion and holiday traditions, language, verbal and nonverbal communication, expression of emotions, moods, and problem-solving strategies (including conflict resolution, child-rearing, definition of family, and family boundaries and obligations) (Biever et al., 1998; Hsu, 2001). In addition, differences in terms of age, race, social class, and "minority/majority status," to name a few, may also contribute to an intercultural couple's distress.

Factors related to initial attraction can also become a source of conflict. Often, couples may have unrealistic or misguided expectations about other cultures. When there is a gap between their fantasies and reality, confusion and resentment may surface. An Asian woman from a more traditional family and culture, for example, may marry a North American man, assuming that he will hold more liberal views regarding women and gender roles. But he may expect his Asian wife to be more deferential to his male authority (Crohn, 1998).

Migration-Related Factors

In addition to the macro and micro influences outlined above, issues related to acculturation become relevant if one or both partners have experienced migration. Many immigrants and refugees resettle in countries that are culturally very different from their homeland. After an initial period of elation and excitement, migrants often find themselves experiencing culture shock (Oberg, 1960). This phase is characterized by confusion regarding cultural norms, values, and roles; changes in the living environment (e.g., housing, diet, climate); and language difficulties. In addition, they are faced with the challenge of learning how to navigate largely foreign government agencies, such as the social, financial, and legal services, and the educational system. Securing employment may also be stressful due to discriminatory hiring practices, and lack of language skills or job experience in the country of resettlement (Winter & Young, 1998). Although many resettle successfully, most do experience, at some time or other, feelings of uncertainty, loneliness, homesickness, and general psychological distress (Al-Issa & Tousignant, 1997). Other related difficulties include substance abuse, marital distress, family violence, depression, and anxiety (Negy & Snyder, 1997; Winter & Young, 1998).

In the case of refugees, who typically have emigrated for involuntary reasons (e.g., war, persecution, torture, genocide), resettlement may be particularly difficult. In addition to these preimmigration traumas, refugees have often experienced additional horrific experiences during flight (e.g., rape, losing family members, being attacked). Those who are successful in fleeing often spend years in refugee camps, where day-to-day life is exceedingly difficult and precarious (e.g., shortages of food and water, overcrowded conditions, physical and sexual violence). Not surprisingly, many refugees are at higher risk for posttraumatic stress disorder (PTSD), adjustment disorder, depression, substance abuse, and family violence. Both immigrants and refugees are also often targets of prejudice, discrimination, and racism, which negatively affect their well-being (Beiser & Hyman, 1997; Tousignant, 1997).

EFT for Intercultural Couples: Forging Secure Attachment Bonds

Providing therapy to intercultural couples in distress presents unique challenges. Although there has been an increase in attention toward this subpopulation of couples, few clinical guidelines currently exist. One approach that has been found to be relevant and effective is Emotionally Focused Therapy (EFT). The sections below provide an overview of the EFT approach in work with intercultural couples.

Attachment Theory and Intercultural Couples

EFT for couples targets sadness, loneliness, and stress directly. EFT is based on adult attachment theory, which stipulates that *all* people, regardless of their culture of origin, have innate needs for safety, comfort, and emotional closeness; that relationships with significant others provide these necessary emotional connections; and that the need for safe, nurturing emotional bonds remains salient across the lifespan (Bartholomew & Horowitz, 1991; Bowlby, 1969; Hazan & Shaver, 1987). According to attachment theory, the survival of the human race necessitates the formation of these emotional bonds with a few trusted others. In adulthood, romantic partners tend to take on the role of primary attachment figure (Johnson & Whiffen, 1999), particularly in the highly individualistic North American culture (Putnam, 2000). Couple distress therefore arises when people are unsure of the emotional engagement and emotional responsiveness of their partners, who are generally their primary sources of support. This attachment distress can become particularly salient in intercultural couples in which one partner from a collectivistic, community-oriented culture in sources of emotional support abound finds himself or herself not only in an individualistic environment that emphasizes independence and personal resolve over interdependence and community, but also in a couple relationship devoid of emotional closeness. The loneliness that people in such situations feel is often excruciating and terrifying, due to unmet basic attachment needs for emotional closeness that they once satisfied through other significant relationships in their culture of origin.

Research on marital satisfaction and distress in North America reflects this attachment perspective. On one hand, the high level of emotional engagement and emotional responsiveness from primary attachment figures that typifies secure attachment is a key predictor of relationship satisfaction. In contrast, interaction patterns tainted by a preponderance of negative emotions such as anger, in which partners either attack or become numb and emotionally distant, are related to relationship dissatisfaction and dissolution (Gottman, 1991; Gottman & Driver, 2006; Huston, Caughlin, Houts, Smith, & George, 2001). From an EFT perspective, these interaction patterns represent a core struggle wherein partners attempt to regulate the strong negative emotions associated with the absence of secure attachment in the couple: The pursuing partner becomes angry and critical in an effort to engage the other emotionally, and the withdrawn partner shuts down and avoids in order to regulate the fear generated by the critical partner's hostility (Johnson & Greenman, 2006). For this reason, the forging of interactions characterized by safe emotional responses between partners is the main task of EFT.

EFT With Ethnic Minorities

A major advantage of EFT in work with people from minority cultures is its emphasis on the fundamental attachment needs and basic emotions that typify the human experience. Needs for safety, comfort, and closeness appear to be universal (Ainsworth, 1967; van IJzendoorn & Sagi, 1999, 2001), as do the six basic emotions: surprise, fear, shame, anger, joy, and sadness (Ekman, 2003). It is also worth noting that patterns of attachment in couples tend to be consistent across cultures (Gaines et al., 1999; Troy,

Lewis-Smith, & Laurenceau, 2006). Yet EFT therapists do not neglect the role of intrapersonal or cultural factors in the development and healing of couples' problems. On the contrary, the EFT approach encourages the understanding of all couple relationships as unique cultures in themselves, in which individual differences—whether they are the products of genetics, upbringing, or cultural norms—can play an important part in the genesis and resolution of the core attachment struggle between partners.

However, although emotions and attachment needs appear to be universal, the rules that govern which emotions and needs can be displayed in interpersonal contexts seem to vary from culture to culture (Rothbaum, Weisz, Pott, Miyake, & Morelli, 2000; van IJzendoorn & Sagi, 2001; Wang & Mallinckrodt, 2006). These cultural rules can constrain couples' interactions, shape their cycles, and affect communication in therapy. EFT therapists must therefore be particularly sensitive to cultural norms surrounding the display of emotion and the expression of needs, because these can have an enormous impact on the development and restructuring of couples' interaction patterns. For instance, the literature suggests that therapists working with people from Asian cultures must pay particular attention to cultural inhibitions regarding the expression and discussion of feelings and personal relationships, and to the stigma associated with consulting a mental health professional (Hwang, 2006). Our clinical experience with couples of Sicilian background indicates that themes such as revenge and honor can play an important role in determining how partners from that culture react to each other when they feel hurt, or when their attachment needs are not met. These clients have shared with us a strong sense of shame surrounding emotional injury that goes unpunished. It seems that, in Sicilian culture, it is important to respond in kind when hurt by another person in a relationship in order to save face. This can create a pervasive attack–attack pattern in which both partners become hostile and defensive, and neither one feels safe in the relationship.

EFT: Stages and Steps

EFT is an experiential and systemic intervention. As is typical of experiential therapies, EFT features active therapist–client collaboration that lends new meanings to clients' experiences (Johnson & Greenman, 2006). The theory of change in EFT is thus geared toward understanding and expanding on people's unique experiences of themselves and their relationships. In work with intercultural couples, this involves helping both partners to recognize the culturally driven norms, values, and expectations that contribute to their personal construction of, and emotional experience in, their relationship. Once the impact of culture on each person's experience of the relationship becomes clear, EFT therapists then invite partners to integrate these elements into their relationship directly and openly in order to encourage a stronger emotional connection, all the while providing them with empathic support.

The systemic component of EFT involves the therapist's construal of couples' problems as the result of rigid, self-reinforcing interaction patterns triggered by context cues and specific partner behaviors related to attachment needs. Whereas the theory of change that informs EFT emphasizes uniqueness and individual differences, the theory of relationships espoused in this approach (i.e., attachment theory) stipulates that the interaction patterns observed in couples reflect the level of satisfaction of fundamental human needs for safety and emotional closeness that are not unique to one particular culture. Therapy with intercultural couples therefore consists of helping partners identify any culture-specific ways of meeting basic needs for closeness and comfort, and reacting to their absence in the relationship. Typical strategies encountered clinically include pursuing one's partner aggressively and engaging in hurtful behaviors when attachment needs remain unfulfilled; becoming jealous, controlling, or overprotective; or refraining from discussing deep-seated longings for the other, and instead stonewalling and withdrawing. Throughout the stages and steps of EFT, the therapist guides intercultural couples' discovery of the manner in which such strategies might actually undermine a sense of closeness.

EFT consists of three stages: cycle de-escalation (Stage I), restructuring interactional positions (Stage II), and consolidation/integration (Stage III) (Bradley & Johnson, 2005; Johnson, 2004). Within each stage of EFT, the therapist follows a prescribed set of steps in order to help couples recognize and combat their negative interaction cycles, and establish a secure emotional connection.

Stage I: Steps 1–4

A total of nine steps make up the EFT process. The first four steps constitute Stage I, and are geared toward diminishing the impact of the couple's negative cycle. The therapist aims at this juncture to reflect the couple's pattern and to illustrate how each partner's behavior and expressed emotions (usually frustration and anger) in the cycle prevent safety and closeness. In so doing, the therapist helps uncover each person's unique construction of the relationship, which can stem in large part from cultural norms and expectations surrounding couple relationships and their partner's behavior. The focus in Stage I is also on uncovering the primary emotions (e.g., fear, sadness, shame, panic) that each partner feels in problematic interactions with the other, which normally underlie their anger or emotional withdrawal, and on framing the couple's difficulties as the result of their negative cycle, replete with the underlying emotions and attachment longings that are present but not yet openly integrated into their interactions. In work with intercultural couples, EFT therapists validate the cultural influences on partners' behaviors and expressed emotions, but they also simultaneously reflect the impact of the same on the couple's negative cycle.

Stage II: Steps 5–7

EFT therapists are most active during Stage II of EFT. First, they support one partner at a time to deepen his or her primary emotions, attachment longings, and sense of self in the relationship, and to express these to the other partner. Then they help the other partner hear, receive, and integrate this information, which is often hard to take in because it is so new. Finally, the therapist attends to the specific wants and needs that emerge, and assists in their expression. During Stage II, the therapist choreographs the couple's interactions (enactments) with an emphasis on asking them to express directly to each other their primary emotions (e.g., sadness and fear when uncertain of the other's love) and needs for closeness. The goal is to help the withdrawn partner to become emotionally engaged in the relationship and the pursuing partner to become less hostile and critical.

In work with intercultural couples, the main focus here is on identifying culture-specific ways of achieving attachment security and the potential impact of these on each partner's sense of the emotional availability of the other. Depending on the level of emphasis on personal privacy typical of clients' culture of origin, the change events in Stage II of EFT might be dramatically apparent, replete with tears and expressions of love and longing, or more subtle, with expressions of need for the other and fear of loss taking on a more reserved tone. It is important to note that in either case the basic underlying processes of helping partners seek each other out in times of need is the same, in accordance with the tenets of attachment theory.

Stage III: Steps 8–9

The final stage of EFT builds upon the first two. By Stage III, the partners have reestablished safety and security in the relationship, or they have fashioned a secure base for the first time. They are now able to return to and solve long-standing problems such as money, sex, and child rearing because these issues no longer have the attachment significance they once did. The therapist's role is to facilitate the problem-solving process, and to reflect and heighten partners' new responses to each other (e.g., husband now speaks openly of his fear and asks for comfort instead of withdrawing; wife now expresses her vulnerability and need for safety instead of criticizing).

Empirical Support for EFT

A number of studies conducted in North America have provided empirical support for the clinical efficacy of EFT. For example, the results of a meta-analysis of four randomized clinical trials in which EFT was compared with other couple therapies and two control groups indicated a highly significant effect of EFT on the reduction of marital distress (Johnson, Hunsley, Greenberg, & Schindler, 1999). Other studies have shown that 86–90% of couples who participate in EFT exhibit significant increases in relationship satisfaction, that 75% of them are no longer distressed by the end of therapy (James, 1991), and that the effects of therapy tend to endure following termination (Gordon Walker, Johnson, Manion, & Cloutier, 1996). In fact, one investigation of couples at high risk for marital distress due to their children's illnesses revealed that the vast majority of those who received EFT continued to improve over the two years following the end of treatment (Cloutier, Manion, Gordon Walker, & Johnson, 2002). Finally, more recent results suggest that EFT might be an effective treatment for problems such as depression (Dessaulles, Johnson, & Denton, 2003), chronic illness (Kowal, Johnson, & Lee, 2003), and relational aspects of PTSD (MacIntosh & Johnson, in press). The following case study illustrates in detail the effect of cultural norms on the evolution of a couple's problematic interaction cycle and the power of EFT to help the partners alter it.

CASE EXAMPLE

Scott and Sameera had been married for 15 years when they began therapy. Scott was White and a member of the English Canadian majority culture, whereas Sameera was of Middle Eastern origin. Many of her friends and acquaintances shared her cultural background. Sameera and Scott had no children. They sought help for what they described as a communication problem in their relationship.

Scott indicated that he often became frustrated with Sameera because, according to him, she would criticize him angrily and incessantly for no apparent reason. Sameera, on the other hand, said that Scott's inattention to her emotional needs, especially in their interactions with members of his family, left her no choice but to point out to him the various ways in which he needed to improve. The couple had heated arguments three to four times a week, usually about how abandoned Sameera felt when Scott tried to "keep the peace" during family conflicts. The content of the arguments then often turned to financial concerns, whether or not to have a baby, and the lack of closeness between the couple. The arguments ended when Scott would leave the room or the couple's home altogether, either to meet up with friends or to take a walk to "cool off." When he would return, he and Sameera would apologize to each other and try to continue as if nothing had happened. However, they both reported feeling as though nothing was ever resolved, which made them feel distant from each other. Despite their difficulties, they both demonstrated a strong desire to work on their relationship in an effort to rediscover the emotional closeness that was present when they first became a couple.

Stage I: Cycle De-Escalation and the Influence of Culture

After an exploration of their history and of some details of their interactions, the therapist conceptualized the couple's problems as the manifestation of a pursue–withdraw pattern and the lack of a secure connection. The therapist reflected that when the couple got caught in this cycle, Scott felt inadequate, unsure of Sameera's love for him, and desperately afraid of losing her. She noted that he would pull back from Sameera out of fear and adopt a defensive posture in their interactions. Sameera, on the other hand, often felt alone, unimportant, and unloved. She expressed doubts about whether or not she could rely on Scott. The therapist underscored that when Sameera felt this way, she tended to express her anger and frustration toward Scott in an attempt to reengage him emotionally, which unfortunately only exacerbated the problem.

Cultural elements accentuated the impact and the rigidity of this problematic cycle. For example, Sameera confirmed our clinical experience with people from Middle Eastern countries when she explained that, in her culture, people regularly experience and express strong emotions. Sameera indicated that her family members and friends of Middle Eastern background understood intuitively that displays of intense affect were ephemeral phenomena that tended to dissipate once expressed openly. She said, "I can love you one day and be passionate, and the next day I want to kill you and divorce you. But I'm not serious. Once I get it out, it's over."

Scott, on the other hand, grew up in a predominantly White, upper-middle-class area of English Canada. As is typical of men in the North American majority culture, Scott did not generally express his intense emotions openly, nor was he comfortable in affectively charged situations. He worked hard to control and to regulate his strong feelings and those of others; he did not tend to ask directly for his emotional needs to be met. Thus, cultural norms surrounding displays of emotion and appropriate ways of meeting attachment needs had an enormous effect on Scott and Sameera's interactions: The more he stifled his feelings and withdrew, the more intense and critical her expressions of emotions became, and vice versa. They each acted according to the cultural templates that they knew.

For this reason, the therapist focused on helping Scott and Sameera recognize the cultural impact on their respective positions in the pursue–withdraw cycle. In addition to the usual Stage I tasks of creating a therapeutic alliance with both partners, and delineating the emotions and attachment needs underlying their behavior toward each other, she also spent a great deal of time reflecting the manner in which their respective cultures of origin influenced how they expressed and regulated their own emotions, how they dealt with each other's expressions of affect or lack thereof, and how they went about seeking the closeness that they needed from each other. For example, the therapist framed Sameera's displays of intense emotion as normal for people of Middle Eastern background, whose culture informs them that it is necessary and appropriate to experience and express strong feelings as a way of garnering the support and closeness they need from others. At the same time, the therapist portrayed Scott's attempts to quell his fear in the face of Sameera's strong feelings by withdrawing from her as a typical response for North American men, whose culture teaches them that it is important to remain strong and to solve problems in order to make their relationships work. True to the attachment perspective that defines EFT, the therapist emphasized that

Scott and Sameera's basic needs for safety, security, and a sense of the other partner's emotional presence were essentially the same, but they each went about fulfilling those needs within the couple in ways that actually created a distance between them. In their case, cultural differences added to the confusion and sense of loneliness common to couples entrenched in negative cycles of interaction.

One of the strengths of EFT is this capacity to integrate cultural information into the conceptualization of couples' difficulties without radically altering or abandoning the theoretical framework that explains and helps alleviate them. Culture becomes yet another element that shapes the individual and affects his or her behavior in the couple's attachment dance. Scott and Sameera's relationship started to improve once they recognized and began talking openly about their cycle, and about how they each felt constrained by their typical ways of responding to each other, which were the products of temperament, personal history, *and* culture. Once they achieved this de-escalation, Scott and Sameera moved into Stage II.

Stage II: Restructuring Interactions in Culturally Appropriate Ways

Couples must recognize and respond to their partners' vulnerabilities effectively in order to establish a secure bond. At this stage, it is essential that each partner identify his or her emotional needs and ask directly for them to be met in the relationship. This work constitutes Stage II of EFT. By the end of Stage I, Scott was beginning to express his fears and insecurities more openly and directly with the therapist's support and guidance. On a number of occasions, he said, "I'm fearful and insecure. When she gets so angry like that, when her emotions get really big and she attacks me, I can't come back from it. I guess I'm too sensitive so I just pull away." At the same time, Sameera was also starting to take a more vulnerable stance in the relationship. She began expressing how alone she felt and how much she relied on Scott for support ("I love and need you so much but you disappear so often!").

At this juncture, the therapist helped Scott deepen and talk in the session about his fears of losing Sameera and his sense of inadequacy. However, as often happens at this stage of EFT, this was at first difficult for Sameera to hear because she was not used to Scott talking about any feelings at all. When the therapist initially reflected Scott's sense of vulnerability and paraphrased his statements to this effect (e.g., "I feel like such a failure, so I get out of there as fast as I can"), Sameera maintained her aggressive stance and continued to criticize him. Therefore, before asking Scott to speak directly to Sameera about his fears and specific needs in the relationship, the therapist first had to help Sameera experience Scott's vulnerability as a sign of her great importance to him, and to help her understand that her intense expressions of criticism were actually preventing her from getting the support and comfort that she stated she was looking for in the relationship.

In order to accomplish this, the therapist first validated Sameera's experience and her reactions. She then framed Scott's expressions of fear in terms of a deeply rooted longing for Sameera, and speculated that it must be difficult for Sameera to hear or believe this because she was so used to Scott withdrawing from her. Once Sameera demonstrated openness to Scott's vulnerability, the therapist then directed Scott to speak to her directly about his emotions, needs, and attachment longings. The following exchange illustrates this process:

Therapist: It's hard for you, Sameera, to hear Scott talk about how he feels like such a failure sometimes. It's hard to take in that you're so important to him that he gets scared he'll lose you when he feels inadequate like that, so scared that he withdraws because he doesn't know what else to do (*Reframe*). You're not used to seeing that side of him; it's new. And when you do see this other side, well that's kind of scary for *you* because it's unknown. It's like you say to yourself, "How can he be there for me if he's so afraid?" Is that it?

Sameera: That's right. And then I just get afraid myself, so afraid of being abandoned *again*, that I start to get angry with him and I let him know it!

Therapist: Right. You show him that anger, and you use it to try to bring him back to where you are, to make sure he's there with you. And from what you've told me about your culture, it's perfectly normal that you let your strong feelings out as a way of getting what you need. You're not accustomed to that having such an impact on the people you're close to. Usually, you

	express your feelings and that's the end of it (*Validation*). But now you're hearing that it actually sometimes frightens Scott, it frightens him because you're so important to him and he wants so badly to be with you and to make things work (*Reflection of cultural elements in the couple's cycle; reframe*). But right now, he deals with that fear by moving away from you, which just makes it harder for you, doesn't it? It just makes you want to shake him even harder to let him know you're there. Your feelings of fear and anger get really big, really strong then, don't they?
Sameera:	Yes. (*pause; to Scott*) Is that true? Is that true what she said about me being so important?
Scott (*tentatively*):	Of course. (*turns to therapist*) I just want to be there but sometimes I don't know how. And it's hard for me to be there when I feel like no matter what I do, it's no good. I'm just a failure.
Therapist:	Can you turn to Sameera and tell her that, Scott? Can you turn to her, right now, and say "You're so important to me and I want so badly to be there for you. It scares me to think that I might lose you because I'm not good enough. I need to feel that you love me too. Then I can be there."
Scott (*to Sameera with tears in his eyes*):	You're the most important thing to me and I want to do everything in my power to take care of you. But it's hard for me to do that when I feel like I'm no good. I get scared. I need you too. Can we be there for each other?
Sameera (*tenderly*):	Oh . . . Yes. I realize now that all of this fear and sensitivity, it's because I'm so special to you, aren't I? I don't usually see that, but now I do.

This excerpt illustrates the important change events of withdrawer reengagement (Scott) and blamer softening (Sameera). Sameera began to perceive Scott's vulnerability as a sign of her importance, and started to understand that she would receive the support she needed from him if she stopped criticizing him and took the risk of showing her own vulnerabilities and asking for her needs to be met. In the sessions that followed, the therapist helped Sameera to deepen and express her own attachment fears to Scott and to ask him from a position of vulnerability to be more supportive and emotionally present. Sameera's concerns about abandonment stemmed from her stressful experiences as an immigrant when she was a young girl, along with the basic fear of emotional abandonment common to all humanity according to attachment theory. These notions guided the therapist's questioning during the Stage II sessions. When Sameera approached Scott directly from a position of vulnerability, he was able to reassure and comfort her instead of withdrawing. The therapist also helped each partner to recognize the impact on their relationship of the typical ways of expressing and regulating emotions that they acquired in their respective cultures. She helped Scott learn to recognize when he was "shutting off and shutting down" in order not to feel, as North American men of European descent tend to do, and the effect this had of isolating Sameera and preventing her from feeling close to him. The therapist helped Sameera identify when her emotions were becoming intense and critical, and how this alienated Scott at the very moments when she needed him the most. At the time of writing, the couple was preparing to move into Stage III of EFT.

Tips for Clinicians

The case of Scott and Sameera illustrates the importance of considering the influence of culture when conducting EFT for couples. In order for this therapy to be effective for couples from minority groups, or for couples in which the partners have different cultural backgrounds, it is essential for therapists to ask the question, "How, in this cultural context, do people generally go about meeting their needs?" This awareness of culture-specific ways of acquiring necessary emotional support from significant others, and of expressing and dealing with the strong emotions that characterize attachment relationships, facilitates a solid understanding of couples' cycles. Such understanding, in turn, permits the therapist to identify appropriate interventions, and to adjust the pace of therapy if necessary.

In the case of Scott and Sameera, for example, the therapist first had to recognize the cultural elements that were playing a role in the exacerbation of the couple's difficulties, then to reflect and validate each partner's responses as products, in part, of their cultural background, and finally to take these cultural dimensions into account when utilizing EFT interventions. The therapist in this case spent a great deal of time reflecting and validating Sameera's emotional responses, all the while respectfully indicating that they were reinforcing the couple's negative interaction pattern. She worked hard to help Sameera access and express her fears and vulnerabilities, and made sure not to ask Scott to risk speaking directly to her about his own until Sameera understood them to represent his deep love and longing for her. The key element in this case was a concentrated effort on the therapist's part to help each partner see and respond to the other's vulnerability. This involved a great deal of work assisting them with the processing of their emotions and finding appropriate words to express their needs to each other. Once again, this entailed moving at a slower pace than the one to which the therapist was accustomed.

EFT and Ethnicity, Oppression, and Privilege

Clinicians must understand and actively acknowledge the legacy of racism, sexism, and classism, both historical and current, in order to provide effective services to intercultural couples (Bobes & Bobes, 2005). EFT, with its systemic underpinnings, is well suited as a therapeutic approach to deal with such issues. EFT therapists, as well as other clinicians, therefore have a responsibility to increase their awareness not only about biases toward certain groups and systems of privilege at the level of society, but also their own biases, including prejudices and stereotypes (Hays, 2001). Furthermore, interactions between the therapist and each member of the couple exist within a cultural context. These interactions will vary depending on the race, class, culture, level of education, and gender of the therapist and clients.

Multiple scenarios are therefore possible, each with its own inherent issues of power, oppression, and privilege (Bhugra & De Silva, 2000). For example, therapy with a couple in which the woman is Filipino, the husband is an American soldier, and the therapist is White American will present its unique set of expectations and problems. Likewise, an African American therapist conducting therapy with a Latino man and a White woman will create a different set of issues. We encourage readers to consult the numerous books that have been published on the topic of multiple identities and their impact on the therapeutic process (e.g., Hays, 2001; Robinson, 2005) for more detailed information on this important issue.

Implications for Educators, Students, and Future Research

In our experience, it is important for EFT supervisors to ensure that students move more slowly through the steps of EFT than they may be initially inclined to. Often, students' enthusiasm for the process of EFT and their sincere desire to help couples improve their relationships drive them to move too quickly through the steps and to employ certain interventions (e.g., enactments) before the couple is ready. Respect for the timing of interventions becomes all the more crucial when conducting EFT with couples in which one or both partners are members of an ethnic minority group, or when cultural differences between them play a clear role in their attachment struggle. Educators, supervisors, and students must therefore be acutely aware of the potential influence of cultural factors on the development of negative interaction cycles in couples, and of culturally defined ways of dealing with and expressing strong emotion. Such awareness will help ensure that EFT interventions are applied appropriately.

At present, the basic text on EFT for couples (Johnson, 2004) has been translated into Chinese, Korean, and Latin American Spanish. Practitioners from all over the globe currently teach EFT and conduct it with couples of various cultural origins. It will therefore be important in the future to examine systematically how to apply EFT to members of minority cultures. It would be interesting to discover, for instance, whether supplementary steps or interventions are necessary in the majority of cases, and whether these could be applied effectively to couples of diverse ethnic backgrounds. Research in this area is currently lacking and would prove useful.

Topics for Reflection

Although providing couple therapy to intercultural couples is a rich and rewarding experience, it is essential that couple therapists acquire the necessary multicultural competency skills before embarking in this work. Since Sue, Arredondo, and McDavis's seminal paper in 1992, there has been a proliferation of clinical research in the area of multicultural therapy and multicultural competencies. In addition to over 500 articles on the topic (Trimble, 2003), there are two comprehensive handbooks dealing specifically with multicultural competencies (Pope-Davis & Coleman, 1997; Pope-Davis, Coleman, Liu, & Toporek, 2003). The various models of cultural competence are essentially based on the following three dimensions: (1) cultural awareness—a sensitivity and understanding of one's own culture; (2) cultural knowledge—acquiring knowledge of other culture's beliefs, values and practices; and (3) cultural skills—developing the skills to interact effectively with diverse cultures.

Conclusion

EFT for couples targets what appear to be universal aspects of marital harmony and marital distress: emotions and attachment needs as they affect partners' responses. EFT is both specific and systemic; those who practice it respect and validate individual differences and they recognize how such differences affect interpersonal interactions. Cultural elements can play an important role in the development and exacerbation of problematic cycles of couple interaction. EFT therapists must take these cultural influences into account when assessing and treating couples in order to ensure the efficacy of the intervention. This normally involves careful attention to culture-specific rules about the expression of emotion and the fulfillment of fundamental needs for safety and security.

Additional Resources

To provide culturally relevant and culturally sensitive EFT interventions to intercultural couples, clinicians will need to develop competence in the above dimensions and to familiarize themselves with current ethical guidelines endorsed by the American Psychological Association (2003) and by other professional organizations (e.g., Canadian Psychological Association, 2000). In addition, Hays's (2001) book, *Addressing Cultural Complexities in Practice,* and Robinson's (2005) volume, *The Convergence of Race, Ethnicity, and Gender: Multiple Identities in Counseling,* are extremely useful for any clinician interested in ensuring the cultural relevance and sensitivity of their interventions. Van IJzendoorn and Sagi's (1999) chapter in the *Handbook of Attachment* on cross-cultural aspects of attachment is also relevant for those who wish to apply EFT to couples with diverse backgrounds.

There are also many resources available for those interested in learning EFT for couples. The basic text is Johnson's (2004) book, *Creating Connection: Emotionally Focused Couple Therapy* (2nd ed.). More recently, Johnson and colleagues published *Becoming an Emotionally Focused Couple Therapist: The*

Workbook (Johnson et al., 2005), which is full of specific instructions and exercises and complements the basic text nicely. Information about other resources, including additional publications on EFT, EFT training tapes, and a DVD of a five-day EFT externship, is available on the Center for Emotionally Focused Therapy Web site (www.eft.ca). Sue Johnson has also recently published *Hold Me Tight* (Johnson, 2008), a self-help guide for couples based on decades of EFT research and clinical experience.

References

Ainsworth, M. D. S. (1967). *Infancy in Uganda: Infant care and the growth of love.* Baltimore, MD: Johns Hopkins University Press.

Al-Issa, I. (1997). Ethnicity, immigration, and psychopathology. In I. Al-Issa & M. Tousignant (Eds.), *Ethnicity, immigration, and psychopathology* (pp. 3–15). New York: Plenum.

Al-Issa, I., & Tousignant, M. (Eds.). (1997). *Ethnicity, immigration, and psychopathology.* New York: Plenum.

Bartholomew, K., & Horowitz, L. (1991). Attachment styles among young adults. *Journal of Personality and Social Psychology, 61,* 226–244.

Beiser, M., & Hyman, I. (1997). Southeast Asian refugees in Canada. In I. Al-Issa & M. Tousignant (Eds.), *Ethnicity, immigration, and psychopathology* (pp. 35–56). New York: Plenum.

Bhugra, D., & De Silva, P. (2000). Couple therapy across cultures. *Sexual and Relationship Therapy, 15,* 183–192.

Biever, J. L., Bobele, M., & North, M.-W. (2002). Therapy with intercultural couples: A postmodern approach. In S. Palmer (Ed.), *Multicultural counseling: A reader* (pp. 73–81). Thousand Oaks, CA: Sage.

Bowlby, J. (1969). *Attachment and loss volume 1: Attachment.* London: Pelican.

Bradley, B., & Johnson, S. M. (2005). An integrative contemporary approach. In M. Harway (Ed.), *Handbook of couples therapy* (pp. 179–193). Hoboken, NJ: Wiley.

Bratter, J. L., & Eschbach, K. (2005). Race/ethnic differences in nonspecific psychological distress: Evidence from the National Health Interview Survey. *Social Science Quarterly, 86,* 620–644.

Cloutier, P. F., Manion, I. G., Gordon Walker, J., & Johnson, S. M. (2002). Emotionally focused interventions for couples with chronically ill children: A 2-year follow-up. *Journal of Marital and Family Therapy, 28,* 391–398.

Crohn, J. (1998). Intercultural couples. In M. McGoldrick (Ed.), *Re-visioning family therapy* (pp. 295–308). New York: Guilford Press.

Dessaulles, A., Johnson, S. M., & Denton, W. H. (2003). Emotion-focused therapy for couples in the treatment of depression: A pilot study. *American Journal of Family Therapy, 31,* 345–353.

Ekman, P. (2003). *Emotions revealed.* New York: Henry Holt.

Falikov, C. G. (1995). Cross-cultural marriages. In N. S. Jacobson & A. S. Gurman (Eds.), *Clinical handbook of couple therapy* (pp. 231–246). New York: Guilford.

Frame, M. W. (2004). The challenges of intercultural marriage: Strategies for pastoral care. *Pastoral Psychology, 52,* 219–232.

Gaines, S. O., & Agnew, C. R. (2003). Relationship maintenance in intercultural couples: An interdependent analysis. In D. J. Canary & M. Dainton (Eds.), *Maintaining relationships through communication: Relational, contextual, and cultural variations* (pp. 231–253). Mahwah, NJ: Lawrence Erlbaum.

Gaines, S. O., Granrose, C. S., Rios, D. I., Garcia, B. F., Youn, M. S. P., Farris, K. R., & Bledsoe, K. L. (1999). Patterns of attachment and responses to accommodative dilemmas among interethnic/interracial couples. *Journal of Social and Personal Relationships, 16,* 275–285.

Gaines, S. O., & Ickes, W. (1997). Perspectives on interracial relationships. In S. Duck (Ed.), *Handbook of personal relationships* (pp. 197–220). Chichester, UK: Wiley.

Gaines, S. O., & Liu, J. H. (2000). Multicultural/multiracial relationships. In C. Hendrick & S. S. Hendrick (Eds.), *Close relationships: A sourcebook* (pp. 97–108). Thousand Oaks, CA: Sage.

Gaudet, S., Clément, R., & Deuzeman, K. (2005). Daily hassles, ethnic identity and psychological adjustment among Lebanese-Canadians. *International Journal of Psychology, 40,* 157–168.

Gordon Walker, J., Johnson, S., Manion, I., & Cloutier, P. (1996). Emotionally focused marital intervention for couples with chronically ill children. *Journal of Consulting and Clinical Psychology, 64,* 1029–1036.

Gottman, J. M. (1991). Predicting the longitudinal course of marriages. *Journal of Marital and Family Therapy, 17,* 3–7.

Gottman, J. M., & Driver, J. L. (2005). Dysfunctional marital conflict and everyday marital interaction. *Journal of Divorce and Remarriage, 43,* 63–78.

Hays, P. A. (2001). *Addressing cultural complexities in practice: A framework for clinicians and counselors.* Washington, DC: American Psychological Association.

Hazan, C., & Shaver, P. (1987). Conceptualizing romantic love as an attachment process. *Journal of Personality and Social Psychology, 52,* 511–524.

Ho, M. K. (1990). *Intermarried couples in therapy.* Springfield, IL: Charles Thomas.

Hsu, J. (2001). Marital therapy for intercultural couples. In W. S. Tseng & J. Stresetzer (Eds.), *Culture and psychotherapy: A guide to clinical practice* (pp. 225–242). Washington, DC: American Psychiatric Press.

Huston, T. L., Caughlin, J. P., Houts, R. M., Smith, S. E., & George, L. J. (2001). The connubial crucible: Newlywed years as predictors of marital delight, distress, and divorce. *Journal of Personality and Social Psychology, 80,* 237–252.

Hwang, W. (2006). The psychotherapy adaptation and modification framework: Application to Asian Americans. *American Psychologist, 61,* 702–715.

James, P. (1991). Effects of a communication training component added to an emotionally focused couples therapy. *Journal of Marital and Family Therapy, 17,* 263–276.

Johnson, S. (2008). *Hold me tight: Seven conversations for a lifetime of love.* New York: Little, Brown and Company.

Johnson, S. M. (2004). *The practice of emotionally focused couple therapy: Creating connection* (2nd ed.). New York: Brunner-Routledge.

Johnson, S. M., Bradley, B., Furrow, J., Lee, A., Palmer, G., Tilley, D., & Woolley, S. (2005). *Becoming an emotionally focused couple therapist: The workbook.* New York: Brunner-Routledge.

Johnson, S .M., & Greenman, P. S. (2006). The path to a secure bond: Emotionally focused couple therapy. *Journal of Clinical Psychology: In Session, 62,* 597–609.

Johnson, S. M., Hunsley, J., Greenberg, L., & Schindler, D. (1999). Emotionally focused couples therapy: Status and challenges. *Clinical Psychology: Science and Practice, 6,* 67–79.

Johnson, S. M., & Whiffen, V. E. (1999). Made to measure: Adapting emotionally focused couple therapy to partners' attachment styles. *Clinical Psychology: Science and Practice, 6,* 366–381.

Killian, K. D. (2001). Reconstituting racial histories and identities: The narratives of interracial couples. *Journal of Marital and Family Therapy, 27,* 27–42.

Kowal, J., Johnson, S. M., & Lee, A. (2003). Chronic illness in couples: A case for Emotionally Focused Therapy. *Journal of Marital and Family Therapy, 29,* 299–310.

MacIntosh, H. B., & Johnson, S. M. (in press). Emotionally focused therapy for couples and childhood sexual abuse survivors. *Journal of Marital and Family Therapy.*

Molina, B., Estrada, D., & Burnett, J. (2004). Cultural communities: Challenges and opportunities in the creation of "happily ever after" stories of intercultural couplehood. *The Family Journal: Counseling and Therapy for Couples and Families, 12,* 139–147.

Negy, C., & Snyder, D. K. (1997). Ethnicity and acculturation: Assessing Mexican-American couples' relationships using the Marital Satisfaction Inventory—Revised. *Psychological Assessment, 9,* 414–421.

Oberg, K. (1960). Cultural shock: Adjustment to new cultural environments. *Practical Anthropology, 7,* 177–182.

Pope-Davis, D. B., & Coleman, H. (1997). *Multicultural counseling competencies: Assessment, education and training, and supervision.* Thousand Oaks, CA: Sage.

Pope-Davis, D. B., Coleman, H., Liu, W. M., & Toporek, R. L. (Eds.). (2003). *Handbook of multicultural competencies in counseling and psychology.* Thousand Oaks, CA: Sage.

Putnam, R. D. (2000). *Bowling alone: The collapse and revival of American community.* New York: Simon & Schuster.

Robinson, T. L. (2005). *The convergence of race, ethnicity, and gender: Multiple identities in counseling.* Upper Saddle River, NJ: Pearson.

Rothbaum, F., Weisz, J., Pott, M., Miyake, K., & Morelli, G. (2000). Attachment and culture. *American Psychologist, 55,* 1093–1104.

Silove, D., Manicavasagar, V., & Coelle, M. (2005). PTSD, depression, and acculturation. *Intervention: International Journal of Mental Health, Psychosocial Work & Counselling in Areas of Armed Conflict, 3,* 46–50.

Steffen, P. R., Smith, T. B., & Larson, M. (2006). Acculturation to Western society as a risk factor for high blood pressure: A meta-analytic review. *Psychosomatic Medicine, 68,* 386–397.

Sue, D. W., Arredondo, P., & McDavis, R. (1992). Multicultural counseling competencies and standards: A call to the profession. *Journal of Counseling and Development, 70,* 477–486.

Sullivan, C., & Cottone, R. R. (2006). Culturally based couple therapy and intercultural relationships: A review of the literature. *The Family Journal: Counseling and Therapy for Couples and Families, 14,* 221–225.

Thomas, V., Karis, T. A., & Wetchler, J. L. (Eds.). (2003). *Clinical issues with interracial couples: Theories and research.* New York: Haworth.

Tousignant, M. (1997). Refugees and immigrants in Quebec. In I. Al-Issa & M. Tousignant (Eds.), *Ethnicity, immigration, and psychopathology* (pp. 57–70). New York: Plenum.

Trimble, J. E. (2003). Cultural sensitivity and cultural competence. In M. Prinstein & M. Patterson (Eds.), *The portable mentor: Expert guide to a successful career in psychology.* New York: Kluwer Academic/Plenum.

Troy, A. B., Lewis-Smith, J., & Laurenceau, J. (2006). Interracial and intraracial romantic relationships: The search for differences in satisfaction, conflict, and attachment style. *Journal of Social and Personal Relationships, 23,* 65–80.

Tseng, W., McDermott, J. F., & Maretzki, T. W. (Eds.). (1977). *Adjustment in intercultural marriage.* Honolulu, HI: University Press of Hawaii.

van IJzendoorn, M. H., & Sagi, A. (1999). Cross-cultural patterns of attachment: Universal and contextual dimensions. In J. Cassidy & P. R. Shaver (Eds.), *Handbook of attachment: Theory, research, and clinical applications* (pp. 713–734). New York: Guilford Press.

van IJzendoorn, M. H., & Sagi, A. (2001). Cultural blindness or selective inattention? *American Psychologist, 56,* 824–825.

Waite, L. J., Bachrack, C., Hindin, M., Thomson, E., & Thornton, A. (Eds.). (2000). *The ties that bind: Perspectives on marriage and cohabitation.* New York: Aldine de Gruyter.

Waldman, K., & Rubalcava, L. (2005). Psychotherapy with intercultural couples: A contemporary psychodynamic approach. *American Journal of Psychotherapy, 59,* 227–245.

Wang, C. D. C., & Mallinckrodt, B. S. (2006). Differences between Taiwanese and U.S. cultural beliefs about ideal adult attachment. *Journal of Counseling Psychology, 53,* 192–204.

Winter, K., & Young, M. Y. (1998). Biopsychosocial considerations in refugee mental health. In S. Kazarian & D. R. Evans (Eds.), *Cultural clinical psychology: Theory, research, and practice* (pp. 348–376). New York: Oxford University Press.

Nine

Brief Strategic Family Therapy

Treating the Hispanic Couple Subsystem in the Context of Family, Ecology, and Acculturative Stress

Olga E. Hervis, Kathleen A. Shea,
and Silvia M. Kaminsky

B rief Strategic Family Therapy (BSFT) is nationally recognized by the U.S. Center for Substance Abuse Prevention and the National Institute on Drug Abuse, both in the U.S. Department of Health and Human Services, and the Office of Juvenile Justice Delinquency Prevention in the Department of Justice. In 2000, it was identified by the Center for Substance Abuse Prevention (CSAP) as a Model Program at its Exemplary Substance Abuse Prevention Awards Ceremony. BSFT was developed in response to the needs of the Hispanic immigrant community in South Florida, and has undergone extensive refinement and testing over the past 30 years. Today, it is being replicated and tested in service-delivery systems across the nation, working with diverse minority as well as mainstream communities. BSFT is based on a belief in systemic contextualism, which recognizes that individuals and couples are part of a larger family system, which is in turn a part of a larger social system. At the broadest level, BSFT was developed to identify and incorporate in treatment those cultural factors that are intrinsically related to the couple's problems, as well as those that can be used as a resource for their recovery.

The authors' backgrounds include research, teaching, and clinical practice over a long period of time. Olga E. Hervis, MSW, LCSW, is the co-author and co-developer of BSFT. The model was initially developed under the auspices of the University of Miami Center for Family Studies, which Ms. Hervis co-founded in 1974. While with the Center, she conducted research, developed the therapeutic models, and designed training programs for clinicians. In 2003, she founded the Family Therapy Training Institute of Miami as a private effort to disseminate the models and clinical findings of 35 years of research and practice in this field. Silvia Kaminsky, MS, LMFT, CAP, is the first Master Trainer in BSFT. She has conducted training throughout the United States in the model, as well as providing clinical supervision for BSFT trainees. She maintains a private practice and currently serves on the Board of Directors of the American Association for Marriage and Family Therapy (AAMFT). Kathleen A. Shea, PhD, is an administrator with a background in research and evaluation. Her particular interest is organization development and large-scale change processes.

Setting the Context for Treating Hispanic Couples

The Hispanic population in the United States has become the largest ethnic minority group in this country. According to U.S. Census data, the total population grew by 13% from 1990 to 2000, while the Hispanic population grew by 58%, now comprising over 13% of the nation's population (U.S. Census, 2003). Hispanics have migrated to the United States from Central and South America, with the largest migration coming from Mexico, Puerto Rico, and Cuba. This immigration process profoundly affects families. Many families immigrate in stages. For example, it is not uncommon for one mate to come to the United States alone to get established and then be joined by his or her partner, children, and others. For many families, this process is protracted, and they are often separated for years. Partners are continually disappointed when confronted with significant emotional detachment and relentless stress. Treatment often involves reestablishing bonds and alliances, creating new and more functional structural arrangements in response to adaptation needs, and bridging the internal acculturation gaps that often accompany the family crisis.

In our work with parenting couples, BSFT is dedicated to the task of executing structural changes in a manner that preserves the family by balancing change, growth, stability, and consistency. Due to the BSFT therapist's focus on changing interactional *processes*, while enabling the clients to manage their own specific *content(s)*, the couple's idiosyncratic definition of how this balance is to be achieved is protected. BSFT recognizes the influence of cultural factors in the development and maintenance of interactional dysfunction (e.g., differential levels of acculturation, separation of parents for several years, and so on).

The work of BSFT with the couple subsystem, within the framework of the family's therapy, is crucial to the efficacy of the model. Children who are "out of control" reflect parents who are "not in control." Typically, the loss of parental control is a consequence of the dysfunctionality of the parental subsystem. Among Hispanics in the context of American life, this inadequacy is one of the chief consequences of the hardships that accompany migration and adaptation. The normal challenges of maintaining relationships and adjusting to life-cycle changes are exacerbated by the stressors of acculturation imbalances between mates, immigration, separation, ecological adjustments, and losses. The couple's competency is injured; the work needed is to repair it. The goal is to help couples adaptively address these stressors, reconstruct the couple subsystem, empower mates in their interactions with larger social systems, and resolve the important underlying vulnerabilities to these stressors.

The remainder of this chapter introduces Brief Strategic Family Therapy, a nationally recognized evidence-based practice. We present the theoretical foundations for BSFT, discuss relevant research data, present BSFT treatment interventions through case vignettes, and finally discuss the BSFT training program for clinicians.

Research and Literature

Although clinicians have long been encouraged to include family members in treating clients with a variety of disorders, few specific couple-family therapies exist, and outcome research is limited. Even less information is available for treating Hispanic couples within the family subsystem, yet because of strong family ties among Hispanic couples, inclusion of family members in treating this population increases the likelihood of meaningful and enduring change.

Acculturation and gender roles are important factors in treating Hispanic couples. Miranda, Bilot, Puluso, Berman, and Van Meek (2006) describe how acculturation has evolved from a one-dimensional to a multidimensional construct, and how families mediate between acculturation and health for Latinos. Traditional gender roles in Hispanic culture also affect marriages and families (Skogrand, Hatch, & Singh, 2004). Few evidenced-based models exist that explicitly address how perceptions of ethnicity influence the therapeutic process. BSFT and its accompanying training model were designed to address the disparity in perceptions of ethnic and cultural differences between practitioners and couples in distress. Halford (2001) calls for a "new model of couple's therapy" that enables couples to help themselves. In BSFT, the therapist actively directs couples to create individual, interactional, and contextual changes themselves.

Brief Strategic Family Therapy

BSFT is best articulated around three central constructs: system, structure/organization, and strategy (Szapocznik, Hervis, & Schwartz, 2003). From this perspective, in BSFT couples are viewed as subsystems of the larger family organism. This organism comprises parts (individuals and subsystems) that are interdependent and interrelated. The behaviors of these parts synergistically work together to organize the family system. The set of repetitive patterns of interactions that are idiosyncratic to a family is called *structure*. In BSFT, the couple dyad is seen as a subsystem with its own unique interactive and complementary patterns that organize the couple's structural arrangement. Partners are engaged in repetitive circular patterns of action–reaction that give style and form to their relationship. If this circularity is maladaptive, symptoms emerge within the dyad. The goal of BSFT is to change these symptom-producing, repetitive interactions within the couple, between the couple and other family subsystems, and between the couple and their social context. This emphasis on the nature of social interactions between partners in a couple is referred to as the couple's *process*. BSFT focuses on changing process. The third and strategic theoretical foundation of BSFT is that interventions are practical, problem-focused, and deliberate.

Our earlier studies in value-orientation (Szapocznik, Scopetta, & King [Hervis], 1978; Szapocznik et al., 1986) and treatment expectations among Hispanics pointed us in this direction of a treatment model that is family-oriented, in which therapists take an active, directive, and present-oriented leadership role. We suggested that the problems within Hispanic families needed to be examined in the context of immigrant families that had been immersed in mainstream American culture. Our approach to this early challenge was consistent with a movement within psychology that suggests behavior is best understood in the social context within which it occurs. This *contextualism* view is concerned with the interaction between the organism and its environment (Bronfenbrenner, 1979, 1987, 1988).

For parenting couples experiencing acculturative stress, normal family processes combined with acculturation processes result in an exaggerated distancing and disengagement, and an increase in conflict. BSFT can address these powerful stressors that impact couple functioning (Santisteban, Muir-Malcolm, Mitrani, & Szapocznik, 2002) and is consistent with a strong family orientation found in research with Hispanics (Marin, 1993; Sabogal, Marin, Otero-Sabogal, Marin, & Perez-Stable, 1987). Some of the most fundamental aspects of successful couple interactions include communication, cohesion, alliance, and congruous parenting practices. These aspects of a couple's life are notably affected by stressors such as migration, disruption of support systems, discrimination and social inequalities, separation, and acculturation disparities.

Brief Strategic Family Therapy: An Exemplary Model Approach to Working With Hispanic Parenting Couples

Hispanic immigrant couples often become adversaries around a struggle that is culturally flavored: Americanism vs. Hispanicism. For a Hispanic immigrant couple living in a bicultural context, recurring processes converge that create acculturative conflict between them. Each partner is striving for personal adaptation and survival, while trying to preserve systemic integrity. In this scenario, a discrepancy develops between tenacious adherence to Hispanic cultural values for cohesion control, and rejection of

Hispanicity in favor of successful social adjustment. The additive effects of individual rates of adaptation and differences in acculturation result in increased conflict and emotional alienation between the partners.

To effectively work within this paradigm, BSFT first relies on accurate assessment of the interactions that are giving rise to or maintaining the dysfunctional behavior. Assessment is based on direct observation of the couple interacting in the session. This is called an *enactment*. Enacted interactional sequences take place when the therapist is able to effectively *join* with the couple. The therapist then diagnoses the interactions in terms of distribution of power, imbalances, openness and directness of communication, alliances, triangulations, developmental stage, boundaries, negativism, and conflict resolution patterns (Szapocznik et al., 2003). The therapist then formulates a treatment plan that is specifically designed to reverse the maladaptive interactions and to produce their functional counterparts. To this end, BSFT relies on a set of treatment strategies that include joining, highlighting, reframing, and tasking. The successful performance of directed tasks is achieved through careful *micromanagement* of the interactional sequences that emerge between the mates while in the process of doing the task.

Joining

Joining refers to both the actions of the therapist as well as the nature of the therapeutic relationship that must be achieved between the therapist and the couple. It gets the couple ready for change, and alleviates the normal resistance to change. There are hurdles to overcome in achieving a "joined to the couple" position, which are exacerbated when working with Hispanic immigrant couples. This joining task demands a high level of cultural sensitivity on the part of the therapist.

The therapist needs to understand and expect that the Hispanic couple comes to treatment with unacceptable feelings of guilt and anxiety, and in a defensive stance. From both the man's *machismo*[2] standpoint and the woman's *marianismo* perspective, having to come to therapy is experienced as a failure. They expect criticism and labeling. Consequently, their position is one of defensiveness, secrecy, and even a reluctance to participate. Equally important is the fact that it is culturally inappropriate to "lay out any dirty laundry." In all, the Hispanic couple is particularly reticent to display spousal conflict, especially as these conflicts may be related to problems with their children.

To overcome these hurdles, BSFT offers a set of joining strategies that ensure a working therapeutic alliance. The therapist does not challenge the existing structure, or presenting frames, but rather offers support and empathy to both spouses. The therapist must show respect to both, and to their cultural orientations, even when these may differ, and must remain open to each spouse's definition of the problem and agendas for change.

Research evidence suggests that empathy and respect are at the core of effective clinical work (Duncan, Miller, & Hubble, 1998; Duncan, Solovey, & Rusk, 1992). Similarly, a respectful and empathic stance is basic to therapeutic cross-cultural sensitivity (Jordan, 2000). A trustworthy engagement of both partners with the therapist is a necessary, basic, and essential condition of therapeutic success. In the case of couples where each partner has acculturated at a different rate, achieving and maintaining a joined position to both mates can become a challenging therapeutic task. Because values and styles, as they refer to acculturation, are viewed by, BSFT as *content*, the therapeutic dilemma is resolved by focusing on each partner's *process*. For example, Clara, who is more acculturated, may be arguing with Miguel about allowing their daughter to go to a school dance without a family chaperone. In the process of this arguing, the therapist notes that they interrupt each other constantly, that other tangential topics are brought up, and that they criticize each other. The BSFT therapist will empathize with their mutual commitment to their daughter's well-being and highlight that interruptions, diffusions, and finger-pointing are not helping them to come to a mutually satisfactory solution. She will then ask them to continue their discussion while making sure that they are listening carefully to each other, staying on the topic at hand, and refraining from criticism. At the end of each successfully completed task, the therapist will offer positive reinforcement and ask the partners to do the same for each other.

Highlighting

The purpose of this intensification is to create a scenario of STOP, LOOK, and LISTEN that will bring a specific transaction into focus that would otherwise be lost in the stream of repetitive activity that underlines the couple's processes. The first order of business in signaling a need for change is to develop a heightened awareness of what is occurring. Along with this increased awareness, the couple must perceive their interactions in a new way, one that allows for a "different" experience of what is happening.

As we go through life, we most often move on "autopilot." We increase our tolerance and decrease our sensitivity. We especially anesthetize that which is painful or in any way uncomfortable or intolerable. We shroud ourselves with a blanket of "awareness anesthesia" in order to continue to operate in the usual manner. This anesthesia, this increased tolerance, reduces or eliminates our motivation for change; it makes change a concept, and not a need. It is distressing to admit that people are most often motivated to change by the experience of pain or discomfort, rather than by the lure of improvement. For these reasons, BSFT signals the beginning of a change operation by a therapeutic process referred to as *highlighting*, which is a form of affective manipulation. It is the drama in the therapy. It intensifies a transaction so that it is felt or experienced differently by both spouses. Its aim is to remove the anesthesia, decrease the tolerance, and take each spouse to a place of awareness. It is then that they are open and ready to try something new.

Intensity can be created by the following behaviors:

- Forcefulness that challenges the couple's threshold
- Changing of affect, tone, or volume
- Repetition—the same theme in different contexts or in different ways
- Extending the normal duration of a transaction
- Word choice—crisp phrasing, powerful words ("You sound like attorneys in a courtroom rather than concerned parents.")

Therapists too often dilute their interventions and render them ineffective by overqualifying, apologizing, rambling, explaining, or lecturing. Couples often have to be "hit over the head" in order to get their attention, much more than individual clients, since they know how to trigger each other and set off a series of sequential interactions that serve to cover up or obscure the underlying significant issues.

Reframing

To "reframe," the therapist offers the couple a "different" perspective (frame) of their behaviors, views, and feelings. The new frames offer an alternative explanation or understanding of what the couple has perceived in their lives, and must support new actions and reactions that the therapist needs to elicit from the couple. For example, an angry husband may be reframed as intense and passionate in his concerns, while his passive wife may be reframed as sad, overwhelmed, and needing a lot of support. New frames must be presented in a convincing manner and "sold" to the couple. Then they can be used to elicit new behaviors, and thus create change in the interactions. The therapist increases motivation and redirects behavior by first convincing the couple that "something is different from the way they have been seeing it." Simply telling people that what they are doing is wrong does not produce change: Often it only increases resistance and distances the client from the therapist. The goal of BSFT reframing is not to educate or to gain insight, but rather to facilitate behavioral change by changing perspectives. Therefore, these new perspectives must be congruent with the new behaviors being elicited.

The challenges of reframing when working with Hispanic couples are augmented by the couples' increased resistance to change given the threats to the stability of their relationship that they have already experienced as a result of acculturation, migration, separation, and adaptation to a new milieu. A central and common "reframe" that often underlies all therapy with Hispanic couples relates to the issue of acculturation and adaptation. To address this issue, BSFT encourages the concept of *biculturalism.* The goal of biculturalism is to help couples retain their ethnic identity and traditions while simultaneously embracing new adaptations to the patterns of the host, mainstream culture. The central theme in this reframe is that there is no need for a struggle between Hispanicity and mainstream culture, but rather that there are many ways to "keep the old, while adding the new."

In working with Hispanic couples, we have consistently observed that high levels of negativity interfere with effective problem solving and communication. *Reframing* is most effective in transforming negative interactions into positive ones. Some commonly used reframes include anger as pain or loss; highly conflictive relationships as close or passionate; crises as opportunities; feeling overwhelmed as a signal that one must recharge one's batteries; impulsiveness as spontaneity; and insensitivity as "telling it like it is."

The BSFT Change Equation

In BSFT, change is effected by the trifold process of changing affect (highlighting), changing cognition (reframing), and changing behaviors (restructuring tasks) (Szapocznik et al., 2003). Because BSFT is a systemic therapy predicated on the principles of circularity and feedback processes, the order and manner in which these therapeutic maneuvers reinforce, support, stimulate, and complement each other is not important. Changes in any one yield changes in the other two. BSFT views changes in all three orders of human experience as essential to bringing about successful and permanent transactional changes.

Tasking

The use of tasks is central to all BSFT work. It is the mechanism by which enactments are elicited, and more importantly it is the vehicle for the creation of new and more functional interactions. Tasks are used both inside and outside the counseling sessions as the basic tool for orchestrating change. Tasks serve as the vehicle through which therapists choreograph opportunities for the couple to behave differently and more effectively, thus creating new and healthier interactions and increasing their level of mastery and sense of competence.

Everything we ask a person to do is a task: "Please have a seat," "Tell me what brought you here," "Ask your wife to please let you finish without interrupting," "Talk together about what will be the curfew for your daughter and come to an agreement about it." As a general rule, the BSFT therapist must assign transactional change tasks to be performed within the therapy session, where he or she has an opportunity to observe, assist, and facilitate the successful conduct of the task (micromanage).

Micromanaging requires careful observations of emerging processes that prevent the task from being accomplished. Then the therapist directs subtasks to ensure final success. For example, "Decide together what will be the consequences if your son skips school again. Come to an agreement about that" (task). A diffusion occurs: "Don't change the topic, stay on this for now" (subtask). The mother states that Dad is just being mean and vindictive in his intentions: "Ask your wife what makes her distrust your intentions and help her to trust you again" (subtask). The mother is somewhat reticent to be so firm: "Help your wife with her feelings until you two can come to a plan that feels comfortable to both" (subtask). This micromanagement and subtasking process continues until the initial task is completed. Success is then followed by positive reinforcement given both by the therapist to the partners and by one partner to the other. The therapist should not try to accomplish too much in a single leap, instead moving step by step with the couple.

Hope for the Best, but Be Prepared for the Worst

When tasks are assigned, therapists should always hope for the best, but be prepared for the worst. After all, a task represents a new behavior for the couple. It represents a behavior that is very different from what they have been doing. As the couple attempts a task, the therapist should assist each of them in overcoming obstacles to accomplishing the task. BSFT views obstacles to achievement as homeostasis in operation. Homeostasis is the mechanism by which systems maintain stability and equilibrium. Therapy disrupts equilibrium in order to insert change. These obstacles are also a great source of information regarding the manner in which the system is structured, and point the way to other transactions that must be considered as targets for change.

CASE EXAMPLES

These vignettes focus both on the identification of maladaptive interactions and the specific intervention plans. The BSFT methodology for diagnosing and treating Hispanic immigrant couples is designed to expressly address their idiosyncratic needs, structures, and relational value orientation.

Case Example 1: "He Thinks I'm Trash!"

The husband/father is Carlos, a 45-year-old born in Venezuela. He has lived in the United States for 22 years, and owns a small construction company. The wife/mother is Esther, 43 years old, born in Puerto Rico. She came to South Florida 18 years ago and does not work outside the home. They live in a blue-collar section of town that has a considerable drug problem and is substantially Hispanic. Carlos speaks English well, but is more traditionally Hispanic in his views, behaviors, and values. Esther's English is not very good but she has more acculturated views and considers Carlos to be old-fashioned. She is very active in her church as a volunteer; Carlos is not particularly religious. The couple has not established a working relationship with their children's school. They have three children: Tomas, Esther's oldest son by a previous relationship, raised by Carlos from age 2, now 20 years old, who lives alone, uses and sells drugs, and is very close to his younger brother; Carlito, the couple's 15-year-old son, the Identified Patient in this case, who is using drugs and is a truant; and Alina, the couple's 12-year-old daughter, who is doing well.

Reason for Referral

Carlito has been referred by the juvenile court for family therapy because of his school problems, truancy, and associated drug use. The family has attended two conjoint family sessions that included all members except Tomas, and Carlito has since run away from home to live with his oldest brother, continuing to be truant from school. In the two previous sessions, the therapist has noted that the couple relationship is highly conflictive, and their lack of parenting as a unit is central to their inability to help their sons. The therapist had been planning to see each partner of the couple alone, but Carlito running away precipitated the start of the couple sessions.

BSFT Diagnosis

Organization. Parents have lost their power within the family and cannot exercise effective behavior control. As their marital conflicts increased, their parental alliance broke down. Esther sees Carlos as old-fashioned, too rigid, negative, and lacking in compassion and understanding. She wants him to have a more "modern" way of dealing with the kids through discussing and lending a hand rather than simply "closing himself off to discussions and putting his foot down." Carlos sees Esther as weak, enabling, easy for the boys to manipulate, and never giving him (Carlos) any backing or support, "like a wife should." When talking, the partners do not listen to each other, often interrupting or talking over each other.

Resonance. Parents are enmeshed, though the quality of the interactional intensity is negative and conflictual. They exhibit patterns of mind reading, interruptions, simultaneous talking, and constantly attempting to control one another.

Developmental Stage. Esther accuses Carlos of treating her like a child, "always reprimanding me and correcting me as if I was one of the kids."

Identified Patienthood. They are equally negative toward each other, and each blames the other for the way the kids are acting and for the problems between them. They are critical of each other from an acculturation perspective. Carlos states that Esther has become too "free and permissive." Esther indicates that Carlos simply wants to impose his views on everybody, which pushes her and the kids away.

Conflict Resolution. There is a high level of conflict between them, and these conflicts are never resolved; instead, they diffuse, constantly going from one topic to another.

Ecology. Esther is overinvolved with her church, which takes up all her free time. Both are underinvolved with the school system.

BSFT Treatment Plan

Organization. Form a couple alliance; empower parents by helping them formulate and implement effective plans to bring Carlito back home and return both boys to therapy; develop clear and open communication patterns.

Resonance. Eliminate interruptions, mind reading, and the use of personal control; replace this with interactions that increase mutual awareness of the other, such as active listening.

Developmental Stage. Establish clarity about roles and age-appropriate behavior toward each other. Substitute parent–child interactions with partnering ones. Reframe the differences in their styles as acculturation differences, and then move them toward a bicultural position.

Identified Patienthood. Eliminate mutual criticisms and substitute recognition of each other's individual skills and contributions. Eliminate negativity and increase positivity from one to the other. Help them to recognize the value that both cultural styles have to offer instead of being critical of either traditional Hispanic or mainstream culture.

Conflict Resolution. Eliminate diffusion by making them stay on one topic at a time. Increase their conflict resolution skills—for example, negotiation, listening before responding.

Ecology. Engage the couple in the school system. Disengage Esther from at least *some* of the church time. Stimulate the couple to spend more free time together.

In their first couple session, Carlos immediately made it known that he was only interested in working on the problem of the boys. He admitted that he and his wife had problems, but stated that they would see to those themselves and that he wanted only to talk about the boys. It is common among Hispanic men to deny the need for help and to maintain marital issues as private. In BSFT, the therapist does not confront or challenge this position, but simply reframes the therapy in a manner that is syntonic and acceptable to each client. Esther agreed with Carlos that the boys were the primary concern. To join, the therapist agreed that the children were the most important, highlighted that indeed these boys were in a lot of serious trouble and something had to be done immediately, and then reframed the therapy job as a need for the parents to become a team. The therapist pointed out that in previous sessions she had observed that they were not working as a team, and that since these boys needed to be rescued, they needed to become a "rescue team." When they agreed to this new frame, the therapist assigned the task of them developing a plan together regarding how they were going to approach the boys and begin the conversation of returning home and going to therapy.

In the performance of this task, all of the above outlined interactional patterns were observed in enactments. Before they could come up with a plan agreeable to both, issues such as their opposing views on how to parent were reframed into a new theme of each one having more expertise in one part of parenting. It was agreed that Carlos was a better disciplinarian, and Esther was more nurturing and patient. This was then reframed: "Together you make an unbeatable team! The problem is that instead of cooperating, you have been competing as to who is a better parent." In their discussion, patterns of interruptions, simultaneous talking, diffusion, and an unwillingness to listen to each other were micromanaged in order to eliminate them. They were helped to listen to each other actively, to hear not just the words but the message behind them. Esther was able to say that her lack of trust was due to the fact that she did not believe that Carlos understood that Tomas had an underlying psychiatric disorder and that she felt Carlos wanted the police to deal with Tomas instead of a therapist. Like the "peeling of the onion," the couple was able to bring into the open the hurts and misunderstandings that kept them apart. At one point Esther said that Carlos "thinks I am trash!" This was highlighted by the therapist via repetition of the phrase slowly and emphatically as "there is no way you can trust and stay married to a man who thinks you are trash; you would be spending your life trying to prove that you are not." And the therapist added the task, "Ask your husband whether he is either foolish enough or of such low self-esteem that he would marry and stay married for 18 years to someone whom he thought was trash."

There exists among the various Hispanic groups a regrettable phenomenon of discrimination by class and nationality. Esther felt that Carlos thought of himself as better because he came from a middle-class Venezuelan family while she was from a more economically deprived Puerto Rican family. It took a series of careful and poignant questions from Esther for Carlos to convince her otherwise. His reprimanding, critical style was reframed as perhaps one that needed some modifications so they could work better together, but simply the "way in which he was raised by his strict and demanding family; it is just the language that he learned and now we have to show him a new one that works better for you." Then Carlos was given the task of telling Esther all the things that he loved and appreciated about her. When asked how often he did that, Esther quickly replied "Never!" He did his task with enthusiasm. After he gave a number of praises and compliments, the therapist asked him, "Do you like the way she mothers?" "No!" was the reply. Then, "do you like the loving part of her mothering?" "Yes!" he quickly recognized. Then the initial task was repeated in a new frame; "If you plan together to use his strictness and her lovingness, you will not fail, because together you are a winning team." The couple then proceeded to join hands and begin to plan together how they were going to approach the boys. A plan was made by them and "sealed with a kiss."

The couple was seen one more time alone. The issue of having a meeting with the school vice-principal and Carlito's teacher was discussed, and Carlos's initial move to let Esther handle this was replaced by his recognition that tackling the school issues also required their combined strengths and talents. In this session, the couple was also asked to discuss how they could plan to spend more of their free time together. The couple made plans for some part of their weekend and to make sure that they had dinners together. Following the first session, Esther and Carlos went to visit their sons at Tomas's apartment on two occasions and, working as a team, were able to bring Carlito back home and to therapy, and to work with Tomas in committing himself to an in-patient drug treatment program.

Case Example 2: "So You're Just Using Me!"

Hernan is a 51-year-old African Hispanic male born in the Dominican Republic. He has lived in the United States for six years and works as a waiter. His wife is Selma, 46 years old, also an African Hispanic born in the Dominican Republic. In the United States for 16 years, she works as an administrative assistant for a medium-sized company. They live in a middle-class community in Connecticut, in which there are more African Americans and non-Hispanic Whites than Hispanics. Both Selma and Hernan speak fluent English, albeit with a heavy accent. Hernan and Selma were physically separated during the first 10 years of their marriage (Selma came first with their son Mateo— then an infant, now 16 years old), and she worked as a domestic in the United States until she was able to train to be an office worker. She is very proud of her accomplishments. Hernan joined them 6 years ago. He works in a restaurant during the day. Selma and Mateo were able to visit Hernan a couple of times early in their marriage, but financial and legal difficulties kept them from going back to visit Hernan.

Reason for Referral

Mateo has been referred because of truancy and associating with a gang (African American). Selma complains that Mateo has become secretive and withdrawn and she disapproves of his new "friends." Hernan states that Mateo never listens to him and their relationship is not good. The family has attended three conjoint sessions, where the therapist observed the couple's dysfunctionality. Thus, the couple was asked to come to therapy alone.

BSFT Diagnosis

Organization. Mother and son have had an alliance against the father that has empowered Mateo. Now that Mateo is older, his mother has lost her control over him. Father never had power, given the physical distance, so the parents cannot exercise effective behavior control. There is no spousal or parental alliance. Selma sees Hernan as too hands off and negative toward Mateo, and thinks he prefers to work rather than spend time with either her or Mateo. She blames him for Mateo's recent problems. Hernan sees Selma as always "on Mateo's side" and never his. He invites her to come with him on days off to play dominoes with friends, but Selma does not want to go because she does not like those gatherings. Their communication is also problematic. Hernan is painfully quiet, and Selma tends to lecture him. He interjects a few words when he disagrees with her. This sends Selma off on another round of lecturing.

Resonance. Parents are disengaged emotionally and physically. Selma speaks of needing his time only "for the family."

Developmental Stage. Selma treats Hernan like a child, lecturing and reprimanding him. Hernan, in turn, makes immature remarks such as, "You like Mateo more than me."

Identified Patienthood. They are equally negative toward each other, and each blames the other for Mateo's behavior. Selma is critical of Hernan from an acculturation perspective, stating that "Hernan expects Mateo to respect him solely because he is his father, and not because he spends quality time with him or attending his sporting activities." Hernan retorts that "Selma does not back him up with Mateo and that she never wants to do what he wants." He claims that she has "become too independent and does not need him, except to bring in more money."

Conflict Resolution. The couple avoids their marital issues, which they detour through the son's problems. In discussing Mateo, they diffuse the issues and never come to any resolutions.

Ecology. Selma is involved in Mateo's activities, but does not socialize with Hernan. Hernan does not attend Selma's work events or Mateo's games.

Practice Exercises

1. Given the systemic diagnosis presented above, what would be your treatment plan/goals for this couple?

2. How would you join with Hernan? With Selma?

3. Which interactions would you highlight? How?

4. What are some reframes you could use to help Hernan see his relationship with Selma differently? What reframes would you use to change Selma's perception of Hernan?

5. What are some interactional tasks that you would prescribe for this couple? What obstacles can you foresee to successful completion of these tasks? How would you micromanage those interactional sequences when they arise?

Implications for Training and Supervision

The advantage of BSFT is that it has considerable flexibility, and for that reason it is extremely adaptable to a broad range of problems and levels of acculturation. The disadvantage of BSFT is that it is not a simple-to-follow recipe (a pinch of empathy and an ounce of joining). Rather, BSFT is an advanced clinical model that requires considerable skill and training on the part of the therapist. Training in BSFT has two major foci: (1) developing the necessary skill levels in all components of the model to ensure adherence in implementation (e.g., diagnostics, enactment development, joining, reframing, restructuring change maneuvers and tasks) and (2) achieving a shift in theoretical and practice paradigms (individual to systemic, linear to circular, content to process, history to present, discussion to action, isolationist to contextual). Training to become certified as a BSFT therapist consists of a program that includes a series of workshops and a weekly videotaped supervision consultation that typically lasts from six months to a year. Training, training materials, and resources are available through the Family Therapy Training Institute of Miami in both English and Spanish. Several of these are listed in "Additional Resources."

Notes

1. The perennial debate over the use of the term *Hispanic* vs. *Latino* centers around the question of bridging designations of race and ethnicity. The terms *Hispanic* and *Latino* may now be used interchangeably according to standards issued by the Office of Management and Budget in 1997 that were implemented in 2003 (Federal Register Notice, October 30, 1997). We use the term *Hispanic* throughout this chapter to describe individuals and couples distinguished by their language, culture, country of origin, or ancestry, and who may be of any race.

2. *Machismo* refers to the maleness or manliness, and it is expected that a man be physically strong, unafraid, and the authority figure in the family, with the obligation to protect and provide (de Rios, 2002; Falicov, 1998a, 1998b; McGoldrick, Preto, Hines, & Lee, 1991; Vega, 1990). *Marianismo* refers to a woman's self-sacrificing, religiosity, and responsibility for running the household and raising the children (Falicov, 1998a, 1998b; Vega, 1990).

Additional Resources

Readings

Szapocznik, J., Hervis, O. E., & Schwartz, S. (2003). *Brief strategic family therapy*. Rockville, MD: National Institute on Drug Abuse. This manual details the research and practice of BSFT, winner of the 2000 exemplary Model in Substance Abuse Prevention Award by the Center for Substance Abuse Prevention in Washington, DC.

Web Sites

BSFT model published by the U.S. Department of Justice: www.ncjrs.gov/html/ojjdp/jjbul2000_04_3/contents.html

BSFT Treatment Manual online: www.nida.nih.gov/TXManuals/bsft/BSFT1a.html

Family Therapy Training Institute of Miami: www.bsft-av.com

References

Bateson, G. (1972). *Steps to an ecology of mind: Collected essays in anthropology, psychiatry, evolution, and epistemology.* Chicago, IL: University of Chicago Press.

Bronfenbrenner, U. (1979). *The ecology of human development: Experiments by nature and design.* Cambridge, MA: Harvard University Press.

Bronfenbrenner, U. (1987). Ecology of the family as a context for human development: Research perspectives. *Developmental Psychology, 22,* 723–742.

Bronfenbrenner, U. (1988). Strengthening family systems. In E. F. Zigler (Ed.), *The parental leave crisis: Toward a national policy* (pp. 143–160). New Haven, CT: Yale University Press.

Coatsworth, J., Santiestaban, D., McBride, C. K., & Szapocznik, J. (2001). Brief strategic family therapy versus community control: Engagement, retention, and an exploration of the moderating role of adolescent symptom severity. *Family Process, 40,* 313–332.

de Rios, M. D. (2002). *Brief psychotherapy with the Latino immigrant client.* New York: Haworth Press.

Duncan, B. L., Miller, S. D., & Hubble, M. A. (1998). Is the consumer always right? *Family Therapy Networker, 81,* 95–96.

Duncan, B. L., Solovey, A. D., & Rusk, G. S. (1992). *Changing the rules: A client-directed approach to therapy.* New York: Guilford Press.

Falicov, C. J. (1995). Training to think culturally: A multidimensional comparative framework. *Family Process, 34,* 373.

Falicov, C. J. (1998a). *Latino families in therapy.* New York: Guilford Press.

Falicov, C. J. (1998b). The cultural meaning of family triangles. In M. McGoldrick (Ed.), *Re-visioning family therapy: Race, culture, and gender in clinical practice* (pp. 37–49). New York: Guilford Press.

Haley, J. (1976). *Problem-solving therapy.* San Francisco: Jossey Bass.

Haley, J., & Richeport-Haley, M. (2003). *The art of strategic therapy.* New York: Brunner-Routledge.

Halford, W. K. (2001). *Brief therapy for couples: Helping partners help themselves.* New York: Guilford Press.

Jordan, J. (2000). The role of mutual empathy in relational/cultural therapy. *Journal of Clinical Psychology, 56,* 1005–1018.

Knobloch-Fedders, L. M., Pinsoff, W. M., & Mann, B. J. (2004). The formation of the therapeutic alliance in couple therapy. *Family Process, 43,* 425–442.

Madanes, C. (1981). *Strategic family therapy.* San Francisco: Jossey-Bass.

Marin, G. (1993). Influence of acculturation on familism and self-identification among Hispanics. In G. P. Knight (Ed.), *Ethnic identity formation among Hispanics and other minorities* (pp. 181–196). Albany, NY: SUNY Press.

McGoldrick, M., Preto, N., Hines, P. M., & Lee, E. (1991). Ethnicity and family therapy. In A. S. Gurman & D. P. Kniskern (Eds.), *Handbook of family therapy* (pp. 546–582). Philadelphia, PA: Brunner Mazel.

Minuchin, S. (1974). *Families and family therapy*. Cambridge, MA: Harvard University Press.

Miranda, A. O., Bilot, J. M., Puluso, P. R., Berman, K., & Van Meek, L. G. (2006). Latino families: The relevance of the connection among acculturation, family dynamics, and health for family counseling research and practice. *The Family Journal, 14*, 268–273.

Office of Management and Budget. (1977). *Standards for the Classification of Federal Data on Race and Ethnicity*. Statistical Policy Directive #1.

Office of Management and Budget. (1997, October 30). *Federal Register Notice Revisions to the Standards for the Classification of Federal Data on Race and Ethnicity*.

Sabogal, F., Marein, G., Otero-Sabogal, R., Marin B. V., & Perez-Stable, E. J. (1987). Hispanic familism and acculturation: What changes and what doesn't? *Hispanic Journal of Behavioral Sciences, 9*, 397–412.

Santisteban, D., Muir-Malcolm, J., Mitrani, V. B., & Szapocznik, J. (2002). Integrating the study of ethnic culture and family psychology intervention science. In H. Liddle, R. Levant, & J. Bray (Eds.), *Family psychology: Science-based interventions* (pp. 331–352). Washington, DC: American Psychological Association Press.

Santisteban, D. A., Suarez-Morales, L., Robbins, M., & Szapocznik, J. (2006). Brief strategic family therapy: Lessons learned in efficacy research and challenges to blending research and practice. *Family Process, 45*, 259–271.

Skogrand, L., Hatch, D., & Singh, A. (2004). *Strong marriages in Latino culture*. Logan, UT: Utah State University.

Szapocznik, J., Hervis, O. E., & Schwartz, S. (2003). *Brief strategic family therapy*. Rockville, MD: National Institute on Drug Abuse.

Szapocznik, J., Santisteban, D., Rio, A., Perez Vidal, A., Kurtines, W., & Hervis, O. E. (1986). Bicultural effectiveness training (BET): An intervention modality for families experiencing intergenerational/intercultural conflict. *Hispanic Journal of Behavioral Sciences, 6*, 303–330.

Szapocznik, J., Scopetta, M. A., & King [Hervis], O. E. (1978). Theory and practice in matching treatment to the special characteristics and problems of Cuban immigrants. *Journal of Community Psychology, 6*, 112–122.

Vega, W. A., Kalody, B., & Valle, R.(1990). Marital strain, coping, and depression among Mexican-American women. *Journal of Marriage and the Family, 50*, 391–403.

Ten

Cultural Considerations in Evidence-Based Traditional and Integrative Behavioral Couple Therapy

Mia Sevier and Jean C. Yi

In recent years, two innovative movements have emerged in the field of counseling and clinical work. Both have been carried forward by enthusiastic pioneers who seek to improve the ways we help couples and families in distress (i.e., Baucom, Shoham, Mueser, Daiuto, & Stickle, 1988; Christensen & Heavey, 1999; McGoldrick, Giordano, & Garcia-Preto, 2005; Snyder, Castellani, & Whisman, 2006). The push to provide evidence that our treatments work, and hence provide therapy that is known to be effective, coincides with efforts to acknowledge the role of culture and promote culturally competent intervention for clients from diverse backgrounds. Despite developing concurrently, and having much to offer toward improving our treatments, these two perspectives have yet to converge in the field of couple therapy.

In this chapter, we seek to open discussion about the interplay of evidence-based therapies and cultural considerations in working with couples. By focusing on two empirically investigated treatments, *traditional behavioral couple therapy* (TBCT) (Jacobson & Margolin, 1979) and *integrative behavioral couple therapy* (IBCT) (Jacobson & Christensen, 1996), we suggest an approach toward integrating empirical work with cultural competence. Although these treatments focus on couples who are already in distress, some of our conclusions may extend to research-based premarital distress-prevention programs, such as PREP and CARE (Markman, Stanley, & Blumberg, 2001; Rogge, Johnson, Lawrence, Cobb, & Bradbury, 2002), which include similar strategies.

Under the mentorship of IBCT developer Andrew Christensen, both authors of this chapter earned doctoral degrees in psychology conducting research on couples and couple therapy as part of the UCLA/UW Couple Therapy Project. We have also studied and taught on issues of culture, minority mental health, and racism. Dr. Yi is currently coauthoring a book about the development of racism in children. Perhaps because of our own ethnic minority backgrounds and our special interests in minority mental health and culture, we have noted the need for research-based therapy to connect with issues of culture, which promoted our desire to write this chapter.

Overview of Empirical Research

Empirical investigations can provide evidence for whether our theories about how to help couples are in fact helping in the ways we hope. Evidence indicates that both TBCT and IBCT do indeed help the majority of couples improve their relationships. TBCT, which is based on a behavior-change and skills model, has the most empirical support of any couple treatment (Baucom et al., 1998) and has met the highest standards associated with evidence based treatments (ESTs; Baucom et al., 1998; Chambless & Hollon, 1998). IBCT expands upon the traditional model by including a new focus on building acceptance in relationships. Results of the largest study of couple therapy to date, including 134 couples who were randomly assigned to treatment, and the largest sample of ethnic minority couples in a clinical trial, indicate that TBCT and IBCT produce similar outcomes after 26 sessions of therapy. About two thirds of the couples demonstrated clinically significant gains at the end of treatment (Christensen et al., 2004). Results also indicated differing patterns of change over time between the treatments. TBCT couples made more rapid gains early in treatment and then leveled off through the rest of the sessions, while IBCT couples made slower but steadier gains throughout their time in therapy. Yi, George, Atkins, and Christensen (2006) examined response to treatment between ethnic minority partners (22% of the sample) and their European American partners (78% of the sample) and found no outcome differences.

Following the TBCT and IBCT couples over time, researchers found that clinically significant gains from before treatment to two years after treatment were maintained for 60% of TBCT couples and 69% of IBCT couples (Christensen, Atkins, Yi, Baucom, & George, 2006). While all couples experienced an immediate decrease in relationship satisfaction right after therapy ended, both groups of couples showed gradual increases over the course of time. In general, IBCT couples who stayed together had less of a drop in satisfaction when therapy ended and had higher levels of satisfaction than TBCT couples. Yi and colleagues (in preparation) examined the maintenance of gains over time and found that there was no difference between European Americans and the ethnic minority groups in the sample. Couples are being followed for a total of five years after therapy ends, so future results will indicate whether there are additional differences over time. This body of research indicates that TBCT and IBCT are indeed helpful treatments for couples in distress.

Overview of Culture

Culture has received little attention in the couple therapy literature, and there is little research to guide clinical practice. In fact, most research studies have focused primarily on White and middle-class Americans (Baucom et al., 1998; Christensen & Heavey, 1999). A review of the major marriage and family therapy journals between 1984 and 1993 found that less than 5% of the articles focused on ethnic minorities (Bean & Crane, 1996). A more recent review of two major journals in the field, the *Journal of Marital and Family Therapy* and *Family Process*, between 1970 and 2000 found that 11.2% of the articles focused on diversity issues (Leslie &

Morton, 2001). Of that 11.2%, 29.8% pertained to race and ethnicity. Although empirical investigations more recently have attempted to include a wider diversity of ethnic backgrounds (e.g., Christensen et al., 2004) and treatment approaches have been created specifically for minority couples indirectly (e.g., Bean et al.'s 2002 treatment for African American couples), cultural variables have yet to be specified and directly studied in couple therapy.

Before focusing more on culture, it is useful to first define and differentiate this construct. Culture includes physical aspects, such as architecture, roads, and other structural elements, as well as subjective aspects that are psychological and behavioral in nature (Betancourt & Lopez, 1993). Hence, culture can be understood as including values, such as personal control, collectivism, or spirituality, and social norms such as gender roles, communication patterns, and emotional styles, as well as beliefs and attitudes. Although related, it is important to note that ethnicity, or regional or national identity, and race, a socially constructed concept based on prevailing, but primarily incorrect, beliefs about underlying genetic differences, are not the same as culture. Rather than ethnicity or race, culture is expected to be most useful in considering applications of therapy, as this construct directly includes more psychological processes and focuses on the social world, while ethnicity and race offer more distal estimates. Betancourt and Lopez suggest we go beyond ethnicity or race, or just naming cultures in our studies, to examining the specific cultural process involved, such as individualism or collectivism, to improve our understanding of the influence of culture.

Although often left unexplored, psychological and counseling theories typically reflect the cultural, as well as other contextual variables, of founding theoreticians that may or may not translate to effective practice across cultural groups. Treatment approaches are not culture or value free (Hays, 1995). TBCT and IBCT were developed by highly educated Euro-Americans, and it is likely that theoretical elements reflect the values, norms, and beliefs of their makers. Treatment concepts and strategies may be universal, or etic, and may work equally well with all clients. Alternatively, they may be culturally specific, or emic, and work well only within particular cultural contexts. By directly specifying and examining the cultural assumptions of TBCT and IBCT, we can begin to explore the potential for culturally competent application of these treatments to a wide range of clients.

To examine issues of culture in these evidence-based couple therapy approaches, we follow a model developed by Lopez and colleagues (Lopez, 1997; Lopez, Kopelowicz, & Cañive, 2002) which highlights three important domains in the helping process that often vary cross-culturally. The first domain is engagement, or the initial process of forming a helping relationship with a couple while defining problems and determining the helper model. Definitions of problems are likely to vary across the perspectives of the clients and therapists, and across cultural sets. For example, TBCT might define a couple's relationship problem as a lack of constructive communication skills, while one partner might define the problem as the other partner being too emotional, while the second partner views the other as being too vocal. Helper models can also vary greatly. In certain cultures, clients may seek an authoritative expert, while others may desire a collaborative self-disclosing ally. The second domain to examine culturally is theory, or the reasons for problems and ideas on how to solve them. Couples may believe they are distressed because one partner is not carrying out proper gender role obligations, while a treatment model may suggest the couple is distressed because of a lack of positivity in their relationship. The third domain to be explored to assess for cultural compatibility includes treatment methods. There is a wide variety of possible ways to intervene with relationship problems, such as open discussion, skills training, third-party intervention, or focusing on emotionally laden issues. True cultural competence involves shifting between different perspectives to find a way to help (Pinderhughes, 2002).

Cultural Competence in Traditional Behavioral Couple Therapy

We start our examination of cultural variables in evidence-based couple therapy by focusing on TBCT. This treatment is a structured, directive, and action-oriented approach. Some have argued that these types of strategies would work best with ethnic minority clients (Vera et al., 1995), but that assertion has not been empirically tested. However, the more important issue may be how well TCBT matches with the culture of diverse clients.

To assess the potential for cultural congruence within Lopez et al.'s model (1997, 2002), we start by examining the engagement in treatment domain, including problem definitions and the helper model. According to TBCT, relationship problems include lack of positive reinforcement value, or couples not doing things that please one another, and skills deficits, including not knowing how to communicate or solve problems constructively. The focus is on behaviors, rather than proximal variables such as family history or culture. Therapists need to test these assumptions with clients to see whether this view of problems matches with how the clients view their problems. For example, a partner might assume that the problem is caused by too much pressure from an in-law or lack of respect. When views differ between clients and practitioners, clients may not readily engage in the treatment process. A therapist can give the rationale for TBCT at the beginning of treatment, and then ask the couple how the rationale fits, or not, with their conception of distress.

In the TBCT helper model, the therapist is seen as an instructor or coach who teaches the couple particular skills and offers advice on how to fine-tune their behaviors. This role may work well with couples who have cultural helper models that are prescriptive, like a doctor, or directive, like a ruling elder, but may be in contrast with helper models that are more about listening and forgiving, like a priest. To engage diverse clients in therapy, it may be useful to ask clients what their expectations are for the role the therapist will take and how therapy will proceed, as well as educating clients about the procedures.

During the engagement process, couples are expected to openly discuss their relationship conflicts with the TBCT therapist, who will start a formal assessment upon the start of treatment. However, this task may be culturally incongruent for some couples. For example, Ross (1987) described an Asian Indian couple from an arranged marriage who were reluctant to talk about personal matters in therapy. However, after the couple gained her trust, they were able to open up to her and talk about their problems. Encouraging couples to talk about their problems with a therapist who is a stranger could be particularly uncomfortable for some couples. Therapists may need to proceed slowly in therapy and assume that some information will not be easily revealed and that in some contexts, secrets may be held to respect the family (Shibusawa, 2005).

Next, we examine cultural assumptions in the TBCT intervention domain. TBCT interventions tend to be highly structured and rule based. There tends to be clear expectations about what "good" relationships are like, and strategies that are applied in an etic manner across relationships. TBCT's lack of flexibility in intervention techniques could be a weakness when striving toward culturally competent applications.

Techniques

Behavioral Exchange

The first technique, behavioral exchange, is often utilized at the beginning of TBCT therapy. It is designed to increase positive emotion and collaboration in relationships. In behavioral exchange, partners are encouraged to do things that will please one another. Research suggests that this technique can be very effective, even when utilized as a stand-alone therapy, although the results are not long lasting when used without other techniques (Jacobson, Schmaling, & Holtsworth-Munroe, 1987). This technique may reflect Western notions of healthy relationships that are often based on the notion of romantic love, or romantic and positive feelings generated between two individuals. Not all cultures subscribe to this view of relationships, with some cultures taking a more pragmatic or practical view (Contreras, Hendrick, & Hendrick, 1996). However, behavioral exchange still may be relevant to cultural groups who prefer positively focused action strategies rather than confrontation, insight-oriented, or emotional-exploration-type strategies in therapy.

CPT

The next two interventions in TBCT are designed to teach highly structured skills to communicate and solve problems. Communication training teaches couples to use assertive communication, stating feelings, desires, and thoughts respectfully and directly as well as using active listening skills such as paraphrasing and checking for comprehension to talk to one another. Problem-solving training includes a set of steps including defining a specific behavioral problem, brainstorming solutions, negotiating, and agreeing to behavior changes in order to find solutions to problems. Although communication and problem-solving training (CPT) are taught sequentially, we will discuss the pair together as we examine issues of cultural competence.

In CPT, there is an underlying assumption that direct and explicit communication is beneficial for relationships. However, not all cultures value talking openly about problems, and this assumption could violate cultural norms. Key factors to consider are individualism and collectivism, and related differences in preferred communication strategies (Gudykunst, Matsumoto, Ting-Toomey, & Nishida, 1996; Perel, 2000). CPT reflects individualistic culture, emphasizing individual experiences and goals. Individualistic cultures tend to use low-context communication, or explicit and direct forms of communication, as taught in CPT. However, in collectivistic cultures, which focus on connection with other people and group goals, high-context communication is typically employed. High-context communication involves implicit and indirect forms of communication. For example, tone and body language may be used rather than direct verbal expressions of frustration, conflict, or personal desire (Perel, 2000). Many Asians value interpersonal harmony (Flores, Tschann, van Oss Marin, & Pantoja, 2004), as well as saving the face of the self and others, or avoiding embarrassment that could be caused by directly pointing out faults (Ting-Toomey & Oetzel, 2002), and hence may discourage using assertive and direct strategies to talk about conflict. In addition, *familismo* is a Latino value that describes the strong orientation toward family bonds with a placement of family interests over individual interests (Bernal & Shapiro, 2005; Santiago-Rivera, 2003), and *simpatia* is a value toward smooth and pleasant relationships (Falicov, 2005); both of these may make talking openly about problematic areas and personal desires culturally irrelevant. Indeed, research shows that collectivistic cultures, including Asian and Latino/a Americans, use avoiding strategies and third parties more than White Americans to solve problems (Ting-Toomey et al., 2000). Hence, in collectivistic cultures, openly discussing conflictual issues in a relationship as expected by the CPT intervention could be difficult and could violate cultural norms (Lee & Mock, 2005; Markus & Kitayama, 2001; Ohbuchi, Fukushima, & Tedeschi, 1999).

Lack of cultural congruence in intervention strategies is a dilemma for clients and therapists. Research says that communication and problem-solving training are useful techniques, but these procedures may clash with the worldview of some clients. An uninformed therapist, as part of the therapy, could inadvertently encourage behavior that is not consistent with a couple's cultural background; this could lead to treatment failure or harm a couple's relationship. A careful balancing act by the therapist is needed when proceeding. The first step is recognizing cultural assumptions in the treatment. The next step is to work carefully with clients, with a willingness to be flexible in applying strategies and an open eye for when interventions do not seem congruent.

When considering using CPT, the acculturation of the couple is an important variable to consider. For example, a study by Flores, Tschann, van Oss Marin, and Pantoja (2004) indicated that more acculturated

Mexican Americans were able to express conflict more directly than their less-acculturated peers. In addition, more acculturated Mexican American husbands reported more conflict, and conflict related to specific issues. Vega, Kolody, and Valle (1988) found that less-acculturated Mexican American women were less likely to use negotiation as a way of alleviating marital conflict than those who were more acculturated. Thus, it is always important to consider the within-group variability and acculturation that may be a useful indicator of the potential effectiveness of CPT.

As an example of the importance of cultural competence skills in working with CPT, imagine that a therapist teaches communication skills to a couple that typically uses high-context communication. The therapist asks the couple to practice during the week and checks on the homework at the next session, which is common in TBCT. The couple reports that they did not do the assignment. At this point in the therapy, the therapist can make a few different attributions. The therapist could think: (1) The couple forgot to do it; (2) the couple is lazy; or (3) the assignment did not match the values of the couple, where direct confrontation of problems is not valued. The therapist needs to do a careful assessment of *why* the homework was not done, rather than making attributions that are not culturally appropriate. Here is an example of what could transpire in therapy:

Therapist: So, I noticed that the two of you did not do the paraphrasing homework that we practiced in the last session. What happened?

Partner 1: Well, we just did not have time this week to practice.

Therapist: If that is the case, why don't we spend some time setting a specific time to practice?

Partner 2: I do not see time in the upcoming week either to practice.

Therapist: I am wondering about something. Sometimes couples find that paraphrasing uncomfortable. Is it like that for the two of you?

Partner 1: Well, maybe.

Therapist: Some families just don't typically directly talk about things, but might be more subtle. Is it like that in your family?

Partner 2: Yes, we usually don't talk like that in our family.

Therapist: I appreciate you telling me that. I may ask the two of you to do some things that might be contrary to how you have been interacting. And I want you to tell me about it, so that the three of us can work together and find things that will be most beneficial for you.

In this example, the therapist takes a nonjudgmental stance and works within two frames: the assumptions of the therapy and assumptions on the part of the couple to seek a useful balance. By proceeding in a tentative manner, the therapist noticed the clients' negative reactions. Clients in TBCT could be misinterpreted as noncompliant, when it could be due to clients feeling uncomfortable going against their culture and also telling a therapist their conundrum. They may not want to embarrass themselves or the therapist. Therefore, the therapist may have to be more willing to suggest different problems and draw a couple out rather than expecting the couple to directly inform the therapist. In openly exploring strategies that the couple and their family typically use to manage conflict, cultural differences between the clients and CPT expectations may become clear. This therapist may now make adaptations to CPT or switch to a different strategy to assist this couple.

Another cultural variation to consider has to do with power, distance, hierarchy, or egalitarian values. TBCT has been shown to be more effective for couples who are more egalitarian (Jacobson & Christensen, 1996) and these values are clearly embedded in the treatment strategies. For example, a reciprocal, or approximately equal, exchange is expected. If one partner does something nice, it is expected that the other partner will do a nice act as well. In addition, through direct negotiation, there is expected to be a weighing and equal exchange of behavior changes. However, clients of color often come from backgrounds that emphasize hierarchy and position (McGoldrick et al., 2005). Thus, encouraging couples to be more egalitarian could actually *cause* more conflict, rather than ameliorating it. Careful assessment of each partner's perspective and reactions to positions of power are called for. The therapist must walk a fine line between using what is helpful, but also not offending clients or blindly imposing values upon them if partners are satisfied with their roles.

In considering power, issues of gender are also useful to consider. Cultures vary greatly in levels of patriarchy. For example, *marianismo* is said to be a value in Latino culture, where the women are expected to be self-sacrificing (McLoyd, Cauce, Takeuchi, & Wilson, 2000). This value could prevent a woman from openly speaking about her problems because it is her duty to bear those problems. However, Mexican American wives who were more acculturated were more likely to express their power in their relationships directly, rather than less-acculturated wives who expressed their power in indirect ways (Flores et al., 2004). For therapists to be culturally competent, they walk a fine line between interventions that have demonstrated efficacy and people who may not value the same assumptions as the therapy.

Some diverse cultural characteristics could be consistent with CPT. While African Americans may value "keeping up appearances" (Boyd-Franklin, 1989, p. 222), which could create initial resistance to seeking couple therapy, once couples are in treatment, therapists report that communication techniques are particularly useful for African American couples (Boyd-Franklin, 1989). In the TBCT frame, problem solving works best when both partners are collaborative and willing to compromise. Oetzel (1998) found that Latino community college students were more willing to compromise than the White students. This finding suggests that formal problem solving may be effective with this group. Thus, a major theme that could be reiterated for various ethnic groups is that once they come to the therapist's office and stay, TBCT techniques may be of use to couples. But there is not nearly enough evidence to be able to say definitively whether, and how and when, TBCT can be maximized for diverse clients.

Cultural Competence in Integrative Behavioral Couple Therapy

In this section, we examine the cultural assumptions and potential for culturally competent application of IBCT. We suggest that IBCT is a more emic approach than TBCT, in that it is ideographically tailored to each couple through careful assessment and in collaboration with the couple. IBCT therapists expect that unique dynamics underlie each couple, ask questions to find out about differences, and are accepting of differences. Hence, IBCT therapists are likely to include clients' cultural notions in their counseling strategies. However, there are also underlying treatment assumptions that need to be considered carefully when applying the treatment to ethnic minority couples.

According to IBCT theory, couples have problems because of their reactions to natural differences in their relationships (Jacobson & Christensen, 1996). For example, partners may have different ideas about how to parent, emotional communication styles, or preferences for spontaneity or planning in addition to differences that may arise because of values, power, gender, or religious backgrounds. The openness of the IBCT perspective to a wide range of differences is a strength in application to diverse populations—as diversity is, in its essence, all about differences. Happy couples successfully manage differences, while unhappy couples react in ways that lead to polarization and conflict. Unhappy couples often also have issues of vulnerability around differences in their relationships. For example, a difference in a couple around expected gender roles would be especially painful for a man who does not consider himself a man unless he is in charge. Repeated change efforts, vilification of differences, and negative behaviors are expected to emerge as unhappy partners unsuccessfully attempt to change one another. This aspect of the theoretical perspective may or may not apply to couples from diverse cultural backgrounds, as some cultural groups may handle conflict by using avoidance strategies (Ting-Toomey & Oetzel, 2002), and hence may not try to directly change or vilify one another. However, given the careful assessment process, IBCT therapists are likely to discover unique patterns and integrate them into treatment conceptualizations.

Although both of the major IBCT theoreticians are from Western backgrounds, Jacobson and Christensen (1996) relate that exposure to Eastern culture impacted their thinking in developing this theory. On describing his exposure to Eastern ideas, Christensen (Jacobson & Christensen, 1996) recalls, "These influences had shown me that the Western idea of direct attack, of changing the things that upset you, was not the only way to resolution. Acceptance of the world as is was an alternative" (p. xiii). A primary focus on acceptance and secondary focus on behavior change in IBCT represents dual cultural influences, and allows for more flexible intervention strategies than in the traditional behavioral model.

Emotional acceptance is demonstrated when a partner tolerates, or even embraces, differences and corresponding behavior because of a deeper understanding of the self, the partner, and the larger context of their relationship. Partners who demonstrate acceptance react to differences with openness, curiosity, and/or empathy. Through exploration, the impact and meaning of these differences for each partner are uncovered, and couples build intimacy as they deepen their awareness and understanding of one another. Although "letting go" of the struggle to change partners can be a sign of acceptance, this concept is different than resignation, which involves submission or yielding.

While acceptance in this theory relates to understanding of the other, we suggest that, in some cultures, some values may naturally create acceptance without deep understanding, as collectivistic couples seek interpersonal harmony. For example, Abela, Frosh, and Dowling (2005) describe how, in Maltese culture, tolerance, sacrifice of oneself for the other, unconditional regard for the other, and a willingness to suffer and adjust for the other are common values. In the context of these values, partners may be less inclined to attempt to try to change their partners, and more willing to accept them for who they are. This is in contrast to more individualist cultures, such as Northern American and Northern European, where values tend to focus on the self and personal needs or expectations, as well as personal power and fair exchange. Individualist cultures include values that encourage each partner to strive for what is personally desired, and hence couples may encounter difficulties with lack of acceptance and desire to change one another to achieve what each individual seeks. Couples with Western cultural values may require the most encouragement to develop acceptance, while it may seem more familiar to couples from collectivistic cultures.

The helper model in IBCT is of a therapist who is a collaborative and accepting expert. The therapist works with the salient issues that clients bring to the session and wish to discuss, but guides the focus of the discussion. Importantly, the therapist models and values acceptance during therapy, taking a stance with each partner that is nonblaming, validating, and compassionate. Most client characteristics, values, desires, and so on are considered potentially acceptable (with issues like domestic violence or substance abuse clear exceptions). The therapist does not take on the role of deciding what is appropriate, but instead models the understandable nature of each client's experiences, and encourages each partner to define what is personally acceptable during exploration. If couples have cultural helper models that are more prescriptive or more directive, there may be some incongruence with the stance the IBCT therapist takes. For example, Chinese clients may react to nonjudgmental listening and neutrality as signs of a therapist not caring, lacking interest, or lacking confidence (Lee & Mock, 2005). However, if the client's model is one of a priest or confessor (Barry & Bullock, 2001), the IBCT stance may offer more natural congruence, as there are elements of confession and forgiveness built into therapist roles. Some writers suggest that some therapist self-disclosure may help clients engage with the therapist in cultures where a desire for more mutual exchange in relationships is expected (Hays, 1996). IBCT therapists will

interact with the most cultural competence by being aware of client expectations for the therapist role, by asking them directly as well as observing
their reactions, and considering the pros and cons of different positions.

A clear strength of the initial IBCT engagement process is that problems
are defined in collaboration with clients through careful assessment and discussion. IBCT allows for variability among couples, and hence allows for
possible cultural differences between therapist and clients. After assessment,
feedback is given to the couple, which invites the couple to join in a collaborative discussion of the accuracy of the therapist's views. As some cultures
highly value respect for authority figures and discourage direct disagreement, in working cross-culturally, therapists will need to be sensitive when
looking for signs of the accuracy of their impressions. For example, couples
who don't raise questions or disagree with a therapist may be indicating that
they have heard, but not that they agree (Shibusawa, 2005).

Although IBCT maintains a secondary focus on the behavioral change
strategies utilized in TBCT, the major focus is on creating emotional
acceptance in relationships. All three major IBCT intervention categories
are designed to increase acceptance. When TBCT interventions are used,
they are applied in a less structured and rule-based manner, allowing for
more flexible application. Therapy methods are individually tailored for
each couple, which allows for consideration of cultural variables.

Techniques

Unified Detachment

Unified detachment interventions help couples shift away from heated
negative emotional reactions to a more intellectualized analysis of differences and unpleasant partner behavior in their relationship. Differences
that may underlie repetitive conflicts are explored and presented as being
understandable.

As discussed in the above section on TBCT, cross-culturally, couples may
vary greatly in their preferences for open discussion of sources of negative
emotion or areas of conflict versus using other strategies, such as avoidance
of overt discussion, preference for indirect and nonconfrontational communication, or third-party intervention for solving problems (Al-Krenawi
& Graham, 2005; Gudykunst et al., 1996; Perel, 2000). In fact, some couples
may present with a pattern of mutual withdrawal or avoidance rather
than engaging in direct conflict. In contrast, IBCT includes a cultural

assumption that directly focusing on and exploring problems and talking about emotions are the best strategies for relationships. To work competently across cultures, the therapist must consider potential differences in desires for direct and open communication, explore differences, and try out different strategies in collaboration with couples while carefully observing the impact. For example, if a couple in therapy has two members who both prefer indirect communication, or high-context communication, with one another but are willing to use a third party to intervene, the therapist could adapt the treatment by initially taking on the role of the third party. By scheduling individual sessions, the therapist could promote open exploration of problematic issues in a less threatening environment than with both partners present, and individually explore each partner's ideas for ways to improve their relationship without direct communication. In addition, if partners seemed to react well to this strategy, as the therapy continued, this therapist could explore promoting communication by speaking for each partner to the other. In addition, it would be wise to openly suggest and gently explore possibilities for more direct communication while noting and respecting each partner's preferences.

CASE EXAMPLE

Differences in communication preferences between partners may at times create problems in couples' relationships. In the following case example, imagine that a cross-cultural couple enters therapy. Partner 1 has a cultural background that values independence and low-context communication, while Partner 2 is from a culture that values interdependence and high-context communication. Upon entering therapy, the therapist determines that one major issue revolves around differences in communication strategies around relationship problems that might be related to culture. Here, the therapist uses unified detachment to discuss this issue with the clients.

Partner 1:   So this week we had another big fight just like we always do. I was really unhappy with the way that our schedules are working, so I tried to bring it up and discuss it. Instead of talking about it like I wanted to, suddenly I was left all by myself in the room. I don't understand why we can't just talk about things. I get so frustrated by all of this game playing.

Therapist: Okay, so this sounds like the common pattern we've started to talk about. This pattern of approach and withdraw we've started to notice. I suspect this might reflect some real differences between both of your backgrounds and the way your families approached conflictual topics. I'd like to hear more how both of your families solved problems when they emerged.

Partner 1:   Well, we'd talk about it. Everyone would state their views and what they wanted. There might be some raised voices or something, but then we'd discuss the different options and decide what would be best to do.

Therapist: Yes, this is one way to solve problems, to be assertive and directly ask for things. When both people communicating have this strategy it can work very well. However, it is only one way to communicate. In some cultures, people are more subtle. They might gently suggest something without being very direct, to avoid embarrassing the other, and expect that others might hear the gentle message and accommodate. [To Partner 2] Which strategy do you think your family took?

Partner 2:   Well, I guess it was sort of more like you were just saying. I don't remember anyone directly saying something they weren't happy about, because we wouldn't want to offend anyone. I'd try to listen and please my parents or sister if it seemed like they wanted something. I don't remember ever having to say no to anyone. I think we'd just shift away from the topic or something instead.

Therapist: Okay, so it sounds to me like the two of you might have very different strategies toward approaching problems. One approach might be to directly discuss, and another strategy might be to use more subtle communication. Both strategies worked in your family, but I can see why the process gets confusing between the two of you! There might be some real cultural variations in your approaches that I think we should talk more about.

In this unified detachment example, the therapist helps the couple explore and deepen their understanding of the way they approach problems in their relationships by starting to explore cultural differences. The goal is not necessarily to promote change in the way each partner communicates, but ultimately to promote acceptance of this understandable difference. Acceptance of differences often leads the couple to move naturally toward the midpoint of the difference. For example, an outspoken partner might become less direct, while an indirect partner might become more direct. The therapist suspects a cultural difference and uses this knowledge to open up exploration with the couple.

Empathic Joining Interventions

The next set of IBCT techniques, empathic joining interventions, encourages partners to explore areas of vulnerability and "soft" emotions, such as hurt, insecurity, or sadness, which often lie behind displays of "hard" emotions such as hostility or anger. Expression of soft emotions is hypothesized to foster empathy and intimacy in relationships, while hard emotions create distance or conflict. This technique is expected to be helpful for couples engaging in openly hostile battles.

In considering this technique, it is useful to note that, although there are universal aspects to emotional displays—for example, a facial expression of happiness can be interpreted similarly across cultures—research also indicates that there are clear differences in cultural display rules that differ between high and low context cultures (Matsumoto, Franklin, Choi, Rogers, & Tatani, 2002). Individualistic cultures tend to promote direct expression of emotions that are experienced, while collectivistic cultures tend to promote masked displays. Hence, the intensity of a display may not indicate the intensity of an emotion that a partner in counseling feels. In addition, cultures vary on several other display rules, such as how much negativity is expressed and how much emotionality in general is expressed to in-group members and to outsiders. For example, while European Americans may feel more comfort expressing emotion to family members than to strangers, Costa Ricans were found to feel equally comfortable with emotionality in both situations (Stephan, Stephan, & Cabezas De Vargas, 1996). To be culturally competent, a therapist must consider his or her own expectations about displays of emotion and those of each partner to accurately explore, comprehend, and encourage emotional experiences.

However, we suggest that empathic joining interventions be applied with caution across cultures. The expression of vulnerability may be especially threatening and potentially culturally incongruent. For example, in patriarchal family structures, this technique might confuse or violate gender norms for men, which require men to be unemotional and appear strong (Williams & Best, 1990). Lopez (1997) describes how a father from a culture that valued machismo, or manliness, reacted with anger toward the therapist during family therapy when a vulnerable state was suggested. Hence, we suggest therapists carefully consider whether this new type of experience would be helpful or not to the particular couple, given cultural factors, rather than blindly imposing the strategy and expecting it to be successful.

Tolerance-Building Interventions

The last set of IBCT techniques, tolerance-building interventions, helps couples tolerate potentially aversive partner behavior, except in cases of abuse or harm. Positive aspects of differences are highlighted. For example, a husband and wife who vary on their preferences for saving versus freely spending money may have many conflicts around this subject. However, because one prefers to save, they may have been able to afford to buy a house. Alternatively, because one prefers to spend, they may have been able to go on vacations and enjoy pleasures in life. This type of focus on the positive benefits of differences may be culturally congruent for couples who prefer to focus on positive elements of their relationships. Another toler-ance intervention is encouraging greater self-care. This intervention may work well for couples who define problems as having a more individual rather than interpersonal basis. In addition, tolerance-building interventions may encourage partners to role-play negative behavior in session or fake negative behavior at home to encourage the couple to observe and discuss them. This process also desensitizes partners to problem triggers. This particular tolerance technique again may be irrelevant or more challenging for couples who prefer avoidance or less direct exposure to problem areas.

Training and Supervision

Opportunities to gain training or supervision in both of these approaches can be found on the IBCT Web site, which lists trained therapists, workshops on IBCT, and research on IBCT. Additional readings and the Web site are listed in the resources section below.

In learning to practice TBCT or IBCT, the development of cultural competence skills is essential in working with diverse couples. Cultural competence is both a content area, including having knowledge of one's own personal cultural background as well as that of diverse clients, and a process, in which clinicians thoughtfully consider possibilities for cultural differences in therapeutic work (Sue, 2006). As outlined below, training should emphasize all facets of cultural competence. The supervisor will want to foster the kind of environment where trainees feel free to be able to talk about cultural issues. For example, the supervisor may want to begin this type of conversation as the supervisee could be uncomfortable in doing so because of the power differential between the supervisor and supervisee.

The first area of cultural competence includes expanded awareness and knowledge of the counselor's own culture and how this may impact the decisions and treatments they provide (Sue, 2006). For example, counselors' personal beliefs about gender roles, the relative importance of children, or relationship fidelity may inadvertently impact the direction of the therapy provided to couples who are struggling with these issues. Clinicians who are aware of their personal beliefs may avoid blindly assuming there is a "right" way to proceed and may instead focus on discovering and evaluating the couple's preferences. A supervisor can help to foster this area of cultural competence by asking the supervisee what his or her values are in intimate relationships. This awareness is important, as it helps the supervisee become more cognizant of the values that he or she possesses about relationships. For example, does the supervisee value staying together? If so, talking with the supervisor about how this value could affect the course of therapy is an important learning tool for the supervisee.

Second, cultural competence training needs to include a wide background of cultural knowledge (Sue, 2006) and lessons about how to seek such knowledge out in order to be helpful with diverse clients. For example, if a clinician from a primarily individualistic culture is working with a couple from a collectivistic culture who want to include extended family in decision-making processes, this clinician would best serve the couple by being knowledgeable about the possible cultural appropriateness of this possibility. Asking the supervisee about his or her training or previous experience working with people of diverse backgrounds helps to get a sense of cultural knowledge. If a situation arises where the supervisor or trainee is out of his or her competence zone, modeling consulting or suggesting resources to the supervisee is critical, as no one person can be expected to know everything about a particular culture.

To impart knowledge of cultural variations, several particularly value-laden issues are worthy of particular focus and discussion during training. For example, cultures vary in the importance of keeping relationships together regardless of all circumstances versus freely allowing divorce or separation. In addition, cultural views about the immorality or acceptability of infidelity vary widely, and some cultures may sanction multiple sexual partnerships for married men, but not women (e.g.,

Brice-Baker, 2005). When affairs are not mutually sanctioned by both partners in a relationship, and one partner has disclosed a secret affair to the therapist, ethical issues of honesty in treatment and balance in equally serving the needs of both partners may incline a therapist to force disclosure or end therapy. However, when both partners sanction undisclosed affairs, the situation may call for a different stance from the therapist. Violence and aggression in relationships, which may be more normative in some cultures than others, is another particularly challenging issue. While it is clear that a therapist should work to end all severe violence and protect partners who are being battered, perhaps by encouraging individual treatment rather than couple therapy, in situations of ongoing low-level violence that is unlikely to escalate or lead to bodily harm, the stance taken by a therapist may be less clear. Supervisors can help trainees by focusing on developing awareness and understanding of cultural variations on these challenging issues.

The third area of cultural competence, and perhaps the most important, involves applying cultural awareness and knowledge in a culturally competent way. Trainees need to learn to hold many potential hypotheses in mind about possible cultural or noncultural factors, to consider whether cultural knowledge actually applies to their current clients, to allow for open discussion of cultural issues with couples, and to avoid blind application of cultural notions and stereotyping. Training can help clinicians learn to "shift lens" or how to move between the professional therapist and the couple's cultural views, while purposefully considering varying meanings and implications (Lopez, 1997). By modeling a process of open communication and consideration about cultural issues between supervisors and trainees, supervisors can help trainees develop these skills while also encouraging a similar process between trainees and couples. Trainees should be directly encouraged to openly discuss cultural issues with their clients, with direct questions about culture and discussion with couples about different implications of cultural variations.

Conclusion and Future Directions

In this chapter, we have highlighted cultural considerations that could enrich work with evidence-based couple treatments with the goal of encouraging culturally competent practice. However, we wish to end with a cautionary note about the dangers of utilizing evidence-based treatments or cultural knowledge in an insensitive way. Typically, empirical work and cultural knowledge focus on understanding groups of people. In practice, we see unique couples who have their own specific needs and characteristics. Assumptions about etic and emic characteristics of treatments must be suspended until evidence is uncovered. In addition, clinicians must avoid mistakes of underpathologizing, or not seeing existing problems because of cultural stereotypes, and overpathologizing, or seeing problems when experiences are in fact culturally sanctioned and normal in the cultural context (Lopez & Hernandez, 1986). Truly culturally competent practice with empirical treatments includes developing a wide base of knowledge, but careful and observant practice in applying it. Practitioners would do well to consider themselves "researchers" in their work with all clients, shifting between cultural perspectives, making hypotheses based on theories about how a couple functions and what will help, and seeking evidence along the way.

We see this chapter as a first step toward connecting empirical work and issues of culture and cultural competence. Much is left to be done to promote true integration of these domains. More theoretical work, like that offered in this book, and more research to make sure theoretical notions are correct, is clearly called for. We hope that others will be inspired to join us as we continue in this important direction.

Topics for Reflection

1. To build the self-awareness necessary for culturally competent practice, consider your own cultural values about relationships. What do you think constitutes a "healthy" relationship? Why do you think problems emerge in relationships?

2. Where do you and your family stand on the following issues: high- or low-context communication strategies, egalitarian or hierarchal power structures, and gender-related expectations for men and women in relationships?

3. Are there areas in your close relationships where you have sought direct behavior change in your partner, or have you demonstrated any acceptance? How did each process go?

4. Think about distressed couples you have seen. How could you integrate direct behavior-change strategies and acceptance-based strategies? Do you think cultural factors would play a role in your choice of strategies? How would you practice being culturally sensitive in using TBCT or IBCT techniques?

5. When deciding on how to help a couple, a counselor could consider personal intuitions, evidence-based strategies, or cultural considerations. Which would you be more likely to follow and why? How can a practitioner integrate these three perspectives?

Additional Resources

Readings

Christensen, A., Atkins, D. C., Berns, S., Wheeler, J., Baucom, D. H., & Simpson, L. E. (2004). Traditional versus integrative behavioral couple therapy for significantly and chronically distressed married couples. *Journal of Consulting and Clinical Psychology, 72,* 176–191; and Christensen, A., Atkins, D. C., Yi, J., Baucom, D. H., & George, W. H. (2006). Couple and individual adjustment for 2 years following a randomized clinical trial comparing traditional versus integrative behavioral couple therapy. *Journal of Consulting and Clinical Psychology, 74,* 1180–1191. Research articles on post-treatment and two-year follow-up outcome studies on TBCT and IBCT.

Christensen, A., & Jacobson, N. S. (2000). *Reconcilable differences.* New York: Guilford Press. A self-help book for partners based on IBCT.

Christensen, A., Wheeler, J. G., & Jacobson, N. S. (in press). Couple distress. To appear in D. H. Barlow (Ed.), *Clinical handbook of psychological disorders* (4th ed.). New York: Guilford Press.

Gottman, J. M., Notarius, C., Gonso, J., & Markman, H. (1976). *A couple's guide to communication.* Champaign, IL: Research Press. A self-help book for partners based on TBCT strategies.

Jacobson, N. S., & Christensen, A. (1998). *Acceptance and change in couple therapy: A therapist's guide to transforming relationships.* New York: Norton. A treatment guide for practitioners on IBCT.

Jacobson, N. S., & Margolin, G. (1979). *Marital therapy: Strategies based on social learning and behavioral exchange principles.* New York: Brunner/Mazel. A treatment guide for practitioners on TBCT.

Web Site

Web site with treatment information, referrals, and training events: http://ibct .psych.ucla.edu/home.htm.

References

Abela, A., Frosh, S., & Dowling, E. (2005). Uncovering beliefs embedded in the culture and its implications for practice: The case of Maltese married couples. *Journal of Family Therapy, 27,* 3–23.

Al-Krenawi, A., & Graham, J. R. (2005). Marital therapy for Arab Muslim Palestinian couples in the context of reacculturation. *The Family Journal, 13,* 300–310.

Barry, D. T., & Bullock, W. A. (2001). Culturally creative psychotherapy with a Latino couple by an Anglo therapist. *Journal of Family Psychotherapy, 12,* 15–30.

Baucom, D. H., Shoham, V., Mueser, K. T, Daiuto, A. D., & Stickle, T. R. (1998). Empirically supported couple and family interventions for marital distress and adult mental health problems. *Journal of Consulting and Clinical Psychology, 66,* 53–88.

Bean, R., & Crane, D. R. (1996). Marriage and family therapy research with ethnic minorities: Current status. *American Journal of Family Therapy, 24,* 3–8.

Bean, R. A., Perry, B. J., & Bedell, T. M. (2002). Developing culturally competent marriage and family therapist: Treatment guidelines for non-African American therapists working with African American families. *Journal of Marital and Family Therapy, 28,* 153–164.

Bernal, G., & Shapiro, E. (2005). Cuban families. In M. McGoldrick, J. Giordano, & N. Garcia-Preto (Eds.), *Ethnicity & family therapy* (pp. 202–215). New York: Guilford Press.

Betancourt, H., & Lopez, S. R. (1993). The study of culture, ethnicity, and race in American psychology. *American Psychologist, 48,* 629–637.

Boyd-Franklin, N. (1989). *Black family in therapy: A multisystems approach.* New York: Guilford Press.

Cai, D. A., & Fink, E .L. (2002). Conflict style difference between individualists and collectivists. *Communication Monographs, 69,* 67–87.

Chambless, D. L., & Hollon, S. D. (1998). Defining empirically supported therapies. *Journal of Consulting and Clinical Psychology, 66*(1), 7–18.

Christensen, A., Atkins, D. C., Berns, S., Wheeler, J., Baucom, D. H., & Simpson, L. E. (2004). Traditional versus integrative behavioral couple therapy for significantly and chronically distressed married couples. *Journal of Consulting and Clinical Psychology, 72,* 176–191.

Christensen, A., Atkins, D. C., Yi, J., Baucom, D. H., & George, W. H. (2006). Couple and individual adjustment for 2 years following a randomized clinical trial comparing traditional versus integrative behavioral couple therapy. *Journal of Consulting and Clinical Psychology, 74,* 1180–1191.

Christensen, A., & Heavey, C. L. (1999). Interventions for couples. *Annual Review of Psychology, 50,* 165–190.

Christensen, A., & Jacobson, N. S. (2000). *Reconcilable differences.* New York: Guilford Press.

Christensen, A., Jacobson, N., & Babcock, J. (1995). Integrative behavioral couple therapy. In N. Jacobson & A. Gurman (Eds.), *Clinical handbook of marital therapy* (pp. 31–64). New York: Guilford Press.

Christensen, A., Wheeler, J. G., & Jacobson, N. S. (in press). Couple distress. To appear in D. H. Barlow (Ed.), *Clinical handbook of psychological disorders* (4th ed.). New York: Guilford Press.

Constantine, M. D., Juby, H. L., & Liang, J. J. (2001). Examining multicultural counseling competence and race-related attitudes among White marital and family therapists. *Journal of Marital and Family Therapy, 27*, 353–362.

Contreras, R., Hendrick, S. S., & Hendrick, C. (1996). Perspectives on marital love and satisfaction in Mexican American and Anglo-American couples. *Journal of Counseling and Development, 74*, 408–415.

Falicov, C. J. (2005). Mexican families. In M. McGoldrick, J. Giordano, & N. Garcia-Preto (Eds.), *Ethnicity & family therapy* (pp. 168–182). New York: Guilford Press.

Flores, E., Tschann, J. M., van Oss Marin, B., & Pantoja, P. (2004). Marital conflict and acculturation among Mexican American husbands and wives. *Cultural Diversity and Ethnic Minority Psychology, 10*, 39–52.

Gottman, J. M., Notarius, C., Gonso, J., & Markman, H. (1976). *A couple's guide to communication.* Champaign, IL: Research Press.

Gudykunst, W. B., Matsumoto, Y., Ting-Toomey, S., & Nishida, T. (1996). The influence of cultural individualism-collectivism, self-construals, and individual values on communication styles across cultures. *Human Communication Research, 22*, 510–543.

Jacobson, N. S., & Christensen, A. (1998). *Acceptance and change in couple therapy: A therapist's guide to transforming relationships.* New York: Norton.

Jacobson, N. S., & Margolin, G. (1979). *Marital therapy: Strategies based on social learning and behavioral exchange principles.* New York: Brunner/Mazel.

Jacobson, N. S., Schmaling, K. B., & Holtsworth-Munroe, A. (1987). Component analysis of behavioral marital therapy: 2-year follow-up and prediction of relapse. *Journal of Marital and Family Therapy, 13*, 187–195.

Hays, P. A. (1996). Cultural considerations in couple therapy. *Women & Therapy, 19*(3), 13–23.

Lee, E., & Mock, M. R. (2005). Asian families: An overview. In M. McGoldrick, J. Giordano, & N. Garcia-Preto (Eds.), *Ethnicity & Family Therapy* (pp. 269–289). New York: Guilford Press.

Leslie, L. A., & Morton, G. (2001). Family therapy's response to family diversity: Looking back, looking forward. *Journal of Family Issues, 22*, 904–921.

Lopez, S. R. (1997). In C. E. J. Watkins (Ed.), *Cultural competence in psychotherapy: A guide for clinicians and their supervisors* (pp. 570–588). Hoboken, NJ: John Wiley & Sons.

Lopez, S. R., & Hernandez, P. (1986). How culture is considered in the evaluation of mental health patients. *Journal of Nervous and Mental Disease, 175*, 143–151.

Lopez, S. R., Kopelowicz, A., & Cañive, J. M. (2002). Strategies in developing culturally congruent family interventions for schizophrenia: The case of Hispanics. In H. P. Lefley & D. L. Johnson (Eds.), *Handbook of psychotherapy supervision* (pp. 61–90). Westport, CT: Praeger/Greenwood.

Markman, H. J., Stanley, S. M., & Blumberg, S. L. (2001). *Fighting for your marriage.* San Francisco: John Wiley & Sons.

Markus, H. R., & Kitayama, S. (1991). Culture and the self: Implications for cognition, emotion, and motivation. *Psychological Review, 98,* 224–253.

Markus, H. R., & Kitayama, S. (2001). The cultural construction of self and emotion: Implications for social behavior. In W. G. Parrott (Ed.), *Emotions in social psychology* (pp.119–138). Philadelphia, PA: Psychology Press.

Matsumoto, D., Franklin, B., Choi, J., Rogers, D., & Tatani, H. (2002). Cultural influences on the perception and expression of emotion. In W. B. Gudykunst & B. Mody (Eds.), *Handbook of international and intercultural communication* (pp. 107–126). Thousand Oaks, CA: Sage.

McGoldrick, M., Giordano, J., & Garcia-Preto, N. (2005). *Ethnicity & family therapy* (2nd ed.). New York: Guilford Press.

McLoyd, V. C., Cauce, A., Takeuchi, D., & Wilson, L. (2000). Marital processes and parental socialization in families of color: A decade of research. *Journal of Marriage and Family, 62,* 1070–1093.

Oetzel, J. G. (1998). The effects of self-construals and ethnicity on self-reported conflict styles. *Communication Reports, 11,* 133–144.

Ohbuchi, K., Fukushima, O., & Tedeschi, J. T. (1999). Cultural values in conflict management: Goal orientation, goal attainment and tactical decision. *Journal of Cross-Cultural Psychology, 30,* 51–71.

Perel, E. (2000). A tourist's view of marriage: Cross-cultural couples—challenges, choices, and implications for therapy. In P. Papp (Ed.), *Couples on the fault line: New directions for therapists* (pp. 178–204). New York: Guilford Press.

Pinderhughes, E. B. (2002). African American marriage in the 20th century. *Family Process, 41,* 269–282.

Rogge, R. D., Johnson, M. D., Lawrence, E., Cobb, R., & Bradbury, T. N. (2002). The CARE program: A preventive approach to martial intervention. In N. S. Jacobson & A. S. Gurman (Eds.), *Clinical handbook of couple therapy* (3rd ed., pp. 420–435). New York: Guilford Press.

Ross, J. R. (1987). Cultural tensions in strategic marital therapy. *Contemporary Family Therapy, 9,* 188–201.

Santiago-Rivera, A. (2003). Latinos values and family transitions: Practical considerations for counseling. *Counseling and Human Development, 30,* 1–12.

Shibusawa, T. (2005). Japanese families. In M. McGoldrick, J. Giordano, & N. Garcia-Preto (Eds.), *Ethnicity & family therapy* (2nd ed., pp. 339–348). New York: Guilford Press.

Snyder, D. K., Castellani, A. M., & Whisman, M. A. (2006). Current status and future directions in couple therapy. *Annual Review of Psychology, 57,* 317–344.

Stephan, W. G., Stephan, C. W., & Cabezas De Vargas, M. (1996). Emotional expression in Costa Rica and the United States. *Journal of Cross-Cultural Psychology, 27,* 147–160.

Sue, S. (2006). Cultural competency: From philosophy to research and practice. *Journal of Community Psychology, 34,* 237–245.

Ting-Toomey, S., Oetzel, J. G., & Yee-Jung, K. (2001). Self-construal types and conflict management styles. *Communication Reports, 14*(2), 87–104.

Ting-Toomey, S., Yee-Jung, K. K., Shapiro, R. B., Garcia, W., Wright, T., & Oetzel, J. G. (2000). Ethnic/cultural identity salience and conflict styles in four US ethnic groups. *International Journal of Intercultural Relations, 24,* 47–81.

Vega, W. A., Kolody, B., & Valle, R. (1988). Marital strain, coping, and depression among Mexican American women. *Journal of Marriage and Family, 50,* 391–403.

Vera, M., Vila, D., & Alegria, M. (2002) Cognitive-behavioral therapy: Concepts, issues, and strategies for practice with racial/ethnic minorities. In G. Bernal, J. E. Trimble, A. K. Burlew, & F. T. L. Leong (Eds.), *The handbook of racial and ethnic minority psychology* (pp. 521–538). Thousand Oaks, CA: Sage.

Williams, J. E., & Best, D. L. (1990). *Measuring sex stereotypes: A multination study.* Thousand Oaks, CA: Sage.

Yi, J. C., George, W. H., Atkins, D. C., & Christensen, A. (2006). *Ethnic minorities in couple therapy.* Manuscript in preparation.

PART III

Ethnicity and Couple Therapy

Section D

African American and Black Couples

Eleven

Premarital Counseling With Middle-Class African Americans

The Forgotten Group

Anthony L. Chambers

This chapter will address the growing, understudied population of middle-class African Americans in the context of premarital counseling. Specifically, it will discuss the unique challenges this population faces in terms of mate availability, gender, power, and vulnerability. Moreover, the chapter will provide therapists with a culturally sensitive intellectual framework for conducting premarital counseling with middle-class African American couples. It will also highlight the unseen financial challenges that middle-class African American couples face that therapists may unwittingly underestimate because of the couple's educational attainment. The impact of those financial strains on the couple's ability to maintain a satisfying relationship is significant.

In the spirit of providing the reader with some personal context, I am a clinical psychologist by training who entered the field with a proclivity toward systemic thinking. My passion for working with African American couples started when I was 16 years old when my parents were selected to be on the *Oprah Winfrey Show* as one of the 25 best couples in America! Although this was embarrassing at the time, I reaped the benefits of their strong marriage. I also grew up in a middle-class family, and often felt that some of the struggles I faced were not adequately captured by the existing literature on African Americans. Once I began college at Hampton University and started thinking about the numerous problems facing African Americans, I came to realize that two factors were critical to the survival of African Americans: family *and* education. The absence of either factor has deleterious consequences. I chose to focus on the family, specifically the marital subsystem, as I view the adult subsystem as critical to family functioning. I chose to complete my PhD at the University of Virginia under the tutelage of Dr. Melvin Wilson, who is renowned for his work with African American extended families. In addition to being a clinical psychologist, Dr. Wilson is also a community and developmental psychologist. Hence, I examine African American marriages through the lens of prevention and development, which may explain my passion for examining premarital couples and the importance I place on context and socioeconomic status (SES). I completed my internship and clinical residency at Harvard Medical School and Massachusetts General Hospital, under the tutelage of Dr. Anne Fishel, who is the director of their Couples Therapy Program. She taught me her model for assessing couples (Fishel, 2000), which is an approach that I have adapted and will reference later in the chapter. I hope this description provides a window into my perspectives and biases, which I believe is important for evaluating any scholarly work.

Sociological Considerations

To understand the cultural backdrop African American couples face, it is important to grasp the current sociological and cultural zeitgeist of African American marriages. U.S. Census data (2000) and sociological research have consistently found that African Americans have the lowest rates of marriage and lower marital stability than all other ethnic groups. Some 41% of African American adults are married compared with 62% of Whites and 60% of Hispanics. In fact, the marriage rate among African Americans has decreased by 20% over the past 50 years (Tucker & Mitchell-Kernan,

1995). This pattern is even more pronounced among subgroups. In 1940, almost 40% of African American men between the ages of 20 and 24 were married; this decreased to 11.6% in 1990 (James, 1998). There have been a number of explanations offered for the disproportionately low marriage rate among African Americans, including one emphasizing the higher rates of unemployment and bleak economic prospects for African American men, resulting in a decreased interest in marriage due to their inability to fulfill the provider role, which makes them less attractive to women as husbands (Tucker & Mitchell-Kernan, 1995). Consistent with this viewpoint, research has noted that it is not possible for every African American college graduate to find a mate with similar education, which has been found to explain the disproportionately low marriage rate (Lichter, Anderson, & Hayward, 1995; Pinderhughes, 2002).

An understudied, though important, subgroup of African Americans currently garnering increased interest from researchers, particularly sociologists, is middle-class African Americans. A major finding from this literature is that African Americans' position in the middle class is significantly more tenuous than that of Euro-Americans in the middle class (Pattillo, 2005). For instance, the average middle-class African American person resides in a neighborhood where the median household income is $35,306 compared with $51,459 for Caucasians (Pattillo, 2005). Another study that found that middle-class African Americans have 2.6 times higher odds of having a poor sibling than middle-class Euro-Americans, which results in an increased likelihood of middle-class African American families sharing their financial resources (Heflin & Pattillo, 2006). The upshot of this research is that being middle class and African American does not mean one is free of financial and familial challenges.

Psychological and Interpersonal Considerations

One of the most important constraints confronting young African American couples coming in for premarital counseling is that many do not have a healthy model of marriage, as evidenced by the fact that 46% of African American families are headed by females (Darity & Myers, 1995; Tucker & Mitchell-Kernan, 1995). The central task of marriage is the management of differences. Managing differences requires couples to be flexible and to accept influence from the other, which is easier when couples have clearly identified gender roles. However, given the disproportionately high divorce rate and high rate of out-of-wedlock births among African Americans (Tucker & Mitchell-Kernan, 1995), one or both members of the couple may have been reared by a single parent and therefore lack a model for how to manage differences in a marital context.

Given the gender disparities and unbalanced sex ratio among African Americans, delineating gender roles can be particularly challenging. It has been well documented that the challenges often manifest themselves in terms of power struggles and conflict over leadership (i.e., Black, 1999; Boyd-Franklin, 2003; Boyd-Franklin & Franklin, 1998; Hatchett, Veroff, & Douvan, 1995; Pinderhughes, 1998, 2002). There are at least a couple of layers to this issue. First, the traditional male role as the provider is not only compromised, but challenged or surpassed, by the woman. Second, the woman often maintains the role of primary caregiver of their children (Pinderhughes, 2002; Tucker & Mitchell-Kernan, 1995). Given her unique role of being the mother, she may also assume the role as "house manager." Researchers have documented that gender role confusion can place a significant stress on the dyadic subsystem, as the woman may understandably feel overwhelmed, and the man may understandably feel emasculated and as though he has little to no influence in decision making (Hatchett et al., 1995; McLloyd, Cauce, Tacheuchi, & Wilson, 2000).

Another significant issue disproportionately affecting middle-class African American couples is that of sharing financial resources with family members (Heflin & Pattillo, 2006). If couples do not have a clear expectation of how much money they will share with extended family members, and when this will occur, there is an increased likelihood of resentment and disappointment. Moreover, the lack of a shared understanding around how to help family members without breaking the bank can constrain the formation of an "us," which is a critical task during the transition to marriage. To be clear, I am not suggesting that couples refuse to help their families. In fact, I espouse a both/and versus an either/or paradigm when working with African American couples (Hardy & Laszloffy, 2002). That is, I try to help couples find a way that protects their marital subsystem while maintaining a mutually agreed upon relationship with their respective families of origin.

Framework for Working With Premarital Middle-Class African American Couples

I use a systemically informed psycho-socio-cultural conceptualization for understanding and working with premarital middle-class African

American couples. One psychological construct that I believe is important to understand is the paradoxical nature of vulnerability. African Americans are frequently given messages throughout society and in their workplace that if you want to be successful then you must not show any weaknesses or vulnerabilities. Although minimizing one's weakness is necessary to be successful in one's career, the paradox is that trying to manage and hide your vulnerabilities in an intimate relationship is exactly the thing that can destroy it. In fact, there is another paradox involved here: Increasing one's vulnerability in a *healthy* relationship can actually increase the safety and intimacy in the relationship because it sends the partner the message that "you love me even when I show you my vulnerability," which is extremely validating (Christensen & Jacobson, 2000). The role of money and finances highlights the importance of helping middle-class African American couples grasp the importance of expressing vulnerabilities because without that awareness money and finances can often be a vehicle to inappropriately "act out" their struggles with vulnerability. Hence, my approach is first to assess the couple's capacity for expressing vulnerabilities and then to help them develop a new paradigm for understanding the utility and necessity of expressing vulnerability in a marital relationship.

The issue of gender disparities is a sociological one with interpersonal implications. With a disproportionate number of African American women obtaining college and graduate degrees relative to men, issues of gender identity and leadership infinitely complicate a couple's ability to appropriately express vulnerability. Hence, it is important to understand each person's conceptualization of gender roles in the context of a marriage, as well as to assess how gender roles have currently been defined in their relationship.

A psychological construct related to vulnerability that also has cultural meaning is the role of trust. There has been a lot written on the historical evolution of African Americans' "healthy paranoia" (Combs et al., 2006). Although there are several benefits to having a "healthy paranoia," a mistrustful disposition that leaks into the marital relationship can have devastating deleterious effects. Hence, it is critical for therapists to closely examine not only the couple's articulation of trust, but to examine each person's history with having trust broken and restored.

A psychosocial issue that is particularly germane to middle-class, African American couples is their coping strategies for handling racial discrimination. This point is particularly salient in light of research documenting the pervasive effects racism has on relationships in terms of the type and quality of problems and situations they have to negotiate (Orbuch, Veroff, & Hunter, 1999). Hence, I believe it is important for clinicians to help couples *turn toward* their partner rather than *turn away* during times of stress, especially when the stressor is racism on the job.

It is also important to keep in mind the intergenerational effects of divorce, marital instability, and marital dissatisfaction in African American families. Given the disproportionately high divorce rate among African Americans, and the disproportionately high number of out-of-wedlock births, it is important to recognize that clinicians will come across a not-insignificant number of highly educated, accomplished African American couples who have very few, if any, positive marital examples in their immediate family. Many middle-class African Americans who have college, graduate, and professional degrees have come from families where education was the primary, if not exclusive, value taught to them. The consequence is that the children grow up inadvertently adopting an individualistic worldview, and do not have a clue about how to be in a healthy relationship—which requires vulnerability and interdependency. It is therefore critical that therapists provide African American premarital couples with a clear, healthy roadmap toward achieving marital happiness, while helping them to create their own vision for what they want their marriage to look like, which can be quite empowering.

As a metaprinciple, I am always looking for individual and couple stories of overcoming obstacles, as resilience has a long, historical place in the minds and hearts of African Americans. Hence, it is important for the clinician to not only encourage those stories but to use those stories as mechanisms for increasing flexibility and hope, which are both important for marital happiness.

Premarital Counseling Approach

I employ a four-session evaluation with all couples, where I meet with the couple together for the first session, then I meet with each of them individually, and then I meet with them conjointly in the fourth session to provide them my feedback.[1] After the assessment, we commence with the premarital counseling, which is informed by the four-session evaluation. In terms of my premarital counseling method, I use a content-driven, psychoeducational approach that I have found to be particularly helpful with premarital middle-class African American couples. The benefit of a psychoeducational approach with this population is threefold. First, as stated earlier, many middle-class African American couples come from families in which they did not have a clear model of how to have a healthy marriage. In addition, middle-class African American couples who did come from healthy two-parent families have an outdated model of what a healthy marriage looks like due to the increasing incidence of women in the workforce making as much money as, if not more than, their male counterparts. Hence, there is a need for both types of premarital couples to have a clear vision of what contemporary healthy marriages look like, and that need fits nicely with a psychoeducational approach.

Second, African Americans in general, and especially educated African Americans, are used to—and, in my experience, receptive to—a didactic format. Hence, using a content driven approach that covers the main areas and is tailored to the couple's specific background is very helpful. In addition to the content areas I address with all couples, such as the transition to marriage, transition to parenthood, parenting, and sex, there are content areas that are especially germane to African American couples, which include *trust, money, gender roles and power,* and *boundaries.*

Third, I find that a psychoeducational approach has the capacity to deescalate intense fighting among couples. Therapists who conduct premarital counseling know that although many couples state they are coming in for premarital counseling, which carries an expectation that there are no significant problems and they just want to protect their investment, many couples also come in with some fairly intense differences that they want to resolve before the wedding. The latter type of premarital couple can be particularly explosive because there is a commitment to getting married, which can prevent objectivity, there is the stress of planning a wedding, and there is an intense urgency for sameness because of the upcoming wedding. With these types of couples, a didactic format can be an efficient method to convey important information while maintaining their receptivity to the information.

Cultural Relevance of Content-Driven Approach

Given the disproportionately high divorce rate among African Americans (U.S. Census, 2000), many African Americans did not grow up with a healthy model of how a marriage should work (McLanahan, Garfinkel, Reichman, & Teitler, 1999). In these circumstances, it is important that premarital counseling provides the couple with a sense of what type of marriage they envision, what is the etiology of that model, and how realistic their model might be. A didactic, content-driven approach is able to provide that for the couple. Following are specific areas of content that are especially culturally relevant for premarital middle-class African American couples.

Trust

The importance of trust in a relationship is not breaking news. However, when it comes to the history of mistrust between African Americans and numerous facets of our society combined with normative challenges everyone faces when trust has been broken, it is no wonder that trust among African Americans is sometimes challenging to foster. In fact, research has cited that nonclinical paranoia among African Americans stems from a long history of racism and discrimination (Combs et al., 2006). The actual incident that creates the mistrust between African American couples usually does not differ from couples of any race or ethnicity (i.e., money, affairs, violence, etc.) (Allen & Olson, 2001); however, what is sometimes different is the process of forgiving. Thus, it is especially important that trust be one of the content areas covered when conducting premarital counseling with middle-class African American couples. Using a didactic approach that discusses the cultural and historical context of trust can be helpful. Moreover, the therapist must help the couple to develop a shared understanding of what trust means to each of them and how they will go about protecting that trust. Consistent with a recent trend in the marital field, it can be particularly helpful to spend sessions discussing forgiveness (Finchman, Stanley, & Beach, 2007), for both small and large offenses.

Gender, Leadership, and Power

In light of the prevalent gender disparities among African Americans, ones that often run counter to those in the rest of American society, particularly with respect to education and income, it is important that gender, leadership, and power be central content areas for premarital counseling. Hence, it is important that the therapist facilitates a discussion of each person's conceptualization of gender, and how their conceptualization may impact their upcoming marriage in terms of division of household labor, parenting, money, and sex. Similarly, given the disproportionate number of African American couples where the woman is more educated and makes more money than the man, it is important to discuss the role of leadership as a way to prevent conflict (Hatchett, Veroff, & Douvan, 1995; McLloyd et al., 2000). Helping the couple to develop a rubric for making decisions, both major and minor, can help them to create an "us."

Similarly, helping the couple to not only delineate gender roles, but learn how to accept influence from the other, is also very important.

Family of Origin/Extended Family

Although the support and influence of the extended family among African Americans can be a source of strength (Wilson, 1989), it can also have a paradoxically constraining effect on the marriage, as it can prevent the couple from forming an "us." The formation of an "us" is a critical task during the transition to marriage, which includes the ability to "separate" from the family of origin to form a new family. To be clear, I am not suggesting that the formation of an "us" and separating from family of origin is an either/or proposition, but rather a both/and proposition. That is, the therapist is to help the couple create a set of guidelines around the type of information they will share with their families of origin and the type of information they will keep private. Similarly, in light of research suggesting that middle-class African Americans are more likely to have an impoverished sibling (Heflin & Pattillo, 2006), the economic strain this potentially places on the middle-class sibling who is in a relationship can present an allegiance struggle with feelings of being confused and torn between providing for his or her nuclear family and providing for his or her extended family. Again, this does not have to be an either/or decision, but rather should be a decision tree that the therapist can help delineate.

CASE EXAMPLE

As I have noted throughout this chapter, there are many issues that couple therapists have to consider when conducting premarital counseling with middle-class African American couples. I have chosen a case in part because it illustrates the overriding theme of this chapter: the complex psycho-socio-cultural dynamics that exist among premarital middle-class African American couples and the elucidating benefit of a content-driven, didactic approach. To protect the confidentiality of the clients, all identifying information has been altered.

Bill and Terri were a couple in their late 20s. They had both completed graduate school and had a newborn son. They came in for premarital counseling at Terri's initiation, though Bill agreed premarital counseling would be a good idea. They were an attractive, athletic couple. Both agreed that they had intense difficulty with communication, where neither of them felt like the other listened to them, and neither of them felt like the other appreciated what they did. They did not have a wedding date set because they both felt they needed to address their issues before committing to a date. However, there was some urgency in that they were moving out of state in four months for occupational reasons.

During the initial conjoint session, it was clear that this couple was having a hard time containing their frustrations as they were both loud and aggressive in their speech and, although never with the intention of hurting him, she would frequently put her hands on him when she was frustrated and felt that he was not understanding her viewpoint. A more thorough assessment of violence was conducted during the individual sessions.

In Terri's individual session, she denied that Bill had ever hit her, but admitted that he had pushed, grabbed, and restrained her. She also adamantly denied ever being scared of him. However, she admitted that she was more physical than he was, and that she has punched him on several occasions. She also admitted to being verbally abusive. In Bill's individual session, he admitted that his primary reason for agreeing to premarital counseling was to get help controlling her anger, as he often felt his masculinity was being challenged in this relationship because he "doesn't allow anyone to put their hands on me," but he has been taking it from her. He also corroborated Terri's description of never hitting her but admitted that he had previously grabbed and restrained her. Pertinent negatives include no history of sexual abuse or rape, no substance abuse, no medical or health issues, and no history of severe mental illness. When asked, "What kept you in this relationship?" they both articulated that they loved each other, admired the other's intellect, and saw a lot of potential in this relationship. The strongest factor keeping them in the relationship was their son. Bill went as far as to say he would not be in this relationship if it were not for his son.

Gender, Leadership, and Power in the Relationship

In terms of character, Terri can be described as a very strong-willed, independent, emotionally expressive woman who has to be in control. Lack of control engendered feelings of vulnerability, which made her very anxious and engendered physical outbursts of anger and frustration. She also possessed a carefree spirit. Bill, on the other hand, had a stoic disposition and a strong work ethic. He valued being organized and on time. He also had an intense need to be right, which motivated his frustration when they argued, and made it difficult for him to empathize. Their different personality styles created conflict around leadership, as they were frequently involved in power struggles about who was in control and whose decision-making skills were "better." During disagreements, Bill would frequently state "I am a man" to justify why his opinion was superior.

Families of Origin and Trust

There were both proximal and distal etiological factors that helped inform my conceptualization of this case. In terms of proximal factors, the couple was experiencing a pile-up of stressors: They had recently moved across country, moved in with Terri's mother, negotiated the transition to parenthood and the transition to marriage at the same time, and struggled with perceived racism at work. Moving into Terri's mother's house significantly constrained their ability to formulate an "us," as Bill frequently reported that he did not feel comfortable and felt that Terri shared too much information about their problems with her mother. This made it difficult for Bill to trust that what he told Terri would stay between them. Distal factors included the fact that both of them were raised by their mothers and never knew their fathers; Terri reported that she "had no men in her life because they all went to jail"; they were both first-generation college graduates; Terri's first boyfriend had stalked her and been physically abusive toward her; and several of Terri's peers encouraged her to be independent and not accept too much influence from Bill, as they believed men would abuse this. The combination of the distal factors made it difficult for Terri to trust Bill, as she had a proclivity to view all men as undependable and dangerous.

My initial impression was that this was a volatile couple who struggled to manage their natural feelings of vulnerability. They were also in a power struggle that manifested itself in every decision, small or big, that had to be made. Similarly, the couple struggled with gender roles that became particularly salient when negotiating the division of household labor and parenting. Furthermore, the lack of a model of how husbands and wives should relate to each other interacted with misinformation coming from peers. Their real protective factor was that they both had a great sense of humor.

The counseling started first with a contract of no violence, and going over timeout procedures and teaching them anger management skills. Although they understood the skills, they had a hard time employing them outside of session. Moreover, the couple came in each week with a new crisis and often entered sessions fairly dysregulated. The ability to work on communication skills was further constrained by their complete inability to tolerate differences. For instance, Bill and Terri could not even describe a full incident because they would argue over the facts of the incident. Even my immense presence at 6'5" could not alter their relationship inertia.

After eight sessions of spinning our wheels, I changed the format. It seemed as though they were incapable of being in the room at the same time. In an act of desperation, I offered the idea of changing to a didactic format for the various reasons mentioned above. To my surprise, they not only agreed to the format, but reported being enthusiastic about the format as they both valued learning!

In conjoint sessions, I handed out one of my PowerPoint presentations, which included three slides per page and lines to the right of each slide for taking notes. Because this was a high-conflict couple, I started out by going over conflict resolution strategies. The order of the topics covered and the length of time spent discussing each topic is not as important as the content. The range of topics discussed and the length of time spent on each topic was based on the couple's areas of strengths and challenges reported during the four-session evaluation. The conflict resolution slides included how to take a timeout as well as the speaker listener technique (Markman, Stanley, & Blumberg, 2001). The next set of slides focused on mate selection and compatibility with an overarching belief that the most important criteria for mate selection is that you must "know yourself" (Nielsen et al., 2004). The areas of compatibility focused on money (Hamburg, 2000), division of household labor, and the role of families of origin. The next set of slides addressed the tasks and issues associated with the transition to marriage and the transition to parenthood. The final set of slides focused on how to prevent relationship distress and maintain commitment.

It was amazing to watch them being so receptive and diligent about asking questions and taking notes. Most of all, there was no fighting! I then met with each of them individually to help them apply the information we had covered. Although this could have been done conjointly, I thought the individual sessions would increase their receptivity and openness to admit fault without fear of being shamed by their partner. After the first week, which was on conflict resolution, the couple actually reported a decrease in the amount of conflict. After the second week, which was on the transition to marriage and how to develop an "us," the couple actually reported not only the absence of negativity but the presence of positive interactions. When asked how they accounted for the change, each of them reported using some skill or piece of information I taught them. By the third session, Terri also reported a shift in her understanding of relationships, which I interpreted as an indication that she now had a script and model for how to approach their relationship. By the end of counseling, they not only reported a higher level of relationship satisfaction but both reported an increased commitment to the relationship and had even started discussing wedding plans!

Tips for Clinicians

My Money Is Our Money

It is no surprise that money is the number one reason couples get divorced (Hamburg, 2000). Given the interesting juxtaposition of money in African American marriages, money takes on special meaning. Part of the reason is because money highlights our vulnerabilities and inextricable dependency in the context of a marriage. However, there is also the opportunity to use money to help facilitate the transition to marriage. I find it helpful to emphasize the importance of merging a couple's finances, at least conceptually. That is, couples need to think about it as "our" money, and there needs to be transparency around the money so that each person knows where their money is going. Of course, the ability for each person to make the cognitive shift of "my money" to "our money" highlights the issues of trust and interdependency. I utilize a diagram by Stuart (1980), which he calls the *Powergram*, which provides a visual aid to explicate how to maintain the choice to buy things each partner individually wants without jeopardizing "us"—that is, how to successfully manage the difficult task of independence versus interdependence.

Focus on Happiness, Not Fairness!

As mentioned throughout this chapter, power struggles are especially prevalent in African American marriages, given the gender disparities. Hence, I find it helpful—particularly for premarital middle-class African American couples—to help them focus on happiness rather than fairness. I utilize the legal system as an example by telling them that the legal system is designed to promote fairness, but very few people who go through that system would describe the legal system process as happy. That simple example appears to resonate with many couples, and can stimulate a shift in their thinking.

Implications for Training, Supervision, and Further Research

Given that the approach described in this chapter does not require specialized training like with other specialized forms of therapy, it is simply a matter of the clinician being committed to strive toward cultural sensitivity. This involves being aware of one's own assumptions and biases, as well as being committed to educating oneself on issues germane to race and SES specific to premarital middle-class African American couples. To that end, I believe that employing a scientist-practitioner approach can help actualize cultural sensitivity. That is, using one's knowledge of the contextual constraints facing a particular population to formulate hypotheses of a couple's difficulties, and then, most importantly, *to test out those hypotheses,* is an excellent method for actualizing cultural sensitivity. This requires supervisors to help trainees to develop a "Colombo" style, curious, investigative approach toward assessment and intervention.

In terms of research, there are numerous significant implications. Although the low marriage rate among African Americans has largely been examined through a sociological lens by documenting structural barriers, which has important policy implications, research has not sufficiently examined the psychological and interpersonal barriers to marriage. Examining this problem on an interpersonal, microsystem level of analysis is integral, as no policy can repair the fragility of African American relationships. Furthermore, it is important to examine the interaction between macro and microsystem variables in order to have a more complete understanding of the relationship difficulties confronting premarital middle-class African American couples.

Past research has understandably focused largely on marriage. However, to treat marriage as a categorical variable without recognizing that relationships begin prior to the wedding date is misleading (Karney & Bradbury, 1995). Hence, examining the development of premarital relationships, including the impact of whom individuals select as a mate, is important in order to ultimately reduce divorce rates and disparities, as well as promote stable relationships (Markman et al., 1991). We know virtually nothing about the long-term effects of mate selection on marital functioning. Furthermore, past research on mate selection and premarital relationships has been done largely with European American samples, and given the relationship difficulties disproportionately affecting African Americans, this is a significant gap in the literature.

Experiential Exercises

One of the experiential exercises I have premarital couples do is interview their parents. The idea behind interviewing their parents is that the couple will better assess their own past and baseline assumptions about relationships that they bring to their current relationship. The procedure and list of questions for this exercise is described in an article by Nielsen and colleagues (2004), and is one of the experiential exercises for an undergraduate course titled "Marriage 101" that I co-teach. Couples often describe this exercise as very meaningful.

I also think this exercise can be helpful for all individuals who conduct premarital counseling with middle-class African Americans. All families have to negotiate and deal with issues of social class, money, and power. All families also have to delineate gender roles. Hence, by interviewing your own parents and/or your current spouse with special attention paid to how salient, easy, or difficult it was/is for your parents/spouse to negotiate those issues, the more sensitive you will become to the pervasive effects such issues have on marital and family functioning.

Note

1. I have a version of the assessment model that is specifically tailored for African American couples. Interested readers who would like to read about my assessment model are referred to a book chapter (Chambers & Lebow, in press).

Additional Resources

Film

Wiley, A. (Director) (2006). *Soulmate,* available from www.soulmatefilm .com/about.htm. This is a movie describing the personal struggles of the growing number of single African American women.

Readings

Hamburg, S. (2001). *Will our love last? A couple's road map.* New York: Scribner. This is an excellent book for premarital couples on compatibility.

References

Allen, W. D., & Olson, D. H. (2001). Five types of African-American marriages. *Journal of Marital and Family Therapy, 27*(3), 301–314.

Black, L. W. (1999). Therapy with African-Americans. In P. Papp (Ed.), *Couples on the fault line* (pp. 205–221). New York: Guilford Press.

Boyd-Franklin, N. (2003). *Black families in therapy: Understanding the African American experience* (2nd ed.). New York: Guilford Press.

Boyd-Franklin, N., & Franklin, A. J. (1998). African American couples in therapy. In M. McGoldrick (Ed.), *Re-visioning family therapy: Race, culture, and gender in clinical practice* (pp. 268–281). New York: Guilford Press.

Breunlin, D. C., Schwartz, R. C., & Mac Kune-Karrer, B. (1997). *Metaframeworks: Transcending the models of family therapy.* San Francisco: Jossey-Bass.

Chambers, A. L., & Lebow, J. (in press). Common and unique factors in assessing African American couples. *Toward a science of clinical psychology: Laboratory evaluations and interventions.* Hauppauge, NY: Nova Science.

Christensen, A., & Jacobson, N. S. (2000). *Reconcilable differences.* New York: Guilford Press.

Combs, D. R., Penn, D. L., Cassisi, J., Michael, C., Wood, T., Wanner, J., & Adams, S. (2006). Perceived racism as a predictor of paranoia among African Americans. *Journal of Black Psychology, 32*(1), 87–104.

Darity, W. A., Jr., & Myers, S. L., Jr. (1995). Family structure and the marginalization of Black men: Policy implications. In M. B. Tucker & C. Mitchell-Kernan (Eds.), *The decline in marriage among African Americans* (pp. 263–308). New York: Russell Sage Foundation.

Fincham, F. D., Stanley, S. M., & Beach, S. R. H. (2007). Transformative processes in marriage: An analysis of emerging trends. *Journal of Marriage and Family, 69*(2), 275–292.

Fishel, A. (2000). Couples therapy. In T. A. Stern & J. B. Herman (Eds.), *Psychiatry: Update and board preparation.* New York: McGraw-Hill.

Hamburg, S. (2000). *Will our love last: A couple's roadmap.* New York: Scribner.

Hardy, K. V., & Laszloffy, T. A. (2002). Couple therapy using a multicultural perspective. In A. S. Gurman & N. S. Jacobson (Eds.), *Clinical handbook of couple therapy* (3rd ed., pp. 569–593). New York: Guilford Press.

Hatchett, S., Veroff, J., & Douvan, E. (1995). Marital stability and marriage among Black and White couples in early marriage. In M. B. Tucker & C. Mitchell-Kernan (Eds.), *The decline in marriage among African Americans* (pp. 177–211). New York: Russell Sage Foundation.

Heflin, C. M., & Pattillo, M. (2006). Poverty in the family: Race, siblings and socioeconomic heterogeneity. *Social Science Research, 35,* 804–822.

James, A. D. (1998). What's love got to do with it? Economic viability and the likelihood of marriage among African American men. *Journal of Comparative Family Studies, 29*(2), 1–13.

Karney, B. R., & Bradbury, T. N. (1995). The longitudinal course of marriage and marital instability: A review of theory, method, and research. *Psychological Bulletin, 118,* 3–34.

Lichter, D. T., Anderson, R. N., & Hayward, M. D. (1995). Marriage markets and marital choice. *Journal of Family Issues, 16*(4), 412–431.

Markman, H. J., Stanley, S. M., & Blumberg, S. (2001). *Fighting for your marriage.* San Francisco: Jossey-Bass.

Markman, H. J., Stanley, S. M., Floyd, F. J., Hahlweg, K., & Blumberg, S. (1991). Prevention of divorce and marital distress. In L. E. Beutler & M. Crago (Eds.), *Psychotherapy research: An international review of programmatic studies* (pp. 115–122). Washington, DC: American Psychological Association.

McLanahan, S., Garfinkel, I., Reichman, N., & Teitler, J. (1999). *Unwed parents or fragile families? Implications for welfare and child support policy.* Working Paper no. 00–04. Princeton, NJ: Bendheim-Thoman Center for Research on Child Well-being, Princeton University.

McLloyd, V., Cauce, A., Tacheuchi, D., & Wilson, M. L. (2000). Marital processes and parental socialization in families of color: A decade review of research. *Journal of Marriage and the Family, 62,* 1–27.

Nielsen, A., Pinsof, W. M., Rampage, C., Solomon, A., & Goldstein, S. (2004). Marriage 101: An integrated academic and experiential undergraduate marriage education course. *Family Relations, 53*(5), 485–494.

Orbuch, T. L., Veroff, J., & Hunter, A. (1998). Black couples, White couples: The early years of marriage. In E. M. Hetherington (Ed.), *Coping with divorce, single parenting, and remarriage: A risk and resiliency perspective* (pp. 23–43). Mahwah NJ: Lawrence Erlbaum.

Pattillo, M. (2005). Black middle-class neighborhoods. *Annual Review of Sociology, 31,* 305–329.

Pinderhughes, E. B. (1988). Treatment with middle class Black families: A systemic perspective. In J. Coner-Edwards & J. Spurlock (Eds.), *Black families in crisis* (pp. 215–236). New York: Brunner-Mazel.

Pinderhughes, E. B. (2002). African American marriage in the 20th century. *Family Process, 41,* 269–282.

Pinsof, W. M. (1995). *Integrative problem-centered therapy: A synthesis of family, individual, and biological therapies.* New York: Basic Books.

Stuart, R. B. (1980). *Helping couples change: A social learning approach to marital therapy.* New York: Guilford Press.

Tucker, M. B., & Mitchell-Kernan, C. (1995). Trends in African American family formation: A theoretical and statistical overview. In M. B. Tucker & C. Mitchell-Kernan (Eds.), *The decline in marriage among African Americans* (pp. 3–26). New York: Russell Sage Foundation.

U.S. Census Bureau. (2000). *Statistical abstract of the United States: 2000* (120th ed.). Washington, DC: Bernan.

Wilson, M. N. (1989). Child development in the context of the Black extended family. *American Psychologist, 44*(2), 380–385.

Twelve

Joining, Understanding, and Supporting Black Couples in Treatment

Shalonda Kelly and Nancy Boyd-Franklin

A controversial topic in the African American community is that of male–female couple relationships. Given the widespread negative portrayals of African Americans, and the high levels of segregation in the United States, many well-trained therapists of all backgrounds may encounter unexpected difficulties when treating African American couples. Despite the great need for viable interventions with this population, relatively little literature has addressed this topic (Boyd-Franklin, 2003; Kelly & Floyd, 2006).

All treatments should include a multicultural, systems-oriented, and strengths-based approach, and these are commonalities in our treatment of African American couples and families. Kelly applies a family systems and a cognitive behavioral framework, while Boyd-Franklin applies a family systems and a multisystemic perspective. Our backgrounds have shaped our approaches; we both grew up in two-parent, working-class homes, where the extended family, community, and education were valued. We both come from fairly expressive Southern roots and Baptist traditions. Boyd-Franklin has both an African American and a Jamaican heritage, and Kelly's family of origin broke from the church in her youth. We are both African American, yet experience has taught us that culturally sensitive therapists of any ethnicity can work well with African American couples.

Space considerations limit the scope of this chapter to heterosexual African American couples. Our focus on African American couples is partially because the Black couples of Caribbean and African descent who make up 5% of the Black U.S. population are at less risk for divorce (Phillips & Sweeney, 2006). We also consider nonmarried couples because many unmarried African American male partners are treated as invisible, and their women and children are considered to be single-parent families by well-meaning therapists (Boyd-Franklin, 2003; Kelly, 2003). Finally, we note the tremendous diversity in country of origin, racial and ethnic identification, experiences, in-group participation, socioeconomic status, and level of acculturation within the African American community, such that our interventions need to be tailored to these differences.

Relevant Research and Scholarly Literature

Evidence-based couple therapy and data on the nature of marriage have been developed on predominately White, middle-class couples (Boyd-Franklin, 2003; Karney, Kreitz, & Sweeney, 2004; Kelly, 2003). For example, in one study of newlyweds (Karney et al., 2004), despite advertising, African American couples sought treatment at significantly lower rates than their proportions of the population surrounding the treatment site. Also, the study criterion of childlessness excluded all of the African American couples who sought treatment (Karney et al., 2004). Kelly (2006a) notes that cognitive-behavioral therapy, an evidence-based approach, may usefully be applied to African Americans, given its emphasis on nonjudgmental, collaborative problem solving and the use of environmental supports. Yet evidence-based approaches have not been used with African American couples and thus do not consider their unique needs.

Current treatments need to be supplemented with in-depth knowledge of African American couples. Well-known negative statistics from nationally representative studies show that African Americans have higher never-married and divorce rates, lower remarriage rates, more complaints of negative partner behavior, and lower relationship quality compared with their White counterparts (e.g., Harknett & McLanahan, 2004; Philips & Sweeney, 2005). These statistics must be contextualized to prevent pathologizing of African American couples. Data substantiate the adverse effects of racism (e.g., Utsey, Chae, Brown, & Kelly, 2002), poverty and financial strain (e.g., Conger et al., 2002), lower education levels (Phillips & Sweeney, 2006), and the shortage of African American men (Phillips & Sweeney, 2006) on African Americans' individual and couple adjustment. Even with these impacts, much variance in African American couple relationships still remains unexplained, and thus we concur with research suggesting that unexplored contexts may impact African American couples (e.g., Orbuch, Veroff, Hassan, & Horrocks, 2002). We explore these contexts below.

Adverse Contexts Commonly Experienced by African Americans

Challenges reflected by the above statistics may be related to ongoing racism and oppression. From slavery to the present, unsubstantiated claims that African Americans are inferior have been used to justify negative treatment toward them (see Pinderhughes, 2002, for a review). For example, much racism was not banned until the Civil Rights and Voting Rights Acts of the mid-1960s, meaning that many Americans have experienced times when all African Americans were denied basic human rights. While public awareness focuses only on individual acts of verbal and physical abuse as racism, more pernicious types of racism exist. Institutional racism reflects policies and practices that result in disparities in benefits across racial groups (Jones, 1997), such as discriminatory practices against African Americans in education, health care, employment, housing, and the media (e.g., Coleman, 2003). Cultural racism refers to values, beliefs, and practices that determine social acceptance (Jones, 1997), such as the dominant value for emotional restraint over the emotional expressiveness that is valued by many African Americans.

African Americans' individual and couple adjustment suffers as a result of racism. Their reports of racism magnify the negative impact of stressors on their relationships (Murry, Brown, Brody, Cutrona, & Simons, 2001), and are positively associated with destructive communication, such as verbal aggression and violence (LaTaillade, Baucom, & Jacobson, 2000). The stress of stigmatization has led to substance use, incarceration, and death for many African American men, resulting in a sex ratio imbalance between African American men and women (Kelly, 2003). This shortage of men is associated with lower relationship quality, lower partner quality, less traditional gender role attitudes, and having children with multiple partners (Harknett & McLanahan, 2004). Another consequence is the tendency for some African Americans to see themselves and their group as inferior. In fact, anti-Black attitudes and a mixture of pro- and anti-Black attitudes are associated with individual and relationship distress for African Americans (Kelly, 2004; Kelly & Floyd, 2006), while marriage is associated with more positive racial attitudes for African Americans (Kelly, 2006b).

These social ills are partly attributable to adverse socioeconomic situations. African Americans have significantly less income and education than their White counterparts (Saegert et al., 2006), and their poverty rates are among the highest (Kelly, 2003). At comparable income levels and with similar jobs, African Americans have significantly fewer financial resources and assets that are passed down through generations than their White counterparts (Saegert et al., 2006), and they have disproportionately suffered from the decline in blue collar jobs since the 1960s (Pinderhughes, 2002). Studies show that financial dissatisfaction and stress consistently contribute to negative couple interactions and experiences (e.g., Conger et al., 2002). Also, socioeconomic differences between the partners tend to be less than those within White couples (Saegert et al., 2006), which can adversely affect gender roles within the couple (e.g., Pinderhughes, 2002).

Strengths and Cultural Values Commonly Held by African Americans

African culture emphasizes family and community ties, which create in-group bonds despite oppression (e.g., Boyd-Franklin, 2003). For African Americans, family can include anyone with whom they feel very close, such as nuclear and extended family and friends who are close enough to seem "like family" (Boyd-Franklin, 2003). African American extended families are interdependent; they may live in the same house or on the same street, share money and resources, turn to each other for help with marital and other problems, and share decision making (Boyd-Franklin, 2003). Similarly, African Americans' involvement in community organizations such as churches, fraternities, or sororities and in Black professional and self-help groups provides them with mentoring, resources, and services.

This self-help orientation is related to African Americans' strength of role flexibility and egalitarianism. For example, African Americans report higher satisfaction in husband- than wife-led couples (Gray-Little, 1982), but they also report favorable attitudes toward sharing breadwinner, decision-making, and family roles (e.g., Orbuch & Eyster, 1997). Of course, most African American women have had to contribute to the family income since slavery (Boyd-Franklin, 2003). Early in the marriage, the husband's household work is related positively to relationship quality for both spouses. Further, endorsement of egalitarian norms and greater wife income relative to that of the husband predicts more male participation in female-typed household tasks (Orbuch & Eyster, 1997).

National data show that African Americans' religiosity and church attendance are higher than those of other groups (e.g., Taylor, Mattis, & Chatters, 1999). Many African American couples pray together for inspiration, support, and a positive moral compass in dealing with problems. The Bible for Christians or the Koran for Muslims may be used as a road map for shared gender role ideals. Some African American churches have marriage ministries that use long-term couples as mentors to struggling couples. They provide marriage-enrichment classes, pastoral and premarital counseling, and activities for couples. In fact, many distressed African American couples go to the church or a Christian counselor, rather than to a therapist. In addition, many African Americans are not religious, but have a spiritual orientation; this can include importance placed upon morals, honesty, respect, and community service (Boyd-Franklin, 2003; Kelly, 2003).

The ability to maintain a positive ethnic and racial identity and self-concept in the face of societal stressors is a great strength for African American couples. African Americans' positive ethnic identity is associated with multiple mental health indices (e.g., Carter, Sbrocco, Lewis, & Friedman, 2001). For African Americans, a positive ethnic identity and racial socialization by the family each acts as a buffer against the effects of perceived discrimination and racism on the mental health of African Americans (Fischer & Shaw, 1999; Wong, Eccles, & Sameroff, 2003).

Expressiveness and creativity also are positive ethnic and cultural traditions (see chapters in McGoldrick, Giordano, & Garcia-Preto, 2005). There is a community-wide dislike for phoniness and a value for saying what one feels (Kelly & Boyd-Franklin, 2004), evidenced by known phrases such as "keeping it real" and "testifying," in which slang and distinctive phrases are used and positive or negative raw emotions are given voice (Kelly & Boyd-Franklin, 2004). Often, nonverbal expressions communicate much, such as with gesticulating and clapping to show pleasure and rolling or cutting of the eyes, loud sighs, and sucking of teeth to show displeasure. Expressiveness values also may be related to the higher rates of self-disclosure in African American couple relationships compared with those of their White counterparts (Oggins, Veroff, & Leber, 1993).

Achievement barriers erected by oppression have led many African Americans to survive by learning from their experiences and focusing upon the present (e.g., Kelly, 2006a). Many African Americans are adept at observing "vibes," which are signs of respect and acceptance, or the lack thereof (Boyd-Franklin, 2003). They also have learned how to "hustle," meaning the strength of finding positive, nontraditional ways to get their immediate needs met, such as with multiple jobs, or meaning negative and illegal means of supporting themselves, as often portrayed in the media (e.g., Majors & Billson, 1992). Notably, the values for learning from experience, focusing on the present, and positive "hustling" to get needs met can be adaptive during times of stress. Yet values for self-reliance also may steer African American couples away from treatment.

Adapting Treatment: A Multicultural, Systemic, and Strengths-Based Approach

A multicultural, systemic, and strengths-based approach has many benefits. A multicultural approach ensures that therapists have useful knowledge of African American cultural tendencies and their history of oppression and White supremacy. Often, those who work with African American couples may focus treatment only on the couple. Systems approaches help therapists to understand the meaning of family and community relationships, and use them as resources. Often African American couples' strengths are overshadowed by media stereotypes and adverse circumstances that may be falsely attributed to cultural deficits, or they may not be recognized or elicited by the therapist. A focus on strengths helps therapists to notice egalitarianism, role flexibility, and other strengths that may not be valued by the larger society.

Our adaptation approach to couple therapy involves the use of knowledge, skills, and awareness, which are crucial areas of therapist growth in conducting cross-cultural treatment (Sue, 2001). Each of these areas is presented in Table 12.1. These methods are not necessary for

Table 12.1   A Multicultural, Systemic, and Strengths-Based Knowledge,
Skills, and Awareness Approach

Factors to Know and Assess

Knowledge

Know history, values, religious and spiritual beliefs, and views on treatment and illness

Assess couple relationship, obtain family genograms, and assess family boundaries

Assess SES, ability to meet basis needs, and other stressors

Assess racial/ethnic identity, acculturation, racial pride, and shame

Assess individual, couple, family, and community strengths

Skills

Join, orient, and match treatment to the couple's preferences

Acknowledge and address racial and cultural differences

Advocate to help address other needs assessed above

Notice ethnic and cultural positives; utilize the strengths identified in the assessment

Develop lightly held emic and etic hypotheses

Label relevant racism, cultural differences, and stressors

Be a cultural broker

Restructure cultural shame perspectives and balance gender roles

Awareness

Learn about own racial/ethnic heritage, and White supremacy, privilege, and oppression

Know the limitations of using measures not normed on the group

Know common negative therapist reactions and own cross-cultural biases

Obtain supervision, consultation, and experiences with in-group members and experts

every couple, and they are particularly indicated when therapists feel a lack of connection with a couple in treatment, hold negative feelings or views of either partner, or notice any negative reactions to treatment by the couple. We do many of these interventions subtly or informally, but for didactic purposes they are labeled separately for therapists to assess whether they have used or can use them in treatment.

Knowledge of African American Couples in Treatment

In-depth knowledge such as that presented above is essential to understand potential treatment enthusiasm or reluctance. Studies show that African American couples are more likely to agree to participate in relationship enhancement and educational programs than their White counterparts (Rogge et al., 2006). This receptiveness must be contrasted with a common bias against "therapy," which may be seen as being for crazy people. Many African Americans have a "healthy cultural suspicion" of Whites and their motives, related to oppression (Boyd-Franklin, 2003) and substandard health and mental health care (U.S. Department of Health and Human Services [USDHHS], 2001). There are also community values against sharing family secrets with outsiders (Boyd-Franklin, 2003; Kelly, 2003; LaTaillade, 2006). For poor African Americans, treatment reluctance may stem from experiences with intrusions from social service agencies, police, schools, and other institutions. Finally, many tend to pray on their problems and then give them up to God, so entering nonpastoral treatment may seem like a lack of faith or a reliance on others who do not respect their religious values.

Often, African Americans' relationship distress may be associated with family relationships and boundaries, and both must be assessed. One example is that of "baby mama drama," which involves co-parenting with ex-partners. While many African Americans in blended families do co-parent well with their ex-partners, some couples have difficulties setting healthy boundaries and cooperative relationships between the two families, and mistrust and issues in addressing finances, visitation, and child custody across each family can result (Boyd-Franklin, 2003).

Therapists can better assist with "baby mama drama" when they assess the key contexts listed in the knowledge section of Table 12.1. After trust has been established, genograms—also known as family trees—can convey interest in who the family comprises, who lives with or is important to whom, and who are role models for their couple relationship and how these models may affect their relationship problems (McGoldrick, Gerson, & Shellenberger, 1999). Beyond education, occupation, and income, therapists should assess the couple's perceived ability to meet their basic needs, as well as the presence of other stressors that adversely impact their relationship quality (Kelly & Floyd, 2006). For example, African Americans may have more health issues than Whites (e.g., USDHHS, 2001), and extended family values suggest that therapists might disproportionately encounter

African American couples who assist extended family members with emotional and financial problems. Because racism is pernicious, it is important to assess cultural pride and shame (Hardy & Lazloffy, 2002), as well as the presence of individual, couple, family, and community strengths, such as religion and community self-help tendencies.

Skills in Treating African American Couples

To combat treatment reluctance, therapists must join with African American couples and orient them to their treatment roles. The systems intervention of joining occurs when therapists use empathy, warmth, respect, and genuine attempts at understanding, while being themselves without use of unfamiliar slang or mannerisms (e.g., Nichols & Minuchin, 1999). This can induce positive "vibes" in the session (Boyd-Franklin, 2003). If a religious statement is made, therapists can show interest in how it has been helpful to the couple. Many African American couples may be unfamiliar with treatment, and clarification of roles and expectations can prevent misunderstandings.

Several simple adaptations can help therapists match treatment to the couple's preferences. Questions about a Christian therapist can be used to discuss whether and how to use the couple's religious or spiritual strengths in treatment, such as via obtaining a release to speak with and include their minister or members of their "church family" in the sessions (e.g., Boyd-Franklin, Kelly, & Durham, 2008). Assessment is important; however, many seek information prematurely, before joining has occurred. The assessment should occur after joining, and the depth should be altered to fit the couple's comfort level and prevent early drop-out (LaTaillade, 2006; Rogge et al., 2006). Scales assessing the partners' racial identities can indicate their likely level of acceptance of therapists of varying backgrounds and signal if more joining is needed (e.g., Boyd-Franklin et al., 2008). In future sessions, after trust has been estab-lished, the partners can be asked how they feel about working with someone from the therapist's background to allow clarification and counteracting of negative expectancies. Therapists also can advocate with agencies to assist couples in addressing socioeconomic needs and other stressors that may comprise systemic contributions to their rela-tionship problems. Finally, therapists can use family, community, and other resources identified in the assessment to support the couple's goals (e.g., Boyd-Franklin et al., 2008)

Therapists should understand couples from the dominant cultural view, such as from one's theoretical orientation, as well as from an emic, or within-group, view. Use of both skills is likely to best fit the couple's circumstances (Sue, 2001). For example, systems concepts can lead to unfair judgments about some African American partners as being enmeshed with their families, when a multicultural view shows that the value placed on family closeness may be expressed with clear, predictable roles. Therapists must accept beliefs that racism negatively affects their lives, and prepare for possible negative affect around racial topics, partner disagreement about the role of racism, and partner blaming that ignores the role of racism in their lives. In response, therapists can ask each partner how similarities and differences in their racial views play a positive role or cause conflict in the relationship. Next, therapists should notice and label the racism that the partners may experience. It is typically a systems case of "both/and," wherein racism adversely impacts the couple, *and* they need to act in spite of it and build skills in addressing it. Once racism-related issues are openly labeled, the therapist can be a cultural broker and help the couple to negotiate agreement on shared values, and explore how to enact those values so as to stay united against racism (for clinical examples, see Boyd-Franklin et al., 2008).

Many African American couples also struggle with maintaining group value systems and meeting societal standards in the face of oppression. Oppression leads many African Americans to experience a lack of respect and power in their daily interactions outside of the home (e.g., Boyd-Franklin, 2003). Many African American couples respond to adversity with a combination of in-group pride, egalitarianism, religious support, and role flexibility, wherein they rely appropriately on themselves and significant others. Thus, their homes become safe spaces to "pull out the arrows" of racism and heal from the burden of making Whites comfortable in their presence (Boyd-Franklin, 2003). Therapists should make treatment a safe place to "pull out the arrows," and not take venting and expressions of the pain of oppression personally.

For African American couples in treatment, often these strengths have gone awry, resulting in issues around gender roles. For example, the combination of high marital ideals, negative in-group stereotypes, adverse socioeconomic conditions, and negative comparisons with Whites can lead to fairytale views of relationships. As one couple stated, "Why can't we have the Brady Bunch family? My White coworkers receive flowers at work. Why don't I?" The sex-ratio imbalance can lead to infidelity, man sharing, competition, or worries about these issues (Boyd-Franklin et al., 2008). For example, for some African American men who cannot meet society's provider ideal, infidelity can be a maladaptive way of proving one's manhood (Majors & Billson, 1992). Or some men may stereotypically perceive their wives as emasculating when they are not submissive, despite African American women's historical survival skill of assertiveness (e.g., Pinderhughes, 2002). Similarly, as Black faces and bodies are often deemed unattractive in the media, some African American women may feel unworthy of fidelity, believe stereotypes that African American men are undependable and unfaithful, and/or believe in raising children without a partner (Boyd-Franklin, 2003; Harknett & McLanahan, 2004). One or more generations of distressed single parenthood or poverty may exacerbate these views (e.g., Harknett & McLanahan), as these situations may limit exposure to the positive African American couple and family role models that exist.

Therapists should explore and decrease partners' negative within-group views, which can contribute to gender role problems. Many African American couples pool their resources well, have positive self- and group concepts and balanced gender roles, behave according to spiritually grounded morals, and empathize with each other's experiences of adversity. Yet in-group shame can lead to partner blaming without recognizing the tolls taken by social and economic stressors. Donohue et al.'s (2006) brief scales and methods help to assess and respond to feelings of in-group pride and shame. Kelly (2006a) and LaTaillade (2006) provide examples of adapting cognitive behavioral treatments to the uniqueness of African Americans. Also, solution-focused systemic techniques can challenge the couples' negative views of their in-group and their partners. These include reinforcing positive behaviors, normalizing their problems and educating them about the contexts that affect them, positively reframing the problem, such as with the application of a developmental framework, and eliciting positive "exceptions" and solutions to their problems (Friedman & Lipchik, 1999).

CASE EXAMPLE

Therapist Kelly saw Jordan and Lena, an African American couple who had been married for three years. Their son, Gene, was 18 months old. Jordan was an insurance adjuster, and Lena was a nurse. They sought treatment after an incident where he stayed out playing basketball with his friends at the local community center and got home later than expected, whereupon a serious argument ensued over time with his friends versus time at home with his family.

The first session was characterized by high negative affect and attempts by both to "tell my side." Kelly joined with both, stating that her concern was not to find out who was right, but to find out what could make them happy as a couple and as individuals. Lena desired that they co-parent more effectively, and that Jordan express more appreciation for her. Jordan wanted more frequent sex and for Lena not to "take things so personally all of the time." Jordan stated that he met Lena at a party, where "I got Lena to loosen up, and she's still uptight even now." Then Lena began to cry, stating that "I didn't know that it was this bad between us." For the fourth time, Kelly directed the couple to positives, distinguishing current bad feelings from the things that initially attracted Jordan to Lena. Then Jordan visibly relaxed and spoke about her caring and giving nature, and the couple spoke fondly of their early times together.

Feedback was given after reviewing their questionnaires and meeting individually with each spouse. Kelly gave a developmental reframe of how impressed she was because they had weathered many stressors and transitions in the past few years. These included earning bachelor's degrees, marrying, buying a home, and having a child. Because of this pileup, she stated that they were still managing individual versus couple time, and figuring out the division of labor and their respective roles. She noted that, as with many couples, they were working to regain their former sex life after having their son. She gave heavy rationales for using standard cognitive-behavioral and systemic interventions, such as a functional analysis of the different role that sex played for each. She also noted how their pattern of mutual attack overshadowed their positive initial intentions.

Kelly did a genogram in the fifth session and found that both spouses had few healthy couple role models upon which to draw. Their relationship ideal was "50/50 all the way," but Jordan revealed that Lena's strict determination to stay independent in their first year of marriage hurt their relationship. He partially attributed it to Lena's mom "telling her not to become dependent on a man." They both discussed the "divorce climate," where their closest African American friends were not married or were unhappily married, and Lena often expressed fears that their relationship might not survive. For example, she saw the incident that led to treatment as a sign that he was becoming tired of her and didn't care for having a family, preferring his best friend's carefree "single" life. She reported that Jordan did not sacrifice for the relationship as she did. For example, she did not go out much with her friends, despite Jordan's urging. Jordan reported that "I've always done the right thing, but she never gives me any credit for it." He revealed a history of "rescuing" Lena by getting her mind off her problems, but stated that Lena had begun to treat him as if he were undependable. Finally, both grew up receiving spankings, yet Lena wanted to learn other ways of parenting, and Jordan did not.

Kelly responded to this information by helping the couple to identify their relationship strengths, and test their assumptions and attributions against objective facts. For example, despite their fears, neither had ever reported a desire to divorce. In fact, Jordan was surprised that Lena worried about the divorce climate. He stated that he loved being married and saw how his friends had lots of problems being single.

Second, Kelly helped the couple to set clear boundaries around their relationship, their nuclear family, and their relationships with extended family and friends. Lena's friendships were found to be solid, but mostly maintained over the phone. She was thus encouraged to do more with a local chapter of her sorority, which Jordan supported, and Kelly helped them to negotiate these changes. These outings were heavily normalized to challenge Lena's beliefs in self-sacrifice for the relationship. Kelly then worked with the couple on outlining couple and individual goals, and negotiating appropriate amounts of time to spend on each. She also praised Lena's bond with her mother, and noted how she wanted Lena to benefit from her own relationship mistakes to the extent that at times she would become very critical of Jordan. Kelly then asked Lena whether she felt dependent upon Jordan. Lena said no, that she actually loved how Jordan used to come to her rescue back in college. Kelly told the couple that they had a dilemma of deciding how much to tell their families about their relationship concerns, given the consequence of greater outside input and negative views about the spouse. Using a standard problem-solving task, the couple agreed on four solutions. First, they would tell their parents one negative only in the context of saying three positives about the other spouse. Second, they identified friends that both trusted who were not affected by the "divorce climate." They agreed to first discuss relationship concerns with those friends before turning to a parent. Third, they agreed to separate and pray on their problems when heated. Finally, they agreed to set a time to talk about problems within 24 hours of feeling strongly about them.

Third, Kelly asked the couple to talk about their experiences of corporal punishment as a child. Both recounted times when their parents had gone overboard, such as leaving temporary marks on their bodies. Still, Jordan reported that he had "turned out fine." Thus, Kelly noted how spanking in the African American community often helps couples keep their children in line, particularly given that they could grow up and get killed by the police for stepping out of line. The couple agreed. Then she contrasted that with the fact that in today's climate, many people who spank run the risk of having child protective services called in when they spank their children, even when they don't go overboard and have good intentions, because other effective methods exist. Kelly then invited them to discuss other pros and cons of spanking and how others they knew handled it. From the discussion, they decided together to explore other methods of parenting and determine whether the other methods would be effective with their son.

Fourth, Kelly was concerned about Jordan's feelings that Lena saw him as undependable, given that he was highly responsible. At first, Jordan labeled himself as the "total man" who could rise to meet any need that she expressed, and he denied ever feeling helpless or burdened. Finally, Kelly raised the question of whether or not it had been harder to meet Lena's needs since college, in the light of all of the stressors that they had faced, to which he reported, "sometimes." Until this point, Lena continued to express periodic desires for more emotional intimacy, given that Jordan tended to shut down whenever their problematic pattern surfaced. More than wanting Jordan to do more household work, she said she felt needy and wanted him to appreciate her. Thus, Kelly continued with the "life transition" reframe, and stated that in their current life phase, the challenge was one of redefining what it meant to "rescue" Lena. She told the couple that it appeared that, now both were getting so many work and home needs met, Lena needed Jordan to "rescue" her by comforting her and helping to soothe her with stories of their large store of positive experiences whenever her fears of the "divorce climate" would arise. To facilitate this, homework was given whereupon Jordan would express appreciation, and Lena would express feeling a lack of it to teach him the cues to identify when she felt that way.

Upon termination, Kelly worked with the couple to develop their "bible," which consisted of their list of positive maintenance behaviors and thoughts, such as "Speak your assumptions, and ask each other if they are true." Their relationship quality had increased significantly into the nondistressed range, and remained in that range three months after treatment. Both reported 6 out of 7 for treatment satisfaction.

Discussion

Some readers unfamiliar with African American culture may see this case as representative of all couples, and miss the subtleties related to African American culture. Therapists should use theory to guide treatment, such as with the cognitive-behavioral and systems approach used with this case. Yet Kelly also used the adaptation approach described above. Some adaptations are minor, such as with use of cultural themes and language important to the couple in applying standard interventions. For this case, Kelly problem solved around issues of closeness and distance with the couple versus family members, and helped them to create their spiritual "bible" toward maintaining treatment gains. At other times, adaptations may be much more involved, or they cannot be done without some cross-cultural skills and knowledge, as with the examples below.

First, extensive joining is important. Kelly gradually grew to know the couple, all the while emphasizing their strengths and respecting their goals and preferences. Thus, the genogram was not done until the fifth session, and all interventions had heavy positive rationales. While both partners had strong positive ethnic identities and sought an African American therapist, these identities did not allay Lena's fears that their relationship would fall prey to the negative stereotypes of African Americans, as had her parents' relationship. Thus, she periodically catastrophized their problems and received messages to stay independent despite the strength of her relationship. It was crucial for Kelly to acknowledge and address the cultural context, as well as family and friend influences.

Second, Kelly emphasized strengths at every step. For example, in the face of their negative trait-based attributions, the main reframe was one of transition and the need to adapt to it, which is a normalizing reframe. In fact, in a later session, the couple seemed to need a strong reminder of their strengths, and so for part of the session they listed all of the major stressors that had occurred in the past three years, and it helped them to see that the list was long and not trivial. Even in her mention of unhelpful family influences, Kelly noted their positive intentions, and countered negative images.

Notably, we have obtained the couple's permission to show their clips in one of our courses. Each time we show clips from the first session, some students from other ethnic groups report feeling overwhelmed by the couple's situation and at Jordan's initial anger. Also, students commonly make negative predictions about their relationship stability. This underscores the value of repeated selective attention to overlooked cultural positives. For example, Kelly noted that they worked harder than most couples on their relationship, before, during, and after treatment.

At times, a racial reframe can replace or supplement a strengths-based developmental reframe. As racism often operates in stressful but subtle ways in the lives of African Americans, one only needs to look for it. For example, Jordan's insistence on being the "total man" and his need to address Lena's needs perfectly and be without reproach may stem from attempts to overcompensate for negative stereotypes, which we have seen with many married African American men. Jordan, and to a lesser extent Lena, felt that they had to "make up" for negative racial images by "always doing right." We find that some Black men try so hard that they are devastated to find a need that their family or partner has that they have not met or cannot address. In this case, Jordan felt that, given the shortage of Black men (Boyd-Franklin, 2003), Lena did not appreciate his hard work in the relationship. So it was important for Jordan to be able to "rescue" Lena, and it is likely that their treatment entry stemmed from the breakdown of his ability to be the perfect partner. Thus, he would attack or withdraw in the face of Lena's change requests and relationship "check ins," even when her approach was reasonable. While Lena's fears of relationship failure and tendency to check in stemmed from her concerns about the cultural context, for Jordan they represented another message that he was not being a good husband. Given these contexts, it was crucial to help Jordan to find a safe way to identify and meet Lena's new needs, and have the couple accept that "bumps in the road" did not have catastrophic meanings for their relationship.

Multicultural Awareness

All therapists who work with African American couples can grow via increasing their own multicultural awareness. Therapists may fail to recognize or elicit cultural factors, feel discomfort in using them, or feel uneasy acknowledging deficits in knowledge. Discomfort can be overcome through reading and direct experience, first about one's own racial and ethnic heritages, and then about White privilege, racism, and oppression (e.g., Hardy & Lazloffy, 2002). Therapists must learn the serious limitations of using scales that are not normed on African Americans. They should learn about common therapist reactions and their own cross-cultural biases, especially via supervision and consultation with multicultural experts.

Experiential Exercises and Additional Resources for Clinicians

We have noticed that unequal relationships such as the therapist–client relationship can foster notions of the inferiority of those one treats. Thus, one experiential exercise that we often suggest is for therapists who are not African American to seek cross-cultural experiences with African American nonclients of equal or higher educational, occupational, and income statuses outside of treatment. This can include behaviors such as attending predominately Black churches or African American–themed festivals, but it is best when cross-cultural friendships with African American equals are undertaken. Also, non–African American couple researchers and therapists can build partnerships with African American researchers and therapists who are established within the community and/or build networks with community leaders, which also may increase cultural knowledge. After such experiences, therapists can ask themselves how many of the aforementioned strengths and values of African Americans they have noticed. What barriers have they noticed that they may not face personally? How can they use this knowledge in treatment?

Resources such as positive African American media presenting their couple and family relationships can provide good information about African American contexts. Three examples are Tyler Perry's movie *Daddy's Little Girls*, Lorraine Hansberry's play *A Raisin in the Sun*, and the late August Wilson's play *Radio Golf*.

Conclusion

Evidence-based treatments generally do not consider the unique needs of African American couples. Thus, a multicultural, systems-oriented, and strengths-based adaptation can enhance the therapist's ability to treat African American couples. These adaptations build the therapist's knowledge of adverse contexts faced by African American couples, and the strengths and values that they bring to their relationships. Important therapist skills and awareness factors are also outlined, and a case example illustrates how they may be used to match treatment to African American couples' needs.

References

Boyd-Franklin, N. (2003). *Black families in therapy: Understanding the African American experience.* New York: Guilford Press.

Boyd-Franklin, N., Kelly, S., & Durham, J. (2008). African American couples in therapy. In A. S. Gurman (Ed.), *Clinical handbook of couple therapy* (4th ed., pp. 681–697). New York: Guilford Press.

Carter, M. M., Sbrocco, T., Lewis, E. L., & Friedman, E. K. (2001). Parental bonding and anxiety: Differences between African American and European American college students. *Anxiety Disorders, 15,* 555–569.

Coleman, M. G. (2003). Job skill and Black male wage discrimination. *Social Science Quarterly, 84,* 892–905.

Conger, R. D., Wallace, L. E., Sun, Y., Simons, R. L., McLoyd, V. C., & Brody, G. H. (2002). Economic pressure in African American families: A replication and extension of the family stress model. *Developmental Psychology, 38,* 179–193.

Donohue, B., Strada, M. J., Rosales, R., Taylor-Caldwell, A., Hise, D., Ahman, S., et al. (2006). The semistructured interview for consideration of ethnic culture in therapy scale: Initial psychometric and outcome support. *Behavior Modification, 30,* 867–891.

Fischer, A. R., & Shaw, C. M. (1999). African Americans' mental health and perceptions of racist discrimination: The moderating effects of racial socialization experiences and self-esteem. *Journal of Counseling Psychology, 46,* 395–407.

Friedman, S., & Lipchik, E. (1999). A time-effective, solution-focused approach to couple therapy. In J. M. Donovan (Ed.), *Short-term couple therapy* (pp. 325–359). New York: Guildford Press.

Gray-Little, B. (1982). Marital quality and power processes among Black couples. *Journal of Marriage and the Family, 44,* 633–646.

Hardy, K. V., & Laszloffy, T. A. (2002). Couple therapy using a multicultural perspective. In A. S. Gurman & N. S. Jacobson (Eds.), *Clinical handbook of couple therapy* (3rd ed., pp. 569–593). New York: Guilford Press.

Harknett, K., & McLanahan, S. S. (2004). Racial and ethnic differences in marriage after the birth of a child. *American Sociological Review, 69,* 790–811.

Jones, J. M. (1997). *Prejudice and racism* (2nd ed.). New York: McGraw-Hill.

Karney, B. R., Kreitz, M. A., & Sweeney, K. E. (2004). Obstacles to ethnic diversity in marital research: On the failure of good intentions. *Journal of Social and Personal Relationships, 21,* 509–526.

Kelly, S. (2003). African American couples: Their importance to the stability of African American families, and their mental health issues. In J. S. Mio & G. Y. Iwamasa (Eds.), *Culturally diverse mental health: The challenges of research and resistance* (pp. 141–157). New York: Brunner-Routledge.

Kelly, S. (2004). Underlying components of scores assessing African Americans' racial perspectives. *Measurement and Evaluation in Counseling and Development, 37,* 28–40.

Kelly, S. (2006a). Cognitive-behavioral therapy with African Americans. In G. Y. Iwamasa & P. A. Hayes (Eds.), *Culturally responsive cognitive-behavioral therapy: Assessment, practice, and supervision* (pp. 97–116). Washington DC: American Psychological Association.

Kelly, S. (2006b). The influence of demographic, marital status, and racial factors on Black couples' relationships. *Humbolt Journal of Social Relations, 30,* 161–181.

Kelly, S., & Boyd-Franklin, N. (2004). African American women in client, therapist, and supervisory relationships: The parallel processes of race, culture, and family. In M. Rastogi & E. Wieling (Eds.), *The voices of color: First person accounts of ethnic minority therapists* (pp. 67–89). Thousand Oaks: Sage.

Kelly, S., & Floyd, F. J. (2006). Impact of racial perspectives and contextual variables on marital trust and adjustment for African American couples. *Journal of Family Psychology, 20,* 79–87.

LaTaillade, J. J. (2006). Considerations for treatment of African American couple relationships. *Journal of Cognitive Psychotherapy, 4,* 341–358.

LaTaillade, J. J., Baucom, D. H., & Jacobson, N. S. (2000, November). *Correlates of satisfaction and resiliency in African American/White interracial relationships.* Paper presented at the symposium The Influence of Culture and Context of the Intimate Relationships of African Americans (J. J. La Taillade, Chair), annual convention of the Association for Advancement of Behavior Therapy, New Orleans, LA.

Majors, R., & Billson, J. M. (1992). *Cool pose: The dilemmas of Black manhood in America.* New York: Simon & Schuster.

McGoldrick, M., Gerson, R., & Shellenberger, S. (1999). *Genograms: Assessment and intervention.* New York: W.W. Norton.

McGoldrick, M., Giordano, J., & Garcia-Preto, N. (Eds.). (2005). *Ethnicity and family therapy* (3rd ed.). New York: Guilford Press.

Murry, V. M., Brown, P. A., Brody, G. H., Cutrona, C. E., & Simons, R. L. (2001). Racial discrimination as a moderator of the links among stress, maternal psychological functioning, and family relationships. *Journal of Marriage and Family, 63,* 915–926.

Nichols, M. P., & Minuchin, S. (1999). Short-term structural family therapy with couples. In J. M. Donovan (Ed.), *Short-term couple therapy* (pp. 124–143). New York: Guilford Press.

Oggins, J., Veroff, J., & Leber, D. (1993). Perceptions of marital interaction among Black and White newlyweds. *Journal of Personality & Social Psychology, 65,* 494–511.

Orbuch, T. L., & Eyster, S. L. (1997). Division of household labor among Black couples and White couples. *Social Forces, 76,* 301–332.

Orbuch, T. L., Veroff, J., Hassan, H., & Horrocks, J. (2002). Who will divorce? A 14-year longitudinal study of Black couples and White couples. *Journal of Social and Personal Relationships, 19,* 179–202.

Phillips, J. A., & Sweeney, M. M. (2005). Premarital cohabitation and marital disruption among White, Black, and Mexican American women. *Journal of Marriage and Family, 67,* 296–314.

Phillips, J. A., & Sweeney, M. M. (2006). Can differential exposure to risk factors explain recent racial and ethnic variation in marital disruption? *Social Science Research, 35,* 409–434.

Pinderhughes, E. B. (2002). African American marriage in the 20th century. *Family Process, 41,* 269–282.

Rogge, R. D., Cobb, R. J., Story, L. B., Johnson, M. D., Lawrence, E. E., Rothman, A. D., et al. (2006). Recruitment and selection of couples for intervention research: Achieving developmental homogeneity at the cost of demographic diversity. *Journal of Consulting and Clinical Psychology, 74,* 777–784.

Saegert, S. C., Adler, N. E., Bullock, H. E., Cauce, A. M., Liu, W. M., & Wyche, K. F. (2006). *APA Task Force on Socioeconomic Status final report.* Washington, DC: American Psychological Association.

Sue, D. W. (2001). Multidimensional facets of cultural competence. *The Counseling Psychologist, 29,* 790–821.

Taylor, R. J., Mattis, J., & Chatters, L. M. (1999). Subjective religiosity among African Americans: A synthesis of findings from five national samples. *Journal of Black Psychology, 25,* 524–543.

U.S. Department of Health and Human Services. (2001). *Mental health: Culture, race, and ethnicity—A supplement to mental health: A report of the surgeon general.* Rockville, MD: SAMHSA.

Utsey, S. O., Chae, M. H., Brown, C. F., & Kelly, D. (2002). Effect of ethnic group membership on ethnic identity, race-related stress, and quality of life. *Cultural Diversity and Ethnic Minority Psychology, 8,* 366–377.

Wong, C. A., Eccles, J. S., & Sameroff, A. J. (2003). The influence of ethnic discrimination and ethnic identification on African American adolescents' school and socioemotional adjustment. *Journal of Personality, 71,* 1197–1232.

Section E

Asian American Couples

Thirteen

Drawing Gender to the Foreground

Couple Therapy With South Asians in the United States

Mudita Rastogi

This chapter will focus on the role of gender, power, and privilege in couple/marital problems in South Asians in the United States. I believe that couple therapists working with this population cannot afford *not* to examine gender in therapy. I will highlight how South Asian couples and families are impacted by gender, and how they in turn construct gender within their relationships. Drawing upon the literature on ethnic identity, acculturation, and cultural views of mental health, I will examine couple problems and larger family conflicts from the lenses of gender, power, and privilege. Utilizing case material, I will illustrate how these gender issues impact difficulties experienced in couple relationships. Finally, I will discuss interventions that are effective in working with the above issues. Please note that while most of the available clinical literature focuses on

Asian Indians, I have tried to expand the discussion to include South Asians (including many overseas Pakistani, Bangladeshi, Sri Lankan, and Nepalese clients). Furthermore, all names and identifying information in the case material have been changed to protect confidentiality.

Author's Background

I am a licensed marriage and family therapist, an educator and a clinician of Indian origin. I have dual citizenship and consider myself as having two homes, namely, India and the United States. This bicultural and binational existence has led me to integrate and switch between multiple perspectives. It also helps me coach my clients to see other viewpoints, and appreciate their challenges as they try to balance loyalty toward various segments of their family and ponder questions of belongingness. In my clinical work, I integrate feminist and multicultural perspectives with intergenerational and Emotionally Focused Therapy (Johnson, 2004) perspectives.

History and Assessment of South Asians

Since the abolition of the national origins quota system via the Immigration Act of 1965, there has been a regular flow of Asian Indian immigrants from a wide range of educational levels and backgrounds into the United States. According to the 2000 census, Asian Indians constitute about 1.8 million of the U.S. population (Barnes & Bennett, 2002). Readers are referred to Chapter 14 in this book for a detailed discussion of the demographics and history of South Asian immigration to the United States. There is a great deal of heterogeneity among South Asians along the lines of social class, region, religion, and immigration status. There are also some common threads in values that influence the vast majority of clients with whom I have worked in my clinical practice in the Midwest. For example, most South Asians value maintaining close relationships with kin, and a great deal of give and take is considered to be a norm and an ideal. Further, extended family needs are often taken into account in one's decision-making processes (Rastogi, 2007). Couple relationships are intricately embedded within this network of extended family exchanges, and a marriage is frequently deeply impacted by the opinions and input of, and interactions with, in-laws. Further, it is common to see gender and cultural issues deeply color the presenting problems among this group. These issues are examined below in detail.

Immigration, Acculturation, and Ethnic Identity

A study by Sodowsky and Carey (1988), using Berry's (1980) bidirectional model of acculturation, classified Asian Indians into three groups: traditional, bicultural, and "Americanized." Most Asian Indians fell into the first two groups; the last group was very small, and its membership was not related to how long one had lived in the United States. The authors concluded that most Asian Indians tend to retain significant aspects of their culture of origin in their daily lives.

Making the transition to a new culture is associated with acculturative stress (Krishnan & Berry, 1992). Factors like current age and age at the time of immigration are important factors in determining acculturative stress. To summarize the literature, the major factors that reduce acculturative stress for Asian Indians are involvement with and acceptance by the dominant culture and one's English language and cultural skills (Mehta, 1998; Sodowsky & Ming Lai, 1997). Asian Indians who are of low socioeconomic status, as well as those who do not have family support, report higher levels of acculturative stress. Finally, differential acculturation among family members can add to family conflict and acculturative stress (Rastogi, 2007, in press).

It is important to examine ethnic identity along with acculturation when assessing a client's mental health needs. Ethnic identity involves defining one's own ethnic membership, and is central to how people see themselves. Ethnic identity has two components (Sodowsky, Kwan, & Pannu, 1995): external—that is, one's language(s), friends, and so on; and internal—for example, one's cognitions, morality, and affect. These dimensions vary independently so, for example, an Asian Indian immigrant might socialize with friends from the majority culture but still maintain her traditional values regarding arranged marriages. Furthermore, both the acculturation and ethnic identity of South Asians are closely tied to the degree of importance they place on their extended family (Durvasula & Mylvaganam, 1994). Therefore, any attempts at intervention with South Asians must include an assessment of acculturation, ethnic identity, immigration history, and relationships with the extended family and community (Das & Kemp, 1997; Durvasula & Mylvaganam, 1994).

Gender

At every stage of the family life cycle, males and females in South Asian families hear gendered messages about their roles, tasks, and expectations. For example, Kakar (1981) discusses how boys of a certain age are "banished" from the world of their mothers and expected to join the world of grown boys and men outside the home. For men, masculinity is frequently defined as the avoidance of anything feminine; vulnerability is seen as shameful. Other common themes for men include the centrality of being the provider, exercising emotional restraint, and asserting privilege.

Common themes of conforming, caretaking, nurturing, and maintaining relationships emerge for women (Bumiller, 1990). Studies on women's mental health in India show high levels of symptoms among the 25- to 39-year-old women (Chakraborty, 2001; Hegde, 2001). In particular, financial dependence and failure to meet feminine role expectations are correlated with mental illness (Addlakha, 2001). The authors delineate how demands to prioritize the needs of various family members and adherence to societal norms of femininity put women at risk. These findings can easily be generalized to other South Asian women.

A solid body of literature on the mental health of Indian, Pakistani, and Bangladeshi populations in the United Kingdom exists (Beliappa, 1991; Bhui, 1999; Bhui, Chandran, & Sathyamoorthy, 2002). A review of the literature on "Asians" by Bhui (1999) found the following patterns from the studies: Overall, women are at a higher risk than men. Upwardly mobile females in the Asian population are especially at risk. Asian Indian women go to physicians with physical problems and then often pursue alternate treatment for psychological issues through practices such as prayer. However, the isolation of women and their lack of access to culturally appropriate resources is a problematic issue. Studies (Beliappa, 1991) show that Asian women will bear psychological and physical pain silently, as they both consider this a part of "womanhood" and assume physical symptoms can reside in the mind due to their understanding of the mind–body connection. There are significant social class differences, however, with more educated women suspecting mental health to be defined as society's expectations of their behaviors.

Comparisons by Bhui (1999) show that, in general, Asian Indians were reported to have a lower rate of mental health disturbance than the control group in the United Kingdom, and prevalence rates were also lower than those reported by studies conducted in India. Asian men in the United Kingdom are more likely than Whites to seek help for health issues, but deny more severe or long-term problems. The author also discusses this somatic expression of distress among Asian Indian men using three possible explanations: (1) that the language of psychological and somatic symptoms overlap for these men, (2) that these two sets of symptoms correlate more closely for this group, and (3) that suffering is consistent with some aspects of Eastern spiritual beliefs, and thus descriptions of suffering cannot be seen as pathological. These findings raise important methodological issues, and readers are referred to Bhui (1999) for a detailed discussion of these. The author concludes that the experience of somatic symptoms and the presentation of somatic symptoms are separate processes.

Some authors discuss differential socialization of South Asian girls and boys in North America and the gendered experiences of second-generation immigrants from India (Almeida, 2005; Dugsin, 2001; Guzder, 2002). Some articles discuss the cultural angle to couple problems, such as the role of extended family members (Nath & Craig, 1999), the fallout of globalization (Sonpar, 2005), and how immigration-related transitions are impacted by gender (Rastogi, 2007). Maker, Mittal, and Rastogi's (2005) chapter stresses the central importance of considering gender issues when clinicians assess the presenting problems in South Asian clients, and also offers a model of assessment. Other authors highlight the importance of considering gender when intervening with Asian Indian families in general (Rastogi & Wampler, 1998, 1999), and family violence in particular (Almeida & Dolan-Delvecchio, 1999). However, some gaps remain. First, there is a paucity of published material that considers gender issues—both men's and women's issues—from a feminist perspective. Second, there are very few publications that consider gender issues in clinical work with these couples. Third, a literature search did not find any specific materials pertaining to conducting couple therapy with South Asians in the United States. However, it is necessary to tie together the existing research on gender issues for South Asians with specific clinical implications for therapists and clients. It is this third area that will be addressed via this chapter.

Family Structure and Gender Socialization

In my clinical practice with South Asian couples and families, I have noticed that people's social class, education, and level of acculturation affect their self-reported adherence to patriarchal traditions. A majority of clients are clearly more progressive around gender issues compared with their own families of origin. However, I have also observed that family/community dynamics such as valuing male children, demanding, accepting or offering dowry, setting different sets of rules for male and female teenage children, and giving male family members greater privileges have little correlation with income. Thus, I will argue that a great deal of explicit gendered socialization takes place, even for second-generation South

Asian children. Further, these second-generation children also observe gendered relationships modeled within their homes and communities, and thus continue to internalize these roles at multiple levels.

Types of Presenting Problems

The vast majority of South Asian couples with whom I have worked in my practice are heterosexual. Same-sex couples of South Asian origin are likely to experience some of the aforementioned problems due to their cultural background, but they also face additional difficulties due to their sexual orientation (Almeida & Dolan-Delvecchio, 1999; Greene, 1994). There is a huge gap in the literature in the area of therapy with South Asian gay and lesbian couples.

Common presenting problems at my private practice include "communication difficulties" and infidelity, as well as relational problems related to depression, anxiety, or another *DSM* disorder. While on the surface these might seem quite similar to the presenting problems of my Euro-American clients, the context makes the former quite different. For example, it is very common for South Asian couples to experience the above problems as stemming from their difficulties with their in-laws, even when the latter live on another continent. In fact, it is rare to have an Indian couple *not* mention in-law problems. Female partners generally report "in-law" problems with greater frequency; daughters-in-law report feeling persecuted or judged harshly; and sons-in-law often report that their in-laws "meddle in the marital relationship."

Second, many immigrant clients define themselves as *Indians* (or *Asian Indian) living in the United States.* Their self-perception as "outsiders" in the United States is often reinforced by their experiences with a mainstream society that treats them as "other," and micro-aggressions (Sue & Sue, 2007) affect their couple interactions. Finally, many clients, regardless of their own financial situation, consider it their obligation to help their extended family members financially and otherwise. Frequently, a greater amount of help is both expected by and extended to the husband's side of the family. Negotiating this can be difficult for couples, and can lead to tensions between the partners.

The problems of these couples may be understood in multiple ways. When listening to my clients' stories, I choose to pay attention to the presenting problems from a gender perspective. Second, I have to set aside Eurocentric notions of health and wellness to understand their problems within their cultural context. At times, a new model or a culturally sensitive adaptation of an existing approach to working with couples using a multicultural and systemic perspective is better suited to my clients. For example, see the assessment model for South Asians proposed by Maker et al. (2005) and the use of a culturally specific construct "trust in hierarchy" (Rastogi, 2002).

Third, I note contextual factors such as their education, income, cultural orientation, religion, and immigration status. My belief is that the intersections of these various types of diversity affect not only the clients' experiences with oppression and their perception of their own sense of privilege, but also the very definition of their problems, and the range of solutions acceptable to them. I prefer to discuss assumptions of privilege, gendered beliefs that are linked to a couple's overt behaviors in the realm of financial, sexual, and emotional interactions.

CASE EXAMPLE

Kris (short for Krishna), 29, and Trisha, also 29, had been married for five years and had a 1-year-old daughter. They sought couple therapy following Kris's infidelity. Both originally came from the same city in Eastern India. Kris had lived in the United States for seven years and Trisha for six. They met as graduate students at a university in the United States. At that time, Kris was already engaged, and his marriage had been arranged by his parents to a woman who was known to the family. Upon meeting Trisha, Kris broke that engagement, and against his parents' wishes decided to marry Trisha. Trisha felt that her in-laws hated her for "taking away" their son.

Their marriage had been rocky from the start. They fought about money, extended family issues, and housework. A few months before their first therapy session, Trisha suspected something was amiss. Eventually, Kris confessed that he had had sex with a prostitute at an out-of-town bachelor party. At this point, Trisha insisted that Kris move out of the house to live in an apartment. Kris apologized profusely to his wife for his behavior and promised to change. A month later, the couple decided that divorce was not an option for them, given their cultural beliefs. They decided to give their marriage another chance, at which time Kris moved back home. They chose to see me for therapy since they felt that a therapist unfamiliar with their culture would not be able to appreciate the cultural nuances impacting their relationship.

Trisha was raised in a close-knit, frugal family, with a widowed mother and a younger sister. Living in a female-headed household had been hard, as the local community in this town in India did not always treat them kindly. Financially, too, life was difficult. At times, Trisha's mother was not invited to weddings or certain extended family celebrations as her widowed status was perceived as bringing bad luck. However, Trisha also gained a feminist perspective due to these experiences, and valued her independence. Prior to having her daughter, Trisha worked full-time in a large corporation and was currently working part-time from home. Trisha reportedly had a host of friends, but most of them lived out of state and she kept in touch with them via phone and e-mail. She often came to therapy wearing a mix of Indian and Western casual clothes and, while she spoke with me in English, she often switched to her mother tongue when addressing her husband.

Kris worked in a very well-paid job in the field of finance. He was raised in an affluent family in India and both his parents were alcoholics for most of his childhood. (His parents were currently sober.) Due to the stigma related to women of her social class consuming alcohol publicly, Kris's mother kept her drinking a secret from nonfamily members, and frequently feigned illness to mask her behavior. Kris reported emotional neglect throughout his childhood, as well as some physical abuse by his father. His father was also very controlling of the entire family, and Kris could not wait to leave home at the age of 17. He described his lonely childhood as a "desert," and even as an adult had few friends. He was cut off from his older brother who was also an alcoholic. Kris appeared far more "Westernized" than his wife, and preferred to listen to jazz music and hang out at clubs. I found him to be articulate and very perceptive regarding the nuances of his own emotional states while in the therapy room. However, he reportedly had difficulty opening up with his wife at home.

Negative Interactional Cycles: The Influence of Gender and Culture

At the start of therapy, the couple discussed Kris's infidelity and its impact on them. Trisha was angry and humiliated, and did most of the talking. While doing EFT (Johnson, 2004) with them, I noticed that Kris appeared withdrawn due to shame regarding his own infidelity and fear that he had lost Trisha's trust. She interpreted this distance as abandonment, and demanded apologies and explanations. Trisha easily appeared to be the pursuer in the relationship due to the intensity of her speech and the raised tone of her voice. She did not modulate her interactions to match Kris's affect, even when he spoke softly or sparsely. This made Kris anxious and led him to become even more secretive about his inner thoughts and the details of his daily life, such as credit card bills and entertainment expenses. Trisha would then fear that Kris was contemplating cheating on her again, and she responded by angrily questioning him about his every move. The couple was frequently hurtful, angry, and blaming toward each other.

During the course of the first five or six sessions, we discussed Kris's avoidant, dismissive attachment style and Trisha's anxious, preoccupied style. I was able to help the couple understand their negative inter-actional cycles, and link these conflict cycles with their attachment styles and past experiences. In time, they understood each other's needs better and negotiated for more caring and functional responses from each other. Kris repeatedly asked for forgiveness, and offered to express his anger and fear during conflict in constructive ways. He was able to share some of his vulnerability and shame, and also ask for comforting from Trisha. This was especially hard for Kris as he preferred to leave the house instead of staying to talk things through. He understood how his child-hood experiences, as well as later notions of masculinity, affected his expression of emotions and his behavior. Kris's expression of emotions led Trisha to soften her blaming stance. She listened more intently, and began to ask for intimacy and reassurance when she perceived he was pulling away. These conversations were healing for the couple as they worked through the infidelity.

Growing up, Trisha had been exposed to cultural messages regarding the centrality of men and marriage in the lives of women. Consequently, at times she felt guilty and responsible for their marital discord. In ther-apy, she struggled with whether she was staying in the marriage "for the sake of tradition" or out of love. Further, she had grown up with a mother who, due to circumstances, was fairly independent and outspoken. However, even when Trisha felt some aspect of their relationship was unfair, she was unsure whether demanding change in an open, assertive manner was "appropriate" for women in relationships. She had few role models for her marriage and from her culture. For example, she often checked in with me whether it was okay for her to ask Kris to make certain changes. I encouraged them to discuss and negotiate many issues, and my "permission" gave Trisha a lot of validation.

Table 13.1   Gendergrams for Trisha and Kris

Name: Trisha
Relationship: Mother (same gender)

Relevant Events	Life Cycle Stage	Roles, Patterns, Themes
The family worrying about money at the end of each month Purchasing gifts for family weddings and birthdays	Adolescence	• Women can support their families. • Money is a scarce resource. • Use money wisely; save money. • Financial problems can be discussed openly within family. • We could afford more luxuries if Dad were alive.

Name: Kris
Relationship: Father (same gender)

Relevant Events	Life Cycle Stage	Roles, Patterns, Themes
Asking for money for school fees and allowance	Adolescence	• Money is power. • Control money tightly. • Always have plenty of money for yourself and your family. • Indulge yourself. • Spend lavishly on others to buy favors for the future. • Saving money is so "middle class."

Gender Issues in the Relationship

Since Kris and Trisha frequently argued over each other's spending habits, I decided to draw gendergrams (see Table 13.1) for each of them on their attitude toward money. Gendergrams help clients and therapists examine gender-related patterns and roles in clients' families of origin. (For a detailed explanation of this tool, see White & Tyson-Rawson, 1995.) Table 13.1 presents an example of a gendergram for Trisha's and Kris's relationships with their same-sex parent during adolescence, and lessons learned regarding money.

By examining what each partner had internalized regarding money and power in their growing-up years, the couple gained a better understanding of their current conflicts around money. Given Trisha's financially tight childhood and the early loss of her father, she admitted that she wanted both financial independence and also, paradoxically, a husband who would provide her with financial security. For example, she saved her salary in a personal savings account, considered it her own "spending money," and refused to contribute to the mortgage or car payments. Kris, on the other hand, used his substantial financial assets as a way to exert power over Trisha. He had also grown up in a home where secrets abounded, and he found it hard to be transparent. Through therapy, Trisha was able to see the links between her attitude toward money, being raised by a single parent in a very patriarchal community, and her fear of being abandoned by Kris. I was able to help them explore Kris's feelings regarding money, power, and masculinity. Since he handled money at work, too, many aspects of his identity were tied up in managing money. In particular, Kris believed his role as husband and father was to "take care" of his daughter and wife, but also felt this entitled him to manage "his" money as he saw fit. Over several sessions, both members of the couple were able to see how their attitudes kept them distant from each other. Eventually, Kris and Trisha negotiated how to split their bills fairly and create greater financial trust in the relationship.

Another gendered area of conflict for this couple was the division of housework and child care. Kris declared himself unable to cook or change diapers and, if pressured to do other chores, would procrastinate until Trisha got tired of waiting and did them herself. Trisha complained bitterly about this since she was quite literally left holding the baby in addition to working part-time and doing all the cooking and laundry. She also noted that Kris did not engage the baby in play for more than a few minutes at a time, and appeared bored or aloof when required to do so. This alarmed her, as she knew Kris had experienced emotional neglect in his own childhood. Occasionally she tried to discuss this topic, and to get Kris to open up emotionally. However, Kris saw any conversations on this topic as angry criticism of him, and as an attack on his parents, and either withdrew or defended his family.

I sensed that Kris had been raised in a household where all the daily chores were done by maids and servants, and I questioned whether he felt household chores were "beneath" him. Kris jokingly asserted that he was simply born without the "diaper-duty gene." I added to the humor by quoting an imaginary study whereby surgeons could treat this deficit by implanting a special gene in men. We went on to discuss Trisha's feelings about this imbalance. She saw Kris's unwillingness to share housework as an unwillingness to be loving toward her, and by extension toward their daughter. This led to a further discussion of Asian Indian women's and men's traditional roles, versus the current reality of Kris and Trisha's life in the United States. I empathized with Kris's experience of having been raised as an upper-class male child with privilege and power, but reframed these values as changeable. Kris also acknowledged that he needed help learning how to stay engaged with the baby. In the therapy room, Kris admitted that his painful childhood memories hindered his ability to be a better father. This led to considerable "softening" (Johnson, 2004) on Trisha's part, and husband and wife agreed to support each other in this area.

Cultural Issues

In addition to discussing how gendered socialization might have impacted the development of their attachment styles and conflict cycles, we also talked about cultural issues. Specifically, Trisha and Kris were immigrants and did not have any extended family or many friends nearby on whom they could rely. Both articulated how lonely each felt when they had conflict in their marriage, as they only had each other to turn to. This added a great deal of pressure and intensity to their relationship. They talked about how much they missed having relatives and extended family members in their life. Had they lived in India, Trisha felt she could have sought advice and support from her mother and sister. Her sense of isolation, in combination with her attachment style and Kris's behaviors related to infidelity, had led her to fear abandonment. Kris, too, was quietly fearful of his own dependence on Trisha.

We discussed at length how they might each gain support from friends and the community so as to feel less isolated. Trisha decided to deepen her friendship with an older Indian colleague who was like an aunt to her, and also occasionally seek childcare advice from that lady. Kris did not have any close friends, but agreed to go out to lunch more with his colleagues. The couple also decided to go to the local temple every Saturday, both to socialize and to begin teaching their daughter about their own religious traditions.

Extended Family and In-Law Issues

Before going on a short vacation to India, Trisha reported that her fears of betrayal and abandonment were magnified due to Kris's family's dislike of her. She had always wanted his family's approval, and had tried to measure up to their expectations of the ideal daughter-in-law. However, Kris's parents had said unkind things about Trisha's family's social standing. In the past, she had tried harder to please them but now she had given up on her in-laws. Trisha was angry that Kris would not confront his parents. While Kris disliked his parents' behavior, he disliked confrontations even more. However, Trisha perceived Kris's unwillingness to stand up for her as an act of abandonment. She urged Kris to spend less time with his parents and more time at her own mother's home with Trisha and the baby. Kris felt crowded by Trisha's need for reassurance, and wanted more space to interact with his family. He withdrew from her criticism of his family as he took this criticism very personally.

Trisha and Kris discussed their obligations to parents, as well as to each other. In this area, Trisha came across as far more acculturated, and she thought of their nuclear family as her primary obligation. She hated that Kris was not more forceful with his parents about their treatment toward her. Although he initially talked about "respect for one's parents," Kris discussed the dynamics in his alcoholic family of origin and his fear of disappointing his parents. Kris was also able to acknowledge Trisha's feelings of rejection and humiliation, and her need to feel protected. She understood his longing to reconnect with his parents, and his need to spend time with them without her being present. Just before they left for the trip, Kris called his parents to state that he wanted them to treat Trisha better. After coming back from their vacation, the couple reported that things were going well for them, and a few weeks later therapy was terminated.

Discussion

In the above case, a gender and cultural framework was helpful in identifying and resolving multiple areas of conflict:

1. Finances, highlighting issues of dependence vs. independence

2. Extended family/in-law issues of idealization vs. feelings of persecution

3. Division of housework and childcare stemming from gendered privilege vs. traditional gender roles

4. One's place in the community stemming from isolation vs. seeking connection

5. Developing a sense of self from expression vs. subjugation

For each area, the couple had to deconstruct their gender role socialization, the influence of their attachment styles, and cultural/familial expectations, and then negotiate their own needs in the context of the couple relationship. Kris and Trisha had to learn new ways of building their relationship in a different country and in the face of expectations vastly different from those placed on their own parents. They did all this while relatively isolated from family and their support system.

While I primarily used Johnson's (2004) EFT approach with this couple, I assessed for gender and cultural issues from the start, as recommended by Maker et al. (2005). This was essential, as Trisha and Kris defined their problems using their own cultural lens. For example, their perspectives on what were possible solutions for their marital crisis, their sense of self and definition of family, and their roles vis-à-vis each other were all colored by their experiences of being South Asian immigrants in the United States. Additionally, they differed from each other in terms of their acculturation on various dimensions, such as language usage, tastes in music and food, attitude toward family, and traditional gender roles. As their therapist, my challenge was also to incorporate their differing perspectives on these issues with the techniques of EFT. I did this by frequently focusing on how gender, cultural, and other factors intersected with attachment issues in their lives. A similar approach is recommended to clinicians who use any other couple therapy approach. The basic processes or underpinnings of a theoretical model will look quite different when intersecting with gender, culture, and other dimensions of diversity (Rastogi, 2002).

As can be seen from their gendergrams, this couple's experiences were impacted by both their life events and the gender and cultural issues salient in their upbringing. Thus, in modifying their interactions, I needed to consider how attachment, gender, and culture interacted with their needs and abilities to respond to each other. I had to weigh how the factors of culture and gender would "demand" certain types of responses from each partner. For example, in encouraging the couple to empathize with each other, it was important to recognize that Kris and Trisha needed to have empathy not just for each other but also for the other's extended family and relationship with that family. Thus, the couple learned to be empathic toward each other's role as son/daughter/son-in-law/daughter-in-law.

Similarly, the couple's conflict around housework and childcare was not simply about male privilege or childhood attachment issues. It also involved social class issues whereby Kris could not see himself changing diapers, taking care of a baby, or cooking and cleaning, based on the social standing of his family of origin. Both his attachment style and his sense of entitlement emanating from being raised as an upper-class Asian Indian male impacted his ability to perform certain functions in the couple relationship. As for Trisha, she wanted the financial independence that she coveted in adolescence; however, paradoxically, she also wanted Kris to pay all the bills. Societal expectations, media messages, and the early loss of her father all went into this being a hot-button issue for her. Once this problem was framed in terms of trust and power, she was better able to override the messages learned via gender role socialization and cultural norms.

Recommendations for Clinicians, Educators, and Supervisors

I would recommend that educators encourage students to learn about the heterogeneity of the South Asian population in the United States and the diaspora, as this community subscribes to highly diverse languages, customs, religious beliefs, and values. In addition to familiarizing themselves with the mental health literature, students are encouraged to explore the resources listed below. Supervisors should encourage trainees to explore the clients' perspectives on the causality of emotional/ relational presenting problems.

When working with South Asians, it is helpful to explore how immigration experiences and acculturation and ethnic identity impact parenting practices, couple interactions, and relationships with the extended family and community. In conducting therapy, I would suggest clinicians find ways to link their interventions with culturally syntonic perspectives regarding the role of therapy, and the mind–body connection. In particular, I suggest utilizing concepts of balance and homeostasis in helping clients understand their symptoms. Clinicians will need to empathize with the roles into which clients have been socialized, but also reframe them as changeable. Finally, it is useful to stress the significance of mutuality, partnership, and emotional growth as the opposites of alienation, inequality, and status quo. Some mistakes to avoid in therapy include not asking about gender, extended family, and cultural issues upfront, not learning about the clients' cultural and religious practices, and applying Eurocentric notions of autonomy and independence to clients of South Asian origin.

Experiential Exercises and Topics for Reflection

1. Create a gendergram for yourself or a role play client (see White & Tyson-Rawson, 1995, for details). Discuss both gender and cultural issues.

2. In what ways would you like your children's gender socialization to be different from yours? Why? Write down your thoughts.

3. Picture yourself leaving your entire family and circle of friends to live halfway across the globe. You can only take two suitcases with you. It is unlikely that you will see your loved ones for about two years. Note your thoughts and feelings in a journal as you visualize this scenario.

4. Imagine that you are living in another country where the culture is quite different from your own. You and your partner have decided to seek couple therapy there. Picture yourself sitting down with a therapist, trying to explain the presenting problem to him or her. Your therapist says, "I don't know much about your country and culture. I am hoping to learn from you. Please tell me about your culture." How would you feel/respond to this? Note down your reactions.

5. Visit an area in your city or state that has a large concentration of South Asians, such as "Little India" in New Jersey, or Devon Street in Chicago, Illinois. This is helpful for familiarizing yourself with the food, clothing, and customs of the Asian Indian community.

Additional Resources

Films

The following commercially available films are excellent for exploring family and couple relationships, as well as themes of immigration, identity, and racism:

Agnihotri, V. (2007). *Dhan Dhana Dhan Goal.* UTV Motion.

Chadha, G. (2002). *Bend It Like Beckham.* Bilb/Road Movies.

Nair, M. (2001). *Monsoon Wedding.* iDream Productions.

Nair, M. (2007). *The Namesake.* 20th Century Fox International.

Readings

It is useful to read fiction written by Asian Indian authors. A search for these works can easily be done on the Internet or at your local library.

Web Sites

Resources on books about and by South Asians: www.lib.berkeley.edu/ SSEAL/SouthAsia.

Highly recommended for further information on South Asians and South Asian scholarship: http://southasia.uchicago.edu.

Information and resources for the South Asian GLBT community: www .salganyc.org.

References

Addlakha, R. (2001). Lay and medical diagnosis of psychiatric disorder and the normative construction of femininity. In B. V. Davar (Ed.), *Mental health from a gender perspective* (pp. 313–333). Thousand Oaks, CA: Sage.

Almeida, R. (2005). Asian Indian families: An overview. In M. McGoldrick, J. Giordano, & N. Garcia-Preto (Eds.), *Ethnicity and family therapy* (pp. 377–394). New York: Guilford Press.

Almeida, R., & Dolan-Del Vecchio, K. (1999). Addressing culture in batterers intervention: The Asian Indian community as an illustrative example. *Violence Against Women, 5,* 654–683.

Barnes, J., & Bennett, C. (2002). *The Asian population: 2000.* Retrieved September 21, 2007, from www.census.gov/prod/2002pubs/c2kbr01–16.pdf.

Beliappa, J. (1991). *Illness of distress: Alternative models of mental health.* London: Confederation of Indian Organizations.

Bhui, K. (1999). Common mental disorders among people with origins in or immigrant from India and Pakistan. *International Review of Psychiatry, 11*(2/3), 136–144.

Bhui, K., Chandran, M., & Sathyamoorthy, G. (2002). Mental health assessment and South Asian men. *International Review of Psychiatry, 14*(1), 52–59.

Bumiller, E. (1990). *May you be the mother of a hundred sons.* New York: Random House.

Chakraborty, A. (2001). Mental health of Indian women: A field experience. In B. V. Davar (Ed.), *Mental health from a gender perspective* (pp. 34–60). Thousand Oaks, CA: Sage.

Das, A. J., & Kemp, S. F. (1997). Between two worlds: Counseling South Asian Americans. *Journal of Multicultural Counseling and Development, 25,* 23–33.

Dugsin, R. (2001). Conflict and healing in family experience of second-generation emigrants from India living in North America. *Family Process, 40,* 233–241.

Durvasula, R. S., & Mylvaganam, G. A. (1994). Mental health of Asian Indians: Relevant issues and community implications. *Journal of Community Psychology, 22,* 97–108.

Greene, B. (1994) Lesbian women of color: Triple jeopardy. In L. Comas-Diaz & B. Greene (Eds.), *Women of Color: Integrating ethnic and gender identities in psychotherapy* (pp. 389–427). New York: Guilford Press.

Guzder, J. (2002). Karthikaya: The boy who wished to be Shiva: A case study of an Indian cultural dynamic. In F. J. Cramer Azima & N. Grizenko (Eds.), *Immigrant and refugee children and their families: Clinical, research, and training issues* (pp. 65–91). Madison, WI: International Universities Press.

Hegde, S. (2001). Further consideration of women and mental health. In B. V. Davar (Ed.), *Mental health from a gender perspective* (pp. 99–120). Thousand Oaks, CA: Sage.

Johnson, S. (2004). *The practice of emotionally focused marital therapy: Creating connection.* Philadelphia: Brunner/Mazel.

Kakar, S. (1981). *The inner world: A psychoanalytic study of childhood in India.* New Delhi, India: Oxford University Press.

Krishnan, A., & Berry, J. W. (1992). Acculturative stress and acculturation attitudes among Indian immigrants to the United States. *Psychology and Developing Societies, 4,* 187–212.

Maker, A., Mittal, M., & Rastogi, M. (2005). South Asians in the United States: Developing a systemic and empirically based mental health assessment model. In M. Rastogi & E. Wieling (Eds.), *Voices of color: First person accounts of ethnic minority therapists* (pp. 233–254). Thousand Oaks, CA: Sage.

Mehta, S. (1998). Relationship between acculturation and mental health for Asian Indian immigrants in the United States. *Genetic, Social, and General Psychology Monographs, 124,* 61–77.

Nath, R., & Craig, J. (1999). Practicing family therapy in India: How many people are there in a marital subsystem? *Journal of Family Therapy, 21,* 390–406.

Rastogi, M. (2002). Mother–Adult Daughter questionnaire (MAD): Developing a culturally sensitive instrument. *The Family Journal, 10,* 145–155.

Rastogi, M. (2007). Coping with transitions in Asian Indian families: Systemic clinical interventions with immigrants. *Journal of Systemic Therapies, 26,* 55–67.

Rastogi, M. (in press). Asian Indians in intercultural marriages: Intersections of acculturation, gender and exogamy. In K. Killian & T. Karris (Eds.), *Intercultural couples.* New York: Taylor and Francis.

Rastogi, M., & Wampler, K. S. (1998). Couples and family therapy with Indian families: Some structural and intergenerational considerations. In U. P. Gielen and A. L. Comunian (Eds.), *Family and family therapy in international perspective* (pp. 257–274). Milan, Italy: Marinelli Editrice.

Rastogi, M., & Wampler, K. S. (1999). Adult daughters' perceptions of the mother–daughter relationship: A cross cultural comparison. *Family Relations, 48,* 327–336.

Sodowsky, G. R., & Carey, J. C. (1988). Relationships between acculturation-related demographics and cultural attitudes of an Asian-Indian immigrant group. *Journal of Multicultural Counseling and Development, 16*(3), 117–136.

Sodowsky, G. R., Kwan, K. K., & Pannu, R. (1995). Ethnic identity of Asians in the United States. In J. G. Ponterotto (Ed.), *Handbook of multicultural counseling* (pp. 123–154). Thousand Oaks, CA: Sage.

Sodowsky, G. R., & Ming Lai, E. W. (1997). Asian immigrant variables and structural models of cross-cultural distress. In A. Booth, A. C. Crouter, & N. Landale (Eds.), *Immigration and the family: Research and policy on U.S. immigrants* (pp. 211–234). Mahwah, NJ: Lawrence Erlbaum.

Sonpar, S. (2005). Marriage in India: Clinical issues. *Contemporary Family Therapy, 27,* 301–313.

Sue, D. W., & Sue, D. (2007). *Counseling the culturally diverse: Theory and practice* (5th ed.). Hoboken, NJ: Wiley.

White, M., & Tyson-Rawson, K. (1995). Assessing the dynamics of gender in couples and families. *Family Relations, 44,* 253–260.

Fourteen

Couples in the Desi Community

The Intersection of Culture, Gender, Sexual Orientation, Class, and Domestic Violence

Rhea V. Almeida

The word *Desi,* derived from Sanskrit, means "one from our country; of the homeland." Often affectionate, although sometimes derogatory, and less formal than the term *South Asians*, it is used to refer to people from the sub-continent of India, in particular India, Pakistan, and Bangladesh. Couples in the Desi community are inextricably linked to extended family across the diaspora and to community. The notion of "couples" as we know it in the Western world is something of an oxymoron in the Desi community, particularly in India where parents and in-laws can dictate the meals and patterns of child rearing for their children in the United States.[1]

I belong to the South Asian diaspora, from India to Africa to London and to the United States. My identity spans many complex intersections, and it is this identity that informs my work. I am the founder and director of the Institute for Family Services, Somerset, New Jersey, where much of the work described here originated and continues.

Using the concept of intersectionality as a standpoint for families, I will examine couple relationships where there is domestic violence. Implications for training, supervision, and further research require an interrogation around the misfit between cultural practices and colonial perspectives. This means not only expanding existing conceptions of therapy, but rethinking multicultural practice, and bringing a social justice perspective into the therapy room (Almeida, 2006, 2007; Hernández, Almeida, & Dolan-Del Vecchio, 2005).

Therapeutic constructs offered in this chapter embrace a collaborative context where the dilemmas of gender, race, class, and sexual preferences are untangled within a couple's relationship. By bringing together the struggles of both genders—the privileged and the oppressed—from diverse backgrounds, we dislodge the compartmentalization of experiences through hierarchical separation. Whenever we intervene with couples involved in domestic violence, it is important to keep in mind the relevance and presence of multiple systems: the criminal justice system, the legal system, and the domestic violence shelter system.

Beyond Multiculturalism: Standpoints That Uphold Intersectionality

The past several decades have witnessed the emphasis on cultural competency across multiple disciplines (Van Soest, 1994). This scholarship focused on educating the White therapist/dominant service delivery systems about ethnic and cultural diversity. Cultural competency is defined and legitimized as knowledge about the "other." Knowledge about the "self" as "White" or about the White system of service delivery is obscured entirely. When cultural competency includes an analysis of the "White therapist," it usually refers to ethnicity—for example, Irish, German, or other European origins. Whiteness as a fundamental arbiter of cultural power as difference is never interrogated. Coupled with this omission, multicultural scholarship relies on male Eurocentric models of intervention (Almeida, 2006, 2007).

This pattern of scholarship around ethnic stereotypes does not bring into focus the complex personal, social, and political intersect of couples' lives. In doing this, it disregards the connections of women and men from diverse cultures to their different social contexts embedded within different trajectories of power. Much of the literature, fashioned after dominant models, focuses singularly on the experiences of oppression. While various approaches have elevated voices of the subjugated and oppressed, they do not challenge the domination of oppressors within cultures, nor within the interior of family life. Power, privilege, and oppression in all of its complex arteries of relationship and social location are not a part of, or systemically integrated into, multicultural scholarship (Almeida, Dolan-Delvecchio & Parker, 2007; Almeida & Lockard, 2005; Bograd, 1999; Hernandez, Almeida & Dolan-Del Vecchio, 2005).

Too frequently, the impact of culture is dangerously misunderstood by therapists embedded within treatment systems guided by dominant or White-centric theories. Minimization of the full meaning and impact of culture occurs when culture is theorized as an "added-on" characteristic.

From this perspective, knowledge about cultural norms is expected to provide details helpful for a (presumably White) practitioner to consider when approaching a minority client. The presumption here is, "Those people are just like us [Whites] except for certain idiosyncratic patterns that one needs to keep in mind." Or, "Let's understand how this culture lives their lives." There is no structural power analysis between "their" lives and cultural intersections with mainstream cultural adaptations and lifestyles.

Consider Hansa, an Asian Indian American female and domestic violence victim. A "culturally sensitive" therapist might be bound to the ethnic stereotype that Asian women generally feel more dutifully bound to marriages and extended families. This being true for many women, it does not in any way minimize her desire to be treated like a full human being. This subtle but dehumanized conception of Asian women limits the options for creative solutions. The therapist then expects to have to work harder to persuade Hansa to accept a mainstream solution: create safety by leaving her marriage. Obscured in this cultural analysis, however, is the fact that the therapist is up against the Draconian pull of patriarchy and the community that supports it. This is not unlike Hansa's mainstream counterparts, albeit the patriarchy here is shaped along different trajectories of family and community. Battered women are constrained by their desire for safety and the pressure to uphold the marital and cultural quid pro quo.

Here, culture is encoded and made problematic by therapeutic and outside systems of support to mean "other." Fundamentally conservative and racist, this paradigm of "cultural awareness" strives to meet clients from nondominant minorities where they are, and bring them to where "we" (real Whites) believe they should be. Within this formulation, cultural differences are construed as problems residing within the minority group's differences from Whites, never within the system of group power dynamics that White domination of institutional structures has created. The need for fundamental cultural change is always perceived as existing within the client's domain (Almeida & Dolan-Del Vecchio, 1999; Said, 1993).

A second, and perhaps more pernicious, distortion of the impact of culture occurs when culture is allowed to account for violence. This happens, for example, when South-Asian-American men are allowed to explain violence toward women and children as being culturally normative. No White male of Euro-American heritage would receive a pass from service providers explaining his violence toward his partner as being culturally normative. This impossibility speaks directly to the differing levels of safety our institutions afford: White women versus women of color.

To prevent these types of distortions and racist collusions from occurring within the assessment process, it is necessary to expand perspective on the meaning and impact of culture and cultural differences. An analysis of group relationships must be fundamental to this perspective, one that includes an unflinching exploration of how the group holding power over the structure of service delivery systems relates to less dominant groups. Within this more inclusive analysis, sexism, racism, and heterosexism are also addressed.

For Asian American women, domestic violence is complicated by factors such as language barriers, immigrant status, cultural differences, and racial discrimination—issues that are not addressed by the mainstream domestic violence movement. Moreover, the Asian American community, which does comprehend these complicating factors, has failed to make domestic violence a priority issue. Thus, the unique needs of battered Asian American women are often left unanswered (Abraham, 2000; Ahmad, 2000; Ayyub, 2000; Dasgupta, 2000; Merchant, 2000).

More specifically, one cannot adequately evaluate the impact of one's race apart from one's gender, class, sexual orientation, age, and disability status (Almeida, Dolan-Del Vecchio, & Parker, 2007; Crenshaw, 1994; Spivak, 1989a, 1985).

Figure 14.1 provides a visual of the resulting matrix.

Migration History

According to the 2000 U.S. Census, there are about two million South Asians in the United States, from Pakistan, Sri Lanka, Bhutan, and the

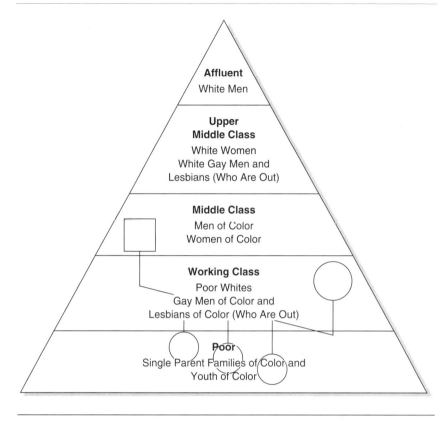

Figure 14.1   Intersections of Patriarchy, Colonialization, and Racism

Caribbean. Their per capita income is $27,000 (U.S. Census, 2000). Median household income for Asian Indians is $65,000, which represents several families living together. Why is this community of immigrants one of the most economically viable?

The first wave of Indian immigration to the United States, mostly made up of farmers, began in the mid-1800s with settlements on the West Coast. A second wave of Indian immigration to the United States took place in the late 1960s. Early participants in this second wave were relatively young (average age about 29 years), highly educated (about 80% had at least four years of college), technically trained, and affluent, with an average income of $24,000 (Lui et al., 2006).

The story of Asian Indians' acculturation process is based on a number of factors specific to their histories, such as preimmigration status, current migration status, economic well-being, religious affiliation, gender representation within the family, educational level, social class, and the ways in which immigrants experience the benefits of the host country simultaneously with the loss of their own country. Some research supports a positive correlation between a higher social class and longer duration of residence in Western countries with a weaker allegiance to traditional gender role preferences (Almeida, 2005). Unlike their Asian counterparts, Asian Indians speak English fluently, which has helped them to cross many barriers. The myth that Asian Indians are a model minority has also served to create competing experiences between them and other racial minorities. In their efforts to assimilate and disconnect from experiences of colonization, many Asian Indians are silent toward racism. Because they are less "other" in appearance than various Asian groups, and have occupied mostly professional roles in this society, Asian Indians have enjoyed a quiet privilege (Almeida, 1998, 2005).

Despite their successful adaptation into U.S. culture economically, community-based studies point to high prevalence rates of domestic violence. In a study of 160 South Asian women living in Massachusetts (Silverman, 2002) who were married or in a heterosexual relationship, 48.8% reported that they had been physically or sexually abused by their current male partners; no significant difference in prevalence of domestic violence reported between arranged and nonarranged marriages. Only 3.1% of the abused women in this study obtained a restraining order against an abusive partner. This rate is substantially lower than women in Massachusetts generally, of whom 33% of those abused by an intimate partner obtained a restraining order.

In New Jersey alone—a state with one of the largest populations of South Asians in the United States—the number of women receiving services rose from 160 in the period July 1996 to June 1997 to 258 for the period July 1998 to June 1999 (Dasgupta, 2000).

Differentiating Culture From Violence

Patriarchal customs vary in form across cultural groups. Dowries, education for the women to increase marketability as brides, the demand for male children, female infanticide, and the devaluing of widows are patriarchal customs common to Asian Indian culture (Almeida, 2005). Among Asian cultures, for example, marriage in all of its prearranged forms replaces the ritual of courtship. The cultural practices of arranged marriage include a number of rites that privilege men's entitlement and power over women's safety and self-determination, although many changes have occurred in this practice, especially in the Western world. Forced marriages, on the other hand, uphold all male rites.

All cultures are carriers of oppressive practices that vary in form. Culture, however, is not synonymous with oppressive practices. There must, therefore, be a distinction between oppressive practices, which range from actual torture to subtle dehumanizing, and definitions of cultural legacies and traditions. Wife battering is not culture. Dowries, wife burning, and female infanticide are not culture. The forced use of *purdah* or veiling for women in Islamic communities is not culture (Almeida, 2005; Lateef, 1990; Mernissi & Lakeland, 1991). These practices cannot be considered culture. Culture is the positive transmission of rituals, celebrations, and stories that makes the general ordering of life familiar for members of a particular group. Even in the face of varying forms of oppression by external forces, culture perpetuates connections for families via particular art forms, food, language, and religious practices.

The following profile is reflective of gender violence within South Asian communities:

1. Domestic violence by multiple abusers—fathers, mothers, brothers, and sisters-in law

2. Immigration-related threats

3. Using and abusing children to inflict harm with threats of international kidnapping of children by family abductors

4. Abandonment with or without divorce

5. Threats of honor killings

6. Dowry-related deaths and burnings

7. Bride price—effectively selling a daughter to the highest bidder

8. Community denial or silence

9. Less attention paid to the education and nutrition of female children and excessive restrictions on their freedom

10. Forced marriages—not to be confused with arranged marriages—that women do not consent to but cannot escape from (Asian and Pacific Islander Institute on Domestic Violence, www.apiah.org/apidvinstitute)

Invasion, Occupation, and Colonization

India's history is one of invasion by Aryans, Persians, and Muslims, and recent colonization imposed by the British, French, and Portuguese. In addition, India has an even older caste system in the religious doctrine of its most populous group. These two factors helped create a national culture organized strongly around social hierarchy. Although relatively brief in the civilization and invasions of India's history, the colonization by the Europeans—the British in particular—set in tow a sense of being beholden to "Whiteness" (Prashad, 2000). This sense of colonial superiority is comingled with a legacy of valuing "other" over self in many areas in life, from education in the Western hemisphere to socializing and integrating mostly with Whites and adapting to Western work patterns and lifestyles. This culturally defined legacy is reinforced by the culture of imperialism (Said, 1993). Only 61 years after independence, the current rate of economic growth for India in the current globalization market might shift some of these "internalized colonial" ideas.

Considering Couple Treatment From a Non-Eurocentric Perspective

Overview of the Cultural Context Model

The Cultural Context Model re-visions multicultural scholarship with links to social justice initiatives. The model transforms family therapy to include the pursuit of justice at every level, using the following tools and techniques:

- Initiate clients' critical awareness of diversity and power.
- Emphasize how "normal" hierarchies of power, privilege,[2] and oppression perpetuate suffering.
- Experientially demonstrate the link between fairness and relational healing.
- Expand the therapeutic encounter to include a community with critical consciousness rather than one family at a time.
- Define *empowerment* in collective rather than individual terms.
- Encourage social action as a means for empowering communities, families, and self.
- Provide *accountability* for all participants, including therapists.
- Create a basis for developing authentic relationships and diverse communities.
- Help people think about ways to connect past, present, and future legacies within the matrix of critical consciousness, empowerment, and accountability.

Critical Consciousness

Critical consciousness refers to awareness of the political foundation of relationship patterns. Transformative family therapy works to develop critical consciousness as both a catalyst and map for positive change. Critical consciousness with clients and trainees is built through social education with the use of film, dialogue, and inquiry (Almeida, 2004).

Paulo Freire (1982) originated the term *critical consciousness*, using it to describe the awakening of his literacy students to the impact of social class dynamics on their life circumstances. As critical consciousness develops, we no longer see current realities as "the unquestioned and unchangeable nature of things." Instead, we see options for change. For example, those who view men as genetically programmed for aggression also accept war and domestic violence as the natural order of things. However, those who view men's aggression as a learned tactic of domination see the possibilities for peace on all systems levels.

Empowerment

Social-justice-based empowerment promotes "power with" rather than "power over." An Asian Indian woman pursues an education not solely to be marketable as a bride, but to fulfill a lifelong dream while also contributing financially to her family. An Asian Indian man gains empowerment by acknowledging the harm he has caused his family through violence, and by bringing accountability and reparative actions to them. He is empowered through just action—and so are those on the receiving end.

Accountability

Accountability begins with acceptance of responsibility for one's actions and the impact of those actions upon others. However, accountability moves beyond blame and guilt. It results in reparative action that demonstrates empathic concern for others by making changes that enhance the quality of life for all involved parties.

Sponsors

Men and women who have participated in this therapeutic endeavor link with new clients, men and women, to raise critical consciousness, support empowerment, and ensure accountability (Almeida & Bograd, 1990; Almeida & Lockard, 2005).

Culture Circles

Another term borrowed from Freire (1982), *culture circles* are heterogeneous helping communities involving members of families who seek treatment, volunteer helpers from the community who work with the families, and a team of therapists. Within the Cultural Context Model, culture circles provide the primary context for treatment. Culture circles promote healing through development of critical consciousness and resistance to norms that maintain hierarchies of power, privilege, and oppression.

Assessing Couples for Gender Inequity and Domestic Violence

Working with heterosexual couples when there is no domestic violence requires that men be divested of their sexist roles and women be encouraged to move beyond traditional prescriptions of family life. When domestic violence is present, it is even more critical to shift these rigidly gendered patterns. All couples, heterosexual and GLBT, are triaged for domestic violence. Couple sessions are scheduled at the discretion of the victim, and only after the perpetrator consistently claims full responsibility for his abuses of power over the victim and in the family. Figure 14.2 describes the multiple dimensions of power and control wielded by a batterer toward a victim. Figure 14.3 specifically shows the misuse and abuse of power toward people of color.

Couple Therapy in the Aftermath of Domestic Violence

Couple therapy that follows a history of domestic violence proceeds only after all forms of violence (verbal, physical, sexual, economic) have stopped, and when the victim—being on a more equal footing—initiates such a request. Ethical standards for treatment of domestic violence require that conjoint counseling (with both partners present) only be considered when the certain criteria are met (Almeida & Durkin, 1999; Almeida & Lockard, 2005; Bograd, 1999, p. 295).

Domestic violence in the Indian Desi culture, not unlike other cultures, is about the domination of women by men and the upholding of traditional family patterns, exacerbated by the problems of immigration status, language barriers, harmful stereotypes, the "White-centered" domestic violence movement, and the silence of men in the community. The caste

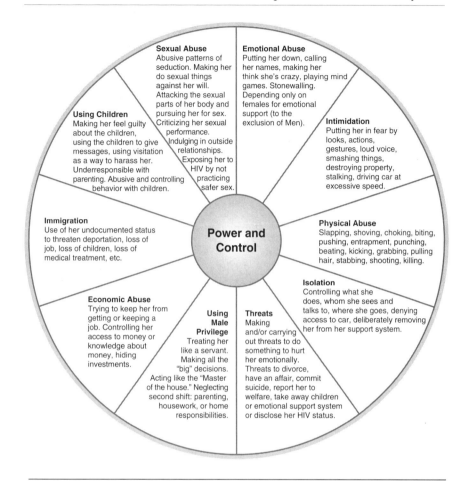

Power and Control

Sexual Abuse
Abusive patterns of seduction. Making her do sexual things against her will. Attacking the sexual parts of her body and pursuing her for sex. Criticizing her sexual performance. Indulging in outside relationships. Exposing her to HIV by not practicing safer sex.

Emotional Abuse
Putting her down, calling her names, making her think she's crazy, playing mind games. Stonewalling. Depending only on females for emotional support (to the exclusion of Men).

Using Children
Making her feel guilty about the children, using the children to give messages, using visitation as a way to harass her. Underresponsible with parenting. Abusive and controlling behavior with children.

Intimidation
Putting her in fear by looks, actions, gestures, loud voice, smashing things, destroying property, stalking, driving car at excessive speed.

Immigration
Use of her undocumented status to threaten deportation, loss of job, loss of children, loss of medical treatment, etc.

Physical Abuse
Slapping, shoving, choking, biting, pushing, entrapment, punching, beating, kicking, grabbing, pulling hair, stabbing, shooting, killing.

Isolation
Controlling what she does, whom she sees and talks to, where she goes, denying access to car, deliberately removing her from her support system.

Economic Abuse
Trying to keep her from getting or keeping a job. Controlling her access to money or knowledge about money, hiding investments.

Using Male Privilege
Treating her like a servant. Making all the "big" decisions. Acting like the "Master of the house." Neglecting second shift: parenting, housework, or home responsibilities.

Threats
Making and/or carrying out threats to do something to hurt her emotionally. Threats to divorce, have an affair, commit suicide, report her to welfare, take away children or emotional support system or disclose her HIV status.

Figure 14.2 Private Context: The Misuse and Abuse of Power Within Heterosexual Relationships

system and its intersection with religion and the family/communal systems also play a role (Almeida, 1990, 1996, 1997, 2005). Women carry the role of "culture bearer." To fulfill this role, women often conspire with their male partners to distort evidence of domestic abuse and deny the long and harsh effects of violence intergenerationally. Because the abuse of women by in-laws in the Desi community is a silent crime, it is important not to label survivors of domestic violence entirely as hapless victims. Instead, women need assistance in evaluating the ways in which they accommodate misuse of power, and personally misuse and abuse power.

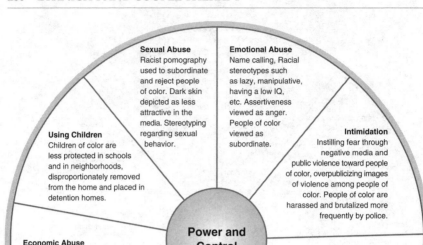

Figure 14.3   White Privilege/Public Context: The Misuse and Abuse of Power Toward People of Color

Women uphold patriarchal practices and structures in many ways. A White mother from a fundamentalist church might justify violence toward her children, saying it is done calmly and serves to teach respect. An Asian Indian woman might argue that in her culture, to keep her daughter-in-law in place, it is important to support the dowry system, subjugate her daughter-in-law, ignore the sexual harassment of her daughter-in-law by the father-in-law, or brothers-in-law, and support her son's violence toward his wife. Regardless of the violence and humiliation directed toward them, mothers from all cultural backgrounds often feel compelled to model respect toward husbands, and respect for traditional male patterns of behavior.

The following case emphasizes the abuse of power and control by an entire family system toward the young bride.

CASE EXAMPLE

Anu and Matmahan, a married couple in their early 30s, were referred because of Matmahan's violence toward Anu, a dental technician and second-generation Indian American. Matmahan, an accountant, grew up and was educated in Bengal, but most of his family lives in the United States. Anu and Matmahan are college educated, and courted other partners prior to this marriage. Following the birth of their son, Matmahan's parents decided to visit for an undisclosed length of time to "help" with the baby. Shortly after her arrival, the mother-in-law began criticizing Anu's cooking, her care of the baby, her care of Matmahan, and the home. The mother-in-law often compared Anu's caretaking to that of "Blacks." Matmahan quickly dropped his support of Anu and aligned with his mother. Matmahan's father did not participate directly in this line of abuse, but did expect his daughter-in-law to care for and pick up after him.

When their baby was about 7 months old, physical battering began. First Matmahan kicked and punched Anu, and then the mother-in-law engaged in numerous hair-pulling episodes. Finally Anu called 911, and Matmahan was arrested. The in-laws remained in the home and blamed Anu for the police involvement. Anu's family came over and both families agreed to have Matmahan go into therapy, on condition that Anu would drop the charges.

At the final hearing, Anu dropped the protective order and asked that the judge mandate her husband into treatment. The judge put a stay on the order and mandated Matmahan to our center.

Anu and Matmahan participated in their own culture circles. Both sets of parents were involved in about 6 to 10 sessions. All family members were exposed to social education, establishing a critical consciousness upon which to build strategies of nonviolence, gender, race, sexual orientation, and class equity. Films included *Radio Flyer, The Great Santini, Kush, Mississippi Masala, Fire,* and *Monsoon Wedding* (see Additional Resources section below). These films were shown with the hierarchy diagram (see Figure 14.1) and the power and control wheels (see Figures 14.2 and 14.3) in the presence of sponsors and other circle members.

This process provides a powerful context for making the private context of family matters public. The conversations between the couple, their families, and sponsors broadened the conversations around multiple perpetrators in the home. This allowed for an interrogation of the system of power and abuse across and between genders. It is important to note here that while women use violence against one another, not against men, men are complicit with this violence.

After a number of months of participation in his culture circle, Matmahan claimed full responsibility for all the ways he had abused his partner. He was required to write a letter to his mother and father as well as to Anu's parents signifying his complicit role in the trajectory of abuse and setting the landscape for a different type of relationship with his parents.

Anu and her two sisters-in-law witnessed Matmahan's letter and reparations. They had never experienced or imagined that an abuser could be held accountable for his violence in a public forum. Matmahan's peers supported him in taking the first steps toward establishing justice in his marriage. He was also given a number of ideas for continuing this work. He was coached on the details of creating an equitable partnership— something most men, and Asian Indian men in particular, lack.

Anu and Matmahan were able to interrupt and change the traditional pattern in their family—a pattern that uses marriage as a family structure to prioritize the bond between the husband, his mother, and his extended family of origin. Women, consequently, are expected to be other focused and to find intimacy primarily within relationships with male children and the families these male children later create. Men are socialized to engage in emotional and economic partnerships with their families of origin.

Changing Intersectionalities Through Changed Alliances

The social justice approach described here, with its focus on community connections, holds the power to offer the couple—the victim in particular— an alternative to the criminal justice system. Men as sponsors of equity in multiple dimensions can call for different ways of being, with rather surprising outcomes.

Situating men who use violence with those who do not provides enormous opportunity for learning and connection. Men who use violence learn to embrace friendships with men who do not support abusiveness. They also get help with parenting their children, negotiating school and medical systems, evaluating the way they manage finances (including the support of dependents), examining their understanding of love, focusing on the value of housework and other second-shift activities, and expanding their range of emotional expressiveness.

When men who have not used violence toward intimates find themselves sitting next to men who have, they more easily confront similarities in their own thinking, as well as choices they have made regarding violence. Men who have not committed acts of physical violence more easily locate their own actions along the continuum of power and control when discussing their patterns with men who have taken control to the extreme. Violence is no longer an abstraction belonging to "others," but a reality demonstrated by the actions of real men, sitting in the very same room—men who seem unremarkable, approachable, and undeniably human.

In brokering common conversations, both sets of men are challenged and encouraged by therapists to place their actions within broader frameworks of masculinity, heterosexism/homophobia, race, and culture. When there is therapeutic accountability, conversations provide a perspective that loosens defensiveness, makes personal accountability less onerous, and clears the way for new choices.

Accountability in the field of domestic violence has frequently included linking the criminal justice and shelter systems with the system, offering intervention to the batterer. All too often, however, accountability focuses exclusively on prosecution and punishment, rather than reparation. We believe there is an important difference between prosecution-oriented domestic violence programs and programs whose centerpiece is redistributive justice. All of these policies require a stronger presence by the South Asian community to speak out against gender violence and accountability on the part of the mainstream domestic violence movement.

This holds true for empowering women as well. By creating forums that privilege the victim's voice and allow her to speak about her experiences, the distribution of power between victim and offender can be rebalanced (Curtis, 2005). This was Anu's experience. We also witnessed a rebalancing of power with Anu's husband, Matmahan, who countered both male and in-law privilege. Couples learn how to join forces to stand up against the in-laws when they cannot get out of the extended family. Men are coached to disrupt the power structures within their family to strengthen the husband–wife relationship.

Therapists encourage women's empowerment by acknowledging their roles within and outside of family life, while at the same time encouraging them to expand self-nurturing patterns. Therapists can also encourage strategizing for economic independence, acknowledging and respecting one's body, striving for leadership, and coming to rely on a collective of conscious women for support. We encourage women to stop overfocusing on their guilt and to begin to experience anger as an appropriate response to control and abuse.

Supervision and Training

As family therapists, we have the ethical responsibility of bridging the scholarship of cultural competency and social justice. The ethical practice of multiculturalism within a social justice perspective requires a simultaneous dismantling of White power and privilege. The tradition of viewing ethnic groups in compartmentalized bubbles negates the complexity of intersectionality and lived experiences of culturally diverse groups. More importantly, it allows White therapists to work from a distance. There is an unspoken boundary of protection for White therapists who are eager to learn about other cultures as they inform therapeutic practices. This boundary of protection continues to endorse multiculturalism, with no demands placed on the dismantling and restructuring of White power and privilege. Understanding Whiteness in all of its dimensions should go hand in hand with cultural discourse and toward re-visioning service delivery systems (Almeida, 1993). If our focus moving forward is to transform client experiences from the intersects of power, privilege, and oppression to liberation, then attending to both sides of the same coin—White privilege and multiculturalism—must be fundamental in our therapeutic endeavors.

Reflective Structure and Questions

It is my belief that White therapists can work with multiple cultures as long as there is a critical consciousness about self and other. Working with students to raise critical consciousness is critically linked to the process with clients. The binary conceptualization of race often forgoes the critical dialogue and inquiry that can greatly benefit students and clients alike. Marginal and immigrant cultures are continuously impacting the lifestyles of mainstream U.S. culture, as reflected in the widespread acceptance of hip-hop, yoga, meditation, and alternative/ integrative medicine. Using film vignettes to bring these powerful dialogues into training and supervision circles offers a rich and stimulating context toward change and action. Framing culture in a multiracial society necessitates the ethics of remembering fundamental historic events. The following topics/questions are some examples of teaching modules that ought to be integrated into the discourse of White power, privilege, and multiculturalism.

- The seizing of Native American land and the genocidal policies that accomplished it
- The enslavement of Blacks
- The internment camps
- The Asian Exclusion Act
- Conditions of the Asian workers building the American railroads, of migrant farm workers and illegal aliens
- The role of the British in the partition of India and Pakistan
- The cultural auditing of social organizations and academic contexts

Conclusion

Couple therapy when there is domestic violence requires a social justice perspective that centers the rights of women as victims. Raising critical consciousness is essential for all family members, bringing the different players, mothers-in-law included, into dialogue and inquiry around the abuse of young women and widows by other women as culture bearers.

Therapeutic changes occur when such dialogue creates empowerment and brings accountability to those harmed, through social action. Expanding the context of therapy to bring in sponsors as witnessing members of the community cements a second-order change.

In the words of Carlos Fuentes, "Culture consists of connections, not of separations: to specialize is to isolate."

Notes

1. The couples described here are heterosexual; however, the conceptual framework is applicable to GLBT couples as well.

2. *Privilege:* One gains an advantage, or privilege, when one possesses certain identity characteristics like White skin, maleness, heterosexuality, middle- or upper middle-class status, and able-bodied status. One loses an advantage, or privilege, when one possesses characteristics like femaleness, queerness, skin with color, and poverty-social class status (Almeida, Dolan-Del Vecchio, & Parker, 2007).

Additional Resources

Films

Carlino, L. J. (Director) (1979). *The Great Santini.* Bing Crosby Productions.
Mehta, D. (Director) (1996). *Fire.* Kaleidoscope India.

Nair, M. (Director) (1991). *Mississippi Masala.* Black River Productions.
Nair, M. (Director) (2001). *Monsoon Wedding.* IFC Productions.
Pratibha P. (Director) (1991). *Kush.* Women Make Movies.
Richard, D. (Director) (1992). *Radio Flyer.* Columbia Pictures.

References

Abraham, M. (2000). *Speaking the unspeakable: Marital violence against South Asian immigrant women in the United States.* New Brunswick, NJ: Rutgers University Press.

Ahmad, K. (2000). Amnesty highlights repression of Asian women. *The Lancet, 355*(9222), 22–29.

Almeida, R. (1990). Asian Indian mothers. *Journal of Feminist Family Therapy, 2,* 33–39.

Almeida, R. (1993). Unexamined assumptions and service delivery systems: Feminist theory and racial exclusions. *Journal of Feminist Family Therapy, 5,* 3–23.

Almeida, R. (2005). An Overview: Hindu, Muslim, and Christian families. In M. McGoldrick, J. Giordano, & N. Garcia Preto (Eds.), *Ethnicity and family therapy* (3rd ed., pp. 395–424). New York: Guilford Press.

Almeida, R. (2006, September). Unpublished presentation to Beyond Multiculturalism Conference, Rutgers University Psychology Program.

Almeida, R. (2007, September,). The ethics and practice of multiculturalism, presentation to NASW conference, New Jersey.

Almeida, R., & Bograd, M. (1990). Sponsorship: Men holding men accountable for domestic violence. *Journal of Feminist Family Therapy, 2,* 243–256.

Almeida, R., & Dolan-Del Vecchio, K. (1999). Addressing culture in batterers' intervention. *Violence Against Women, 5,* 654–683.

Almeida, R., Dolan-Del Vecchio, K., & Parker, L. (2007). *Transformative family therapy: Just families in a just society.* Boston: Allyn & Bacon.

Almeida, R., & Durkin, R. (1999). Couples therapy when there is domestic violence. *Journal of Marital and Family Therapy, 25,* 169–176.

Almeida, R., & Lockard, J. (2005). The cultural context model. In N. Sokolov (Ed.), *Domestic violence at the margins: Readings on race, class, gender, and culture* (pp. 301–319). New Brunswick, NJ: Rutgers University Press.

Almeida, R., Woods, R., Messineo, T., & Font, R. (1994). Violence in the lives of the racially and sexually different. In R. Almeida (Ed.), *Expansions of feminist family theory through diversity* (pp. 3–23). New York: Haworth Press.

Almeida, R. V. (Ed.). (1998). *Transformations of gender and race: Family and developmental perspectives.* New York: Hawthorn Press.

Ayyub, R. (2000). Domestic violence in the South Asian Muslim immigrant population in the United States. *Journal of Social Distress and the Homeless, 9,* 237–248.

Bograd, M. (1999). Strengthening domestic violence theories: Intersections of race, class, sexual orientation, and gender. *Journal of Marital and Family Therapy, 25,* 275–289.

Crenshaw, K. (1994). Mapping the margins: Intersectionality, identity politics, and violence against women of color. In M. Fineman & R. Mykitiuk (Eds.), *The public nature of private violence* (pp. 93–118). New York: Routledge.

Curtis, S. (2005). Gendered violence and restorative justice: The views of victim advocates. *Violence Against Women, 1,* 603–638.

Dasgupta, S. D. (2000). Broken promises: Domestic violence murders and attempted murders in the U.S. and Canadian South Asian communities. In S. Nankani (Ed.), *Breaking the silence: Domestic violence in the South Asian-American community* (pp. 27–46). Xlibris Corporation (www.xlibris.com).

Hernández, P., Almeida, R., & Dolan-Del Vecchio, K. (2005). Critical consciousness, accountability, and empowerment: Key processes for helping families heal. *Family Process, 44,* 105–130.

Lateef, S. (1990). *Muslim women in India: Political and private realities.* Atlantic Highlands, NJ: Zed Books.

Lui, M., Robles, B., Leondar-Wright, B., Brewer, R., & Adamson, R., with United for a Fair Economy (2006). *The story behind the U.S. racial wealth divide.* New York: New Press.

Lynch, O. (1969). *The politics of untouchability: Social mobility and social change in a city of India.* New York: Columbia University Press.

Merchant, M. (2000). A comparative study of agencies assisting domestic violence victims: Does the South Asian community have special needs? *Journal of Social Distress and the Homeless, 9,* 249–259.

Mernissi, F., & Lakeland, M.J. (1991). *The veil and the male elite: A feminist interpretation of women's rights in Islam.* Jackson TN: Perseus Books.

Papenek, H. (1973). Purdah: Separate worlds and symbolic shelter. *Comparative Studies in Society and History, 15,* 289–293.

Prashad, V. (2000). *The karma of brown folk.* Minneapolis, MN: University of Minnesota Press.

Raj, A., & Silverman J. (2002). Intimate partner violence against South-Asian women in Greater Boston. *Journal of American Medical Women's Association, 57,* 87–102.

Said, E. (1993). *Culture and imperialism.* London: Chatto & Windus.

Spivak, G. (1985). The Rani of Simur. In F. Barker et al. (Eds.), *Europe and its others,* Vol. 1 (pp. 128–151). Colchester, UK: University of Essex.

Spivak, G. (1989). A response to "The Difference Within: Feminism and Critical Theory." In E. Meese & A. Parker (Eds.), *The difference within: Feminism and critical theory* (pp. 207–20). Philadelphia: John Benjamins.

Van Soest, D. (1994). Social work education for multicultural practice and social justice advocacy: A field study of how students experience the learning process. *Journal of Multicultural Social Work, 3,* 17–28.

Fifteen

A Multilevel Contextual Model for Couples From Mainland China

Lin Shi and Linna Wang

Couple therapy is considered challenging because many intricate emotional elements are involved in the marital relationship. An even greater challenge arises when a mainstream therapist from the West works with a couple from mainland China. In this chapter, we attempt to provide a multilevel contextual conceptualization that is based on a competent understanding of the culture and its people as well as a unique culturally informed clinical intervention that aims to optimize couples' functioning in the marital context. This model takes into consideration variables such as acculturation and cultural identity, which are absent in the traditional Western models of psychotherapy. The term *multilevel* refers to the influence of the marital relationship from various levels, including cultural, political, extended family, marital, and individual. First, we view the evolving Chinese *culture* as the first and most basic level upon which other unique contexts and characteristics are built. It is important to examine how this culture's principles are applied to the individual, and to marital, family, extended family, and societal levels. The second level is the *influence of the Communist takeover* in 1949 upon the individual, family, and society. The third level is the unique situation faced by *mainland Chinese living in the United States,* and their negotiation between the old and the new, the East and the West.

The guiding belief of this model—that marital and family issues are to be examined and conceptualized in their cultural context—naturally leads to an approach that honors the cultural validity of family relationships and interaction patterns specific to the population of interest. It demands that interventions be drawn from the cultural context, and take a format that validates the cultural experience of the couple. It goes without saying that cultural competence—the ability not only to appreciate other cultural groups but, more importantly, to work with them effectively—is crucial for a desirable clinical outcome. A good cognitive match between the therapist and clients on goals of treatment and coping styles is related to better adjustment in clients and a more favorable evaluation of the sessions (Ito & Maramba, 2002; Zhang, Snowden, & Sue, 1998).

Marriage in the Cultural Context

Chinese culture is one of the very few existing cultures that have lasted thousands of years without interruption or fundamental changes. In its long 5,000 year history, it has resisted numerous foreign invasions and conquerors. It was powerful enough to open itself to absorb the strengths of the cultures that were considered "less civilized" or even "barbaric" by its own standards during turbulent as well as peaceful periods. The culture has thus maintained its core, yet also has evolved with the change of dynasties, and it is the background context for the behaviors of its people and their families.

Extended Family and Group Harmony

An ideal image of the traditional Chinese family is a large extended family residing in the same family estate, with its members strictly following a code of ethics that ensures the well-being of each family member. Even though most modern families do not follow this type of living arrangement, the core value of group harmony remains. Due to this, the focal point for a couple is their relationship with others (Hamaguchi, 1985), namely, the husband's parents, their own children, and the husband's siblings, along with their spouses and children. A marriage is not an independent entity to fulfill the individual emotional needs of the couple; rather, it is additional and subordinate to the extended family hierarchy. A marriage has the superior goal of promoting harmony in the extended family and the practical goal of raising children.

The relationship orientation in such a family is naturally vertical: Energy is invested downward in raising children and upward in taking care of aging parents. Such vertical obligations essentially capitalize on the physical capacity of adults to ensure that the weak and the fragile in the family are cared for. By taking care of the young, one earns merit as a parent. By taking care of aging parents, one pays back the parents' earned merit and demonstrates to the young what is expected of them. Life continues and expands in this organic cycle, which is regarded as being as natural and preordained as the earth itself. The joy derived is *supposedly* heavenly. Any behavior deviant from this cycle is considered to be defying the force of nature, which will incur a serious price, including guilt (Hsiao, Klimidis, Minas, & Tan, 2006) and the social/ moral condemnation of the community, as this mutual obligation is written into the Chinese Marriage Law (National People's Congress, 2001, Article 21).

Loyalty to the extended family is not a preferential choice but a moral commitment to the lives of other members. Interpersonal harmony, therefore, is the key element in maintaining Chinese patients' mental health (Hsiao et al., 2006). This emphasis on group harmony leaves little room for the individual rights that are valued by Western culture (Weatherley, 2002). Indulging in personal freedom is considered by the Chinese to be immature and selfish, as one must carefully consider the impact of a personal decision on the whole of the community.

One can see the work of the principle of group harmony in life events, such as mate selection. The individual decision must be approved by the parents and/or extended family, and parental approval has been found to be one of the unique factors impacting on marital quality in China (Pimentel, 2000). Furthermore, self-sacrifice is expected for group harmony. It is not rare for parents to sacrifice their personal well-being or careers for their children and/or extended family. It is common for couples to live and work in different geographic locations to better provide for the family. The concepts of marital boundaries and personal fulfillment do not exist in the traditional Chinese culture. When children are born, the function of the marital subsystem practically ceases to exist.

Gender Issues in Traditional Chinese Culture

Although the traditional family structure gives males more power in the family, married females who have produced an heir are not necessarily powerless. Confucian teaching leads the young to respect and obey both parents, thus giving the mother almost equal power in some areas. Chinese women may appear to be submissive to their men, such as deferring decision making to their husbands in public, yet most of them know how to use their power at the right moment, and they gain more power as their children grow up. This makes the couple dynamics in Chinese marriage much more complex than may be apparent to a less experienced observer who relies heavily on clients' verbal reports. The gender role in the new social context is explored in the next section.

Political Impact

Decades of political movement have impacted Chinese families and family relations profoundly. A brief history of these movements is enlightening. Following the end of World War II, a civil war erupted between the ruling Nationalist Party and the Communist Party of China. The Nationalist government quickly collapsed under Communist attack and in 1949 retreated to Taiwan. Mainland China was and remains under the complete control of the Communist government as it has gone through numerous political campaigns. The highlight of these campaigns was the Cultural Revolution that traumatized almost every citizen and brought the country to the brink of economic disaster. As a result, a unique cultural variation began to emerge in mainland China.

Gender Roles

Since it came into power, the current Chinese government has been promoting women's equality in workforce participation, education, and political involvement for over half a century. The Chinese Marriage Law of 1953 made a special effort to promote equality between men and women (Marriage Law of the People's Republic of China, 1959). The government started a nationwide movement to "liberate" women. This was driven by the communist ideology of equality as well as the practical need for a workforce after decades of war. It has become the norm for contemporary Chinese women to participate in paid work and to expect the same opportunities as men in education, employment, political involvement, decision making, and compensation. Women have been led to believe that they can "hold up half of the sky." Urban Chinese women had one of the highest workforce participation rates in the world in the 1980s (Bauer, Wang, Riley, & Zhao, 1992). Employment enabled these women to demand equality in the family, and to expect men to pick up their share of the domestic tasks, including child rearing and household chores. Compared with previous generations, Chinese men do more household work and participate more actively in child rearing ("Chinese Husbands," 1999; Da, 2004). The patterns of division of household labor found in most urban Chinese families are consistent with those of the United States (Lu, Bellas, & Maume, 2001).

In mainland China, the social system, political ideology, and governmental policies played a crucial role in reshaping gender and family relationships (Croll, 1995; Hooper, 1989). Changes of this nature, heavily influenced by politics and governmental policy yet without sufficient economic backing, have been difficult to sustain. Since China started to embrace a capitalist economy, the economic force has been reversing the tide of change for women. Although educated Chinese women are still taking the lead in workforce participation in the new economy, and value their independence and identity ("China: Women's Employment Changing," 1995), they may also be seen as less "womanly," and they are struggling to renegotiate their identity as professionals and as women (Thornton & Wang, 1998).

The status of immigrant women, like that of their sisters in China, is being impacted by economic forces as well. Although immigrant Chinese women have a higher education level, they experience a reduction in employment, and many were shocked to find that the gender role to which they were accustomed was not accommodated in the new country, leading them to reorient toward the domestic sphere of the family (Ho, 2006). The economic impact on gender role beliefs held by immigrant Chinese men has been an increased expectation of traditional gender roles and a decreased valuation of professional identity and achievement by their wives.

Limited Mate Selection Criteria

Mate selection in old-fashioned, arranged marriage used to be a group decision based on tangible "conditions," such as educational level, financial resources, and family background, rather than on romantic love or personality match. Even though most marriages today are either based on "free choice" or "negotiated" (Pimentel, 2000), the mate selection criteria remain largely unchanged in that males are expected to be taller, better educated, and more resolute in decision making than their female counterparts (Pang, 1993). This indicates that the change in gender behavior did not necessarily translate into the change in gender belief. Before the 1980s, when China was under tight Communist control, not much variation was allowed in anything in society, including education and financial resources. This further limited selection criteria. Young people were led to believe that their shared Communist ideology, the so-called common language, was a sufficient premise for a good marriage. One of the purposes of marriage, according to the propaganda, was to better serve society. Premarital sex was strictly forbidden until the1990s; it could—and often did—lead to being expelled from a job or college.

Immigrant couples who have selected their mates based on the limited selection criteria may be greatly challenged when they are transplanted to a culture that values romantic love and different behavioral norms of emotional expression. Things that have not mattered much to marital relations, such as social skills, femininity, and ability to adapt, suddenly take on more weight in a marriage. What used to be frowned on, such as comfort in openly expressing affection, may become more desirable than some people can demonstrate.

Immigration Experience

Mainland Chinese have migrated to America in waves in search of economic betterment since the gold rush (Hirschman & Wong, 1981). First they came as laborers, then they remained within the Chinese community and clung to their traditional cultural beliefs and practices in the face of open hostility and discrimination. The makeup of the Chinese immigrants coming to the United States changed significantly in the early 1980s. College-educated professionals joined the process when the United States opened its college doors to mainland Chinese. A typical professional immigrant from mainland China in the 1980s and most of the 1990s was a married man or woman who had left behind his or her spouse and their child, with the hope of eventual reunion. Life was harsh in the new land due to financial hardship, culture shock, and the language barrier. Equally frustrating was the reunion process, which was often delayed for years. The late 1990s and 2000s saw an increase in the number of younger singles who were more financially secure and who had been more exposed to U.S. culture due to the global economy (Wong, 2006).

Unlike earlier immigrants, who usually started their American lives in the cultural enclave of Chinatown, the professional immigrants from mainland China today are much more willing, and better equipped with language ability and transferable skills, to embrace the U.S. lifestyle early in their stay in the new country. A shared experience among them is that they gradually begin to identify with and incorporate some American individualistic cultural values into their existing value system. Examples include, but are not limited to, personal and family boundaries, privacy, self-reliance, and self-actualization. A potential disagreement between them and their family members back in China regarding duties and obligations is almost inevitable.

Acculturation Rate and Its Impact on Gender Role Expectation

One of the challenges encountered by many immigrant couples is the discrepancy in acculturation rate between spouses, as acculturation is an individual process (Côté, 2006). The speed of acculturation process concerns proficiency in language and exposure to the host society (Berry, Poortinga, Segall, & Dasen, 1992). This discrepancy of acculturation rates changes the couple's view of the world, as well as their marriage relationship. A couple that follows more traditional gender role assignments may find this discrepancy less disturbing than a nontraditional couple in which the wife has more advanced language ability and has been exposed to the mainstream culture more than her husband. In such a couple, the less-acculturated husband may be intolerably slow and interpersonally inappropriate to the wife, and the wife may be seen by her husband and his family as too masculine, unloving, and ungrateful. This is more likely to be true in couples in which the wife has migrated first and gained language ability, employment, and sufficient stability to enable her husband to join her, or in couples in which the husband can work only in a Chinese-speaking environment, such as a Chinese restaurant, while the wife has more interaction with American mainstream society by working in a U.S. company. Our clinical observation is that the marriage in which the wife is more acculturated than the husband is less stable than the marriage in which the husband is more acculturated than the wife. This is consistent with the less changed gender belief in mate selection criteria that males are expected to be more educated, more capable, and fluent in coping with the external environment (Pang, 1993), and this phenomenon also testifies that gender role changes during the immigration do not follow a unilinear trajectory along the traditional–modern continuum (Zentgraf, 2002).

Clinical Conceptualization and Treatment Goals

Rather than focusing solely on the nuclear family, a couple's presenting problems must be conceptualized at the multilevel context. However, it should be noted that factors at different levels of the context are dynamically interactive rather than mutually exclusive. General goals include helping the couple to find their appropriate place in the complex net of interwoven contexts, to renegotiate the marital contract in the changed context, and to develop new skills that promote healing and health in the new country.

The goals can be achieved through the following interventions/strategies:

1. Strengthen emotional bonds by prioritizing couple relationship in the context of nuclear and extended family contexts. Provide education by using scientific evidence. A strong marriage is the core of family systems and benefits all, yet a Chinese marriage cannot survive in isolation without mutual nurturing in the context of extended families.

2. Normalize the couple's struggle in the context of immigration and cultural differences. Promote awareness that their marriage also goes through an immigration and acculturation process as they do individually; thus, their struggle is part of the acculturation task in the process.

3. Encourage and facilitate conversations about their extended families, promoting understanding and avoiding parent blaming. If one spouse has strong emotions regarding this, individual sessions can be helpful in venting emotions. The focus of the individual sessions, however, remains on the marital relationship. Personal sacrifice that is likely to come up during individual sessions needs to be acknowledged and credited as a contribution to the family.

4. Explore and establish culturally appropriate ways of expressing love and appreciation, including sexual love. Encourage the couple to develop their own special language that is understood only by them.

5. Explore and process emotional injuries in marriage: externalize injuries; highlight each spouse's contribution to the marriage and their families in the immigration process. Assess for abuse and violence, and assess for sexual difficulties.

6. Utilize the value of acceptance in Chinese beliefs, promoting coping rather than devoting too much energy to attempting to change the unchangeable.

Common Presenting Problems

Marital Disharmony Due to Gender Role Conflict in the New Country

When couples from mainland China immigrate to the United States, their gender roles may not encounter significant challenges during the initial stage. Couples tend to focus on "making it" in the land of opportunity. Masculine qualities such as independence, initiative, and execution are valued and appreciated in this stage. However, gender role conflict tends to erupt after the couple has "made it." When men witness different gender roles and begin to accept the more male-dominated American culture, they begin to expect their female partners to be more submissive and "feminine." Many of the wives start to feminize their roles as well (Ho, 2006). However, those with strong professional identity and/or those whose professional ability and masculinity played a major role in the couple's "making it" usually find the "feminization" requirement offensive. This creates resentments on both sides. Many marital conflicts among mainland Chinese couples find their origin in gender role conflict.

CASE EXAMPLE

Mrs. Wang, a brilliant scientist and considered by many a "genius," migrated to the United States as a graduate student. She chose a less prestigious program over an Ivy League college that had accepted her in order to gain more negotiating power to have her husband accepted in the same school. She graduated first, and then financially supported him through graduate school. Their relationship was satisfying to both and admired by others during their "making it" years. Conflict erupted after they had "made it." Both were hired by prestigious firms and bought a million-dollar house. He started to see her as not feminine enough because she was not good in cooking and decorating, and she was resentful that her contributions and sacrifices were not appreciated and reciprocated. In revenge, she cooked even less and spent her free time on the computer.

Disagreement Due to Circular Obligations to Extended Family

It is not always easy for Westerners to understand the psychological power that Chinese parents exert on their adult children. Under Confucian influence, children are taught that their precious lives are given to them by their parents, and that they should respect their parents' requests and wishes. The ideal children are those who foresee and satisfy their parents' financial, physical, and emotional needs. These obligations are usually felt more by adult males, as they are expected to carry on the family name; therefore, more of their loyalty to the family of origin is expected. One's success is the pride of the whole extended family, and it is meant to be shared with parents and siblings. Immigration to the United States is success in itself, so it is not unusual for parents to want their son to buy them a house and/or other expensive items so that they can show off in their home town what a great son they have, or they may want him to financially support a sibling who is less fortunate. "I can't eat or sleep until your brother is taken care of" is a hint that nobody can miss. While still trying to provide financially for his own family, the son must achieve a delicate balance between his family of origin and his immediate family. Lack of support and understanding from either side is sufficient to make him feel trapped.

CASE EXAMPLE

After seven years of hardship going through graduate school and establishing their careers, Feng and his wife Mei finally settled down in a lovely suburban house. Feeling guilty for not being able to satisfy his parents' and brothers' financial requests while both of them were still in graduate school, Feng (as any grateful and dutiful son would do) shared his success with his extended family by offering a significant amount of money to them each year. Mei was understanding and supportive. Feng's parents began to make more financial requests, including the purchase of an apartment, more money for his siblings, and finally a request for a gift of a large sum of money equivalent to Mei's annual salary in order for Feng's brother to start a business. Mei's objections were fierce, but Feng's parents' plea was strong. Feng had never felt so helpless. He saw Mei's perspective but he could not refuse his parents and brother for fear that he would be viewed in his home town as a heartless man who had refused to take care of his family. He quickly sank into depression and physically attacked his wife in a heated argument. Mei filed for divorce.

Low Marital Satisfaction Resulting From a Discrepancy in Acculturation and Changed Style of Emotional Expression

In the traditional Chinese culture, affection is expressed not by spoken words but by actions and gestures. Overt expression of affection is often frowned upon and considered embarrassing, "graceless," or even disrespectful to others who have to watch. This belief and practice can be strongly challenged in the new society, which values romantic and verbal exchange between lovers. The traditional expression of affection of the Chinese couple may be perceived to be lack of love when compared with American couples. Among nonconflictual couples, it is usually recognized as one of the cultural differences that may trigger some desire to adopt new ways of expressing affection. Among conflictual couples, however, the perception of "lack of affection" may be exacerbated by other existing marital issues and may become an independent reason for complaint.

CASE EXAMPLE

Mrs. Gao, while describing her husband's violence, also complained that he did not know how to express affection. "Look at [an American-born Chinese], he always gives her a kiss of greeting or good bye. My husband never shows any affection to me. That makes me feel I am nobody in his eyes. After over 10 years of loveless marriage, it really doesn't matter if we have or have not this marriage any more."

Here, her marriage is "loveless" in comparison with an American marriage. His Chinese way of expressing affection is totally discounted. While this complaint appears to be independent, it is used as supporting evidence of her husband's other wrongdoings.

Clinical Implications

Seeking Treatment

In the long history of Chinese culture, loyalty to the immediate and extended family has been fostered from the time the child was in the cradle. A general rule is to keep important information within the family system, especially information that does not complement the family image, including marital disputes and parent–child conflict. There is a sense of who is an insider and who is an outsider, using family or close friends as a reference. When there is a marital dispute, for example, the couple is not necessarily hesitant to seek help but is most likely to do so only from the extended family and close friends (Epstein, Chen, & Beyder-Kamjou, 2005). Couples are usually quite open about their complaints against each other and do not necessarily restrain from using emotional language, feeling free to vent to insiders. An extended family member, especially an elder member or a close friend who notices signs of marital distress, may initiate a talk with the couple, with the intent of reducing the marital distress. More often than not, this effort is met with great appreciation by the couple.

Most mainland Chinese immigrants do not have the extended support system that they knew in China. In fact, many live in relative social isolation, without close family and friends nearby to serve as a buffer when there is a marital challenge. Yet seeking help from a mental health professional—an outsider—is alien to the cultural belief to which they were exposed since childhood. It is not surprising that many Chinese couples use therapy as a last resort or are forced by court order to participate in therapy. A strong sense of shame may be experienced when they finally have no options but to ask for external help, fearing that they are being judged by the therapist (an outsider) and that they are betraying their loyalty to their family, which is seen as a sign of weak character or lack of honor. These reservations or concerns may compromise willingness to discuss the problems in the family system openly and constructively.

Joining

Most mainland Chinese who immigrate to the United States in adulthood feel that they are caught in an awkward middle between the East and the West. Families and friends in mainland China see them as too Americanized, even while they themselves may not feel socially comfortable in America. They long to be understood, validated, and accepted. It is important that the therapist join them from the standpoint of a caring professional. Genuine interest in the immigration experience, families left behind, the home visiting routine, the experience of "making it" in the new land, and so forth are promising joining leads.

In addition, the therapist is strongly recommended to learn basic cultural beliefs and practices of Chinese clients, such as responsibility, loyalty, and extended family, and to be aware of major political events, especially the Cultural Revolution, since many current relationship choices, patterns, and emotions are in one way or another connected to those events. One Chinese lady left therapy because her young therapist had never heard of the Cultural Revolution, much less understood her depressive symptoms that resulted indirectly from that political storm.

Cultural Variables for Assessment

The In-Law Variable

A Chinese couple's relationship with extended family is one of the variables that provide insight into their relationship. A couple in conflict usually begins by trying to spare their parents any concern about their "trouble" when the conflict is still contained and is considered manageable. When they do share, the extended family's first socially expected reaction is to hold their own son or daughter responsible for the marital conflict. If the parents are siding with their child's spouse (the wife's parents side with the husband and the husband's parents side with the wife), that is an indication that the extended family on both sides is supportive of the marriage. This variable can be assessed by questions such as, "How much does your family, on each side, know about your difficulties?" "Who did you share with, siblings or parents?" "How do your parents deal with your difficulties?" "Do they side with either of you?"

Parents not siding with their own children is also a show of good faith to the other side of the extended family of their moral support for the couple's marriage (i.e., the connection between the two extended families). The behavior of the extended family members at this moment (e.g., siblings function as go-between peacemakers, parents provide advice) may appear to Westerners to be "enmeshed," a lack of boundary, or interference. Yet these behaviors are socially expected and perceived to be supportive in the Chinese cultural context. Such behavior has been clinically observed to be a protective factor for the marriage and should be considered an available resource.

Balanced "Accounts"

A Chinese marriage is healthy when all "accounts" are balanced: Parents do their duty to nurture the children and the adult offspring to take care of their parents and support their siblings. Guilt and depression may arise when these accounts are not balanced. A son who cannot go home to China to take care of his ailing mother must find other ways to do his fair share in order to release guilt before it festers into depression. Of course, the "other ways" must be agreeable to his wife, who also is expected to fulfill her duty to her parents and siblings. The therapist should assess this balance by asking the couple whether they consider that they are doing their fair share to their extended family and at the same time taking care of their own family, and whether they have any long-term plan to balance any unbalanced account.

Moral Issues

Homogenous cultures, such as the Chinese culture, are conducive to widely shared moral and ethical values. The Confucian belief that conduct should not be regulated by law and punishment but by morals and ethics leads to widely shared moral values that are socially sanctioned and enforced. As mentioned previously, it is written in the Chinese law that adults have *legal and moral* obligations to take care of their parents and their children (National People's Congress, 2001, Article 21). Whether or not a person performs his vertical obligation is often used in character judgment. Thus, when a Chinese person refers to moral obligation, the therapist should understand that such moral obligation has much stronger social significance than a mere personal value statement. Loyalty to the family is one of the fundamental moral obligations for Chinese. This loyalty is not totally due to psychological attachment; rather, it is rooted in the belief and the practice of social reciprocity and interdependence, the shared sense of reciprocal accountability. The therapist should refrain from quickly judging such vertical relationship orientation as pathological but should validate the couple's willingness to self-sacrifice, utilizing this willingness as a source of motivation for the couple to work out their differences.

Culturally Informed Interventions

Based on our clinical experiences and the above analyses, we offer the following suggestions for clinical interventions.

1. Learn more and talk about the couple's emotional history, their expectations for marriage, and how their love is defined and expressed.

2. Explore sexual issues, especially whether and how sexual love is expressed within the relationship to address marital problems.

3. Initiate, facilitate, and encourage conversations about their relationship with parents, especially regarding boundaries; avoid parent blaming.

4. Avoid applying White middle-class values, such as that taking care of family should be the woman's first priority.

5. Work hard on balancing gender roles; help the couple to find their unique voices in their own context.

6. Allow and encourage the couple to communicate in ways in which they are comfortable, not necessarily verbal communication only. Avoid asking them to use love language in sessions.

7. Use and cite research findings to highly educated and high-SES couples.

8. Match the couple's metaphorical style of communication.

A general goal of couple therapy with Chinese clients is not to turn them into American couples, but to help them function in their own cultural context. Affection need not be expressed overtly if the couple does not make it an issue. What needs to be highlighted is the sincere care that the spouses have for each other, so that they do not take each other for granted.

Following the previous example, rather than exploring the possibility for the husband to adopt a new way of expressing affection, the treating therapist asked Mrs. Gao, "Let's imagine that you are sitting on the couch watching TV in the evening. If you were him, how do you think you could express your affection to make your spouse feel loved at this moment?" Mrs. Gao looked around the office, got up and, without a word, made a cup of tea for her husband. This led to the discussion about her Chinese way of expressing her love and her need to be loved and cared for. In the following session, the husband reported that he did try to give her kisses for greetings. Mrs. Gao responded with laughter: "Oh, I am not used to that. That's a bit too much and I had goose bumps!"

Domestic Violence

Our clinical experience shows that many couples who seek professional help are court ordered to do so because of domestic violence and/or child protection issues. With the loss of a social support system and the "face" factor that keeps them from sharing their problems with and seeking help from friends, conflict among Chinese immigrant couples is clinically observed to escalate more quickly to physical violence. In the clinical practice of one of the authors, over 70% of the Chinese couples are seen for these issues. Thus, it is worth discussing the topic of domestic violence separately.

In China, domestic violence is a moral violation but not always a legal offense. Confucian teaching emphasizes that people should be regulated by virtue and moral principles; therefore, the police function as part of the moral system in promoting moral behavior in the community (Jiao, 2001). Mainland Chinese immigrant couples experiencing domestic violence will call 911 for police mediation, not necessarily for legal intervention. They are shocked to learn that, rather than mediating and educating, U.S. police may arrest one of the spouses (usually the husband) and file charges even without the wife's permission, as the law in some states requires. If young children are present during the physical altercation, child protective services will be involved as well. Couples in this situation are usually overwhelmed by the involvement of the social and legal system about which they know very little. When they seek therapy by court order, they are generally confused, resentful, and pessimistic about their future. The immediate concern of the husband is whether the record of the arrest will affect his career, and the wife often feels guilty for having "invited so much trouble" by calling the police, and may sink into self-blame and depression. When word eventually gets out into the Chinese community, couples may feel even more inhibited from seeking help.

In such cases, the therapist may consider stepping out of his or her professional comfort zone and wear many hats: educator, legal consultant, cultural advocate, and so forth. At the same time, the therapist may choose to advocate for them in the system and educate the staff in the legal and social systems about the cultural differences in the definition of, and ways to cope with, domestic violence. In immigrant communities where resources are scarce, therapists should provide help whenever and wherever it is needed.

Another important component of working with Chinese immigrant couples is community preventive outreach and education. The therapist can go to locations that have high concentrations of Chinese immigrants, such as Chinese language schools, Chinese churches, or Chinese holiday celebrations. Couples should learn to step out of their own comfort zone, utilize their cultural strength of networking skills, and create a family-like non-kin support network. In lieu of differences in cultural and social norms, it should be stressed that a couple's behavior has just as many legal implications in the United States as it has moral implications in China. While moral standards can be subjective, legal standards delineate specific behaviors of which couples should be aware.

Conclusion

The essence of the multilevel contextual model is, first, to capture the influence of the culture on the individual, family, and group psyche based on which marital expectations and norms have evolved. The impact of historic and political events as well as immigration experiences should be considered a second layer and interpreted within the cultural context. The magnitude of the impact, however, can be individually unique due to many intricate factors that may be in play. This requires the therapist to avoid a stereotypical approach to culture-related issues and marital distress. This approach, along with many other culture and diversity-informed approaches, continues to call for the training of more well-rounded therapists who not only take an increased desire in serving minority clients, but more importantly commit themselves to perfecting the profession through integrating new perspectives. The following questions are intended to trigger reflection and discussion.

1. During a social event, a Chinese woman complains to her friends about her husband being a workaholic, while her husband smiles. This means:

   a. She is washing dirty linen in public.

   b. He is used to her nagging.

   c. She is praising her husband as a hard worker and good provider.

   d. He is a workaholic, and she is upset about his not spending time with her.

2. A new Chinese immigrant, a single mother who arrived through family reunion, wrote to her boss thanking him for recognizing her hard work with a raise: "Life is so very hard for me and I want to kill myself. Now I am very grateful for your fairness." This note may mean that:

   a. She is suicidal.

   b. Verb conjugation is too difficult for her.

   c. She is blackmailing him for a higher raise.

   d. She is delusional.

3. In a court-ordered case, a young Chinese mother has to demonstrate adequate parenting skills to her baby. It is observed that she often defers to her

mother, who has brought up six children and three grandchildren. This may mean that:

a. Child rearing is shared by the mother and grandmother.

b. She is demonstrating respect to her mother.

c. The child is not cared for well as the mother doesn't know how.

d. A and B.

4. Mrs. Lee has been living and working in the United States with the couple's three children for six years while her husband has worked for a firm in China. He visits the family only a couple of times a year. This may mean that:

a. This is the couple's self-sacrifice for their children and their family.

b. The couple is emotionally distant from each other.

c. This is a sign that the couple has confidence in each other's commitment.

d. B and C.

Correct answers: 1 c, 2 b, 3 d, 4 d.

Additional Resources

Films

Chen, K. (Director) (1993). *Farewell My Concubine*. Miramax Films. This is a dramatic description of how people were forced to betray each other, resulting in the deep wounds and mistrust in the political turmoil that occurred before and after 1949.

Lee, A. (Director), & Hsu, L. K. (Producer) (1994). *Eat Drink Man Woman*. Samuel Goldwyn. Explores relationships in a contemporary Taiwanese family.

Stone, O. (Producer), & Wang, W. (Director) (1993). *The Joy Luck Club*. Hollywood Pictures. Depicts how political turbulence impacted Chinese families and Chinese women during World War II and the subsequent civil war, as well as the immigration impact on family relationships.

Readings

Buck, P. J. (1931). *The Good Earth*. This 1932 Pulitzer Prize-winning novel is still a standout. It portrays traditional family relationships in China's rural areas.

Chang, J. (1991). *Wild Swans: Three Daughters of China*. New York: Anchor Books/Doubleday. An autobiography by a Chinese woman who went through the Cultural Revolution as a teenager, exploring her own life and those of her mother and grandmother over eight decades.

References

Bauer, J., Wang, F., Riley, N. E., & Zhao, X. (1992). Gender inequality in urban China. *Modern China, 18*, 333–370.

Berry, J. W., Poortinga, Y. H., Segall, M. H., & Dasen, P. R. (1992). *Cross-cultural psychology: Research and application.* New York: Cambridge University Press.

China: Women's employment changing (1995). *Women's International Network News, 21*(4), 64.

Chinese husbands spending more time on housework (1999, June 18). China Today: 62.

Côté, J. E. (2006). Acculturation and identity: The role of individualization theory. *Human Development, 49*, 31–35.

Croll, E. (1995). *Changing identities of Chinese women: Rhetoric, experience and self-perception in twentieth-century China.* Hong Kong: Hong Kong University Press.

Da, W. W. (2004). A regional tradition of gender equity: Shanghai men in Sydney, Australia. *Journal of Men's Studies, 12*(2), 133–149.

Epstein, N. B., Chen, F., & Beyder-Kamjou, I. (2005). Relationship standards and marital satisfaction in Chinese American couples. *Journal of Marital and Family Therapy, 31*(1), 59–74.

Hamaguchi, E. (1985). A contextual model of the Japanese: Towards a methodological innovation in Japan studies. *Journal of Japanese Studies, 11*, 289–321.

Hirschman, C., & Wong, M. G. (1981). Trends in socioeconomic achievement among immigrant and native-born Asian-Americans, 1960–1976. *Sociological Quarterly, 22*(4), 495–513.

Ho, C. (2006). Migration as feminisation? Chinese women's experiences of work and family in Australia. *Journal of Ethnic and Migration Studies, 32*, 497–514.

Hooper, B. (1989). The great divide: Gender and Chinese politics. *Review/Asian Studies Association of Australia, 13*, 12–18.

Hsiao, F. H., Klimidis, S., Minas, H., & Tan, E. S. (2006). Cultural attribution of mental health suffering in Chinese societies: The views of Chinese patients with mental illness and their caregivers. *Journal of Clinical Nursing, 15*, 998–1006.

Ito, K. L., & Maramba, G. G. (2002). Therapeutic beliefs of Asian American therapists: Views from an ethnic-specific clinic. *Transcultural Psychiatry, 39*(1), 33–73.

Jiao, A, Y. (2001). Police and culture: A comparison between China and United States. *Police Quarterly, 4*(2), 156–185.

Lu, Z. Z., Bellas, M., & Maume, D. J. (2001). Chinese husbands' participation in household labor. *Journal of Comparative Family Studies, 1*(2), 191–216.

National People's Congress. (1959). *The Marriage Law of the People's Republic of China.* Beijing: Foreign Languages Press.

National People's Congress. (2001). *Marriage Law of the People's Republic of China.* Retrieved February 24, 2008, from www.nyconsulate.prchina.org/eng/lsqz/laws/t42222.htm.

Pang, L. (1993) Matchmaking via the personal advertisements in China versus in the United States. *Journal of Popular Culture, 27*(1), 163–170.

Pimentel, E. E. (2000). Just how do I love thee? Marital relations in urban China. *Journal of Marriage and Family, 62*(1), 32–48.

Thornton, M., & Wang, W. (1998). Sexing modernity: Women in the Chinese legal academy. *Canadian Journal of Women and the Law, 10,* 401–437.

Weatherley, R. (2002). Harmony, hierarchy and duty-based morality: The Confucian antipathy towards rights. *Journal of Asian Pacific Communication, 12,* 245–267.

Wong, M. G. (2006). Chinese Americans. In Pyong Gap Min (Ed.), *Asian Americans: Contemporary trends and issues* (2nd ed., pp. 110–145). Thousand Oaks, CA: Pine Forge Press.

Zentgraf, K. M. (2002). Immigration and women's empowerment: Salvadorans in Los Angeles. *Gender and Society, 16*(5), 625–646.

Zhang, A. Y., Snowden, L. R., & Sue, S. (1998). Differences between Asian and White Americans' help seeking and utilization patterns in the Los Angeles area. *Journal of Community Psychology, 26,* 317–326.

Section F

Latino and Hispanic Couples

Sixteen

Using Art to Co-Create Preferred Problem-Solving Narratives With Latino Couples

Maria Bermúdez, Margaret L. Keeling,
and Thomas Stone Carlson

In memory of Michael White, with gratitude.

For many immigrant Latinos in the United States, transitioning from a traditional partnership to a companionate partnership is often a necessary and desired change. However, it may also be a factor that brings couples into therapy (Falicov, 1998; Repak, 1995). Balancing their relationship or marriage, parenting, family of origin, child rearing, work, economic and acculturation issues, among others, is sure to cause tension among couples. Issues related to immigration and economic hardships are especially difficult for immigrant couples and families (Inclan, 2003), with divorce rates being higher for couples who emigrate together (Repak, 1995). Latino couples must learn to negotiate gender roles and be flexible in order to survive the demands of the new culture. This renegotiation process is easier for some couples than others. For example, immigrants who had affluent status in their country of origin often come with a sense of class consciousness, and are more likely to accept a dual-earner family structure. Such couples understand the need for gender role flexibility, have less distance between themselves and their working-class *paisanos* (people of the same nationality), and are more interested in upholding their ethnic identity and remaining different from the American mainstream (Inclan, 2003). With all of these changes, it is easy to see how relationships are strained by these cultural clashes and transitions. Yet, as Gottman (1994b) points out, the ways in which couples resolve conflict are correlated to marital stability and outcomes. Therefore, helping Latino couples attend to the process of communication and better understanding how to renegotiate their preferred ways of resolving or regulating conflict may result in greater effective communication and greater relational satisfaction.

In terms of the communication process in general, it has been noted that Latinos prefer to avoid conflict, control aggression and violence, and do whatever possible to maintain a sense of peace and harmony among family members (Falicov, 2005, 1998; Garcia-Preto, 1996; Ho, 1987). Latinos generally uphold the values of collectivistic cultures, wherein there is a strong desire to preserve family harmony and to favor indirect, implicit, and covert communications. Being assertive, openly disagreeing, and expressing direct demands for clarification are seen as rude or insensitive to others' feelings (Falicov, 1998). Although Gottman's research (1994) has provided clinicians with a valuable framework for understanding marital conflict styles in Western-based cultures, major questions concerning these traditions still remain to be addressed from a multicultural perspective (Ting-Toomey, 1994). Other researchers question the inherent Eurocentric bias in conflict styles, such as *validating, volatile,* and *avoidance* (Gottman, 1994a, 1994b), and urge others to work toward using culturally responsive approaches to help couples resolve communication difficulties (Bermúdez, Reyes, & Wampler, 2006).

It is our contention that Latino couples will feel less threatened and stigmatized by the clinical process, and thus be more willing to adopt an exploratory—even playful—mind-set, if practitioners provide them with a wider array of options for addressing their communication and relational concerns. In this chapter, we will provide therapists with creative strategies for using narrative therapy and art with Latino couples experiencing communication difficulties. Working from a narrative family therapy lens (Freedman & Combs, 1996; Parry & Doan, 1994; White & Epston, 1990), our goal is to help couples create two pieces of artwork: one representing the externalized problem and the other representing their envisioned solution. The use of art in couple and family therapy has been an emerging clinical approach (Kerr, Hoshino, Sutherland, Parashak, & McCarley, 2007) including the use of narrative approaches with couples (Riley, 2003). In this chapter, we hope to help couples personally and culturally contextualize a narrative in which they can experience greater agency in creating a preferred way of resolving their differences. Various art media can be used, such as drawing, painting, sculpture, collage, assemblage, and a combination of these media. Couples or therapists do not have to perceive themselves as artistic, creative, or innovative in order to benefit from this clinical process (Simmons, 2006). The primary stipulations are that the couple is committed to change and to the relationship, that they trust the therapist, are not in immediate crisis, and are ready to try a different approach to creating solutions. The therapists should also be willing to adapt a creative and artistic mindset to working with couples.

All three authors work in COAMFTE (Commission on Accreditation of Marriage and Family Therapy Education) Couple and Family Therapy programs in the United States, and all employ experiential and narrative approaches in their work. Maria Bermúdez applies social constructionist, experiential, narrative, and feminist-informed approaches in her clinical work, supervision, and research. She is originally from Honduras, and her primary research and clinical work is with Latino couples and families. Maggie Keeling is a narrative therapy practitioner who combines art, expressive writing, and other experiential elements into her therapy practice. She has also combined these elements into innovative interventions for research purposes (Keeling & Bermúdez, 2006; Keeling & Nielson, 2005). As a native Texan, she has conducted therapy with numerous Latino individuals, couples, and families. Her primary clinical and research focus is on the intersection of gender, culture, and power as it influences experiences of trauma. She is also a practicing artist. Tom Stone Carlson works primarily from a feminist/narrative therapy perspective in his work with clients and supervisees. He has published several articles on narrative therapy, and provides regular consultation to agencies interested in adopting narrative ideas. He has provided therapy and outreach services to the Latino community for over 10 years and is

currently the primary investigator of a grant that seeks to provide culturally accountable therapy services to Latino families through the clinical
agency sponsored by the Couple and Family Therapy program at North
Dakota State University.

Narrative Therapy With Latino Couples

The basic assumption of narrative therapy is that people, through the
course of their lives, internalize problematic beliefs about themselves or
others that have the potential to deny them the experience of preferred
narratives (Freedman & Combs, 1996; White, 1995; White & Epston,
1990). This entrapment of the problematic, dominant discourse is significant if we accept the notion that our lives are storied by the internal, contextual, and interpersonal factors that shape our identities and
relationships. With the use of externalizing conversations (White, 1995)
and deconstructive questioning, we help loosen the grip of the dominant,
problematic narratives, and help our clients redefine and restory a preferred relationship and course of action. This preferred way may be
informed by their relational dynamics, culture, contextual influences,
interpersonal or internal conflicts, family or origin patterns, gender
scripts, notions of masculinity and femininity, and reactivity. This creative process serves to generate unique outcomes in relation to a couple's
problem-saturated story (White & Epston, 1990).

We propose an alternative experiential approach for helping Latino
couples coconstruct their own definition of mutually preferred ways of
resolving conflict. Much of the literature related to working with Latino
families and couples in therapy is based on anecdotes and assumptions
about Latino families, with limited recommendations for models that are
culturally appropriate beyond structural family therapy. Other cultural
characteristics may provide clues as to what constitutes culturally competent therapy. For example, Latino cultures are described as being *collectivistic*,
which refers to being meaning- and story-based cultures (Smith & Montilla,
2005). We contend that narrative approaches fit well with Latino families
because narrative ideas cluster around the notion that relationships are
central in the construction of meaning and identity (collectivistic) and
such approaches value collaborative forms of communication. An experiential approach to narrative therapy can help clients collaboratively generate experiences from which new meanings can emerge (White, 1995). It
is our assertion that, by giving couples the freedom to express themselves

through artistic means, they will be able to focus more on their communication *process*, as opposed to specific content. Focusing on the process helps them learn to metacommunicate and to problem-solve in a more effective and preferred manner—that is, they will be able to generate preferred meanings about how they communicate. In addition, having a visual representation of their problem-maintaining process helps remind them of how to accomplish their communication goals when they inevitably revert back to less desirable ways of resolving problems (e.g., yelling, retreating, demand/withdraw pattern, withholding affection or information, keeping secrets, triangulating others, etc.).

Using artistic approaches to restorying a Latino couple's preferred way to resolve or dissolve problems is also consistent with certain cultural values. For example, Latinos are said to value harmony, which can be maintained in various ways. The use of *indirectas* (stating what you want in the third person) helps Latinos indirectly say what they want to say without being disrespectful. *Choteo o bromear* (humor) is also used as a way of making fun of people, situations, or things to by exaggerating or joking to modify tense situations. Additionally, the formation of "light" triangles in the form of gossip and secrets creates alliances that provide an emotional outlet and serve to enhance the stability of marriage and family relationships (Komarovsky, 1967, cited in Falicov, 1998, p. 180). Other harmony-maintaining communications may be seen in the use of positive expression, such as words of endearment and compliments, and the use of *simpatica,* which is the ability to create smooth, friendly, and pleasant relationships to avoid conflict (Falicov, 1998, p. 180). Using artistic approaches to discussing a Latino couple's communication and problem-solving processes is a creative and nonthreatening way to triangle in the art work, use *indirectas,* so as to address difficult issues in an indirect manner, and have opportunities to be *simpatico/a* with each other by praising each other's art work and one's ability to work together in an artistic manner and/or *chotear o bromear* as a way of teasing each other and each other's art work. Working from an artistic and narrative perspective offers Latino couples a culturally congruent alternative to more traditional methods of helping couples resolve conflict.

Several studies and clinical papers have been published highlighting the significance of using art and narrative therapy (Ball, Piercy, & Bischoff, 1993; Barton & Bischoff, 1998; Bermúdez & Bermúdez, 2002; Carlson, 1997; Zimmerman & Shepherd, 1993), and in particular empirical data examining the process of externalizing the problem (Keeling & Bermúdez, 2006;

Keeling & Nielson, 2005). In this intervention, the goal is to help couples experience a collaborative, creative process that helps them describe and externalize a problem-maintaining, problem-solving approach, and co-create a new, preferred way of problem solving. By experiencing this artistic restorying of their conflict process in therapy, couples are able to take home a visual reminder of their preferred narrative and continue to expand upon it, alter it as needed, recruit an audience, and continue to expand the life of a preferred problem-solving process.

CASE EXAMPLE

For the purpose of illustration, we demonstrate how this creative process was implemented with a Latino couple, Armando and Karina. We provide illustrations of their artwork (see Figure 16. 1 and Figure 16.2) and a description of the suggested clinical process (see Table 16.1), deconstructive questions (see Tables 16.2 and 16.3), and reconstructive questions (see Tables 16. 4 and 16.5).[1]

Narrative therapy questions have been provided in both Spanish and English for ease of application for bilingual or multilingual therapists (Aguirre, Bermúdez, Parra, Reyes, & Zamora, 2005; Rivas, Delgado-Romero, & Ozambela, 2005). The questions were written by the first author, and then translated into Spanish. A second reader then used the in-back method of translation to translate the questions back into English (American Psychological Association, 2001). Consistent with Sperber, Devellis, and Boehlecke's suggestions (1994), the translator formulates questions in the original language and keeps in mind the anticipated translation process. Given the subjectivity in language, there is no one correct translation of one word or sentence into another language (Werner & Campbell, 1970); therefore, the goal was to obtain a general consensus among the readers so the translation could be adapted to the heterogeneous nature of the Spanish language (i.e., different countries using different words to refer to the same meaning).

Additionally, similar to the work of Keeling and Bermúdez (2006), and Keeling and Nielson (2005), we wanted to extend the participation experience to a nonclinical population as analog clients. This population is well suited to help us further develop and test an innovative narrative therapy intervention that incorporates deconstructing, externalizing, and reconstructing questions, as well as the co-creation of artwork to represent the externalized problem and the envisioned solution. We also recognize that narrative therapy does not usually follow discrete, sequential stages or phases; however, we portray the following case illustration in that manner for the ease of readers, and to provide a clear basis for clinical interventions and future research. The interview was conducted by the first author and was mostly conducted in Spanish.

Case Background

Armando and Karina had been married for three months. Armando was 30 and from Colombia, and had immigrated to the United States legally when he was just a year old. He was a doctoral student at the time we conducted the interview. Karina was 19 and from El Salvador. She had immigrated to Mexico when she was a child, and then to the United States when she was 16, three years ago. She had a ninth-grade education, was working as a nanny, and was trying to enroll into high school to complete her high school education. Her immigration story was painful, as it is for so many Latina/o immigrants (Bean, Perry, & Bedell, 2001). In general, immigration issues are very sensitive, and therapists need to proceed in their questioning with caution and establish trust due to the fear and mistrust surrounding these concerns. Karina and her family first immigrated to Mexico from Central America, fleeing war-related problems. At the age of 16, after three attempts at crossing the U.S. border illegally with the help of a "coyote" (person, usually male and often exploitive, who is paid to help someone cross the border) and her godfather, she became an undocumented resident. Two days later, she met Armando, and they dated for three years. Because Karina was a minor when she entered the United States, she was able to return to Mexico to apply for a visa on the basis of being engaged to be married to a legal U.S. resident. Nine months later, she was granted the visa to return, and they were married one week later. She stated that in three years she hoped to be granted legal residential status in the United States.

This was a onetime interview; therefore, I (MB) intentionally and respectfully did not delve into depth about many of the contextual issues that influenced their marriage. As mentioned above, the primary purpose of the interview was to implement an alternative method of helping a nonclinical couple attend to the process of problem solving using narrative and artistic methods. Nonetheless, in actually therapy I would have found it necessary to ask the questions related to the following issues:

- How did Karina define herself as a Latina living in the United States?
- What were her life goals, and how did they coincide with those of her partner?
- What were their emigration and residency narratives, and what effects did they have on their relationship dynamics and their problem-solving process?
- What were potential power issues related to their age differences, financial resources, educational levels, and differing immigration status?
- How did those issues affect her sense of power, privilege, and entitlement?
- What truncated her educational attainment?
- What would she need from her partner in order to continue and develop her educational and professional goals?
- How do their families of origin and issues related to language barriers affect their personal and relational well-being?

Although I did not ask these questions, it was apparent that Armando and Karina were struggling more than the average newlywed couple, especially for a couple not presenting for therapy, but they were clearly not in crisis. Their struggles seemed to be related to her immigration status, Karina's trauma related to her immigration history, financial concerns, her language barriers, differing social status, and a clash of marital expectations. The following illustration describes Karina and Armando's process of renarrating and coconstructing a preferred problem-solving process (see Table 16.1).

Phase 1: Choosing the Intervention

After a brief explanation of what we would be doing together, I showed them the list of questions I would be asking. I told them that we would not be focusing on specific content issues, but that if they arose, we could discuss them as a way to better understand their communication process. They both agreed to the intervention and I presented them with a wide array of art supplies. They seemed excited about having the materials and immediately started to play with the Play-Doh and did not stop throughout the entire process.

Phase 2: Describing the Problematic Problem-Solving Process

They both sat down at the table and looked at all of the materials. I told them that, in order to create an artistic expression of their problematic

Table 16.1   Suggested Clinical Process

Phase 1	Couple agrees to do the intervention, and therapist has a wide array of art materials available
Phase 2	Couple describes their problematic problem-solving process
Phase 3	Co-creating the artistic expression of the externalized problem (the problematic problem-solving process)
Phase 4	Naming the externalized problem
Phase 5	Deconstructive questions
Phase 6	Describing the preferred problem-solving process
Phase 7	Co-creating an artistic expression of the envisioned solution
Phase 8	Naming the envisioned solution
Phase 9	Reconstruction questions about the preferred problem-solving process
Phase 10	Therapist requests feedback regarding the client's participation in the process

way of resolving conflict, they first needed to describe their communication process from each of their perspectives. I also normalized that all couples have struggles and that they would continue to have struggles, but they could mutually decide upon and co-create a preferred way of addressing and resolving their conflicts.

When describing the process, Armando stated that he felt like Karina was always "pecking" at him and that, although he felt he was a calm person, she agitated him with her "pecking." If they were in couple therapy, this would have been a time to include a discussion about the intersection of gender and I would have asked the following questions: What cultural messages influencing the term "pecking" would lead a man to describe his partner in this way? What factors helped "the pecking" gain influence and power in their relationship? Karina stated that she felt like "pecking" at him was necessary because he ignored her. She said she would get mad at him because he did not listen to her. Very quickly they were in agreement about the description of the problematic process of communication. Basically, they described their problematic communication process as Karina needing to "peck" at him because Armando did not listen to her when she needed to talk about a particular problem.

Phase 3: Co-Creating an Artistic Expression of the Externalized Problem (the Problematic Problem-Solving Process)

After they were in agreement about the problematic process, I asked them to co-create an artistic expression (externalization) of the problematic process of solving problems. I told them that they could use any or all of the materials available to them. The idea was that when they saw the image, it would be an obvious representation of the problematic communication process between them. They were given 10 minutes to create the artwork. They were left alone in the room to give them space to talk and to co-create the artwork, without any interference. The whole time they were laughing and playing with the Play-Doh. They had a great deal of energy, and Karina told Armando jokingly, "I am going to make you a monster," and he smiled and told her, "I am going to make you a woodpecker." They constructed a line, which represented a wall between them, with the woodpecker and the monster on opposite sides. The monster had the word *Yo* on it, which means "me" in Spanish, and it was holding a sign that said *"No es sierto y defiendo a otros,"* meaning, "It is not true and I defend others." They continually described the elements of the sculptures, such as the big mouth on the monster and the dagger to attack her, and he created the bird with daggers in a belt behind it, in order to be able to secretly attack him. As they were applying the final touches, they were then asked to think about the problem's name, as if it were an entity or thing attacking their relationship (see Figure 16.1).

Phase 4: Naming the Problem

When I returned they proceeded to describe what they had created (see Figure 16.1). They named the problem "the surprise." When I asked why they named it "the surprise," they both stated that they were surprised that they would communicate in that way with each other and that they did not think being married was supposed to be that way. He was surprised that she would "peck" at him and agitate him in the way that she did, and she was surprised that he could be "so mean and ignore her" and not validate her complaints or her feelings. Interestingly, although we were speaking in Spanish, they named the externalized problem in English.

Phase 5: Deconstructive Questions

Next, I told them that I would ask them a series of questions that would help them understand the influence of "the surprise" in their relationship

The Surprise

Figure 16.1   The Externalized Problem: "The Surprise"

(see Tables 16.2 and 16.3). Armando mentioned that "the surprise" did not happen instantly, that it crept its way into their relationship over time and developed slowly. They stated that "the surprise" got stronger when they began living together. They both became animated as they talked about their expectations about marriage, and admitted that their reality did not match their expectations. I normalized the first year of marriage as an adjustment and told them most couples have expectations and hopes for their marriages. Initially, they focused their discussion of the problem in terms of the other person. When this happened, I reminded them that what we were looking at and describing was the problematic problem-solving process, not each partner in the relationship. As time went on, they were able to talk more about the problematic pattern or "the surprise." As they discussed the ways in which "the surprise" separated them, I affirmed that the problem had a lot of power in their relationship and asked them whether this was something that they wanted to change. They said yes, that "the surprise" needed to change and have less power. Our goal was to find ways in which they could work together to defeat the problem and co-create a preferred way of resolving conflict.

Table 16.2 Deconstructive Questions in English

Deconstructive Questions
1. Can you both describe what you created together? What does this artistic representation mean or say about your problematic problem-solving process?
2. When you look at the image that represents your problematic problem-solving process, what name would you give it? How did you decide on this name?
3. When did X (the name of the externalized problem of the problematic problem-solving process) become a problem in your relationship?
4. Do you think X has always interfered with your sense of connection and commitment in your relationship, or has there been a time when it wasn't this way?
5. If your style of resolving conflict was different before, what were the factors that helped X evolve and develop?
6. What effects does X have in your relationship when it is in control of your communication with each other?
7. Does X ever try to convince you that you are no longer in love, friends, or compatible, committed, or attracted to each other?
8. Which one of you would feel most relieved if X's influence diminished in your relationship?
9. Is there ever a time when you feel that X benefits your relationship in some way?
10. When you look at X now, what emotions and thoughts does it evoke in you both?

Table 16.3 Deconstructive Questions in Spanish

Preguntas de Desconstrucción
1. ¿Pueden describir lo que crearon juntos? Que significa o implica la representación artística de su manera de resolver problemas?
2. ¿Cuándo ven la imagen que representa el proceso problemático de resolver conflictos, que nombre le pondrían? Como llegaron a escoger ese nombre?
3. ¿Cuándo se convirtió X (nombre del proceso problemático de resolver conflictos) en un problema en su relación?
4. ¿Creen ustedes que X ha interferido siempre con su sentido de conexión y de compromiso en su relación, o ha habido algún momento en que no fue así?

5. ¿Si su estilo de resolver conflicto era diferente antes, cuáles fueron los factores que ayudaron a X a desarrollarse?
6. ¿Cuáles efectos tiene X en relación cuando X está en control de la su comunicación entre ustedes?
7. ¿Trata alguna vez X de convencerlos que ya no están enamorados, que no son amigos, o que no son compatibles, comprometidos, o atraídos el uno al otro?
8. ¿Quien de ustedes sentiría mas alivio de ver la influencia de X disminuir en su relación?
9. ¿Existe alguna ocasión en la cual ustedes sienten que X beneficia la relación entre ustedes?
10. ¿Cuándo ven ustedes a X ahora, que emociones y pensamientos se pro ducen en cada uno de ustedes?

There were several outcomes from the deconstruction process. One of the main outcomes was that they were able to identify the ways in which they had individually contributed to the life of the problem. When I asked whether there were any benefits of having "the surprise" in their lives, Karina immediately said that there were. Her partner looked surprised. She stated that his anticipation of her behavior (the pecking) kept him from acting in ways that he knew would upset her. He stated that there were no benefits of "the surprise" in his life. We explored whether the possible benefits could also serve to feed life into "the surprise" and give it strength. In general, they did not like seeing the externalized problem when we observed it from different angles and took pictures of it. When I asked what they thought and felt as they saw "the surprise," Karina became emotional and said it was difficult. I assumed that the visual representation of the problematic problem-solving pattern made it more real to them, which made it more difficult to avoid or deny the existence of the problem. I assured them the next process would be more enjoyable, as they were going to do the same thing as before, except that next time the art would represent the solution, their preferred problem-solving process. It is possible that their different cultural contexts (country of origin, immigration process, SES prior to emigrating, educational levels, gender role scripts, culturally informed marital expectations, and language abilities) affected the ways in which they perceived "the surprise" and also how the life of "the surprise" was shaped.

Phase 6: Describing the Preferred Problem-Solving Process

The couple was asked to think about and describe a problem-solving process that they believed was positive, good, helpful, and that they thought would bring them together to denounce the problematic conflict pattern. As they talked, Armando stated that he wanted a process in which there was a win–win outcome, without a loser, and wherein he did not feel forced to solve a problem right away. Karina stated that she wanted to be able to talk about problems, calmly. Once they both agreed on what their preferred problem-solving process should be like, then they created a sculpture to represent the envisioned solution. Both being calm and wanting a win–win outcome are consistent with preferred conflict resolution approaches from people from collectivist cultures (Gabrielidis, Stephan, Ybarra, Dos Santos Pearson, & Villareal, 1997).

Phase 7: Co-Creating an Artistic Expression of the Envisioned Solution

The couple was asked to create an artistic expression or art work that would serve as a representation of their ability to handle a problem or disagreement in a way that was more positive for both of them. This process took longer for them to complete, but it was richer in that there was a lot more energy around talking about the preferred way to resolve problems, rather than the problematic way of resolving problems. Interestingly, they were doing most of the deconstruction work themselves before I could even asked the questions, which they continued to do when I asked the questions. I gave them some time alone to ask each other questions about what they wanted and what they needed. This alone time gave the couple the freedom to express their thoughts and feelings and maintain a sense of privacy. Such a practice respects the *private self*, a phenomenon experienced by Latinos—particularly Mexicans—which is typically protective and evasive (Paz, cited in Falicov, 1998).

During their alone time, both partners were able to express their ideas about their envision solution. Karina stated that she wanted Armando to listen to her, and Armando told her that he wanted her to be more open and understanding and not accuse him so quickly. He said that he wanted to talk in a peaceful manner, in which they could be patient, soft, and *dulce* (sweet). Both of their voices softened during the time they were describing the preferred process. They described what they would be doing if they were resolving conflict in a preferred way: sitting together at a table, being calm, and staying focused on the topic at hand. As they talked, they

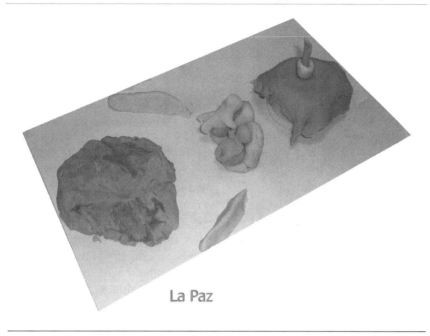

La Paz

Figure 16.2   The Envisioned Solution: "La Paz"

began to create the preferred process. He made a tablecloth out of Play-Doh, and then made a little table. She made the chairs, and a candle to put on the table. They both made the figures and she created a lake to symbolize tranquility. When I returned, I validated them for their creativity (consistent with being *simpatica*) and their ability to come together to create their solution. I also praised them for their willingness to undertake this process, which many couples would find difficult because of the temptation to get stuck in problem talk.

Phase 8: Naming the Envisioned Solution

They named the envisioned solution of their preferred problem-solving pattern "La Paz" (see Figure 16.2). *La paz* means the peace in Spanish. They said they named it "La Paz" because they felt calm and that there were no barriers between them, like when the "the surprise" was present. They were sitting together in front of the lake, and looking on with hope. This process related to their cultural context is several ways. For example, many immigrants move to another country hoping for a better way of life, seeking opportunities that are not present in their countries of origin. In many ways, "La Paz" was an important metaphor for what they were seeking in their lives in general, not only in their relationship. It is also consistent with the value of wanting to keep the peace and maintain harmony, as mentioned above.

Phase 9: Reconstructing a Preferred Problem-Solving Process

When I asked them to describe the factors that gave life to "La Paz," they stated that it was togetherness (*la unión*), faith (*la fe*), not being so busy, and not having so much stress. When I asked what they had to do individually to keep "La Paz" strong in their relationship, Armando stated that he needed to be honest, patient, and conscious of the desired outcome. Karina stated that she needed to be smarter with how she resolved conflict and more aware of her timing. At this point I asked them, "If 'La Paz' were truly alive, and in the room, what advice would it give you?" Karina said that the water would say, "You can be like me, calm and tranquil"; the door/barrier would say, "You can stay open and not create a barrier"; and the candle on the table would say, "You need to keep me lit so that your faith can be alive and never fade." Armando agreed with all she had to say and did not feel he needed to add anything else. I then asked about the emotions they felt at that moment. They were both smiling and looked relaxed, and said they felt peaceful and strong in their ability to deal with whatever problem they had. Armando stated that he felt hopeful that "La Paz" was going to represent the next phase of their relationship, and felt happy because he knew it was possible. Tables 16.4 and 16.5 provide some ideas for reconstructive questions in English and Spanish.

Phase 10: Requesting Feedback

At the end of creating both pieces of artwork and after amplifying the preferred narrative, I asked Karina and Armando to describe what this process was like for them, and whether they could offer suggestions for how the process could be improved. It is important, according to Falicov (1998), to invite Latino clients to provide feedback about the process when a theoretical orientation or type of intervention is used. She stated the following:

> In a culture that emphasizes cooperation and respect for authority, clients may feel that it is impolite to openly disagree with the therapist. Encouraging the family to express both their positive and negative reactions to the therapist's opinion helps to establish a tone of mutuality. (Falicov, 1998, p. 182)

Table 16.4   Reconstructive Questions in English

Reauthoring or Constructive Questions
1. Can you both describe what you created together? What does the artistic representation of your envisioned problem-solving process mean or represent?
2. As you look at the artistic representation of your preferred communication process, what name would you like to give it? Why did you give it this name?
3. What do you both have to do together in order to give life to O (say the name of the envisioned solution: the preferred problem-solving process)?
4. What can you both do individually in order to make O stronger?
5. What other factors (e.g., in your relationship, your lives, work, family, etc.) would help strengthen O's life?
6. What is it about O that makes it a preferred way to resolve your differences?
7. When are you the most receptive or open to letting O influence you instead of X?
8. When was the last time that X could have taken over your communication with each other and you chose O's influence instead?
9. Who would benefit the most from having O influencing your relationship?
10. What does this mean for you that you were able to co-create this preferred way of resolving or discussing your problems?
11. Who is O going to need to support its life in your marriage/relationship?
12. What are you both going to have to do differently to keep O alive in your relationship?
13. How will you know that X is trying to overpower O and creep its way back into your relationship? What will be the signs?
14. If O were to really come to life, what would it tell you about your relationship? What advice would it give you?
15. When you look at O now, what emotions and thoughts does it evoke in you both? How do they compare to the feelings and thoughts when compared with X?

Armando and Karina stated that this process helped them discover new things about each other. Karina perceived Armando to be more open, and she felt closer to him when he shared his thoughts and feelings. She also stated that she appreciated having time alone during the interview, and that this could be an issue for some Latinos who are not accustomed

Table 16.5   Reconstructive Questions in Spanish

Preguntas de Re-autoria o Re-construcción
1.   ¿Pueden ambos describir lo que crearon juntos? Que significa para usteds esta representación artística de su manera preferida de resolver problemas juntos?
2.   ¿Cuándo ven la imagen que representa su proceso preferido de resolver problemas juntos, que nombre le darían y por qué?
3.   ¿Que tienen que hacer ambos en sus vidas para darle mas vida a O (el nombre del proceso de resolver problemas de una manera preferida)?
4.   ¿Que pueden hacer ambos individualmente para que O se fortalezca?
5.   ¿Cuales otros factores (por ejemplo, en su relación, en sus vidas, en su trabajo, familias, etc.) fortalecerían la vida de O?
6.   ¿Que es lo que tiene O que lo hace ser su manera preferida de resolver problemas preferida?
7.   ¿Cuándo están ustedes mas receptivos para que O les influya mas que X?
8.   ¿Cuándo fue la última vez que X pudo haber asumido control de su comunicación y ustedes eligieron la influencia de O en su lugar?
9.   ¿Que otras personas se beneficiarían de tener a O influyendo en la relación entre ustedes?
10.   ¿Que significa para ustedes haber podido crear juntos esta manera preferida de resolver o discutir sus problemas de una manera constructiva?
11.   ¿A quien van a necesitar para que O sobreviva y se mantenga vivo en su matrimonio/relación?
12.   ¿Que van a tener que hacer ustedes diferente para que O se mantenga vivo en su relación?
13.   ¿Cómo van a saber ustedes si X esta tratando de dominar a O, o si esta tratando de volver a controlar su relación? Cuales son las señales?
14.   ¿Si O fuera una persona real, que le diría sobre su relación? Cuales consejos les daría?
15.   ¿Cuándo ven ustedes a O, que emociones y pensamientos se producen en ambos individualmente? Como se comparan con los sentimientos y pensamientos que tienen con X?

to discussing their relationship problems in front of others. She suggested that the therapist could ask the couple whether they wanted her or him to leave so that the couple could talk about a particular issue in more depth. Armando stated that the process was very helpful, but that he did not have more to add to Karina's comments. At the end of the interview, they took the sculptures home as a reminder of the preferred problem-solving process and of what they could achieve together.

There were a few cultural and gender elements that stood out in this case. First, it was interesting to me to see how much power Karina had in their relationship. She was strong, opinionated, and assertive, and did not at all seem to fit the stereotype of a submissive Latina. This was especially significant given their age difference, educational levels (PhD student and ninth-grade education), and other factors that could have created power imbalances (sexist ideologies, immigration status, language barriers, and work status). Second, I was impressed with how quickly they were able to identify the externalized problem and the envisioned solution and with how well they worked together as a team. There did not appear to be an expectation that Armando, as the man, would take the lead. This collaborative process is also inconsistent with the stereotypes about Latino couples that state there is usually a dominant male who prefers to make the decisions. Another nonclinical couple who participated in this process, but was not included in this chapter, was a gay Latino couple. Their process seemed to differ in that the older partner, who was 42, and the younger partner, who was 26, showed greater power differences based on age, with the younger partner often deferring to the older partner.

In terms of working with couples in a clinical setting, we would predict that this process would be very similar to the case illustration provided here. This couple was highly stressed and could easily have met the criteria for a couple seeking therapy. Important contraindications for using this artistic approach to restorying a preferred way to problem solve would be if the couple was in a crisis situation (e.g., domestic violence, currently dealing with addiction, homelessness, needing medical care, etc.) or unable or unwilling to discuss their communication process. We propose that this intervention is best suited to couples and families who want to improve their communication with each other and who are interested in restorying preferred ways to problem-solve in an artistic and creative manner. Table 16.1, above, offers a suggestion for how this narrative process could potentially unfold.

Overall, the combination of narrative therapy and the use of art in therapy offers family therapists hope and an artistic option for helping couples and families learn how to mutually agree upon a definition of their preferred problem-solving process. Additionally, this process can help them to systematically evaluate the ways in which the externalized problem tries to overpower their relationship and rob them of living their preferred narratives. In the following section, we offer a few suggestions for implementing this narrative process and for working with Latino couples in general. Clearly, these suggestions are not exhaustive, nor are they mutually exclusive to Latino/as. We invite the reader to think about what other culturally informed and culturally responsive suggestions could be added to the list, as well as how these ideas could be helpful with other types of clients and various presenting problems.

Clinical Suggestions

Suggestion 1

Do not emphasize the fact that you are doing therapy. This may sound bizarre, but there is still a strong stigma associated with going to therapy. Because of the value of *personalismo*, Latino clients will respond much better if they feel as though they are sitting in your living room, but clearly in the presence of a professional, competent, yet personable therapist. The more relaxed they feel, the greater is the likelihood they will trust you (*tener confianza*) and believe you are capable of helping them with their relational problems, which are often kept private.

Suggestion 2

Create the space for them to have fun! Our experience has been that, although the couple may be dealing with tough issues, this creative process lends itself well to engaging in a creative and artistic activity that helps them work together to focus on the process of communication, without necessarily delving into particular (content) issues. Those content issues are important, but getting at process issues first or simultaneously will help the therapist gain greater insight into the couple's problem-saturated narrative that maintains the problem. Examining the process can be less threatening and is clearly more enjoyable, and because they are expecting therapy to be a heavy and dreaded process, they will more likely be surprised and relieved when presented with an artistic, creative, and collaborative process. Nonetheless, there will be couples who may prefer a more traditional approach, and we encourage therapists to use art in therapy only if the couple or family approves of this way of working. Presenting clients with options regarding how they would like to proceed with therapy is consistent with our values as culturally responsive therapists.

Suggestion 3

Invite the couple to display the artwork as a reminder of their preferred way of resolving conflict. For Karina and Armando, we provided a framed photograph of their artwork as a visual reminder of what they cocreated. This is especially helpful if the artistic medium is Play-Doh or clay, which may not hold up over time. Displaying the artwork at home helps to spread the news of difference. As White and Epston (1990) point out, identifying and recruiting a wider audience is essential for the preferred perspective or story to become a new dominant narrative in the couple's life. Sometimes a new way of problem solving can be tenuous, so when others inquire about the artwork it invites the couple to re-tell their story about how they coconstructed the art, share the meaning it has for them, and in turn give the new narrative more power. Ultimately, it is their decision to share it with others. They may feel it is a personal and/or private process, or it may be something that they may want to share and celebrate with others. Nevertheless, it will still serve as an important reminder for them to extend the preferred narrative into the future.

Suggestion 4

When working with Latino couples, ask about their "couple language" and deconstruct the context in which they speak in Spanish or English, or *code switch* (shifting back and forth to convey a particular meaning). Many couples mention that they prefer to speak Spanish when they convey feeling words and often speak in English to convey thinking or doing words. This is consistent with Guttfreund's (1990) findings in which he proposes that Spanish, being a Latin language, will provide greater opportunities for deeper expression of feelings. Other therapists state that certain Latino clients would use Spanish in sessions when they were experiencing powerful emotions, and English when they were more cognitively focused (Rivas, Delgado-Romero, & Ozambela, 2005). Clearly, more research is needed to enrich and improve the work we do with monolingual or bilingual Latino couples and families.

Training and Supervision

The use of this approach to therapy provides the reader with multiple implications for training, supervision, research, and personal growth. This narrative approach to working with couples in therapy has obvious creative benefits for everyone involved, and can be applied in a multitude of settings.

For illustrative purposes, art and narrative therapy methods can be applied in a classroom setting. The facilitator/instructor can help trainees identify their own problematic conflict processes and create a visual, artistic externalization of the problematic process and the preferred process (Keeling & Bermúdez, 2006). Additionally, as part of a graduate course or clinical practicum, couple and family therapy graduate students have found this type of activity helpful, enjoyable, and meaningful. Graduate students could include their partners or significant persons in their lives, as a way for them to personally experience the clinical intervention and apply it to their lives and relationships. We encourage instructors to help students and supervisors at all developmental levels to deconstruct internalized messages of sexism, racism, sense of agency, oppression, and privilege, and to explore how these internalized scripts or messages are conveyed in their style of communication or ways of resolving conflict. They can also use this artistic narrative approach to further examine how their own biases and assumptions affect their work with Latino couples and families (Bermúdez, 1997).

Conclusion

In this chapter, we attempted to culturally contextualize how language and communication shape the narratives of Latino couples. With the use of narrative therapy, we offered a creative and artistic approach to helping Latino couples attend to their communication process and co-create a preferred way of resolving their differences. It is our hope that this illustration will serve to ignite creativity when dealing with complex communication issues while working with Latino couples in therapy. Additionally, we hope this process can serve as a springboard to expand its use for other purposes, such as for clinical training and supervision, self-of-the-therapist work, and creativity in research.

Note

1. Case study material used with permission by Pablo and Teresa Gore.

References

Aguirre, C., Bermúdez, J. M., Parra, J. R., Reyes, N. A., & Zamora, J. A. (2005). The process of integrating language, context, and meaning: The voices of bilingual and bicultural therapists. In E. Wieling & M. Rastogi (Eds.), *Voices of color* (pp. 189–210). Thousand Oaks, CA: Sage.

American Psychological Association. (2001). *Publication manual of the American Psychological Association* (5th ed.). Washington, DC: American Psychological Association.

Ball, D., Piercy, F., & Bischoff, G. (1993). Externalizing the problem through cartoons: A case example. *Journal of Systemic Therapies, 12*(1), 19–21.

Barton, M., & Bischoff, R. (1998). Rocks and rituals in producing therapeutic change. *Journal of Family Psychotherapy, 9*(3), 32–41.

Bean, R. A., Perry, B. J., & Bedell, T. M. (2001). Developing culturally competent marriage and family therapists: Guidelines for working with Hispanic families. *Journal of Marital and Family Therapy, 27*, 43–54.

Bermúdez, J. M. (1997). Experiential tasks and therapist bias awareness. *Contemporary Family Therapy, 19*(2), 253–267.

Bermúdez, J. M. (1998). Recalling the way we were: Narrative therapy for couples. In L. Hecker & S. Deacon (Eds.), *The therapist's notebook: Homework, handouts, & activities.* New York: Haworth Press.

Bermúdez, J. M., & Bermúdez, S. (2002). The therapeutic use of altar-making. *Journal of Family Psychotherapy 13*(3/4), 329–347.

Bermúdez, J. M., Reyes, N. A., & Wampler, K. (2006). Conflict resolution styles among Latino couples. *Journal of Couple and Relationship Therapy, 5*(4), 1–21.

Carlson, T. D. (1997). Using art in narrative therapy: Enhancing therapeutic possibilities. *American Journal of Family Therapy, 25*, 271–283.

Falicov, C. J. (1998). *Latino families in therapy: A guide to multicultural practice.* New York: Guilford Press.

Falicov, C. J. (2005). Mexican families. In M. McGoldrick, J. Giordano, & N. Garcia Preto (Eds.), *Ethnicity and family therapy* (pp. 229–241). New York: Guilford Press.

Freedman, J., & Combs, G. (1996). *Narrative therapy: The social construction of preferred realities.* New York: W. W. Norton.

Gabrielidis, C., Stephan, W. G., Ybarra, O., Dos Santos Pearson, V., & Villareal, L. (1997). Preferred styles of conflict resolution: Mexico and the United States. *Journal of Cross-Cultural Psychology, 28*, 661–677.

Garcia-Preto, N. (1996). Latino families: An overview. In M. McGoldrick, J. K. Pearce, & J. Giordano (Eds.), *Ethnicity and family therapy* (pp. 141–154). New York: Guilford Press.

Gottman J. M. (1994a). *What predicts divorce? The relationship between marital processes and marital outcomes.* Hillsdale, NJ: Lawrence Erlbaum.

Gottman, J. M. (1994b). *Why marriages succeed or fail, and how you can make yours last.* New York: Simon & Schuster.

Guttfreund, D. G. (1990). Effects of language usage on the emotional experience of Spanish-English and English-Spanish bilinguals. *Journal of Consulting & Clinical Psychology, 58*, 604–607.

Ho, M. K. (1987). *Family therapy with ethnic minorities.* Newbury Park, CA: Sage.

Inclan, J. (2003). Class, culture, and gender in immigrant families. In L. B. Silverstein & T. J. Goodrich (Eds.), *Feminist Family Therapy* (pp. 333–347). Washington, DC: American Psychological Association.

Keeling, M. L., & Bermúdez, J. M. (2006). Externalizing problems through art and writing: Experiences of process and helpfulness. *Journal of Marital and Family Therapy, 32*(4), 405–419.

Keeling, M. L., & Nielson, R. (2005). Indian women's experience of a narrative therapy intervention using art and writing. *Contemporary Family Therapy, 27*, 435–452.

Kerr, C., Hoshino, J. M., Sutherland, J., Parashak, S. T., & McCarley, L. L. (2007). *Family art therapy: Foundations of theory and practice.* New York: Routledge.

Malchiodi, C. A. (Ed.) (2003). *Handbook of art therapy.* New York: Guilford Press.

Morgan, M. L., & Wampler, K. S. (2003). Fostering client creativity in family therapy: A process research study. *Contemporary Family Therapy, 25*(2), 207–228.

Newman, D. (2007). *Identities and inequalities: Exploring the intersections of race, class, gender and sexuality.* New York: McGraw-Hill.

Parry, A., & Doan, R. E. (1994). *Story re-visions: Narrative therapy in the postmodern world.* New York: Guilford Press.

Prouty, A. M., & Bermúdez, J. M. (1999). Experiencing multiconsciousness: A feminist model for therapy. *Journal of Feminist Family Therapy, 11*(3), 19–39.

Repak, T. (1995). *Waiting on Washington: Central American workers in the nation's capital.* Philadelphia: Temple University Press.

Riley, S. (2003). Art therapy with couples. In C. A. Malchiodi (Ed.), *Handbook of art therapy* (pp. 387–398). New York: Guilford Press.

Riley, S., & Malchiodi, C. A. (2003). Solution focused and narrative approaches. In C. A. Ichiodi (Ed.), *Handbook of art therapy* (pp. 82–92). New York: Guilford Press.

Rivas, L. A., Delgado-Romero, E. A., & Ozambela, K. R. (2005). Convergence of the language, professional, and personal identities of three Latino therapists. In E. Wieling & M. Rastogi (Eds.), *Voices of color* (pp. 23–41). Thousand Oaks, CA: Sage.

Simmons, L. L. (2006). *Interactive art therapy: "No talent required."* Binghampton, NY: Haworth Press.

Smith, R. L., & Montilla, R. E. (Eds.). (2005). *Counseling and family therapy with Latino populations.* New York: Routledge.

Sperber, A. D., Devellis, R. F., & Boehlecke, B. (1994). Cross-cultural translation: Methodology and validation. *Journal of Cross-Cultural Psychology, 25,* 501–524.

Ting-Toomey, S. (1994). Managing conflict in intimate intercultural relationships. In D. D. Cahn (Ed.), *Conflict in personal relationships* (pp. 47–77). Hillsdale, NJ: Lawrence Erlbaum.

Werner, O., & Campbell, D. T. (1970). Translating, working through interpreters, and the problem of decentering. In R. Naroll & R. Cohen (Eds.), *A handbook of method in cultural anthropology* (pp. 398–420). New York: American Museum of Natural History.

White, M. (1995). *Re-authoring lives: Interviews and essays.* Adelaide, Australia: Dulwich Centre Publications.

White, M., & Epston, D. (1990). *Narrative means to therapeutic ends.* New York: W. W. Norton.

Zimmerman, T., & Shepherd, S. (1993). Externalizing the problem of bulimia through conversation, drawing and letter writing in group therapy. *Journal of Systemic Therapies, 12*(1), 22–31.

Seventeen

Culturally Informed Emotionally Focused Therapy With Latino/a Immigrant Couples

José Rubén Parra-Cardona,
David Córdova Jr., Kendal Holtrop,
Ana Rocío Escobar-Chew, and
Sheena Horsford

L atinos/as[1] are the largest and fastest growing ethnic minority group in the United States (U.S. Census, 2000). However, Latinos/as continue to be seriously underrepresented in research and service delivery, which

AUTHORS' NOTE: We would like to express our gratitude to Dr. Susan Johnson, developer of EFT, for reviewing this manuscript and offering valuable feedback. We also thank Dr. Mudita Rastogi and Dr. Volker Thomas for their helpful editorial guidance. Finally, we express our sincere appreciation to Dr. Kenneth Hardy, who was the clinical supervisor for this case and who encouraged the first author to overtly address issues of gender with his clients.

prevents them from obtaining the benefits associated with participation in evidence-based practices (Castro, Barrera, & Martinez, 2004). The purpose of this chapter is to present a culturally informed model for the application of Emotionally Focused Therapy (EFT) with Latino/a immigrants. EFT is an evidence-based intervention capable of alleviating couples' emotional distress by promoting individual worth and identity along with relational security and intimacy (Johnson, 2004). We focus on the application of EFT with Latino immigrants because this specific Latino population is significantly underrepresented in clinical research (Castro et al., 2004).

For purposes of clarity, we will first introduce a general theoretical framework that integrates sociological, cultural, and Latin-American feminist theories. These theories identify relevant contextual factors that impact the lives of Latinos/as. Next, we will present a culturally informed model of EFT, followed by a detailed step-by-step demonstration of its clinical application with an immigrant Latino/a couple. Finally, we will propose recommendations for applying EFT among diverse Latino/a populations (e.g., U.S.-born Latinos/as).

Authors' Backgrounds

I (JRPC) am a Mexican native and relocated to the United States eight years ago to pursue my graduate education. I have since completed my graduate studies and become an assistant professor in a graduate family therapy program at a state university. As a first-generation immigrant, I have experienced the excitement and fulfillment associated with accomplishing professional goals that would be very difficult for me to achieve in Mexico, due to the intense contextual challenges that my country of origin continues to face. However, as an immigrant in the United States, I have also experienced the pervasive effects of ethnic discrimination and bigotry that continue to exist in this country.

Based on my life experiences, I am passionate about utilizing clinical interventions that are efficacious and culturally relevant. It is also critical for me to ensure that clinical practice is informed by social justice. Thus, I consider it necessary for clinicians to remain attentive to the ways in which disadvantaged populations continue to face contextual barriers and oppressive legacies that impede them from fully embracing their strengths and cultural richness.

I (DC) am a third-generation Mexican American whose grandparents took the challenging journey of immigration in order to provide more opportunities for future generations. As such, I have benefited from their sacrifices. In particular, I am currently entering my third year as a doctoral student. I have encountered many contextual challenges as part of an ethnic minority living in the United States. For example, I have lived in lower socioeconomic neighborhoods with crime, poverty, and drugs that create many stressors on couples and families. Therefore, I am dedicated to narrowing the gap of educational and health disparities for Latinos through the advancement of evidence-based and culturally appropriate interventions.

I (KH) am a White female who was born and raised in the United States. I am now in my third year of graduate school, working toward my master's— and eventually my doctoral—degrees in marriage and family therapy. I have been seeing clients for almost two years now. Through my personal relationships and clinical work with marginalized populations, I have become aware of and begun to question my privileges in society. For example, as I write this chapter I am sensitive to the fact that most couple therapy intervention is developed and implemented with populations of the cultural and ethnic background to which I belong (e.g., White, middle class, heterosexual), and I struggle with this reality. The many inequities that people of color face motivate me to take responsibility for the promotion of social justice.

I (AREC) am a female international student from Guatemala, Central America. After becoming a licensed clinical psychologist in my country, I decided to specialize in marriage and family therapy in the United States. I am currently a second year master's student. Throughout this process, I have had the opportunity to work with clients of different social status, particularly with low-income families and clients living in multi-stress situations. My professional career has been a path of personal growth through which I have questioned my beliefs and strengthened my commitment toward social justice. My journey to the United States has helped me to experience the importance of using culturally sensitive approaches to help clients effectively.

I (SH) am an African American female graduate student in a marriage and family therapy program. I am in my second year of a nonterminal master's degree. As a racial minority in my graduate program, I constantly question my role and at times find myself silenced by my personal feelings of inferiority. Initially, I began writing this chapter with a bit of hesitation because I did not want another book to alienate and negatively isolate the Latino population as different from other clients. After many discussions with my colleagues, I became aware of the need to acknowledge and embrace the differences of Latino populations as a way to enhance their experiences in therapy. Therefore, I realize it is important that our clinical work is continuously grounded on the histories and experiences that our clients bring to therapy.

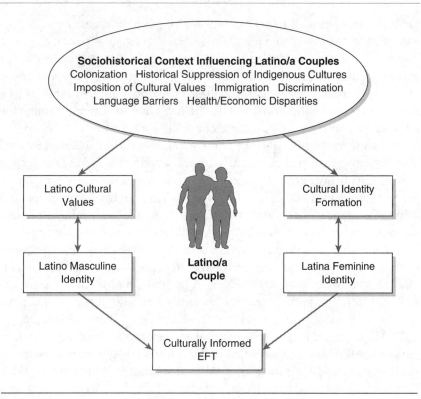

Figure 17.1   Context and Clinical Practice With Latino/a Couples

Context and Clinical Practice With Latinos/as

Figure 17.1 illustrates key contextual factors that impact the lives of Latinos and that should inform clinical practice with Latino/a couples. As illustrated in the figure, a major limitation of our model is that it has been applied only with heterosexual Latino/a couples. We recognize the great need to disseminate and evaluate EFT among LGBT populations, including the LGBT Latino population. We also consider that the adaptation of EFT among sexual minorities should be informed by knowledge of the intense oppressive experiences that they continue to experience (Bepko & Johnson, 2000).

Historical Colonization

The European invasion of the Americas brought genocides and destruction of the Indigenous cultures already established on the continent. The European conquest also promoted an ideology that depicted Native

Americans as inferior "savages without soul," who needed to be taught the "true civilization" as lived by the Europeans (Bacacela, 2006). Scholars have indicated the need to continue to identify the long-term effects of the European colonization. For instance, in the mental health professions there is a risk of considering Eurocentric forms of relationship functioning as the ideal, while minimizing the cultural richness embedded in the relationship dynamics of ethnic minority populations (Castro et al., 2004).

Latino/a Immigration Perceived as a Threat: Perennial Colonization

Latino/a immigrants living in the United States have historically been at best tolerated and at worst persecuted. Some scholars have even suggested that Latino/a immigration represents "a major potential threat to the cultural and political integrity of the U.S." (Huntington, 2004, p. 243). Unfortunately, the depiction of Latino/a immigrants as a burden overlooks the systematic efforts the United States has made over time to attract Latino/a immigrants in order to satisfy U.S. interests. Specifically, a revolving door policy has operated by which immigrants become welcome whenever there are labor shortages in critical areas of the U.S. economy (Nevis, 2002). Despite such realities, Latinos have frequently been utilized as "convenient scapegoats" whenever the United States faces political or economic crises (Nevis, 2002). In response, mental health practitioners should remain attentive to the potential negative impact these contextual stressors may have on Latino/a immigrants, particularly because the couple relationship may be one of the few avenues they have to express the distress associated with these forms of social exclusion (Parra-Cardona & Busby, 2006).

Latino/a Cultural Values and Cultural Identity Formation

Latino Cultural Values

Mental health practitioners should recognize and appreciate important Latino/a cultural values (Falicov, 1998). As summarized by Falicov, *familismo* is understood as dedication and commitment to one's family. For many Latinos/as, a commitment to *la familia* may supersede financial or professional achievements. In addition, rather than considering the nuclear family as the basic family unit, Latinos/as may consider *la gran familia* as their family unit, consisting of both vertical (i.e., multigeneration) and horizontal (i.e., extended) family members. *Respeto* is a Latino value that highlights the deference that is owed to every individual. *Personalismo* refers to the importance of establishing meaningful interpersonal relationships in diverse social settings. Finally, *colectivismo* highlights the importance of evaluating the ways in which one's actions affect the common good (Falicov, 1998).

Cultural Identity Formation

Scholars have highlighted the dangers of utilizing simplistic models of cultural identity formation (Cabassa, 2003). Specifically, rather than considering "assimilation" or "acculturation" to mainstream U.S. culture as an ideal outcome, a more culturally relevant paradigm is to understand cultural identity as a complex process with multiple potential outcomes (Ivey, 1995). For instance, some Latino/a immigrants may develop a cultural identity that embodies a strong identification with either their country of origin or the United States. In contrast, other Latino/a immigrants may want to be identified as bicultural, and choose to integrate elements from both cultures. Unfortunately, the benefits associated with integrative expressions of cultural identity (e.g., biculturalism) continue to be overshadowed in clinical practice, particularly by service providers using theoretical models that identify assimilation as the ideal form of cultural identity (Coatsworth, Maldonado-Molina, Pantin, & Szapocznik, 2005).

Latin American Feminism and Gender Analysis

Latin American Feminism

Feminist perspectives argue that patriarchal societies are structured in ways that ensure the socioeconomic and political superiority of men, while relegating women to subordinate roles (White & Kowalski, 1998). Latin American feminist ideologies share this assumption. In addition, these theories highlight the need to examine the ways in which patriarchy is associated with the diverse forms of historical oppression experienced by Latin American countries (e.g., foreign invasion and colonialism, assassination and alienation of indigenous communities), as well as the need to identify culturally relevant definitions of masculinity and femininity (Ramírez Hernández, 2002).

Latino Masculine Identity

The concept of *machismo* has often been defined in a way that depicts Latino men as domineering toward women (Baca-Zinn, 1982). In objection to this portrayal, Latino/a scholars have expressed the need to identify new culturally relevant definitions of Latino masculinity. For example,

Latino men have reported embracing alternative identities characterized by *positive machismo* and *nobleza* (Tello, 1998; Torres, Solberg, & Carlstrom, 2002). *Positive machismo* and *nobleza* highlight the importance of embracing compassion, tolerance, and perseverance when facing extreme contextual challenges (Tello, 1998). These constructs motivate men to establish interpersonal relationships characterized by open emotional expression, gender equality, and family commitment (Tello, 1998).

Latina Feminine Identity

Latina feminist scholars have expressed concerns that feminist ideologies often overlook the cultural value that ethnic minority women may attribute to traditional gender roles (Torres & Pace, 2005). For instance, Latina women may find their role as primary caretaker empowering and culturally relevant. Thus, scholars have expressed the need to avoid stereotyping such women as submissive or unable to become independent. Instead, Latina feminist scholars advocate for examining the extent to which Latina women feel safe and empowered in deciding their preferred gender roles (Torres & Pacem, 2005).

Culturally Informed EFT

Our proposed culturally informed model of EFT stems directly from the theoretical framework we have just presented. Table 17.1 summarizes this model by indicating how each step of the EFT process can be adapted for clinical work with Latino/a immigrant couples.

Emotionally Focused Therapy (EFT)

EFT is an evidence-based intervention for couples that privileges emotion and attachment (Johnson, 2004). As Johnson explains, the process of EFT seeks to restructure the way in which each partner responds to the attachment needs and emotional reactions of the other, seeking to develop a new interactional cycle that fosters emotional engagement and promotes secure bonding. The practice of EFT traditionally takes place according to nine steps that guide the couple through three stages of change: (1) de-escalation of the negative interaction cycle, (2) building new interactional patterns that promote secure attachment, and (3) consolidating the new cycles of attachment. The reader is referred to the original source for a more detailed description of EFT (Johnson, 2004).

Table 17.1 Overview of Culturally Informed Emotionally Focused Therapy With Latino/a Immigrant Couples

---

Step 1: Joining and Assessment Informed by a Cultural Perspective

Part A: Joining While Attending to Immigration, Gender, and Cultural Identity Issues

Join with the couple in a collaborative and genuine manner.

Obtain a clear history of the couple's immigration experience(s) as well as their individual perceived cultural identities.

Learn about the couple's cultural values and how these may relate to your work together (e.g., role of *familismo*).

Begin to explore how each partner's gender script relates to expressions of emotional vulnerability.

Listen to the couple's story and recognize possible obstacles to secure attachment and emotional connection.

Part B: Assessment of Relational Difficulties

Clarify the presenting problem and identify the couple's goals for therapy.

Notice strengths of relationship.

Assess for appropriateness of EFT (e.g., no ongoing domestic violence, couple wishes to improve relationship).

Step 2: Identifying the Problem Interaction Cycle That Maintains Attachment Insecurity

Utilizing a systems perspective, identify how the actions of each partner interact to form a cycle of distress.

Remain attentive to issues of attachment, cultural identity, immigration, and gender when conceptualizing the cycle.

Confirm this cycle with the couple and begin to elicit their automatic cognitions and self-dialogues associated with it.

Step 3: Preparing the Experience of Emotional Vulnerability and Accessing Unacknowledged Feelings

Part A: Preparing the Experience of Emotional Vulnerability

Understand that gender and culture can play a critical role in influencing couple dynamics.

Recognize that gender socialization may obstruct emotional vulnerability in both males and females.

Respect the contextual necessity of emotional toughness while also expressing how this could prevent intimacy in the couple relationship.

Promote a "both/and" position of gender identity that can respond to cultural strengths and appreciate emotional vulnerability (e.g., by using the *hombre noble* philosophy).

Part B: Accessing Unacknowledged Feelings

Validate and explore the context in which the gender and cultural identity of each partner has developed.

Help each partner identify the primary emotions that are driving the interaction cycle.

Foster a validating and safe atmosphere as the partners in the couple begin to express these emotions.

Step 4: Reframing the Problem in Terms of Emotions, Attachment, and Cultural Needs

Talk through the problem with the couple, explaining it as a cycle that evolves out of each partner's emotional reactions and attachment behaviors.

Encourage continued emotional vulnerability by inviting each member of the couple to share their cultural needs.

Externalize the problem, empowering the couple to work together to combat the distressing interaction cycle.

Step 5: Promoting Identification With Disowned Needs and Integrating Into Relationship Interactions

Enable both partners to continue to explore and express their attachment needs.

Promote interactions that are validating and nonblaming.

Steps 6 and 7: Facilitating Acceptance of Each Partner's Experience and Encouraging Expression of Specific Needs

As each partner begins to disclose his or her underlying attachment and cultural needs, help the other to understand these needs and respond appropriately.

Challenge the myth that each member of the couple must have similar cultural experiences by asking the couple to recognize and accept their cultural identity differences.

Steps 8 and 9: Fostering the Emergence of Unique Solutions and the Consolidation of New Positions

Support each partner as they practice expressing clearer requests for connection and providing validation.

(Continued)

Table 17.1 (Continued)

> Help reinforce new interaction cycles that promote emotional vulnerability and engagement.
>
> Ensure both partners feel fully entitled to their attachment and cultural needs.
>
> Celebrate overt expressions of needs that defy traditional gender and cultural stereotypes and reinforce the value of such expressions within the relational context.
>
> Revisit troublesome issues in the couple's relationship and support each member in addressing these issues using their new patterns of interaction.
>
> Move toward termination (e.g., normalize fears of relapse, reinforce couple's successes, discuss attachment rituals).

Finding Two Homes: Fulfilling Emotional and Cultural Needs

The following clinical presentation describes the implementation of EFT with a first-generation Latino/a immigrant couple affected by immigration stressors, lack of attention to issues of cultural identity formation, and rigid gender socialization. This case study is meant to be an illustration of one way in which culturally informed EFT has been applied with an immigrant Latino/a couple to produce multiple positive outcomes. It is by no means a fixed format that should be followed in every case. Rather, the essence of culturally informed EFT requires that the uniqueness and diversity of every Latino/a couple be acknowledged during the therapeutic process. This model suggests a method by which to accomplish these goals.

CASE EXAMPLE

Pedro (35) and Sofia (33) had been married for six years.[2] Both were first-generation immigrant Latinos/as. Pedro came to the United States five years before under a visa limiting his employment to specific sectors of the labor market (e.g., construction, agriculture). After spending four years as a farm worker, he was promoted to production supervisor in a food processing plant. Sofia immigrated along with Pedro by using a spousal visa and was not allowed to work. However, she had recently enrolled in the community college and was pursuing an associate's degree in nursing. At the time of therapy, they had applied for a new type of visa that would allow Sofia to seek employment.

During the intake session, Sofia reported acute communication problems that had recently become much more frequent and intense. She was also distressed by a marked reduction in her sexual desire. Pedro confirmed the communication difficulties and expressed concern for their decreased sexual activity. He expressed confusion over Sofia's distress and loss of sexual desire. Despite these difficulties, both Pedro and Sofia expressed a desire to rekindle their relationship and pointed to how fulfilling their relationship had been when they had gotten married.

Next, we will apply the case to the EFT steps as suggested by Johnson (2004).

Step 1: Joining and Assessment Informed by a Cultural Perspective

The initial sessions were devoted to clarifying the presenting problem, identifying the couple's goals for therapy, and establishing a collaborative treatment plan. During this stage of treatment, it was particularly important for me (JRPC)[3] to obtain a thorough history of their immigration experiences and perceived cultural identities before proceeding. This allowed me to obtain a clearer understanding of the ways in which contextual and cultural issues were impacting the couple relationship.

Part A: Joining While Attending to Immigration, Gender, and Cultural Identity Issues

Pedro and Sofia were married prior to relocating to the United States, and recalled how their relationship had been stable and fulfilling during the first few years. About a year after their wedding, the couple had decided to come to the United States to escape the financial and safety problems they were experiencing in their home country. Once in the United States, Pedro was subjected to an exhausting work schedule—between 60 and 70 hours per week—but the couple decided to remain here because of the opportunities they had to improve their quality of life. However, Sofia explained that it was difficult for her to only see her family for two weeks each year. Pedro reported similar feelings, but expressed that "unfortunately, that's the price we need to pay in order to have a better future . . . We need to focus on what's ahead of us and not to look back."

When asked about cultural identity issues, Sofia expressed a deep appreciation for the economic opportunities and sense of safety she had experienced in the United States. She especially valued the opportunities for independence and professional development offered to women, which differed from the barriers women continued to experience in her home country. Although she expressed a desire to spend the rest of her life in the United States, she also explained, "I really miss feeling the warmth of my people, the beauty of my country and my culture . . . that is difficult to find here in the U.S."

Pedro focused on describing the challenges associated with being an immigrant in the United States, but also demonstrated a deep appreciation for his job, despite the hardships it entailed. He affirmed that one of his major life goals was to become a U.S. citizen. Although he expressed a strong appreciation for his culture, he also described clear frustrations related to his country of origin, explaining, "We came here [to the United States] because we couldn't find in our country these opportunities . . . a good job and safety . . . and that angers me . . . that's why I want to become a U.S. citizen . . . this country is offering me a home."

I asked the couple what they valued most about being Latinos/as and how they wanted to inform our work based on these issues. Sofia expressed that she strongly valued the importance of having a strong sense of family cohesion and community. Pedro agreed, but explained that the family he had established with Sofia was of primary importance to him because his own family disintegrated after his parents divorced when he was young. Pedro also affirmed the importance of his recent promotion because it would allow him to ensure that all the workers were treated with *respeto*.

Part B: Assessment of Relational Difficulties

As therapy progressed, Sofia expressed how one of her main concerns was that Pedro struggled to understand that sometimes she was not in the mood for sex. Pedro complained that Sofia "was too sensitive" and that she seemed to "keep resentments" from previous fights. When I asked Sofia about her reaction to Pedro's statement, she was clearly upset and expressed how difficult it was to share her feelings with Pedro. In addition, Sofia explained that she realized the advantages of relocating to the United States, but felt that Pedro refused to acknowledge the hardships associated with being an immigrant. She expressed that "Pedro only faces problems by saying 'never look back, always look forward' . . . that is frustrating . . . I wonder if coming to the U.S. was the right thing or not."

Step 2: Identifying the Problem Interaction Cycle That Maintains Attachment Insecurity

Pedro and Sofia were engaged in a pursue–distance pattern. Specifically, Sofia was actively seeking increased emotional connection with Pedro by sharing with him her feelings of distress and loss. However, Pedro dismissed Sofia's feelings by remaining in a withdrawn emotional position, trying to deal with her emotional distress by focusing on the future.

Contextually, issues of cultural identity, gender, and immigration influenced the relational difficulties of this couple. For example, Pedro could be considered a biculturally oriented individual with a strong orientation toward the United States, particularly because of how much he valued the opportunities he had found in his adopted country. Overall, his sense of satisfaction associated with living in the United States was higher than his sense of loss associated with not living in his country of origin. In contrast, although Sofia also had elements of biculturalism, she was clearly oriented toward her country of origin, as demonstrated by the profound sense of loss that she continued to experience by missing her family and culture.

Gender issues were present in two ways. First, Pedro was not validating Sofia's experience and was pushing her to "move on," while trying to impose the need to "focus on the future." Thus, Pedro had not realized the ways in which his male privilege and identity as their sole source of income increased Sofia's pressure to conform to his viewpoints. In addition, it appeared that Pedro had internalized strong gender socialization messages that undervalued the richness of emotional vulnerability.

Important attachment needs were also not being met for each partner, in part because of the difficulties associated with immigration. Specifically, both partners were experiencing attachment losses associated with not living close to their families and country of origin. When coping with these loses, Pedro was adopting a more stoic stance by highlighting the need to "move forward, without looking back," while Sofia was clearly naming the profound negative impacts associated with their lives as immigrants. In addition, Pedro interpreted Sofia's low sexual desire as an indication that she was losing interest in him. This was highly threatening to him because he vividly reported how much he loved Sofia and how she provided the motivation that kept him "fighting in life." Sofia described Pedro as being emotionally unavailable. Thus, she did not experience Pedro as the secure base she needed in order to cope with the contextual stressors she was facing.

I described these patterns to Sofia and Pedro in order to confirm that my impressions reflected their experiences. Next, I asked them to focus on the automatic cognitions and self-dialogues associated with each cycle. Sofia identified that after refusing to engage in sexual intercourse with Pedro she would frequently think, "I wish he would only hug me and understand me more." When I asked her whether she had similar thoughts after attempting to share her struggles as an immigrant with Pedro, she agreed. Sofia explained how she had convinced herself that it was useless to share her distress with him, because "he would only try to focus on the benefits of living in the U.S." Pedro was able to identify a self-dialog informed by a sense of resentment. Specifically, he would say to himself that Sofia was not capable of valuing his daily efforts because she was too immersed in herself. He also expressed that Sofia's decreased sexual desire was a source of anxiety for him. He wondered whether she was losing interest in him or if she wanted to force him to return to their country of origin. As the couple began to disclose their attachment insecurities, I reflected to Pedro and Sofia that their experiences were also a testimony of their desire to be close to each other.

Step 3: Promoting Emotional Vulnerability and Accessing Unacknowledged Feelings[4]

This step is informed by feminist and cultural perspectives. We draw from the contributions of scholars who have documented the importance of engaging Latino/a men by emphasizing the virtues associated with being a *hombre noble* (noble man) as a way to challenge rigid gender socialization. We purposefully focus on engaging males in treatment, especially if we perceive struggles with experiencing emotional vulnerability. We also recognize that being a man conveys privilege in patriarchal societies, and because Latino/a immigrant men are often the main providers in their families, issues of power have a critical role in Latino/a couple dynamics. Thus, we fully agree with scholars who have proposed informing the EFT intervention according to feminist principles, particularly because of the importance of overtly addressing issues of gendered privilege in couple therapy (Vatcher & Bogo, 2001).

Part A: Preparing the Experience of Emotional Vulnerability

To begin to open space for deeper emotional work, I provided Pedro and Sofia with a brief handout to consider prior to our next session. The handout referred to reflections of what constitutes a *hombre noble*. I started the following session by asking the couple about their reactions to the handout. Sofia was enthusiastic after reading that a man who is able to be emotionally vulnerable can also be considered a virtuous man. Pedro expressed that he resonated with the image of a being a *hombre noble* and was intrigued by my emphasis on men, rather than the couple. I explained that after working with many families and couples, it was my belief that men can promote much more happiness in their families when they understand masculinity not only as the capacity to fight for their families in everyday life but, equally importantly, as the ability to help everyone to embrace intense emotions such as fear, sadness, or hurt.

I went on to focus my attention on Pedro and expressed to him that I deeply respected his capacity to face the extremely challenging working conditions he encountered on a daily basis. I asked him to help me understand how he had developed this sense of strength and resilience. Pedro vividly described the numerous ways in which he had to adapt his thinking in response to his work environment. For instance, he had often felt like giving up after a work week of 70 hours in the fields under challenging conditions. He also reported various occasions where he experienced discrimination by supervisors or non-Latino coworkers and decided to remain silent for fear of jeopardizing his immigration status. Pedro shared how he was committed to enduring any hardships in order to secure the future of his family. He said, *"Te tienes que aguantar* (you must tolerate it) . . . you cannot be weak in the fields . . . if they treat you bad because you are an immigrant, you just need to be very strong."

After validating Pedro's strong commitment to his family and virtues, I invited him to reflect on the ways in which his capacity to overcome adversity by hardening his emotions could also represent a challenge to his relationship with Sofia. I clarified how I was concerned that the armor he had developed in order to survive as an immigrant farm worker was also preventing him from experiencing emotional vulnerability in his relationship with Sofia. I encouraged him to maintain this armor as a way of protecting himself from the contextual challenges he had to face, and I also suggested he let his guard down at times with Sofia in order to experience increased intimacy through emotional vulnerability.

Part B: Accessing Unacknowledged Feelings

Pedro shared that he wanted to be a *hombre noble,* but said he did not know how to solve Sofia's problems. When asked about his feelings whenever Sofia expressed distress to him, he responded "I'm afraid . . . I don't know how to make her feel better . . . It's hard for me to hear what she says." I thanked Pedro for embracing emotional vulnerability and asked him whether he was willing to listen to Sofia's experience. He consented. Next, I asked Sofia to express to Pedro her losses associated with being an immigrant, but she insisted that he was aware of her feelings. I validated her hesitation by asking, "Are you afraid that he will not be able to listen and understand you?" She confirmed this fear. In response, I asked Pedro to tell Sofia that he was committed to listening without having to fix anything and that he would focus on fully understanding her struggles.

Sofia provided a description of her emotional distress associated with being an immigrant. Although Pedro spontaneously reached out to her and touched her shoulder, Sofia remained unresponsive to his gesture. I reflected on Sofia's nonverbal response and asked what was keeping her from responding to Pedro. She replied in an angry tone, "It's just that I'm tired of feeling so lonely! . . . Pedro is the only person I have here and I cannot talk to him! . . . I'm afraid of telling him what I feel because he shuts me down by saying 'let's focus on what is good.'" I thanked Sofia for showing her anger, and I asked Pedro to let her know that he was committed to providing a safe space in order for her to continue to share her feelings of loss. I also encouraged him not to find a solution, but to focus on understanding her emotional experience. Before ending the session, I asked the couple to keep talking about Sofia's experience and encouraged Pedro to exclusively focus on validating her feelings.

In the following session, Pedro expressed his strong desire to make Sofia feel better whenever she became sad. He also identified feeling "incompetent for not being able to make her happy." Sofia expressed relief after listening to Pedro's disclosure of concern for her.

After highlighting their accomplishments, we went on to explore the underlying feelings associated with their sex life. Sofia expressed that she wanted to be sexually intimate with Pedro. However, she could not enjoy sex because she "felt disconnected from him." At other times she would just feel angry and did not want to think about having sex. I asked Sofia whether she usually dealt with anger by disengaging from Pedro and asked her whether she would be willing to express her anger to Pedro if she knew he would be responsive.[5] She responded that it was difficult for her to express anger because she was never allowed to do so in her family of origin. I reflected to Sofia that the process of therapy provided a growth opportunity for both her and Pedro. This meant that it was important for her to openly express her anger without taking a blaming stance. In addition, I highlighted to Pedro how critical it was for him to reassure Sofia that she could express any type of emotions whenever she experienced them.

As the process continued, I asked Sofia whether she experienced any other insecurities in her relationship with Pedro. She disclosed that she struggled with fears of not being the type of woman that Pedro wanted as a partner. These concerns left her constantly wondering whether Pedro would abandon her for someone else who could be "more courageous" than she was.

Step 4: Reframing the Problem in Terms of Emotions, Attachment, and Cultural Needs

During the following sessions, we continued to explore the underlying emotions experienced by Pedro and Sofia, as well as the nature of their unmet emotional needs. Sofia continued to express sadness for the losses that she experienced as an immigrant. She also became aware that the more she suppressed her feelings, the more she emotionally distanced herself from Pedro. On the other hand, Pedro felt inadequate for not being able to help Sofia with her experiences of loss. He continued to feel overwhelmed by Sofia's distress and would still resort to his strategy of focusing on the future as a coping mechanism.

By reframing the problem in these terms, I promoted interactions between Sofia and Pedro to communicate their emotional experiences to each other. In addition, I invited them to expand their emotional vulnerability by identifying the unique cultural needs that each one of them considered would make their lives more fulfilling.

Step 5: Identifying Disowned Needs and Integration Into Relationship Interactions

I continued to encourage Pedro and Sofia to focus on themselves and their expectations of each other, rather than adopting a blaming stance. Sofia expressed to Pedro her desire to reach out and share with him her emotional distress. She also described her need to feel safe prior to sharing her feelings of sadness or anger. In addition, Sofia wanted Pedro to reassure her that he did not think she was inadequate and that he was committed to remaining in the relationship. In return, Pedro expressed to Sofia how important it was for him to be validated by her. He explained how this was particularly important because she inspired his commitment to face adversity in life. Pedro also communicated to Sofia that he needed to know that she continued to love him, particularly because he had interpreted their increased emotional and sexual distance as an indication that Sofia was considering leaving the relationship.

Steps 6 and 7: Facilitating Acceptance of Each Partner's Experiences and Expression of Needs

In addition to promoting a mutual acceptance of their attachment needs, I asked Sofia and Pedro to recognize and accept their differences in cultural identity. I invited them to challenge the expectation that they had to feel the same way regarding their cultural experiences, and encouraged them to express their cultural needs to one another. Thus, Sofia expressed to Pedro that she wanted to travel more often to their home country, and to become more involved in local Latino/a community activities. Sofia also talked about her desire to experience more financial independence by obtaining a degree in nursing. Pedro shared with Sofia that he wanted her to pay more attention to the numerous challenges he experienced at work as well as his plans for seeking opportunities for career advancement. He also expressed his desire for Sofia to become more involved with him in social activities related to his work.

Steps 8 and 9: Fostering New Solutions and the Consolidation of New Positions

The final sessions focused on reminding Pedro of the importance of validating Sofia's feelings, particularly because it was challenging for him to remain emotionally responsive without acting on his desire to make Sofia feel better. As Sofia felt more understood by him, she realized that she needed to face the challenge of openly expressing her anger to Pedro, rather than distancing herself from him.

An important breakthrough in the final phase of therapy occurred when Sofia entered nursing school. This experience provided her with a sense of independence that she had not felt before. Pedro's capacity to overcome adversity was very important in helping Sofia face the challenges associated with pursuing her degree. In addition, Pedro and Sofia learned to respect and nurture each other's cultural needs without attempting to change their individual cultural experiences. Thus, Pedro supported Sofia by saving money so she could return to her home country to visit family and friends one additional time per year. Pedro also started to attend several Latino/a community events with Sofia, where they were able to make new Latino/a friends. Sofia accepted that Pedro did not want to maintain the same level of contact with their home country as she wanted to, and she respected his desire to travel with her to their country of origin only once per year. Sofia also became involved in Pedro's professional plans, and she often engaged in conversations with him about possibilities for his professional development.

At termination, Pedro and Sofia reported that they had begun to enjoy a more fulfilling sexual life now that their relationship distress had diminished. They had also agreed to commit to finding time to go out on dates and enjoy each other despite the pressures of other obligations.

Discussion

EFT is one of the few evidence-based practices capable of alleviating emotional distress within couple relationships by promoting the fulfillment of attachment needs. This case study illustrates the multiple positive outcomes that are possible through implementing a culturally informed model of EFT.

The culturally informed model of EFT presented here seeks to become relevant to Latino/a immigrant populations by considering the sociohistorical challenges this group has faced, as well as the cultural experiences that are most relevant to their lives. In addition, we consider it is necessary to overtly address issues of male privilege and power in couple therapy, especially because Latino/a immigrants are often raised in patriarchal societies. However, patriarchy can be observed in multiple ethnic groups, and is not a unique characteristic of Latino males (Baca-Zinn, 1982). Thus, we advocate for a strength-based perspective of Latino masculinity. We have found in our clinical experience that the notion of *hombre noble* can become a strong motivator for change and a precursor of emotional intimacy among Latino men, even among those who have engaged in extremely violent and abusive behaviors.[6]

Application of the Model With Nonimmigrant Latino/a Couples

The case example presented in this chapter focused on a first-generation immigrant Latino/a couple. However, the basic premises of this model can be applied to diverse Latino/a subgroups, provided therapists gain an understanding of the most relevant life experiences of their clients. Thus, it is critical for counselors to learn from clients about the cultural values and forms of cultural identification that are most relevant to them, as well as the ways in which these issues impact their couple relationship and the implementation of EFT. We provide a summary of suggestions for the application of EFT with diverse Latino/a couples in Table 17.2.

Cultural Diversity and Becoming an EFT Therapist: Reflection, Questions, and Additional Resources

Overall, we believe the principles we have used for culturally inform- ing the practice of EFT with Latinos can be extended to diverse minority groups through two main activities. First, clinicians should actively seek to learn from clients the key cultural values and practices that inform their lives. This step will help ensure the cultural relevance of the intervention and facilitate the engagement of clients in therapy. To facilitate this pro- cess, clinicians may ask themselves the following questions:

What assumptions do I hold about the culture and values of the clients I am working with?

How might these assumptions interfere with the clinical work?

What information have I learned from my clients about their culture and val- ues that may challenge my assumptions?

What else must I learn from them in order to fully understand and appreciate the context of their lives?

The second factor we consider essential is maintaining close adherence to the core components of EFT. To this end, therapists should receive close supervision from a professional with a thorough understanding of the EFT model, such as an EFT certified therapist. We refer the reader to the Web site of the International Center for Excellence in Emotionally Focused Therapy (www.eft.ca), as this site contains detailed information on EFT workshops, publications, and the process of EFT certification. We also suggest the book *The Practice of Emotionally Focused Couple Therapy: Creating Connection* (Johnson, 2004) and the companion workbook, *Becoming an Emotionally Focused Couple Therapist* (Johnson et al., 2005), as these resources include numerous case examples, exercises, and specific suggestions for clinical practice.

Table 17.2   Suggestions for the Utilization of EFT With Latinos/as

Conceptualization of the EFT Model

- Counselors should conceptualize the EFT process within a sociohistorical model capable of capturing *past and current* challenges experienced by Latinos/as.

- Counselors should identify specific contextual stressors that may negatively impact the process of therapy.

Latino/a Cultural Values and Cultural Identity Formation

- Counselors should be knowledgeable of relevant Latino/a cultural values.

- Counselors must avoid a simplistic conceptualization of cultural identity by recognizing that Latinos/as may develop diverse forms of cultural identity.

- Counselors should work collaboratively with clients in order to identify which cultural values are most valued by them.

- Counselors should recognize their clients' preferred expressions of cultural identity.

- Counselors should explore with clients the ways in which cultural values and issues of cultural identity influence their couple relationship.

- Counselors should explore with clients the ways in which cultural values and issues of cultural identity can facilitate change and promote emotional intimacy.

Rigid Gender Socialization and the Promotion of Emotional Vulnerability

- If the promotion of emotional intimacy is blocked because Latino male clients adhere to rigid gender identifications, counselors should reach an understanding of the role that such identifications have on their clients' lives.

- Counselors should examine the ways in which gendered privilege and power may be detrimental to the promotion of emotional vulnerability in the couple relationship.

- Counselors should challenge rigid patterns of male socialization that impede emotional vulnerability. However, this process should be informed by strength-based and cultural perspectives that highlight the importance of strength when facing adversity, as well as the way in which integrity can be associated with the expression of emotional vulnerability (e.g., *hombre noble*).

Conclusion

There is a great need to further investigate the ways in which EFT can effectively be disseminated among Latinos/as. We have proposed a culturally informed model that may be useful in the pursuit of this goal. A key premise of this model rests on the assumption that EFT can greatly benefit Latino/a couples, but only if such interventions are implemented in a way that enhances the cultural experiences and strengths that inform the lives of Latinos/as.

Notes

1. We utilize the term *Latinos/as* when making reference to inhabitants or individuals who can trace their origins back to Latin American countries in which Romance languages are predominantly spoken (e.g., Spanish, Portuguese). We also utilize the term *Latinos/as* in order to highlight the Indigenous ancestry of Latino/a cultures. For a more detailed explanation of the term *Latino/a*, we refer the reader to Santiago-Rivera, Arredondo, and Gallardo-Cooper (2002).

2. Original names have been replaced with pseudonyms in order to protect clients' confidentiality. Specific details related to country of origin, immigration status, length of U.S. residence, and occupations have also been modified.

3. The first author (JRPC) was the lead therapist in this case.

4. We have informed our couple and family therapy interventions based on a feminist perspective that approaches males from a strength-based perspective while also challenging patriarchal structures. We have repeatedly confirmed the strong commitment of Latino men toward those they love; however, we have also witnessed the numerous ways in which rigid gender socialization can impact their lives negatively. Thus, we overtly address issues of masculinity and privilege prior to engaging in more emotionally focused therapeutic interventions.

5. It is important to clarify that, although we identify Sofia as the pursuer and Pedro as the withdrawer, in reality partners engage in diverse pursue/withdraw behaviors. In this case, Sofia also distances herself when Pedro seeks sexual intimacy. Our emphasis on identifying Pedro as the main withdrawer refers to the fact that in EFT it is helpful to identify the main pursuer based on an attachment perspective. That is, the negative cycle should be understood as unmet attachment needs that are often expressed through separation protest (Johnson et al., 2005). In this case, Sofia tends to verbally express her need for emotional connection as well as emotional pain associated with her attachment losses, whereas Pedro is more likely to avoid emotional vulnerability.

6. The first author facilitates therapy groups for Latino men referred by the courts for charges of violence against women. He has confirmed the value of presenting the notion of *hombre noble* as a way of promoting vulnerability among Latino men involved in therapy, as well as a way of developing accountability and a commitment to challenge rigid gender identifications that promote violence.

References

Bacacela, S. (2006). *La discriminación de la mujer indígena: Un peso histórico* [The discrimination of the indigenous woman: A historic weight]. Retrieved March 2, 2007, from www.llacta.org/notic/2006/not0308a.htm.

Baca-Zinn, M. (1982). Chicano men and masculinity. *Journal of Ethnic Studies, 10,* 29–44.

Bepko, C., & Johnson, T. (2000). Gay and lesbian couples in therapy: Perspectives for the contemporary family therapist. *Journal of Marital and Family Therapy, 26,* 409–419.

Cabassa, L. J. (2003). Measuring acculturation: Where we are and where we need to go. *Hispanic Journal of Behavioral Sciences, 25,* 127–146.

Castro, F. G., Barrera, M., & Martinez, C. (2004). The cultural adaptation of prevention interventions: Resolving tensions between fidelity and fit. *Prevention Science, 5,* 41–45.

Coatsworth, J. D., Maldonado-Molina, M., Pantin, H., & Szapocznik, J. (2005). A person-centered and ecological investigation of acculturation strategies in Hispanic immigrant youth. *Journal of Community Psychology, 33,* 157–174.

Falicov, C. J. (1998). *Latino families in therapy.* New York: Guilford Press.

Huntington, S. P. (2004). *Who are we? The challenges to America's national identity.* New York: Simon & Schuster.

Ivey, A. E. (1995). Psychotherapy as a liberation: Toward specific skills and strategies in multicultural counseling and therapy. In J. G. Ponterotto, J. M. Casas, L. A. Suzuki, & C. M. Alexander (Eds.), *Handbook of multicultural counseling* (pp. 53–72). Thousand Oaks, CA: Sage.

Johnson, S. M. (2004). *The practice of Emotionally Focused Therapy: Creating connection.* New York: Brunner-Routledge.

Johnson, S. M., Bradley, B., Furrow, J., Lee, A., Palmer, G., Tilley, D., et al. (2005). *Becoming an emotionally focused therapist.* New York: Brunner-Routledge.

Nevis, J. (2002). *Operation gatekeeper: The rise of the "illegal alien" and the making of the U.S.–Mexico boundary.* New York: Routledge.

Parra-Cardona, J. R., & Busby, D. M. (2006). Exploring relationship functioning in premarital Caucasian and Latino/a couples: Recognizing and valuing cultural differences. *Journal of Comparative Family Studies, 3,* 325–344.

Ramírez Hernández, A. (2002). CECEVIM—Stopping male violence in the Latino home. In E. Aldarondo & F. Mederos (Eds.), *Programs for men who batter: Intervention and prevention strategies in a diverse society* (pp. 12:1–12:30). New York: Civic Research Institute.

Santiago-Rivera, A. L., Arredondo, P., & Gallardo-Cooper, M. (2002). *Counseling Latinos and la familia.* Thousand Oaks, CA: Sage.

Tello, J. (1998). *El hombre noble buscando balance:* The noble man searching for balance. In R. Carrillo & J. Tello (Eds.), *Family violence and men of color: Healing the wounded male spirit* (pp. 31–52). New York: Springer.

Torres, G., & Pace, K. (2005). Understanding patriarchy as an expression of Whiteness: Insights from the Chicana movement. *Journal of Law and Policy, 18,* 129–172.

Torres, J. B., Solberg, S. H., & Carlstrom, A. H. (2002). The myth of sameness among Latino men and their machismo. *American Journal of Orthopsychiatry, 72,* 163–181.

U.S. Census Bureau. (2000). *Annual resident population estimates of the United States by race and Hispanic or Latino origin.* Retrieved March 23, 2006, from http://eire.census.gov/popest/data/national/tables/asro/NA-EST2002-ASRO-04.php.

Vatcher, C., & Bogo, M. (2001). The feminist/emotionally focused therapy practice model: An integrated approach for couple therapy. *Journal of Marital and Family Therapy, 27,* 69–83.

White, J., & Kowalski, R. M. (1998). Male violence toward women: An integrative perspective. In R. G. Green & E. Donnerstein (Eds.), *Human aggression: Theories, research, and implications for social policy* (pp. 205–229). San Diego, CA: Academic Press.

Section G

Native and First Nations Couples

Eighteen

The Use of Narrative Practices and Emotionally Focused Couple Therapy With First Nations Couples

Sam Berg

This chapter will explore the integration of Emotionally Focused Therapy for couples and narrative therapy, in order to demonstrate an approach to working with couples of First Nations background in Saskatchewan, Canada.

I hold the position of Professor of Counseling at Briercrest College and Seminary, Caronport, Saskatchewan, where I coordinate and teach in a marriage and family counseling program. I am a Clinical Member and Approved Supervisor of the AAMFT. I am also in private practice at a small agency in a nearby city. My counseling practice is a general one, in which I see individuals, couples, and families. I am also a counselor recognized by the First Nations and Inuit Health Branch of Health Canada, a federal government department, to provide counseling for First Nations clients. I am a first-generation Canadian descendent of German parents whose families both immigrated in the 1920s. I have recently attained senior citizen status.

Theoretical Guidelines

Emotionally Focused Couples Therapy

Emotionally Focused Therapy for couples (EFT) is an empirically supported therapy that was first developed by Les Greenberg and Sue Johnson. Among the earliest literature on this approach is a chapter titled "Emotionally Focused Couples Therapy," which they published in 1986 (Greenberg & Johnson, 1986). The primary current source is Johnson's (2004) work, *The Practice of Emotionally Focused Couple Therapy*, now in its second edition.

EFT is based on two main theoretical streams. The first is the more psychodynamically oriented field of attachment theory, as developed by John Bowlby and Mary Ainsworth (Ainsworth, Blehar, Waters, & Wall, 1978; Bowlby, 1969, 1973, 1979, 1980). While the original research in attachment theory was done with very young children, EFT applies these findings to adult intimate relationships. The second stream comes from family systems theory.

EFT consists of nine steps grouped into three phases that mark the process of therapy. *De-escalation* involves the establishment of the therapeutic alliance, and the validation of each partner's experience in the relational pattern. *Engagement* is the next phase, where the two partners begin to describe their experience to each other and to express feelings to each other that would have been too risky to reveal before. *Consolidation* is the final phase, in which the partners are coached further in their newfound ways of interacting, until these patterns firmly replace the earlier conflicted patterns (Johnson, 2004).

The overarching goal of EFT is the establishment of a secure attachment between the couple to replace the conflicted or distant attachment with which they had presented. As such, EFT works at both the intrapsychic and the interpersonal levels of human experience. As each partner becomes more aware of his or her experience in the interaction—the plethora of emotions and thoughts, feelings and interpretations that happen in an exchange—each partner is also more able to become aware of his or her role in the interpersonal pattern, and discover personal agency in changing that role in the pattern in order to move toward a more satisfying experience of attachment, belonging, and mattering (Crabb, 1986). Bowen describes similar ideas in his description of drives for togetherness and separateness. A well-differentiated person would be one who is able from the experience of a "secure base" to explore the world around her (Bowen, 1985). Bowlby (1979) describes "a strong causal relationship between an individual's experiences with his parents and his later capacity to make affectional bonds, and . . . certain common variations in that capacity, manifesting themselves in marital problems and trouble with children . . . can be attributed to certain common variations in the ways that parents perform their roles" (p. 135).

There are two special situations to which EFT has been applied in which it is more difficult to establish this secure attachment. One of these is where one or both partners have a significant trauma story that they have brought into the marriage or which they have experienced after marriage. Johnson and Keeler-Williams (1998) describe the use of EFT with such couples, demonstrating how trauma-laden emotional responses can be "reprocessed" in the presence of the partner, who can then become a source of comfort.

The other special situation is where there has been an attachment injury, in which one partner has done, or failed to do, something that is seen by the other as an act of betrayal or disloyalty to the relationship. Johnson, Makinen, and Millikin (2001) define an attachment injury as a betrayal in the relationship, such as an abandonment or violation of trust, and demonstrate how the injuring partner can be guided to take a nondefensive stance in order to provide the injured partner with the experience of being heard and comforted, and to offer forgiveness as appropriate.

Characteristics of First Nations Persons That Affect Couple Relationships

Both of these situations—trauma and attachment injury—often pertain to work with First Nations clientele. I want to share here some impressions from my experience over a dozen years of clinical experience as a mental health care provider approved by the First Nations and Inuit Health Branch (FNIHB) of the Department of Health of the Government of Canada. The FNIHB provides "to registered Indians and recognized Inuit, a limited range of medically necessary health-related goods and services which supplement benefits provided through private insurance plans, provincial/territorial health and social programs." The noninsured health benefits include

Mental Crisis Counseling (short-term mental health crisis intervention; www.hc-sc.gc.ca/fnih-spni/nihb-ssna/index_e.html). The FNIHB maintains a list of approved counselors and therapists from a variety of professional backgrounds whom First Nations clients can access, and whose services are then paid for by the FNIHB.

It is a well-documented fact that many First Nations persons have suffered from trauma (Grant, 1996; Miller, 1997; Milloy, 1999). In Canada, there was a century-long policy of removing First Nations children from their parents and homes and placing them in residential schools, where they were required to learn English and to leave behind their native languages and customs in order to be assimilated into Canadian European society. In 1931, there were some 76 such schools in existence in Canada, 14 of which were located throughout Saskatchewan (Milloy, 1999, p. 307). In addition to these inhumanities, the children were often abused physically and sometimes sexually in these schools (Grant, 1996). This left these children with their histories of traumas, and they were often unable to return to their families. Parenting skills were not modeled and passed on to these children and, as they grew up, they often reproduced the abuse with their own children (Milloy, 1999, p. 299). In my own counseling practice, I have not had a single client from the First Nations people who did not have a story of childhood physical and/or sexual abuse.

In addition to the experiences of trauma, as these children grew they also failed to learn by observation about healthy male–female adult relationships. As a result, first pregnancies in the mid-teens are common for women, many men and women have multiple partners in their early adult years, and when couples come for help with a significant relationship at a time when they are reaching their middle years, they come with extended family and stepfamily complications that include histories of trauma and attachment injuries. One teenage woman described her first pregnancy at age 15 as "getting on with my adult life." Another man in his mid-20s had fathered several children by different women.

Narratives of EFT in First Nations Couples: Trauma and Injury

There is a general understanding that EFT is not indicated in cases of violence. Johnson (2004) states that ongoing abuse or violence in a relationship is a contraindication for EFT. This is particularly true where expressions of vulnerability are likely to place the abused partner at more risk. However, this needs to be tempered by an understanding of different kinds and degrees of abuse. This is particularly so with some First Nations couples where there has often been a history of physical violence. While it would be easy to assert no EFT with couples in which there is violence, there is often a strong ongoing desire on the part of the couple to get beyond the violence and bring the relationship to a happier state. Simpson, Doss, Wheeler, and Christensen (2007) have distinguished between "common couple violence" and "intimate terrorism." *Common couple violence* includes pushing, shoving, and slapping that results from frustration and poor problem-solving skills, whereas *patriarchal terrorism* is more consistent with what we usually call battering, characterized by the systematic efforts of one partner to control the other.

My approach has generally been to assess the level of violence, to ascertain whether it qualifies as more or less severe, by hearing the stories that each partner tells about the abusive incident. The ability for each partner to hear the other's story of the abuse, and the stories about how the couple came through the violent interaction in order to come together to therapy, can be an indication that the ideas of EFT may be useful in working with the couple. See the end of the chapter for a list of questions that I use in assessing whether the violence is common or of the patriarchal variety. While there are good reasons for this violence to be termed "patriarchal," it is important to be aware that the female partner may be as, or more, violence-prone than her partner. I always spend some time individually with each partner in order to further assess the extent and danger of the violence. As much as possible, I seek to respect the couple's preference to attend together.

A further consideration with First Nations couples, indeed with all cross-cultural work, is the issue of attachment itself, and the question of whether attachment is a culturally conditioned phenomenon. If it is culturally conditioned, it could be seen as purely a Western, European phenomenon with no relevance for other cultures and EFT would not be useful outside the culture in which it was developed. Johnson (2004), however, maintains that "attachment is an innate motivating force . . . an innate part of being human, and that this perspective can claim considerable cross-cultural validity" (p. 25). Emotionally focused therapists describe our emotional responses as being "hardwired"—that is, that they have a correlate in human biology, and are not simply the product of human culture. The meaning of emotional experience is of course culturally shaped, but emotional experience is part of the human experience. The ideal attachments are "secure," and these secure attachments provide a secure base from which to explore our world.

There is an emerging body of literature that is investigating the universality of emotionality and the cultural contexts in which it is developed and expressed (Brody, 1999; Oatley, Keltner, & Jenkins, 2006). Our secure base forms early in life due to our attachment with our primary caregivers; thus, the form that family life takes in any given culture affects the shape and form of this secure base. Castellano (2002) describes some of the unique qualities of First Nations family life:

> The aboriginal family in traditional, land-based societies was, until very recently, the principal institution mediating participation of individuals in social, economic and political life. The extended family distributed responsibilities for care and nurture of its members over a large network of grandparents, aunts, uncles and cousins. Clan systems extended the networks of mutual obligation even further. Families were the units which exercised economic rights to territory and resources. In village, nation and sometimes confederacy families were represented in councils charge with collective decision-making. (p. 16)

This statement raises the question for the practice of EFT of where in this extended family the "secure base" might be found. In a more individualistic culture such as North American culture of European extraction, the secure base for the young child is the primary caregiver, usually the mother. For adults, that secure base is normally expected to become the couple relationship. Johnson (2004) states that "there can be more than one attachment figure, but for both child and adult there is usually one key primary person who represents a safe haven and secure base" (p. 33). I would suggest that Castellano (2002) poses a counterpoint to this "key person" notion in that her description posits a broader secure base. In other words, while there may be a universal attachment need, and while it may be that we are biologically formed to attach, who we attach to and how we attach are shaped by the cultural context in which attachment is taking place. I would suggest, then, that in the traditional Aboriginal culture the couple relationship may occupy a different role than it does in North American/European culture. For adults, the couple as the nucleus in the nuclear family is replaced in Aboriginal families by a molecular family where the attachment is not just to one other person but to the family as a whole. Derrick (2005) corroborates this view in her description of the "metasystem" in Native cultures as being based on the "circle system," which she describes as a "spiritually centered, child-focused system with a holistic worldview of love and respect and forgiveness for all living things" (p. 56). Indeed, Ainsworth et al. (1978) allow room for this possibility:

> We need to take advantage of cross-cultural studies and "experiments of opportunity" within our own culture in order to investigate how different patterns of infant care affect the attachments of the infant to those involved in a caregiving role, and how variations on the theme of principle caregiver with supplementary and secondary figures show support and reinforcement for each other, compensatory function, or conflict; and we need to show how at least the more common of the many possible variations affect the development of the child. (p. 308)

This more communally shared responsibility for the care of children translates also into where adults might find their secure base. This conjecture of a broader secure base of course will require further research.

While this broader secure base may be true generally, it is important to remember that each couple comes with their own expectations of what couple relationships or marriage should be like. Thus, some Aboriginal couples might expect that their marriages should have the same characteristics as those of their White neighbors. Others will be satisfied to be couples within the context of the band or reserve. Others will find themselves moving from one preference to another: One couple may move toward an appreciation and understanding of more native ways of being a couple, and the other may move in the other direction. This brings to awareness the ever-present possibility that one partner in a relationship might be moving in one direction while the other moves in another.

It is not the therapist's role to prescribe one way of being a couple as opposed to another. It would be a significant temptation for North American/European therapists to bring the expectations and values of a couple-based, individualistic viewpoint to their work with Aboriginal couples. We are not in a position to claim that one way of being a couple is superior to another. For this reason, it is important to add to the practices of EFT another set of practices in working with First Nations couples. These are the practices of narrative therapy.

Narrative Therapy

Narrative therapy is an approach to the work of therapy that pays particular attention to the ways in which persons and cultures construct their worlds. Freedman and Combs (1996) have very succinctly summarized this as follows:

1. Realities are socially constructed.

2. Realities are constituted through language.

3. Realities are organized and maintained through narrative.

Freedman and Combs (1996) actually have a fourth statement, "There are no essential truths" (p. 22), but this statement is formally different than the first three and beyond the scope of this chapter. Michael White (2002) has described this postmodern understanding of the social construction of reality with language through narrative as rather a return to a premodern-era, more experience-near, folk-psychology approach to understanding and working with people. A key notion here is that we understand ourselves through the stories that we tell about ourselves. These stories are our realities, based as they are on our reflections on our experiences in the contexts of our families, communities, and cultures.

Aldred (2002) has described the particular appropriateness of the narrative approach to work with Aboriginal people. Aldred, an Aboriginal and a Christian theologian, describes the failure of both fundamentalist and liberal Christians to relate effectively to Aboriginal peoples because of their individualistic biases. Fundamentalists see truth in propositional statements, and liberals see truth in personal experience. By way of contrast to both of these, he describes an "ethic of storytelling" that still exists in Aboriginal culture. The storyteller, he states, does not just speak for herself or himself, but tells the story as a representative of the community. The storyteller is not simply an autonomous individual, but rather a "representative of something bigger than themselves." The storyteller, further, has entered into an *understanding*. The storyteller does not know something in the sense of having discovered it. Rather, the storyteller has entered into a wisdom that "flowed from the 'Creator' and they were merely entering into a 'river of understanding'" (p. 8). Third, the storyteller's identity includes not only the present community but also those who have come before.

Thus, the essence of narrative therapy is the careful hearing of stories. The therapist's role is that of an audience—an audience whose first task is to enter into and be moved by the story. The several practices that narrative therapists use in their role as audiences include the practices of *externalization*, the discovery of alternative stories, sometimes called *unique outcomes* and *reauthoring*, the practice of "thickening" these alternative stories through richer descriptions, and further retellings in other contexts (Freedman & Combs, 1996; White & Epston, 1990).

These three practices roughly coincide with the three phases of EFT described above. Externalization is the process of describing the problematic interaction cycle with a view to understanding its devices, strategies, and wiles. This results in a deescalation of the conflict. The discovery of unique outcomes corresponds to the reengagement phase, as the partners each discover new stories in their story that counter and disempower the problem story. Reauthoring corresponds to the process of consolidation, where the new preferred story becomes the accepted true story of the couple's relationship.

Reauthoring Through Questions

The key intervention a "narratively oriented" Emotionally Focused Therapist uses is the question. The construction of effective questions is the subject of a number of authors. Brown (1997) has devised the question cube, which helps therapists to think about the form (e.g., open or closed), subject (behaviors, feelings, etc.), and orientation (self or other) of the question being asked. Tomm (1988) describes four styles of questions depending on the intention of the therapist (orienting himself or influencing the client) and on the assumptions of the therapist (lineal assumptions or circular assumptions). Tomm recognizes that every question is influencing. He also describes some kinds of questions as more invasive than others. In particular, he refers to questions that are intended to be influencing and that have an assumption of circular causality as the most generative of client reflection, and the least invasive on the part of the therapist.

A number of authors have also noted that questions are inherently invasive (Freedman & Combs, 1996; McGee, Del Vento, & Bavelas, 2005; Rober, 2005). The inherent power imbalance that exists between client and therapist is exacerbated when further inequalities are part of the therapeutic relationship. Such a power imbalance potentially exists when an Aboriginal couple, both partners of which are members of a minority group, comes to see a White therapist, a member of the dominant culture. The additional danger is the inherent blindness to the effects of the exercise of power due to one's privileged position in the culture. Cooper (2007) describes the investigation by Madonna Constantine on racist remarks made by therapists. The study concludes that therapists are insufficiently aware of their own perks or others' disadvantages, and recommends that "clinicians acknowledge racial differences early in therapy with minority clients, so that these clients will know that it is safe to talk about them in therapy" (p. 15).

These cautions make it particularly important for therapists to recognize the invasive quality of their questions and to take steps to ameliorate those effects. In addition to raising the subject of cultural differences early in the therapy, narrative practices also indicate the importance of situating one's questions so that the therapist's intentions and assumptions in asking a question are clear to the clients. This is often referred to as *transparency*, because the process of therapy and the assumptions of the therapists are often quite opaque to our clients. Freedman and Combs (1996) make this remarkable comment about transparency:

> When we say "situating ourselves" we refer to the practice of clearly and publicly identifying those aspects of our own experience, imagination and intentions . . . that we believe guide our work. In so doing, we enter therapeutic relationships as fallible human beings, rather than as experts. We present ourselves as particular people who have been shaped and affected by particular experiences. We hope that this gives people an idea of how they might want to take what we say and do. (p. 275)

I believe that a willingness to open the question of cultural differences with Aboriginal clients, and the practices of transparency, can be tremendously helpful in establishing a therapeutic alliance, and in leveling the ground shared by therapist and clients.

CASE EXAMPLES

We turn now to a brief consideration of three stories of client couples with whom I have had the privilege of working. Each of these is a composite; the names are fictitious, and I have gained verbal agreement to share their stories.

Ray and Susan

Ray and Susan are a married Aboriginal couple of middle-aged years, belonging to different but neighboring reserves. They had been married for approximately five years. Both had previous relationships that had produced children. At the time of therapy, the household consisted of two of Ray's sons and Susan's only daughter. Both have other children who are living elsewhere, either with previous partners or with extended family members.

Ray and Susan came for therapy because of daily conflict, primarily over Susan's failure to teach her daughter to show proper respect around the house, and especially to Ray. The conflict had turned violent to the point where, on one occasion, the authorities were called. While both were members of neighboring reserves, they lived in Ray's house located on Ray's reserve. They also had religious differences. Susan had been raised in a Christian home and sought to continue practicing her Christian faith. Ray, on the other hand, was interested in traditional spirituality and sought to practice it. This, however, did not seem to be as great a problem for them as the stepparent issues. Both also had stories of previous alcohol and substance abuse, having been sober for a number of years prior to coming for therapy. Further, both had stories of childhood abuse, as the parents of both had been students in residential schools.

My practice is to spend some time at the outset of therapy with each partner individually. It was during this time that I broached the subject of cultural differences. Ray engaged in an interesting conversation about his perceptions of a number of the problems and challenges facing First Nations in Canada, and expressed appreciation that I would be interested in these things. From Susan, I learned of her Christian faith and its importance, and her relative lack of interest in Native spirituality and traditions. I wondered to myself how this might become a subject of further conversations.

The early sessions of therapy, after the relationship had been established, centered on describing the conflict patterns, alternating with stories of childhood abuse and previous relationship stories. The conversational pattern was a reviewing of the events of the interactional pattern alternating with explanatory narratives of abuse or previous relational injuries or disappointments. After several sessions, relative peace was established and the couple discontinued therapy for several months. They returned after a particularly violent episode, which had resulted in a one-month separation. In the aftermath of the violent episode, both had called the police, so there were also charges pending.

I was interested in several things. First, I was curious as to their intentions for the relationship now. They were quite openly ambivalent, as is often the case with conflicted couples. I was also curious as to how the couple had reinitiated contact, whose initiative it had been, and what the intentions were. In other words, I was curious as to what unique outcomes might be lurking in the fact that, in spite of the intense conflict, they were now back in my office. Through a series of questions from me, Ray was enabled to ask Susan what she wanted. Susan had been empowered enough to say that she wanted to come home. This final exchange was conducted by Susan and Ray, with virtually no intervention from me.

This story illustrates the use of narrative practices, particularly the asking of reflexive questions in the application of the ideas of EFT, and the seeking of unique outcomes, as well as the attunement of the therapist to the cultural divide between therapists and clients. It also raises the issue of responding to this couple as a therapist who shared the Christian point of view of one of the partners. I believe that my inherent curiosity about Native spirituality in the conversations helped avoid the impression of taking sides, and hopefully also modeled curiosity about spirituality for both partners.

Mike and Michelle

The second story is about Mike and Michelle, a couple living "common law" with two of Michelle's children. Mike did not have any children. Michelle had two other children who at the time of therapy were in foster care due to Michelle's use of drugs that had interfered with her parenting at an earlier stage in her life. Each partner worked outside the home and both described themselves as hard workers. The couple has been together for about a year. They presented stories of intense conflict, but the conflict was expressed verbally, with no physical violence. The conflict episodes usually ended with Michelle ordering Mike out of the house, an order with which he complied for a couple of days and before returning. This return was followed by reconciliation, and the peace would last until the next episode. The episodes were usually sparked by a suspicion Mike had that Michelle was being unfaithful to him. He pointed to evidence such as clues left around the house—for example, an empty beer bottle the presence of which had no explanation. Michelle would respond with intense anger to these questions. In my office, she stated, "I can't take this any more."

In my individual session with Michelle, she was not willing to talk at any length about her Aboriginal background. She was more interested in telling me about her work. She held down two jobs, she informed me, and was in demand from other potential employers. I wondered to myself whether it was important to her that I know this because of the White cultural discourse about the First Nations work ethic. I learned from Mike, but not from Michelle, about her abusive background, including a period earlier in her life during which she had been led into prostitution by one of her caregivers, when she was around the age of puberty. It was shortly after Mike had shared this with me that Michelle dropped out of attending therapy with Mike. I have wondered, but have not had the opportunity to ask, whether Michelle was aware of what Mike had shared with me and wasn't ready to talk with me knowing that I had this information about her.

However, Mike continued to come. He also had a background of abuse. During one of the conjoint sessions, I was able to ask Mike about this. He shared some difficult stories of beatings at the hands of a violent mother. Our continued conversations had to do with the current state of the relationship with Michelle, and Mike's concern over his career. As I continued to ask reflexive questions, Mike continued to reflect on his role in the relationship with Michelle.

This story illustrates the use of the integrated practices of narrative therapy and EFT, with special attention to the need to attend to prior stories of abuse. In the case of this couple, I expect that I was not able to establish a strong enough therapeutic alliance with the woman so that she could overcome the feelings of shame that she may have experienced as more details of her story came forth, particularly if they were also shared by her partner before she was ready for them to be known.

This story may also illustrate how third-party payers may affect therapy. The funder described above, FNIHB, approves a maximum of six sessions at a time. It is possible to apply for another set of six. However, the inherent message is that solutions to marital issues should be found by the conclusion of six sessions. If this does not happen, the client may infer that therapy has failed, with the attendant belief that the client must be a failure even in this.

Joe and Jill

The third story is about Joe and Jill, a cross-cultural cohabiting couple. Joe came to see me by himself at first, wanting to "fix" himself before bringing his partner to join him in therapy. During the first four sessions, I learned of the children he had from two previous relationships, and of some of his family background.

At the fourth meeting, he brought his partner Jill. Joe is Aboriginal, and Jill is Euro–North American. The couple presented with a typical pursue/withdraw pattern in which Jill quite intensely pursued Joe, wanting a commitment to marriage and to a lifetime together. Joe, on the other hand, withdrew, wanting to preserve "my own space" and not be smothered in the relationship. In addition, shortly after they began the relationship, Joe had become involved briefly in a sexual relationship with another woman who Jill knew, a relationship that he took the initiative to disclose to Jill.

A crisis developed in this relationship when Jill became pregnant. Jill was immediately excited, and Joe was initially dismayed. However, as time went on, he began to look forward to the baby's arrival. Unfortunately, Jill miscarried early in the pregnancy. Joe was very attentive for the first day but after that withdrew again—a further injury as Jill saw it. A second crisis involved an episode with Joe when he had a very mild heart attack and was briefly hospitalized. Jill was equally attentive, but when Joe was released from the hospital, he announced that he needed to move back to another city several hours away so that he could be nearer to his family. Jill was devastated by this announcement.

I wondered to myself—and raised this question—whether this decision illustrated a cultural difference, particularly about where one's primary attachment needs are met, and where one finds a secure base. They both recognized the possibility that Jill would seek her secure base in the one relationship while Joe would seek his in his more extended family network, in which he was more than willing to include Jill. Through these questions, Jill was also able to take a broader viewpoint about what the possibilities for the relationship were with Joe. This story illustrates the use of awareness of cultural differences in guiding the conversation.

Final Reflections

All three of these stories invited my reflection on my status in the relationship with these couples. I am a White male, in all cases a generation or two older than the clients described here. Each of these characteristics bestows on me power and privilege to which is easy for me to be blind. I recall the humbling experience of asking an Aboriginal woman student what it was like for her to hear me ask a particular question. Her reply was that her first thought was that I was an elder, and thus my words carried weight.

Second, as a male, I needed to be particularly attentive to the power I had with respect to the women members of each couple. The fairly high likelihood that each might have had unwelcome attention from other White men had the potential of interfering with the establishment of a therapeutic relationship with these clients that required careful attention to acceptance and a willingness to learn about the lives of these women through the attention to the language they were using and stories they were telling.

Third, as a White male of European background, I stood in danger of recapitulating some aspect of the colonial experience. This was particularly important in the case of those First Nations persons who were interested in reclaiming and benefiting from Native cultural and spiritual resources. I believe that my practice of engaging in a conversation of curiosity about the importance of this, and about the paths that led to these preferences, created the common ground for further therapeutic conversations.

Conclusion

I have found the ideas of EFT in understanding and working with couples to be effective, particularly as the style of questioning and interacting that narrative therapy gives us is used in the conversation. Further, the correspondence between the three main practices of narrative therapy and the phases of EFT is a happy one. Essentially, the correspondence is one in which the ideas of EFT guide the therapist in what he or she needs to be thinking and asking about, while the practices of narrative therapy guide the therapist in how to do the asking. Because narrative therapy attunes so carefully to the language of the clients, and attends to the stories that clients bring, it is particularly appropriate for clients from First Nations communities where there is a growing value placed upon oral traditions.

Exercises and Reflections

1. Review your knowledge of the Aboriginal histories of your community. Are you aware of significant dates, people, and places of events, particularly of the area in which you live?

2. Reflect on recent news items having to do with Aboriginal issues. Can you recall what your initial reaction was—of curiosity, of pain, of celebration? Were you aware of any stereotypical thoughts that may have influenced your immediate reactions?

3. Review a recent conversation or encounter that you may have had with an Aboriginal person. Were you more likely to want to ask something about their lives, or to tell them something that you thought might be helpful to them?

Questions for Assessing Characteristics of Violence

1. What happened? This is a request for the details of the violent incident. I look for the following:
   a. The sequence of events.
   b. The affect each partner displays in the description. In particular, does one partner seem intimidated by the other?
   c. The level of minimization or denial either partner might be displaying. Is there denial or minimization of the fact, memory, responsibility, or impact of the event?
   d. The amount of actual physical force that was used.
   e. Whether there was physical injury.

2. How often does this kind of thing happen? The more often, the greater is the possibility that it is patriarchal.

3. How did it end? The fact that the couple is now sitting with me indicates that there must have been further conversation.
   a. Whose initiative was it to come to see me?
   b. What resources for conversation and conflict resolution might this couple possess that made it possible for them to come together to see a therapist?

Web Site

First Nations and Inuit Health Branch: www.hc-sc.gc.ca/fnih-spni/nihb-ssna/index_e.html

References

Ainsworth, M. D. S., Blehar, M. C., Waters, E., & Wall, S. (1978). *Patterns of attachment: A study of the Strange Situation*. Hillsdale, NJ: Lawrence Erlbaum.

Aldred, R. (2002). *The resurrection of story*. Paper presented at Briercrest College and Seminary, Caronport, Saskatchewan, Canada.

Bowen, M. (1985). *Family therapy in clinical practice*. Oxford, UK: Rowman and Littlefield.

Bowlby, J. (1969). *Attachment and loss: Vol. 1. Attachment*. New York: Basic Books.

Bowlby, J. (1973). *Attachment and loss: Vol. 2. Separation*. New York: Basic Books.

Bowlby, J. (1979). *The making and breaking of affectional bonds*. London: Tavistock.

Bowlby, J. (1980). *Attachment and loss: Vol. 1. Loss*. New York: Basic Books.

Brody, L. (1999). *Gender, emotion, and the family*. Cambridge, MA: Harvard University Press.

Brown, J. E. (1997). The question cube: A model for developing question repertoire in training couple and family therapists. *Journal of Marital and Family Therapy, 23*, 1, 27–40.

Castellano, M. B. (2002). Aboriginal family trends: Extended families, nuclear families, families of the heart. In *Contemporary family trends*. Ottawa, Canada: Vanier Institute of the Family.

Cooper, G. (2007, May/June). Clinician's digest: Do therapists make racist remarks? *Psychotherapy Networker.*

Crabb, L. J. (1987). *Understanding people.* Grand Rapids, MI: Zondervan.

Derrick, J. M. (2005). When turtle met rabbit: Native family systems. In M. Rastogi & E. Wieling (Eds.), *Voices of color: First person accounts of ethnic minority therapists* (pp. 43–63). Thousand Oaks, CA: Sage.

Freedman, J., & Combs, G. (1996). *Narrative therapy: The social construction of preferred realities.* New York: W. W. Norton.

Grant, A. (1996). *No end of grief: Indian residential schools in Canada.* Winnipeg, Canada: Pemican.

Greenberg, L. S., & Johnson, S. M. (1986). Emotionally focused couple therapy. In N. S. Jacobson & A. S. Gurman (Eds.), *Clinical handbook of marital therapy* (pp. 253–276). New York: Guilford Press.

Johnson, S. M. (2004). *The practice of emotionally focused couple therapy* (2nd ed.). New York: Brunner-Routledge.

Johnson, S. M., Makinen, J. A., & Millikin, J. W. (2001). Attachment injuries in couple relationships: A new perspective on impasses in couple therapy. *Journal of Marital and Family Therapy, 27*(2), 145–156.

Johnson, S.M., & Williams-Keeler, L. (1998). Creating healing relationships for couples dealing with trauma: The use of emotionally focused marital therapy. *Journal of Marital and Family Therapy, 24*(1), 25–40.

McGee, D., Del Vento, A., & Bavelas, J. B. (2005). An interactional model of questions as therapeutic interventions. *Journal of Marital and Family Therapy, 31*(4), 371–384.

Miller, J. R. (1997). *Shingwauk's vision: A history of Native residential schools.* Toronto, Canada: University of Toronto Press.

Milloy, J. S. (1999). *"A national crime": The Canadian government and the residential school system, 1879 to 1986.* Winnipeg, Canada: University of Manitoba Press.

Morgan, A. (2002). *What is narrative therapy? An easy-to-read introduction.* Adelaide, Australia: Dulwich Centre Publications.

Oatley, K., Keltner, D., & Jenkins, J. M. (2006). *Understanding emotions* (2nd ed.). Malden, MA: Blackwell.

Rober, P. (2005). Family therapy as a dialogue of living persons: A perspective inspired by Bakhtin, Volosinov & Shotter. *Journal of Marital and Family Therapy, 31*(4), 385–397.

Simpson, L. E., Doss, B. D., Wheeler, J., & Christensen, A. (2007). Relationship violence among couples seeking therapy: Common couple violence or battering? *Journal of Marital and Family Therapy, 33*(2), 270–283.

Tomm, K. (1987a). Interventive interviewing: Part I. Strategizing as a fourth guideline for the therapist. *Family Process, 26,* 3–13.

Tomm, K. (1987b). Interventive interviewing: Part II. Reflexive questioning as a means to enable self-healing. *Family Process, 26,* 167–183.

Tomm, K. (1988). Interventive interviewing: Part III. Intending to ask lineal, circular, strategic, or reflexive questions. *Family Process, 27,* 1, 1–15.

White, M. (2002). *Workshop notes.* Winnipeg, Canada.

White, M., & Epston, D. (1990). *Narrative means to therapeutic ends.* New York: W. W. Norton.

Nineteen

Native Couple Therapy

Connecting, Rebuilding, and Growing Beyond

Jann M. Derrick

S he:kon skennenkowa: Hello and welcome to these words and to their understanding.

I am of Mohawk ancestry. I am the mother of three children and the grandmother of six children. These are my primary roles: Mother and Grandmother.

I am also a learner and a teacher—this is my life focus, my life perspective, and my life's walk. As a learner and a teacher, I have become a member of the Canadian Psychological Association, and a registered marriage and family therapist. I have sat with many Old Ones. I have experienced many teachings, some hard, some soft. All have left their mark on me.

Although my traditional territory is in the East, I live and work in the West where my Grandfather settled when he decided to leave home.

I specialize in working with Native Historical Trauma and recovery from Residential School Trauma. This chapter will focus on couple therapy and include the clinical concepts of Native Historical Trauma, Residential School Trauma, strong deep traditions of cultural circle teachings, and the cultural perspective of regaining our balance—rather than being dysfunctional—to once again become who we truly are (Hart, 2007). It will also provide a culturally appropriate systemic clinical model (Derrick, 1993).

The terms for *Native* vary in Canada and the United States, and currently are in flux, with some being considered more politically correct than others. This chapter will interchangeably use the terms *Native, First Nations*, and *Aboriginal* to refer to any person of Native ancestry. The couples represent several different Native cultures, all of whom reside in western Canada. They are between the ages of 25 and 65. A small percentage of these couples are "two-spirited" (a cultural description implying gay or lesbian). The couples are both urban and rural. Some are legally married; most are "common law" relationships.

Recent Research and Literature

Native/First Nations couple therapy research is small in size and limited in scope. As stated by Turner, Wieling, and Allen (2004), "The socially constructed and politically situated concepts of race, culture and ethnicity have been seriously underaddressed in the clinical and scientific literature" (p. 257). It is only in recent years that family therapy and other social service professions have begun to address the need to understand cultural family differences and to understand that all families cannot be viewed through the European lens and Western middle-class norms (McGoldrick, Giordano, & Garcia-Preto, 2005; Rastogi & Wieling, 2005).

In addition, it is only since the late 1960s that Native/First Nations people have strongly shared their colonizing experience by Europeans during the last 500 years (Gordon-McCutchan, 1991; Moses & Goldie, 1998; Royal Commission on Aboriginal Peoples, 1996).

Cross-cultural literature has focused on creating culturally competent therapists. Generally, this literature presumes the position of the Western/European as the norm position, and reaches from this platform to understand the difference between this norm and the cultures of people of color (Gray, Coates, & Hetherington, 2007; Hays, 1996; Ho et al., 2003). However, Laird (1998) proposes that, rather than focus on cultural differences, the focus shift to understanding our own culture "so as to make us more sensitive to other's cultures" (p. 58). This allows a shift to a "lack of competence" focus with the client as the expert and the clinician in a position of seeking knowledge.

Current Focus of the Literature

Research on Native families is dominated by a focus on alcohol and substance use, violence, suicide, and poverty (Brown & Languedoc, 2004; Dion, Gotowiec, & Beiser, 1998; Jacobs & Gill, 2002; Sack, Beiser, Baker-Brown, & Redshirt, 1994; Trepper, McCollum, Dankoski, Davis, & LaFazia, 2000). Often, Native/First Nations populations are included with other populations of color, all of whom share common factors (O'Farrell & Fals-Stewart, 2006). Not so readily noted in the research are the social and underlying patterns of domination and oppression these populations also share (Hart, 2002). Writing in the social work literature, Hart states it is essential to note history and the impact of "colonization, oppression, and social work's role in these destructive processes" (p. 23).

Outside the research literature is the growing body of writing by Native authors in Canada and the United States. This literature powerfully describes personal, family, community, and cultural experiences. Wagamese (2002) writes, "The lives of Native people in Canada are ones of endless toil, frustration and heartache. This they have borne with great good humour, grace, and dignity. To say that I am one of them is my greatest pride" (introductory page). The authors document the Native worldview and contrast it with the Western worldview. They describe the personal and collective process of reclaiming what has been lost through colonization (Armstrong, 1998; Brant, 1997; Chrisjohn & Young, 1997; Wiebe & Johnson, 1998).

Native academics describe Indigenous knowledge and the importance of research using its holistic perspectives (Hart, 2007). A quote from the Royal Commission on Aboriginal Peoples (1996) goes further: "It is powerful for Aboriginal people to realize that one of their traditional approaches to health (the Medicine Wheel) is now viewed as progressive and crucial by health care educators and policy planners within the United Nations and in Canada" (p. 5).

Native organizations often publish their own manuals and literature for use by service providers and clients. This literature reflects cultural and traditional perspectives, and Native healing and rebalancing approaches. The Family and Child Clinic in the Native American Health Center in San Francisco has published two books, and the Aboriginal Healing Foundation in Ottawa has published research books on topics related to Native issues, Residential School Trauma, and healing.

Genocide and Trauma

What is seldom described in the literature is the underlying relationship between Europeans and Native peoples (Tafoya & Del Vecchio, 2005). It is vital to the therapeutic relationship that both therapist and clients are aware of this genocidal relationship and the level of trauma it has created in Native Peoples, especially if the therapist is of Western/European ancestry. It is also essential for an understanding of the couple relationship and trauma-based behaviors in Native couples. The United Nations Genocide Convention (1946) defines genocide as follows:

1. Killing members of the group

2. Causing serious bodily and mental harm to members of the group

3. Deliberately inflicting on the group conditions of life calculated to bring about its physical destruction in whole or in part

4. Imposing measures intended to prevent births within the group

5. Forcibly transferring children of the group to another group (Chrisjohn & Young, 1997)

Readers should note that all of the above listed forms that constitute genocide have been experienced by Native peoples in Canada and the United States.

It is important for the therapist to know whether either partner in the couple or their family members attended a residential school. The Royal Commission on Aboriginal Peoples (1996) states that the residential schools were "aimed at severing the artery of culture that ran between generations and was the profound connection between parent and child sustaining family and community . . . This was more than a rhetorical flourish as it took on a traumatic reality in the life of each child separated from parents and community and isolated in a world hostile to identity, traditional belief and language" (Vol. 1, Ch. 10, p. 1). The children were forced to attend by law, and were abused physically, emotionally, mentally, and often sexually with no recourse available to them from family or community leaders (Royal Commission on Aboriginal Peoples, 1996).

The resulting traumas from an often horrendous childhood have become multigenerational, and include unresolved loss and grief, a shattered family system, depression, anger and violence, generalized anxiety, panic attacks, somatic disturbances with constant ill-health, reactive attachment, suicide, loneliness, sexual dysfunction, low self-esteem, catastrophic thinking, a belief that death is imminent, and challenges with parenting (Morrisette, 1994; Sutton & Broken Nose, 2005; Tafoya & Del Vecchio, 2005). It is these multigenerational, intergenerational traumas that are collectively referred to as Native Historical Trauma (Brave Heart & De Bruyn, 1998).

Systemic Differences

It is important to emphasize the systemic difference between Native cultures and European/Western cultures. Native cultures are based in a system generally referred to as "the circle," which embraces a holistic worldview (Derrick, 1993). The circle is 180 degrees opposite to the Western/European "box" system. The circle's central features are spirituality, a focus on children, and the relationship between families and their community (Derrick, 2005). It is described below in greater detail.

Recent Native professional literature emphasizes the brilliance of the cultures in science, art, general knowledge, and relationships. This literature both reflects and generates further energy in the reclamation of what has been lost, and a personal process of rebalancing (Dufrene, 1990; Helin, 2006; Mehl-Madrona, 1997; Poonwassie & Charter, 2001; Smith, 2005). McCormick (2005) writes, "Early on in my career [as an Aboriginal psychologist] I made the decision to focus on the tremendous strengths of Aboriginal peoples and their many rich cultures in an effort to balance the body of research that attempted to pathologize and disempower Aboriginal peoples. Aboriginal psychology and healing are considerably older and consequently more complex than Euro-Western therapies" (p. 293). Native couples seeking therapy will usually reflect this growing desire to rebalance, and to rebalance together. Both Krech (2002) and Graham (2002) discuss creating a healthy future for Native people, and finding reasons to reconnect to traditional healing as a means of doing so.

A Clinical Systemic Therapy Model

This systemic clinical model is based on the foundation of the circle as a system—the circle system being the foundation of Native cultures.

The key factors of the circle system are as follows:

1. It is spiritually centered. The belief is that we are spirits first and have come to earth in order to learn and evolve.
2. It is child based. The first circle in the system is the children. All other circles and roles are based on raising the children.
3. It is female led. Most circle cultures are matrilineal, and all honor and respect the women as the givers of life. The men are the cocreators with the women.
4. It processes information by asking "What is true?" The process then takes the following steps: accepting what is true; reflecting on what is true using the four aspects of the circle—the spiritual, emotional, physical, and mental aspects—plus the positive and negative; evaluation; decision making; action.
5. All life forms are accepted as equal in value.
6. Roles bring direction, accountability, and responsibility to all relationships.
7. The primary goal is to become self-aware and self-disciplined, thus allowing each person to live in harmony with all our relations.
8. Relationships are the primary focus. What one person does happens to all. What happens to all happens to one person.
9. The family is the primary building block of the community. All our relatives are our family and our community.

The key factors of the Eurocentric box system are opposite to those of the circle system. Here, the important factors that enter into the clinical process are as follows: The box is financially centered; it is male based and male dominated; it processes information by asking "What is wrong?" The box system then uses negative critical thinking and takes action using judgment, blame, and shame. It defines who we are as what we do, usually in reference to our job: It focuses primarily on the individual.

While these descriptors are mine and based on cultural experience, other authors have observed similar systemic perspectives, including family therapist Virginia Satir (1972), archaeologist Riane Eisler (1998), and psychologist Ann Wilson Schaef (1987).

Systemic Shifts

In the circle, Native couple relationships were a marriage of two families, and often the marriages were arranged. Following contact with the box, and the traumatic events that followed, family relationships were extended to a breaking point. With the forced removal of the children to residential schools, the child base of the cultures imploded, and roles and responsibilities shifted dramatically. Through trauma, the children of the residential school survivors became the "parents of their parents." Those in the third generation following the residential schools, the children of the parentified children, were often fostered and adopted due to their parents' inability to care for three generations: their traumatized parents, their own traumatized selves, and their own biological children. The circle focus of health and walking forward to the next seven generations *reversed,* and the focus instead became the survival of the people in the box. The children were now caring for their parents rather than parents caring for their children; people were lost and relationships broken; and the focus turned to the survivorship of the individual. This, then, is the pivotal point of the clinical work: *working with the couple's relationship from where it currently is in the box and in historical trauma and shifting each relationship issue 180 degrees back to the circle.*

Conducting therapy with a couple with this systemic model allows a multiplicity of tools and paradigms as a clinician. Emotionally focused therapy, cognitive-behavioral therapy, solution-focused, narrative, brief, family, relationship, trauma recovery—all these and more can be used as the couples require them on their path from the box to the circle. It further allows a meta–"working distance" from the heavy emotions and extreme trauma of the genocide, allowing both the clinician and the client to safely move into and out of the depth of the harm. It is large enough for the reclamation of specific Native cultural traditions within the circle system, thus being respectful of the often-private ceremonies and knowledge. The metasystemic view provides such a large perspective that it gives both the client and the clinician a better knowledge of their own cultures, and rises above the "mud" and heaviness of the present Euro/Western and Native relationship. *And the shift is simply choosing to move in the opposite direction from where the client currently sits at whatever level—from a shift in immediate behavior to a shift in relationships over time.* Overall, it gives perspective and room to move clinically, and fits with Native cultures.

It is understood implicitly that the circle that is reemerging in Native relationships and communities does not represent the culture as it once was. Therefore, the couple will be redefining themselves and their relationship as their own unique project. The healing and rebalancing of the relationship will create immediate positive changes in their relationship with their children, and often puts strain on their relationship with their parents. Siblings of the couple may be supportive, reactive, or both. The couple may chose to maintain survivorship roles but create more comfort for themselves, or may choose to work together to create rebalancing for themselves, and thus shift their family system toward the circle.

Common Themes in Native Couple Relationships

Survivorship themes:

- I'm attached with you so I can survive.
- If you'll be my parent, I'll be your kid—just don't abandon me.
- Chaos is comfortable. Let's keep things chaotic.
- One of us is the abuser. The other is the victim. That's the way it is.

Healing/rebalancing themes:

- I want to heal my traumas and be with you as you heal yours.
- We're willing to work on our relationship and be accountable.
- We want our children and both of us to feel safe.
- We want to stop the residential school in this relationship.

CASE EXAMPLES

The following case studies illustrate several of the common themes in Native couple relationships. The therapy makes use of the clinical circle–box model and the awareness of the systemic shifts and traumas of the couples.

Case Study 1

Geri and Dakota are a couple in their mid-30s. She is proud of her Native ancestry, but uncertain from what Nation and culture her family came. Her family moved away from their traditional lands two generations ago and her grandparents purposefully "forgot" their culture and became "White." He is from the local Nation and they live together on reserve. Dakota is third generation from the residential school. He was raised by his grandparents in a "custom fostering" situation while his mother lived a chaotic life. He now wants to be close to his mother but she continues her chaos, is highly manipulative, and steals from him when she is around. He and Geri have had a common-law relationship for 10 years and are raising her children from a previous relationship. Dakota also has two children from a previous relationship whom he sees from time to time at the urging of Geri. Their couple relationship includes continuous use of marijuana, and constant "light" use of alcohol: he is diabetic; she is anxious, has panic attacks, and fears being alone. Their relationship is mellow as long as substances are used moderately. As their use increases or is replaced by work, their relationship immediately becomes verbally abusive. It quickly escalates physically, and neighbors call the police. Dakota is court-mandated to attend a men's violence group and therapy. Geri attends therapy because she wants to learn more about herself. The therapy has evolved to a point where she has decided to leave the relationship physically but maintain the emotional bond with him, with boundaries and limitations on behaviors. The focus of the therapy initially was individual work; it was hampered by the use of substances but moved quickly when Geri began AA. Dakota grieves the loss of his grandparents with his relatives while they drink together. His relationships remain chaotic. Geri hears the circle system teachings and uses them as she can; she uses art therapy to express herself, and has begun to advance herself as an Aboriginal artist. In future therapy, Geri and Dakota are likely to move into the "rebalancing" form of couple work, and seek several additional forms of healing, such as residential alcohol and drug treatment, Residential School Trauma recovery, and ceremonies. It is likely that Geri will want to trace and find her own people and her own culture.

Applying the Circle-Box Systemic Model to This Case

Major goals:

- The child is the center of this family.
- Dakota has refocused his life on inner self-discipline.
- Geri identifies as Native and has reclaimed teachings of her culture.
- Geri and Dakota have a cocreative relationship.

Immediate goals:

- Geri continues in trauma recovery and attaches with her inner child self.
- Dakota achieves sobriety and maintains sobriety.
- Dakota finds Native male resources and a support system.
- Geri and Dakota attend parenting classes with both mainstream teachers and Elders.

Possible interventions:

- Refer and support Dakota in attending a Native alcohol and drug treatment center.
- Support Dakota in becoming part of an Aboriginal men's support group.
- Complex trauma and grief recovery therapy with Dakota.
- Teach circle-based communication to Geri and Dakota. Practice using it together and with their children.
- Coordinate with the Tribal Children's Protection Agency to provide family support to the children and to Geri and Dakota in order to prevent apprehension of the children.
- Support the children's attendance at children's language and culture circles led by Elders.
- Play therapy with the children with either Geri or Dakota present—to encourage deeper understanding of the children, awaken their own "inner child," and increase their parenting skill set.

Case Study 2

Darwin and Evan are a two-spirited couple: Both are women in a man's body (cultural description). Both are strong leaders, politically and artistically. They are jointly raising two children who are relatives. They are comfortable with their relationship, but keep a low profile at home because of the often-derogatory reactions from local community members toward their gender and relationship. However, they are each proud of who they are and of the choices they have made to publicly declare themselves a family. Their children are proud of them and do very well in school. Both Darwin and Evan experience the high stress of meeting home, work, travel, and relationship needs. Each believes in the work he is doing on behalf of First Nations people. Darwin believes in multiple relationships that are very emotionally bonded but nonsexual. Evan believes in an emotionally exclusive partnership and is threatened by the number of close bonds Darwin has. The therapy is focused on resolving Darwin's childhood trauma in foster care and Evan's use of negative critical thinking, judgment, and fear of losing Darwin. The therapy is actively teaching the use of "opposites" in the model of the circle system, namely, moving Darwin—as the traumatized partner—toward greater awareness of himself and his strengths. He has reflected on these questions in therapy: What did each foster home provide as a gift for you, both positively and negatively? What can you now give yourself that you did not receive when you were a child? As the negatively critical partner, Evan is learning to accept what is true—namely, the use of emotional awareness and acceptance, the expression of emotion rather than judgment, appreciation rather than shame, and the art of self-nurturing. As the acceptance of what is true emerges as a commonly used tool in the relationship, the jealousy and fear of loss should diminish. If it does not, then the jealousy will need to be addressed directly. Therapy will focus on problem-solving skills as the relationship becomes more open.

Applying the Circle–Box Systemic Model Application to This Case

Major goals:

- A co-creative mutually rewarding relationship between Darwin and Evan
- Circle-based communication in the relationship
- A willingness to be more active within the community as a two-spirited couple
- A willingness to carry their powerful, respected traditional role as two-spirited leaders

Immediate goals:

- Recovery from a traumatized fostered childhood for Darwin—to a point where it does not actively interfere in his relationship with Evan
- Development of a skill set for continued rebalancing for Darwin
- Deconstruction of authoritative, judgmental communication and behavior by Evan
- A mutually comfortable attachment between Evan and Darwin

Possible interventions:

- Trauma recovery for Evan regarding residential school intergenerational behaviors from his grandparents
- Acceptance of loss and gains for Darwin regarding his fostered childhood
- Reconstruction of safety within a close relationship for Darwin using trauma recovery tools with the triggers he experiences as closeness is gradually achieved with Evan
- Continued communication with communal family members of both Darwin and Evan—developing relationships with healthy boundaries that support their couple relationship

Cultural Core Questions to Ask Native Couples

- Details about their culture and their relationship with it
- Attendance at residential school—by the couple and by family members, and its impact
- Membership in an organized religion/participation in Native spirituality
- Traumatized family relationships

- Previous relationships and the relationship with children conceived in them
- Effects from substance use, violence, FASD, illness, extended hospitalization
- Current and past traumas/losses of each partner
- Cultural shame and identity as a Native person

Core Clinical Skills for Working With Native Couples

- Trauma: genocidal, residual, generational, vicarious, complex
- Attachment disorders
- Comfort with strong emotion
- Shame and recovery
- Grief/delayed/complex/anniversary/anticipatory
- Sex therapy
- Violence/anger/hostility
- Depression/anxiety/phobias
- Dissociative disorders
- Posttraumatic Stress Disorder/Native Historical Trauma
- Family systems/Parenting skills
- Awareness/acceptance of the traditional naming of gender/cultural belief of four genders
- Awareness of the clinician's own culture and its historical interaction with Native culture
- Comfort with spiritual beliefs
- Humor (this is especially important)

Experiential Exercises

1. *Moving 180 degrees.* This is based on the systemic shifts between the box system and the circle system. For example, when feeling alone, switch to the circle by doing the opposite. Move from feeling to action, from aloneness to being in the company of others. Reach out and do something with another person, plant, or animal. When feeling afraid, dance.

2. *Acceptance.* Practice receiving information at any level of emotion, action, and thought as a truth, and simply absorb it as what is true for the person sharing it with you. No judgment or criticism or response is necessary. Simply accept it as a truth for someone else, and as you absorb it into your internal system, observe whether it is true for you.

3. *Curiosity.* Sit in observation and respect and be curious about all that is going on around you—spiritually/energetically, emotionally, mentally,

and physically. Absorb the information you gained while being curious. Store it for future reference or let go of it.

4. *Communication.* A Native traditional teaching is "Listen and communicate with your mouth closed." Practice communication with your ears, and keep your mouth closed. Note the difference in your understanding and appreciation of others, and how much more you actually hear in contrast with the box and "talking" communication.

Tips for Educators and Supervisors

1. Visit Native Elders and sit with them and listen to what they have to teach. Hear their stories and absorb what they have to tell you about their life experiences. If they are comfortable visiting in a classroom, ask them to tell their story to your students. If several Native Elders or families are willing to speak and teach and share their life experiences, this would be an even richer experience. Offer them gifts in exchange for their stories and time.

2. Be culturally appropriate. Ask to learn from local Native People—be prepared to listen, to be uncertain and uncomfortable at times, and perhaps even to be confronted by them. Accept and listen and learn, and apply what is taught to the work with Native couples.

3. Review the precepts of Cultural Safety as initiated and authored by Maori nurse Irihapeti Ramsden (Ramsden, 1990). Learn them and practice them in your teaching and supervision.

4. Ask a local Native natural healer or Elder to be present in the room when you teach cultural therapy methods and/or provide therapy to Native couples. It will be necessary to create clear guidelines for everyone prior to the work, but the learning will be worth it.

Nia:wen, Onen Kiwahi: Thank you, and go well.

Web Sites

Aboriginal Healing Foundation research books (free of charge): www.ahf.ca
Indian Residential Schools Resolution Canada: www.afn.ca/residentialschools/resources.html
Indian Residential Schools Survivors' Society: www.irsss.ca
Royal Commission on Aboriginal Peoples: www.parl.gc.ca/information/library

References

Armstrong, J. (1998). The disempowerment of First North American Native Peoples and empowerment through their writing. In D. D. Moses & T. Goldie (Eds.), *An anthology of Native Canadian literature in English* (pp. 239–242). Don Mills, Canada: Oxford University Press.

Brant, B. (1997). Grandmothers of a new world. In D. D. Moses & T. Goldie (Eds.), *An anthology of Native Canadian literature in English* (pp. 163–174). Don Mills, Canada: Oxford University Press.

Brave Heart, M. H. Y., & De Bruyn, L. (1998). The American holocaust: Historical unresolved grief among Native American Indians. *National Center for American Indian and Alaskan Native Mental Health Research Journal, 8*(2), 56–78.

Brown, J., & Languedoc, S. (2004). Components of an Aboriginal-based family violence intervention program. *Families in Society Journal, 85,* 477–483.

Chrisjohn, R., & Young, S. (1997). *The circle game: Shadows and substance in the Indian residential school experience in Canada.* Penticton, Canada: Theytus.

Derrick, J. (1993). The box and the circle: A model for understanding Native/non-Native issues. *Selected papers from the 1988 and 1990 Mokakit Conferences* (pp. 161–198). Vancouver, Canada: University of British Columbia First Nations Longhouse.

Derrick, J. (2005). When turtle met rabbit: Native family systems. In M. Rastogi & E. Wieling (Eds.), *Voices of color: First-person accounts of ethnic minority therapists* (pp. 43–63). Thousand Oaks, CA: Sage.

Dion, R., Gotowiec, A., & Beiser, M. (1993). Depression and conduct disorder in native and non-native children. *Journal of the American Academy of Child & Adolescent Psychiatry, 37*(7), 736–742.

Dufrene, P. (1990). Utilizing the arts for healing from a Native American perspective: Implications for arts therapies. *Canadian Journal for Native Studies, 1,* 121–131.

Eisler, R. (1988). *The chalice and the lade.* New York: Harper & Row.

Gordon-McCutchan, R. C. (1991). *The Taos Indians and the Battle for Blue Lake.* Santa Fe, NM: Red Crane.

Graham, T. L. C. (2002). Using reasons for living to connect to American Indian healing traditions. *Journal of Sociology and Social Welfare, 29*(1), 55–75.

Gray, M., Coates, J., & Hetherington, T. (2007). Hearing indigenous voices in mainstream social work. *Families in Society, 88*(1), 55–66.

Hart, M. (2002). *Seeking Mino-Pimatisiwin: An Aboriginal approach to helping.* Halifax, Canada: Fernwood.

Hart, M. (2007). Indigenous knowledge and research: The mikiwahp as a symbol for reclaiming our knowledge and ways of knowing. *First Peoples Child and Family Review, 3*(1), 83–90.

Hays, P. A. (1996). Cultural considerations in couples therapy. In M. Hill & E. Rothblum (Eds.), *Couples therapy feminist perspectives* (pp. 13–23). New York: Haworth.

Helin, C. (2006). *Dances with dependency: Indigenous success through self-reliance.* Vancouver, Canada: Orca Spirit.

Ho, M. K., Rasheed, J. M., & Rasheed, M. N. (2003). *Family therapy with ethnic minorities.* Thousand Oaks, CA: Sage.

Jacobs, K., & Gill, K. (2002). Substance abuse in an urban Aboriginal population: Social, legal and psychological consequences. *Journal of Ethnicity in Substance Abuse, 1*(1), 7–25.

Krech, P. R. (2002). Envisioning a healthy future: A re-becoming of Native American men. *Journal of Sociology and Social Welfare, 29*(1), 77–95.

Laird, J. (1998). Theorizing culture: Narrative ideas and practice principles. In M. McGoldrick (Ed.), *Re-visioning family therapy: Race, color and gender in clinical practice* (pp. 20–36). New York: Guilford Press.

McCormick, R. (2005). The healing path: What can counselors learn from Aboriginal people about how to heal? In R. Moodley & W. West (Eds.), *Integrating traditional healing practices into counseling and psychotherapy* (pp. 293–304). Thousand Oaks, CA: Sage.

McGoldrick, M., Giordano, J., & Garcia-Preto, N. (2005). *Ethnicity and family therapy.* New York: Guilford Press.

Mehl-Madrona, L. (1997). *Coyote medicine: Lessons from Native American healing.* New York: Fireside.

Morrissette, P. J. (1994). Holocaust of First Nation People: Residual effects on parenting and treatment implications. *Contemporary Family Therapy Journal, 16*(5), 381–392.

Moses, D. D., & Goldie, T. (1998). *An anthology of Native Canadian literature in English.* Don Mills, Canada: Oxford University Press.

O'Farrell, T., & Fals-Stewart, W. (2006). *Behavioral couples therapy for alcoholism and drug abuse.* New York: Guilford Press.

Poonwassie, A., & Charter, A. (2001). An Aboriginal worldview of helping: Empowering approaches. *Canadian Journal of Counselling, 35*(1), 63–73.

Ramsden, I. (1990). *Kawa Whakarririjai: Cultural safety in nursing education in Aotearoa.* Wellington, New Zealand: Ministry of Education of New Zealand.

Rastogi, M., & Wieling, E. (2005). *Voices of color: First-person accounts of ethnic minority therapists.* Thousand Oaks, CA: Sage.

Royal Commission on Aboriginal Peoples. (1996). Ottawa, Canada. Retrieved from.www.ainc-inac.gc.ca.

Sack, W. H., Beiser, M. Baker-Brown, G., & Redshirt, R. (1994). Depressive and suicidal symptoms in Indian school children: Findings from the flower of two soils. *American Indian and Alaska Native Mental Health Research Journal, 4* (Mono), 81–96.

Satir, V. (1972). *Peoplemaking.* Palo Alto, CA: Science and Behavior.

Schaef, A. W. (1987). *When society becomes an addict.* New York: Harper & Row.

Smith, D. P. (2005). The sweat lodge as psychotherapy: Congruence between traditional and modern healing. In R. Moodley & W. West (Eds.), *Integrating traditional healing practices into counseling and psychotherapy* (pp. 196–209). Thousand Oaks, CA: Sage.

Sutton, C. T., & Broken Nose, M. A. (2005). American Indian families: An overview. In M. McGoldrick, J. Giordano, & N. Garcia-Preto (Eds.), *Ethnicity and family therapy* (pp. 43–54). New York: Guilford Press.

Tafoya, N., & Del Vecchio, A. (2005). Back to the future: An examination of the Native American holocaust experience. M. McGoldrick, J. Giordano, & N. Garcia-Preto (Eds.), *Ethnicity and family therapy* (pp. 55–63). New York: Guilford Press.

Trepper, T., McCollum, E. E., Dankoski, M. E., Davis, S. K., & LaFazia, M. A. (2000). Couples therapy for drug-abusing women in an in-patient setting: A pilot study. *Contemporary Family Therapy Journal, 22*(2), 201–227.

Turner, W., & Wieling, E. (2004). Implications of research with diverse families. *Journal of Marital and Family Therapy, 30*(3), 255–256.

Turner, W., Wieling, E., & Allen, W. (2004). Developing culturally effective family-based research programs: Implications for family therapists. *Journal of Marital and Family Therapy, 30*(3), 257–270.

Wagamese, R. (2002). *For Joshua.* Toronto, Canada: Doubleday/Random House.

Wiebe, R., & Johnson, Y. (1998). *Stolen life: The journey of a Cree woman.* Toronto, Canada: Vintage/Random House.

Index

About the Editors

Mudita Rastogi, PhD, LMFT, is Professor of Clinical Psychology at the American School of Professional Psychology, Argosy University, in Schaumburg, Illinois. She obtained her PhD in Marriage and Family Therapy from Texas Tech University. She has also earned undergraduate and master's degrees in psychology from the University of Delhi and University of Bombay, India. Dr. Rastogi has published in the areas of family and couple therapy, cross-cultural and gender issues, and South Asian families, and is editor of the book *Voices of Color* (SAGE, 2005). She is Associate Editor for the *Journal of Marital and Family Therapy*. Dr. Rastogi has over 15 years of clinical experience in both India and the United States with a highly diverse client population, and is in private practice in Arlington Heights, Illinois, as a Licensed Marriage and Family Therapist. Her clinical interests include couples, families, adolescents, cultural and gender issues, domestic violence, and trauma. She frequently presents workshops nationally and internationally, and also conducts training and consultation in the area of leadership. Additionally, Dr. Rastogi maintains an interest in volunteering and partnering with grassroots, not-for-profit organizations. She is an AAMFT Clinical Member and Approved Supervisor, and a founding member of the Indian Association for Family Therapy.

Volker Thomas, PhD, is Associate Professor of Marriage and Family Therapy in the Department of Child Development and Family Studies at Purdue University, West Lafayette, Indiana. He received his PhD in Family Social Science with a specialization in marriage and family therapy from the University of Minnesota and an MSW from the University of Kassel, Germany. Since 1993, Dr. Thomas has been on the faculty of the COAMFTE-accredited doctoral MFT program at Purdue University and served as its director from 1999–2003. Dr. Thomas has been on the editorial boards of the *Journal of Marital and Family Therapy, The Family Journal,* and *Counseling and Values.* He served as the editor-in-chief of the *AFTA Newsletter* from 1998–2002. His research interests include family assessment, family therapy with economically disadvantaged families, gender and multicultural perspectives in family therapy, family therapy with children, ethical and professional issues, and supervision in family therapy training. Among his many publications are *Family Assessment: Integrating Multiple Perspectives* (with M. Cierpka and D. H. Sprenkle; Hogrefe, 2005) and *Clinical Issues With Interracial Couples: Theory and Research* (with T. Karis and J. Wetchler; Haworth Press, 2003). Dr. Thomas has also published over 60 refereed journal articles and book chapters and has extensive experience as presenter at national and international conferences. He is a Licensed Marriage and Family Therapist in Indiana and has a small private practice in West Lafayette. He is a Clinical Member and Approved Supervisor of the American Association for Marriage and Family Therapy (AAMFT).

About the Contributors

Sheila Addison, PhD, LMFT, is a core faculty member in the MA Counseling Psychology program at John F. Kennedy University, where she heads the couple and family therapy specialization. She has published on sexual identity in supervision, therapeutic interventions with minority gays and lesbians, and interventions with mixed-orientation relationships. She has presented at national MFT conferences on sexual identity and supervision, and at a national legal conference on same-sex domestic violence. Her private practice is also aimed at GLBT clients and couples of all kinds. Her other academic interests include queer theory, feminism, size acceptance/health at every size, and the whole spectrum of gender presentations. In her spare time, she studies American Tribal Style and other forms of belly dance.

Rhea V. Almeida, MS, PhD, LCSW, founder of IFS, is a family therapist and Columbia graduate. She has 25 years' experience as a teacher, therapist, consultant, speaker, and author, and is the mother of two daughters. She is the creator of the Cultural Context Model. Dr. Almeida is the author of *Expansions of Feminist Theory Through Diversity,* and *Transformations in Gender and Race: Family and Developmental Perspectives,* and the co-author of *Transformative Family Therapy: Just Families in a Just Society.* She has been featured in the *Los Angeles Times,* and on CNBC, National Public Radio, *USA Today,* and *Pure Oxygen.* Dr. Almeida was born in Uganda. When Idi Amin seized power in 1970 and decreed the exile of all citizens of Asian Indian heritage, she came to the United States. She has dedicated herself to bringing the connection between justice and healing to her chosen profession.

Sam Berg is Professor of Counselling at Briercrest Seminary, Caronport, Saskatchewan, and has a part-time contracted counseling practice at The Caring Place, a counseling agency in Regina, Sasaktchewan, where he see couples, families, and individuals, as well as supervising students. He is a Clinical Member and Approved Supervisor of the AAMFT, and currently serves as President of the newly formed Saskatchewan Division of Marriage and Family Therapy. He is interested in the use of narrative therapy practices in clinical work, as well as in teaching and in the supervision of trainees. Prior to coming to Caronport, he served as pastor of a church in Ottawa, Ontario. Outside interests include golfing, hiking, movies, and playing with his granddaughter as much as possible.

Maria Bermúdez, PhD, is an Assistant Professor of Marriage and Family Therapy in the Department of Child and Family Development at the University of Georgia. Her work is based on social constructionist, feminist-informed, and culturally responsive approaches to therapy, research, and supervision. She is originally from Honduras, and her research and clinical work addresses conflict resolution and communication processes among Latinos/as, the effects of immigration on Latino couples and families, and experiential approaches to narrative therapy, spirituality, and creativity in therapy.

Nancy Boyd-Franklin is a Professor in the Graduate School of Applied and Professional Psychology at Rutgers University. She is the author of *Black Families in Therapy: A Multisystems Approach* (Guilford Press, 1989); *Reaching Out in Family Therapy: Home-Based, School and Community Interventions* (with Dr. Brenna Bry; Guilford Press, 2000); *Boys Into Men: Raising Our African American Teenage Sons* (with Dr. A. J. Franklin; Plume, 2001); and the second edition of *Black Families in Therapy: Understanding the African American Experience* (Guilford Press, 2003). She is also an editor of *Children, Families and HIV/AIDS* (Guilford Press, 1995).

Thomas Stone Carlson, PhD, is the program coordinator of the Couple and Family Therapy Program at North Dakota State University. He has published several articles and book chapters on narrative therapy, and is currently the coinvestigator of a grant that seeks to provide culturally responsive therapy services to the Latino community through the program's Family Therapy Center.

Anthony L. Chambers, PhD, is an Assistant Clinical Professor in the Department of Psychology, Research Program Coordinator for The Family Institute and the Center for Applied Psychological and Family Studies, and a Licensed Clinical Psychologist on staff at The Family Institute at Northwestern University. He received his BA from Hampton University, and completed his MA and PhD in clinical psychology at the University of Virginia. He completed his internship and postdoctoral clinical residency at Harvard Medical School and Massachusetts General Hospital, specializing in the treatment of couples. Dr. Chambers teaches an undergraduate course titled "Marriage 101" about mate selection and the intricacies of committed, romantic relationships. Dr. Chambers's program of research focuses on the impact of mate selection on relationship development and functioning. He has a particular interest in understanding the unique factors that explain the disproportionately low marriage rate and high divorce rate among African American couples. Dr. Chambers has made frequent appearances in the mass media, talking about the challenges facing today's couples and their marriages.

Deborah Coolhart, PhD, LMFT, is an Assistant Professor of Community and Human Services at SUNY's Empire State College in Syracuse, New York. She is also a private practice family therapist and supervisor. Deb's primary clinical focus is working with queer people and their loved ones, particularly transgender people undergoing gender transition. She has published articles and presented numerous workshops on transgender issues and coming out in family therapy. Her research interests include family processes around queer youth and coming out, stress and the gender transition process, and PTSD as it relates to substance use and combat experience. Academically, Deb focuses on infusing issues of diversity and oppression into the wide range of courses she teaches in human services.

David Córdova Jr. earned his master's degree from Alliant International University and is a doctoral candidate in the marriage and family therapy program at Michigan State University. He currently serves as a research intern at Behavioral Assessment Inc. A student member of the National Hispanic Science Network on Drug Abuse, his interests are in developing, implementing, and evaluating culturally appropriate prevention interventions for high-risk families of color. David's current research projects include examining the effectiveness of an evidence-based prevention intervention for HIV, hepatitis, and substance abuse among high-risk Latino youth in a community agency setting and establishing the psychometrics of a psychosocial stress instrument for Latino youth. He was recently awarded the Michigan Association for Marriage and Family Therapists' Student of the Year Award.

Manijeh Daneshpour is a Professor and the Director of the Marriage and Family Therapy Program at St. Cloud State University in Minnesota. She teaches marriage and family therapy graduate courses and, as a licensed marriage and family therapist, works with individuals and families in her private practice. She provides supervision to postdegree marriage and family therapy students and mentors supervisors in training. She is from Iran and identifies herself as a Muslim feminist. She has done research about the lives of immigrant families, especially Muslim couples and their struggles once they come to the United States. She works with Muslim immigrant and refugee families in Minnesota, and has published articles and has done many presentations related to this topic. Her research interests and her publications are also in the areas of diversity, social justice, third-wave feminism, and the impact of trauma on family functioning.

Jann M. Derrick is a Registered Family Therapist, a member of the Canadian Psychological Association, and a Clinical Member and Approved Supervisor in the American Association for Marriage and Family Therapy. Jann is the mother of three children and the grandmother of six. She is of Mohawk heritage and has been in practice for 30 years in several urban and rural communities in British Columbia. Jann provided groundbreaking work with residential school survivors, presents workshops internationally, and publishes in the areas of relationships, Native trauma, and two metasystems—the box and the circle. Jann also has knowledge of traditional First Nations healing methods. Jann has worked at Round Lake Treatment Centre, and also facilitated a national Aboriginal Focus Group that created a Code of Ethics for the Aboriginal Healing Foundation. Jann was awarded the John Banmen Award for outstanding service and contribution to the Family Therapy Profession in BC.

Sol D'Urso, MA, is a marriage and family therapist intern in the San Diego area. She immigrated to the United States from Argentina in 2000. Sol earned her master's degree in marital and family therapy from the University of San Diego. She currently serves as the student/associate representative for AAMFT.

Ana Rocío Escobar-Chew is an international Fulbright scholar from Guatemala. After becoming a licensed clinical psychologist in her native country, she came to the United States to specialize in marriage and family therapy. She is currently a master's level student pursuing her doctoral degree at Michigan State University. Her thesis in Guatemala involved the creation and implementation of a parenting program, adapted to decrease parental anxiety levels. Her clinical work has been committed to clients from disadvantaged groups, living in multi-stress situations, especially from Latino populations. She has presented at national and international conferences. Ms. Escobar-Chew is currently pursuing multiple research projects as a member of Dr. Rubén Parra-Cardona's research team. This includes exploring the life experiences of immigrant Cuban families as well as evaluating the effectiveness of treatment groups for domestic violence. She is also preparing the implementation of a communication program for Latino couples in Lansing, Michigan.

Paul S. Greenman, PhD, is a Professor of Clinical Psychology at the Université du Québec en Outaouais in Gatineau, Québec, Canada, and a practicing psychologist at the Ottawa Couple and Family Institute in Ottawa, Ontario, Canada. He specializes in EFT for couples in his teaching and clinical practice and he conducts research on the emotional and interpersonal lives of individuals from a range of cultural backgrounds. Dr. Greenman continues to be a major contributor to publications on EFT for couples and the relational dynamics of children and adolescents from diverse cultural backgrounds. Dr. Greenman is also active in the research and application of psychological treatments for individuals and couples suffering from physical illnesses. He is currently directing a project on the integration of psychotherapy into the cardiac rehabilitation program at the Montfort Hospital in Ottawa.

Olga E. Hervis, MSW, LCSW, is the coauthor and developer of Brief Strategic Family Therapy (BSFT)©TMand Family Effectiveness Training (FET). BSFT is a nationally recognized, award-winning, evidence-based approach to reducing problem behaviors, eliminating substance abuse risk factors, and strengthening families. She is also the founder of the Family Therapy Training Institute of South Florida, which has been training clinical staff of mental health service providers throughout the country to implement BSFT. She holds a master's degree from Barry University and has done postgraduate training in New York, Pennsylvania, Louisiana, and Florida, where she is an Approved Supervisor. She is also a clinical member of the AAMFT, a member of AFTA, a Certified Criminal Justice Specialist, and a Master Addictions Counselor. She has won numerous awards for her family therapy clinical research work, including the 2000 Exemplary Model in Substance Abuse Prevention from SAMHSA. She is widely published, both nationally and internationally.

Kendal Holtrop is a doctoral student in the Marriage and Family Therapy program at Michigan State University. Her clinical and research interests focus on cultural competence, intersections of privilege and oppression, and underserved populations, with a special focus on Latino/a subgroups. She is currently involved in research projects exploring processes of accountability and change among Latino men who batter, and culturally adapting an evidence-based parenting intervention for Latino/a populations. She has also had the opportunity to publish and present at professional conferences in relation to her work in these areas. Kendal is contributing to this dialogue on multicultural couple therapy from the perspective of a White female graduate student from the United States. She would like to thank Dr. Rubén Parra-Cardona for his continued mentoring, which has supported her in promoting social justice from this position.

Sheena Horsford is a second-year master's student in the marriage and family therapy doctoral program at Michigan State University. She demonstrates her commitment to social justice through her clinical work, research, and national presentations. Her clinical interests focus on underserved, multistressed populations as well as community-based outreach to families in poverty. In her clinical work, she provides parenting education, family therapy, and advocacy to parents who have temporarily lost custody of their children. She is also involved in a culturally adaptive research project aimed at providing evidence-based parenting interventions to families of color.

Susan M. Johnson, EdD, is one of the originators and the main proponent of Emotionally Focused Therapy (EFT) for couples, now one of the best validated interventions for couples in North America. She is a Professor of Clinical Psychology at the University of Ottawa and Director of the Ottawa Couple and Family Institute and the Center for Emotionally Focused Therapy. Dr. Johnson is a member of the editorial board of the *Journal of Marital and Family Therapy*, the *Journal of Couple and Relationship Therapy*, and the *Journal of Family Psychology*. She is also a Research Professor in the Marital and Family Therapy Program at Alliant University in San Diego.

Silvia M. Kaminsky, MSEd, LMFT, CAP, is a licensed Marriage and Family Therapist and Certified Addictions Professional in the State of Florida. She holds a BA in Psychology from the University of North Carolina at Chapel Hill and an MSEd. from the University of Miami. She has 22 years of clinical experience, the past 18 years in private practice in South Miami, Florida. Ms. Kaminsky has worked as a clinical supervisor in both agency settings and her private practice. She has trained with Olga Hervis at the Center for Family Studies at the University of Miami and is a BSFT Master Trainer and Supervisor for the Family Therapy Training Institute of Miami. Ms. Kaminsky served as President of the Florida Association for Marriage and Family Therapy from 2001–2003 and is currently serving a three-year term (2007–2009) as a Board Member of AAMFT. She is also an AFTA member.

Margaret L. Keeling, PhD, is an Assistant Professor and Director of Clinical Training of Marriage and Family Therapy at Virginia Tech in Blacksburg, Virginia. She is a narrative therapy practitioner who combines art, expressive writing, and other experiential elements into her therapy practice. She has also combined these elements into innovative interventions for research purposes. She received her PhD in marriage and family therapy from Texas Tech University in 2005. As a long-time Texas resident,

Dr. Keeling has conducted therapy with numerous Latino (predominantly Mexican American) individuals, couples, and families. Her primary clinical and research focus is on the intersection of gender, culture, and power as it influences therapeutic practice and utilization. She is also a practicing artist.

Shalonda Kelly is an Associate Professor at the Graduate School of Applied and Professional Psychology at Rutgers University. She received a dual PhD in urban studies and child and family clinical psychology from Michigan State University in 1998. Dr. Kelly publishes empirical and clinical manuscripts related to racial, ethnic, and cultural issues, and couple relationships. She has received NIH and Rutgers University funding to study racial and cultural factors in clinic-referred and university populations. She conducts workshops and consults with organizations working with African Americans, people of color, couples, children, and families. She is a licensed psychologist who conducts and supervises couple and family therapy from a cognitive-behavioral and/or systems orientation.

Larry Jin (Kwok Hung) Lee is a staff psychotherapist in psychiatry at Kaiser Permanente in San Francisco. He received his graduate training at the University of California, Berkeley. He has taught at San Francisco State and the University of California, Berkeley, in their Graduate Schools of Social Welfare. He believes that creating a safe space, especially for oppressed and marginalized patients' narratives of survival and resilience, is at the heart of culturally literate practice. He is a part of the Kaiser Best Practices Workgroup for cultural diversity, planning conferences and training for mental health clinicians. Mr. Lee is a keen writer, with his previous chapter being on "Taking off the Mask: Breaking the Silence—The Art of Naming Racism in the Therapy Room." He is committed to the challenge of transforming psychology from another system of oppression into a liberatory one. He has two children, aged 9 and 18 years.

Israela Meyerstein, LCSW-C, LMFT, a clinical social worker in the Baltimore community, has been in private practice for 30 years. She treats couples, families, and individuals of all ages for a variety of problems, with a special interest in families coping with medical illness and spirituality. As co-founder of the Baltimore Jewish Healing Network, Ms. Meyerstein co-led Spiritual Study/Discussion groups for those struggling with medical illness. Ms. Meyerstein directed the Family Therapy Program at Sheppard Pratt Hospital for 12 years. An Approved Supervisor in the American Association for Marriage and Family Therapy, Ms. Meyerstein has trained mental health professionals of all disciplines and skill levels in both academic and clinical settings. She has lectured and published extensively in the field of family treatment, training, and family life education.

José Rubén Parra-Cardona is an Assistant Professor in the Marriage and Family Therapy program in the Department of Family and Child Ecology at Michigan State University. He is currently involved in research focused on the cultural adaptation of evidence-based parenting interventions for Latino/a populations and collaborates with an international research team in carrying out this line of research in the United States and Mexico. Dr. Parra-Cardona is also a core faculty member of the MSU initiative on violence against women (www.vaw.msu.edu). As part of this initiative, he conducts research with Latino men referred to abuser treatment programs. Dr. Parra-Cardona serves on the editorial boards of three leading journals in the fields of family therapy and family studies, the *Journal of Marital and Family Therapy, Family Process*, and *Family Relations*. He has published in the areas of cultural competence, cultural identity, adult and adolescent Latino/a parenting, and cultural adaptation of evidence-based parenting interventions.

Jo Ellen Patterson is a Professor in the Marital and Family Therapy program at the University of San Diego. She is also Clinical Associate Professor of Family Medicine and Psychiatry at UCSD Medical School. She is the author of three books and numerous articles.

Sandra Reynaga, MA, is a bilingual Marriage and Family Therapist Intern in the San Diego area. Ms. Reynaga is a first-generation Mexican American. Ms. Reynaga earned her bachelor's degree from the University of California, San Diego, in psychology and a master's degree in marital and family therapy from the University of San Diego.

Mia Sevier, PhD, is an Assistant Professor in Human Services, an interdisciplinary department focused on helping students acquire social science knowledge and applied intervention skills, at California State University, Fullerton. She regularly teaches courses on subjects such as counseling theories and techniques as well as research methods for program evaluation. Mia received her doctorate in clinical psychology from the University of California, Los Angeles, specializing in couples and couple therapy. Her scholarly interests include issues of culture, cultural competence, communication strategies, and interventions for couples. As an ongoing research member of the UCLA/UW Couple Therapy lab, she collaborates with Andrew Christensen, a founder of Integrative Behavioral Couple Therapy, to investigate the outcome and process of couple therapy.

Kathleen A. Shea, PhD, holds a doctorate in higher education administration from the University of Miami and a master's in counseling from the University of Dayton (Ohio). Dr. Shea's experience includes university teaching, research, and administration, health care marketing, project management, and consulting. She has consulted with educational and human services organizations on organization development, assessment, and evaluation projects. She has a special interest in organization development from a structural-functional point of view. She is a former Vice President of the National Association of Women Business Owners (NAWBO) and served on the board of directors for National Small Business United (NSBU). She is currently the President and Florida Coordinator for Living Values: An Educational Program, Inc., a global character education program supported by UNESCO and UNICEF.

Lin Shi, PhD, LMFT, is Associate Professor and Program Director of the master's program in Marriage and Family Therapy accredited by the Commission on Accreditation for Marriage and Family Therapy Education within the School of Family, Consumer, and Nutrition Sciences at Northern Illinois University. She received her doctorate from Texas Tech University. Dr. Shi is a clinical member and an Approved Supervisor of the American Association for Marriage and Family Therapy. Her current research and clinical interests include trauma and cross-cultural marital functioning from an attachment theory perspective. In addition, she is interested in clinical application of attachment theory in various cultural contexts. Dr. Shi has published in *Family Process*, the *American Journal of Family Therapy*, and the *Journal of Family Psychotherapy*, among others.

Linna Wang, PhD, was born and raised in China. She lived through the infamous Great Cultural Revolution and the early stage of the economic reform, and experienced and witnessed how social and political forces impacted marriages and families. As one of the new Chinese immigrants described in the chapter, she migrated to the United States for advanced degrees and professional development. She is teaching in a graduate program of marriage and family therapy. Her researches focus on the global psychologies and the impact of immigration process on families. She has extensive experience working with and advocating for Chinese immigrants and their families. It is her belief that immigrants and host countries mutually benefit each other through a constant cultural evolution, a process that produces a third culture that is richer than any two combined. She lives in San Diego with her extended family.

Jean C. Yi, PhD, is currently a postdoctoral fellow at Fred Hutchinson Cancer Research Center, and is mentored by Karen L. Syrjala, PhD. She is also an affiliate postdoctoral fellow in the Biobehavioral Cancer Prevention and Control Training Program offered through the University of Washington's Department of Health Services, under the guidance of

Donald L. Patrick, PhD. Dr. Yi received her doctorate in 2007 through the Department of Psychology at the University of Washington and was mentored by William H. George, PhD. She continues to work with Andrew Christensen, PhD, at the University of California, Los Angeles, on research related to a randomized clinical trial of two behavioral treatments for relationship distress. Her research interests include couples and couple therapy, race and ethnicity, health, and the intersections of these three domains.

Marta Y. Young, PhD, is a Professor of Clinical Psychology at the University of Ottawa in Canada. She also has a private practice providing assessment and treatment services to immigrants and refugees. Dr. Young specializes in cross-cultural psychology, and she conducts research on the acculturation and well-being of immigrants and refugees.